The High School
in a New Era

*Papers presented at the Conference
on the American High School
at The University of Chicago,
October 28–30, 1957*

HENRY STEELE COMMAGER

JAMES B. CONANT

LAWRENCE A. KIMPTON

LAWRENCE G. DERTHICK

DEVEREUX C. JOSEPHS

GILBERT FOWLER WHITE

ALEXANDER J. STODDARD

ALAN T. WATERMAN

THEODORE W. SCHULTZ

REUBEN G. GUSTAVSON

CLARENCE H. FAUST

JOHN I. GOODLAD

JACOB W. GETZELS

WILLIAM H. CORNOG

RALPH W. TYLER

FRANCIS S. CHASE

ROBERT S. GILCHRIST

J. LLOYD TRUMP

LLOYD S. MICHAEL

ARCHIBALD B. SHAW

HENRY H. HILL

ROY E. LARSEN

WILLIAM HENRY SHAW

ERNEST A. GRAY

GEORGE W. CONNELLY

FRANCIS KEPPEL

WALTER L. COOPER

KENNETH W. LUND

HOWARD A. LATTA

CLYDE VROMAN

DOROTHY E. NORRIS

JOHN W. MELCHER

I. JAMES QUILLEN

MARSHALL H. STONE

HOWARD F. FEHR

JAMES G. HARLOW

GERALD B. LEIGHBODY

HENRY TOY, JR.

The High School in a New Era

Edited by **FRANCIS S. CHASE**
and **HAROLD A. ANDERSON**

THE UNIVERSITY OF CHICAGO PRESS
CHICAGO AND LONDON

Library of Congress Catalog Card Number: 58-11947

THE UNIVERSITY OF CHICAGO PRESS, CHICAGO & LONDON
The University of Toronto Press, Toronto 5, Canada

© *1958 by The University of Chicago*
Published 1958. Fourth Impression 1963
Composed and printed by
THE UNIVERSITY OF CHICAGO PRESS
Chicago, Illinois, U.S.A.

Acknowledgments

We desire to record our thanks to the thirty-eight speakers at the Conference on the American High School whose papers made this volume possible. Their willingness to prepare papers for delivery at the conference which would at the same time lend themselves to publication in book form claims the profound gratitude of the larger audience of school men and laymen who may now share the deliberations of the conference.

We wish also to express our indebtedness to Miss Mildred Herrod for her invaluable assistance in preparing the manuscripts for the printer.

Introduction

Under the heading "Chicago Starts Great Debate on Quality," *Better Schools,*[1] in its "Spotlight Report" for December, 1957, commented that the necessity of fulfilling effectively the American commitment to universal secondary education "has become urgently apparent with the pressure of exploding population and of recent international events" and continued:

And so, for the first time since the establishment of the public high school in the mid-nineteenth century, a national conclave of leading citizens and educators got together in Chicago last month to re-examine the role and directions of this American invention. Some 1,100 people—two thirds of them educators from secondary and higher institutions, one third laymen—met to hear outstanding speakers and to concentrate in small group sessions on "The American High School—Challenge of a New Era."

The conference, sponsored by the University of Chicago in collaboration with the National Citizens Council for Better Schools, was planned to provide a national forum through which present needs for education and the means of meeting them might be explored by educational leaders and other citizens who have given more than passing thought to education. It was designed to stimulate creative thought about the possibilities for school improvement rather than to reach any fixed conclusions with regard to what our schools should be. That it succeeded in its purpose has been attested not only by the lively discussions in the many small groups at the conference but also by the reports of a continuation of the discussions in hundreds of communities. Many signs indicate that America may be beginning a new forward movement in education comparable to that which spread the high school into every part of the country.

The American people throughout their history have held great expectations for their schools and have seen them as means to the

[1] Published by the National Citizens Council for Better Schools.

achievement of both individual and national goals and aspirations. The American schools have been wonderfully responsive to these demands. They have extended their reach downward and upward; they have contrived to enrol larger and larger portions of the population; and they have constantly broadened their offerings and services in an attempt to minister to the new needs expressed by society.

Certainly the schools have not realized all the hopes placed upon them; but, by and large, they have been the kinds of schools that the American people wanted and were willing to support. Probably no schools in the history of mankind have ever achieved so wide a range of objectives for so large a portion of the population as have the schools of the United States. Yet there is a growing realization in the United States, as in other countries, that modern man's needs for education are not fully met by any system of schools now existing. Within the past forty years the application of science and technology to the release of energy, the processes of production, the means of transportation, and the mechanics of communication, have projected man into a new era for which he is ill prepared. In contrast, education, the means through which men assimilate the accumulated culture and become children of their own age, tends to remain fixed at the level established by the conditions of the past century. Analysis of the situation makes it doubtful that schools as now constituted and supported can carry the burden of preparing men to cope with the problems and possibilities inherent in the changes already upon us, much less those now taking shape on the drawing boards and in the laboratories.

In the papers presented at the Conference on the American High School three convictions recurred repeatedly: (1) the high school has played an essential role in the notable American achievements of the past fifty years; (2) American life in the next half-century will also be conditioned by the quality of secondary education; (3) the responsibility for improvement of the schools to meet the challenges of the new era rests upon all American citizens.

This volume, through the papers presented at the conference, provides a few backward looks at the contributions of the high school to American society and then proceeds to analyze the new demands to which the high school must respond and to consider how the high school can adapt itself to the new conditions. It is hoped that publication of *The High School in a New Era* will stimulate further thought and discussion as preludes to wise action to strengthen our schools. The suggestions advanced are intended not for uncritical acceptance but as fomenters of a great debate on how the schools, which have served so well in the past, may make themselves equal to the even more exacting demands of the present and the onrushing future.

Table of Contents

The American High School Is Viewed in the Perspectives of History, Comparative Education, Philosophy, and Present Needs

A Historian Looks at
the American High School

It is not chance that the prodigious issue of racial equality should have come to a boil in a case called *Brown* v. *Board of Education* and that it should have boiled over, as it were, in Little Rock High School. Even the most ardent critic of the Supreme Court would not take issue with the obiter dicta of the Brown case:

Today education is perhaps the most important function of the state and local governments. Compulsory school attendance laws and the great expenditures for education both demonstrate our recognition of the importance of education in our democratic society. It is required in the performance of our most basic public responsibilities. . . . It is the very foundation of good citizenship. Today it is a principal instrument in awakening the child to cultural values, in preparing him for later professional training, and in helping him to adjust normally to his environment. In these days it is doubtful that any child may reasonably be expected to succeed in life if he is denied the opportunity of an education [347 U.S. at 493].

This argument, with its brief but comprehensive references to the relation of education to citizenship, culture, special skills, and social adjustment, is an echo of a long series of statements, proclamations, and arguments that began in the 1630's and have re-echoed down the corridors of our history. It takes us back to the justification of the School Act of 1642, "that learning which may be profitable to the commonwealth," and the Act of 1647, "that learning may not be buried in the graves of our fathers in the church and commonwealth," and the commitment to education, not for narrow religious, but for broad commonwealth, purposes throughout the history of the Bay Colony. It found expression, particularly, in the Revolutionary generation: no body of nation-makers were ever so conscious of the role that education should play as were the American Founding Fathers. Thus Jefferson's proposal for "a system of education which shall reach every description of citizen from the richest to the poorest"; thus the provision of the Northwest Ordinance that "religion, morality and knowledge being necessary to good government and the happiness of mankind, schools and the means of education shall be forever encouraged." Thus the ardent Noah Webster's argument: "In our American Republic where government is in the hands of the people, knowledge should be universally diffused by means of schools. Of such consequence is it to society that the people who make laws should be well informed that I conceive no Legislature can be justified in neglecting proper establishments for this purpose."

Characteristic Features of American Schools

The characteristic features of the American educational system emerged early and were in large part the product, or the accident, of circumstances and of environment. By the time the high school made its appearance on the educational landscape, the pattern was pretty well fixed: pluralism, or local rather than centralized control of education; secularism, or separation from religious control; a general or liberal rather than a vocational education; and an education of the general populace rather than of the elite.

If we can, formally, date elementary education from the Massachusetts Act of 1642, we can date the high school from the Massachusetts Law of 1827 (leave aside that both laws were ineffective for a long time). Thus the formal advent of the high school came late in our educational system. In fact, it came a good deal later than these dates would indicate, for not until 1864 did New York State require the maintenance of high schools, and as late as 1890 there were only 2,526 public high schools in the entire nation (this in a population of 63 million).

Yet recent as is the high school on the American educational scene, it is, by comparison with the scene abroad, almost a venerable institution. To be sure, there had been schools called "high" in England as early as the fourteenth century (in Exeter, for example, in 1313), and our own earliest high schools took their name from the high schools of Edinburgh and Glasgow. These were not high schools in our meaning of the word, merely the principal school, and it is true that not until well into the twentieth century did any European country provide an effective system of free public secondary education for all who desired it. (Thus at the beginning of this century, only 109,000 pupils attended the secondary schools of Britain, and not until 1907 was provision made for secondary education for those unable to pay the ordinary fees.) Only since the second World War has Britain begun to provide for its 14–18 year-olds as adequately as the United States did sixty or seventy years ago. And what is true of Britain is true of all continental countries, except possibly Holland, Switzerland, and the Scandinavian nations.

The American high school, then, was the pioneer—the pioneer not only in time but in program was well—and if older European nations do not borrow heavily from our experience, many of the new nations outside Europe do. In the comprehensive high school, in the single curriculum for all, in the amalgamation of preparation for college and for work; in the emphasis on student government and student activities; in coeducation; in the openness of the cur-riculum and of the whole academic course (the easy, almost unconscious merging into college); in the emphasis on doing in the processes of learning—in all these and other things the American high school has been a pioneer.

It is the most hackneyed of observations that schools are a function of society, but we should keep in mind that, as American society differed profoundly from European in the eighteenth and early nineteenth centuries, the functions imposed upon schools differed profoundly from those which older societies imposed upon their schools. The story is familiar, and I need not rehearse it: how, especially in the nineteenth century, we required our schools to train citizens competent to govern themselves (a requirement not urgent in the Old World), to absorb and Americanize millions of newcomers from the Old World and elsewhere, to encourage and strengthen national unity, and to teach the habits and practices of democracy and equality and religious tolerance.

Achievements of the American Schools

Looking back on the American experience in the perspective of a century or so (about the time we have been at the job of compre-hensive education), we cannot, I think, but be dazzled that we have managed so well in so short a time. If we look only to the educational achievement, we see that we have provided more education to a larger portion of society than did any other country in history; we have built a magnificent physical plant and equipped it with educational apparatus, for example, gymnasiums and school libraries; we have supplied more than one million teachers (and who will deny that they are better prepared for their jobs than were the teachers of a half-century or a century ago?). If emphasis seems to be laid too heavily on quantity, may we not add that, qualitatively, the products of the American school system compared favorably with the products of German or French school systems both in competence and in judgment in the great crisis of the World War and its aftermath?

As schools are commonly blamed for the failings or inadequacies of society, perhaps it is not wholly unfair to give them some credit for the larger successes and achievements. After all, Americans, the products of our educational system, succeeded in a great many things which involve intelligence and judgment. They established a nation and held it together, expanding thirteen to forty-eight states with less difficulty than England had with Ireland alone in the same period. They made democracy work reasonably well and did not gratify the expectations of those who were so sure that a majority would inevitably exercise tyranny over minorities. They elected mediocre presidents, but never a wicked or a dangerous one. They never yielded to a military dictator. They settled all their problems, but one, by compromise and concession instead of by violence (and perhaps that one could not be solved by compromise). They adjusted themselves speedily to their responsibilities as a world power. These are not accomplishments that can be confidently traced to the educational system, but it would be absurd to deny that the schools contributed to them.

Not only do our schools deserve some credit for these accomplishments; they deserve some credit for the things they have avoided. Much of our history is, in a sense, an achievement in avoidance—nationalism without "nationalizmus," world power without imperialism, majority rule without majority tyranny, capitalism without class warfare, and so on. The schools, too, have somehow managed to avoid many of the dangers that might have worked irreparable harm to our social or intellectual fabric.

The schools began in New England as exponents of a particular religion but avoided religious fanaticism or too intimate a dependence on the church even in the Colonial period. Since that time, public schools have had no religious dependence, and even private schools have been tolerant. Recollect that as late as the 1860's a Catholic could not attend Oxford or Cambridge Universities and that even Leslie Stephen severed his connection with Cambridge because he could not subscribe to the Thirty-nine Articles. Though the schools are divorced from the church and from formal religion, there has been no failure to inculcate morality.

Though required to take all comers, mass education has not meant a vulgarization of culture or a serious watering-down of the intellectual content of learning. If the American high school does not do as good a job in formal education as the English public school, the French lycée, and the German gymnasium, it is part of an educational process which eventually goes as high as does any other system in the world.

Though the tasks that confronted Americans—and that appealed for educational support—have been intensely practical, there has not been an overemphasis on vocational education in the American system. There has not been a rejection of humanism, or even of classical education, as was threatened by some of the enthusiasts of the Revolutionary period.

Though few societies displayed greater differences and divisions than did the American, our schools have not accentuated, but have mitigated, these differences educationally. We have not separated our students between the many who are called and the few who are chosen, as is still the practice in almost all European countries.

Though upon the schools was placed heavy responsibility for encouraging national unity and inculcating pride in the history and traditions of the nation, the schools were not instruments of chauvinism, nor did they ever, except in the prewar South, allow themselves to become instruments of the state.

It is important that we keep in mind that the school has never been a merely passive agent in the process of serving the needs of our society. Indeed, as a result of the peculiar circumstances of American life, schools have played a somewhat more important role here than elsewhere in setting standards and in creating social patterns: first, because almost from the beginnings of our national history, education has been a secular religion; second, because the schools furnished perhaps the largest and the most familiar framework of experience to a heterogeneous and fluctuating population, and the tendency was strong to adjust to the school; and, third, because in the nineteenth and much of the twentieth century the school, by giving each generation of young a better education than their parents had enjoyed, set standards, as it were, for the parents and persuaded the adult world to yield to those standards and adjust to those demands. In most societies of the Old World (as in more primitive societies), each generation tends to have about the same educational experience as did the preceding generation: children of those who have not gone to secondary school do not themselves go to secondary school; children of those who have not gone to a university do not ordinarily go to the university. But in our society it has almost always been the other way around. In our country, in the game of "schoolmanship," the young know all the plays and have their elders at a disadvantage. This is one of the explanations of that habit which Europeans find so difficult to understand—the grown-ups' habit of yielding to the standards, the demands, the expectations, of their children and conforming to the notions brought home from school.

The Demands of a New Era

Now our entire educational system, but especially our high schools, have entered, or are in process of entering, a new era—an era which demands new things of the school and which requires new things from the school. It is to no point to intone the old litanies. The schools are called upon to play a role closer, perhaps, to that imagined for the academies and colleges in the eighteenth century than to that which they did play in the nineteenth. What are the considerations and conditions which require a rethinking of the functions of our schools?

First, our schools are, in a sense, the victims of their own success. If they are not precisely buried beneath the ruins of their own triumph, they are conditioned and committed by their achievements. Most of what we may call the non-academic functions of the schools in the nineteenth and early twentieth centuries have been performed: to give unity to a heterogeneous population, to create a sense of belonging to, to inculcate democracy and equality. These are never ending problems, and I do not suggest that they are wholly solved: witness the problem which New York City faces with its Puerto Rican school children, or the South with its Negro population. But can it not be said that schools have already formulated solutions to these problems, that their application rests with society?

This suggests a second consideration, one which has not, I think, been adequately assimilated by educators: that the school no longer bears the heavy responsibilities in the non-academic realm that it did in the nineteenth century, that it now shares with many other agencies responsibility for non-academic educational activities, and that it is in a better position to devote its attention to what we may call academic functions than ever before. Schools do not need to educate parents through their children, as they once did; and the parents themselves not only are more sophisticated but have more leisure time for their own responsibilities and duties than they had in the nineteenth century. Most important, scores of other agencies are now doing what the school did in the nineteenth century: the press, radio, television, movies, organizations like the Boy Scouts and Girl Scouts, the churches in their enlarged social functions, and others.

Indeed insofar as schools are agents of social development as well as instruments of society, they have a duty to resist, rather than to yield to, community pressures. Because schools are a function of society, a great many educators think it the primary duty of the schools—and especially the high school, which here occupies a crucial position—to "adapt" the young to the society in which they are to live. Needless to say, if each generation of young is merely fitted to the existing order of things, we shall end up with a Byzantine, not a Western, civilization. A dynamic society cannot stay dynamic if the existing order fixes the standards to which all must conform and into which all must be fitted.

Schools are a part of society, but they should not be a complete mirror of society. They should offer not a repetition of experience but a challenge to, and an extension of, experience. They are not a tranquilizer but a conscience for society. Yet at a time when schools are in a better position to emancipate themselves from community pressures than ever before and when the necessity of challenge and experimentation is perhaps stronger than ever before, our schools seem to make a fetish of adaptation and conformity.

When almost every agency proclaims the merits of "private enterprise," the schools, all too often, weakly yield to pressures from filiopietistic or business organizations to beat the academic drum for private enterprise. When almost everybody reads *Reader's Digest* and *Life* and *Look* and *Newsweek* anyway and the young can be trusted to see them outside the schoolroom, students read these magazines in the schoolroom or the school library, rather than less popular and less readily available magazines which they may otherwise never come to know. When the discussion of current affairs commands the daily press, the radio, television, and most conversation at home, the schools, instead of diverting the young to a contemplation of the affairs of Greece and Rome or of medieval England, meekly concentrate on current affairs. At a time when society is perhaps overly concerned with material things—with business and industry, with roads and automobiles—when things are in the saddle and ride mankind, the schools, too, emphasize the practical and the material rather than the intellectual or the aesthetic.

At a time when almost all the institutions of society are in a conspiracy to suppress individuality and heterodoxy and eccentricity and to produce organization men and women, the schools, too, put the hobbyhorse away in the basement and organize group games, emphasize at every point (but nowhere more than in the high school) the virtues of conformity and adaptability in order to produce organization boys and girls. When society hangs breathless on the prowess of a Lew Burdette or a Walt Kowalczyk, schools, too, celebrate competitive sports. When the climate of nationalism is pervasive and almost stifling and a hundred agencies proclaim, day and night, the superiority of everything American to everything non-American, the schools, instead of encouraging the young to challenge old shibboleths and to develop broader and more spiritual loyalties, tend to join in the parade of ostentatious patriotism. When it is regarded as good manners, almost everywhere, to avoid controversy and blur all differences of opinion, schools, instead of preparing the young for a world of controversy, tend to discourage sharp differences of opinion and meaningful discussion in order to achieve general agreement and contentment.

Third, in this connection it is appropriate to observe that, whatever difficulties schools may have in getting enough money for their needs, they no longer have the elementary task of winning or enlisting community support to their very existence that they had in many communities in the nineteenth century and need not make convulsive efforts to win that support. Everybody takes for granted, now, the necessity of free public education through the high school; everybody takes for granted the desirability of adequate classrooms, libraries, laboratories, playing fields, and so on. Yet in one notorious realm our schools are still engaged in enlisting community interest and support on an elementary level and with crude techniques. I refer, of course, to the emphasis on competitive athletics. I know that sports have other functions than that of exciting community interest, namely, to teach fair play, to provide physical training to all, to furnish a healthy outlet for the competitive spirit, to provide areas in which success and prestige are independent of wealth or family.

But these purposes have been achieved, or are no longer urgent, or are rather frustrated by our current emphasis on sports than advanced by it. A system where a handful of boys devote most of their energy to football while five thousand students sit in stands and watch them, is not designed to provide sound bodies to go with sound minds. A system where victory counts for more than the game is not conducive to encouraging standards of fair play (and I think those standards have gone steadily down in the last quarter-century). Neither wealth nor family insure prestige in our schools today, and the alternative of the playing field is by no means as important as it was. As for the safety valve of competition, our need is rather to restore competition in the classroom and to discourage it on the playing field and elsewhere.

The most dangerous feature of the development of competitive sports in the high school remains: its relation to community interest and support. Instead of being a device whereby the community is persuaded to take an interest in the high school, football and basketball have become, in all too many communities, devices whereby the high school entertains or profits the community. More and more, the athletic tail is wagging the academic dog. More and more, young men who are protected by law from exploitation in the labor market and who would never be allowed to work at night, are exploited even at night for the convenience, the entertainment, or the profit of adults. We would not expect or permit our high-school daughters to entertain the community in a night club or a burlesque show; there is no reason why we should permit our high-school sons to entertain the community by what are, in effect, burlesque performances on the playing field.

Not only do our athletic malpractices—born of sound policy in the nineteenth century—do grave harm to the young by denying to *some* appropriate participation in sports, by fostering unsound standards of sportsmanship, and by distracting attention from more serious academic affairs; but they do grave harm to the whole institution of education. For they constitute, at the high-school and the college level, an acknowledgment on the part of the academic community that interest in, and support for, education is to be won, not on its own merits, but by extraneous means. They constitute a gratuitous and unworthy confession that public support (or alumni support) to education cannot be expected except from appeals on wholly irrelevant grounds.

The amelioration of our current, and vulgar, overemphasis on competitive sports in the high school is drastic but relatively simple. Take away the dollar sign. Do away with paid coaches, and the pressure for victory will abate. Do away with travel expenses, and teams will stay home (where they belong) and schools develop intramural sports. Do away with paid admission, and dependence of "other" sports on basketball and football will disappear. Do away with athletic scholarships or scholarship aid (this is largely but not exclusively a problem of the college), and teams will lose as many games as they win, which will be all to the good. If this seems like a revolutionary program, may I suggest that it is the current American practice that is revolutionary. What I propose is, in effect, a return to the old and tested practices of nineteenth-century England and America and present-day England. It was a calamity that Harvard and Columbia did not follow the example of the University of Chicago in abandonment of intercollegiate football. It will be a calamity if high schools generally do not take to heart the logic of the University of Chicago decision on their own academic level!

Fourth, just as we have not fully assimilated the fact that schools now have community support and that they do not need to use the playing fields as they did a generation ago, so we have not assimilated the fact that the problem of what we may roughly call Americanization has likewise been solved. In the nineteenth and early twentieth century—up to 1914, in fact—when our schools were confronted with the children of immigrants and of freedmen having no knowledge of American history or institutions, and when the problem of creating a harmonious society out of heterogeneous racial and religious elements was a pressing one, the schools were properly required to, and did, take on large responsibilities here. That problem is no longer acute; indeed we may question whether it still exists in any serious sense. Yet just at a time when we have achieved a larger degree of unity than we knew in the nineteenth century; at a time when there are scores of other media to inculcate a knowledge of, and pride in, America; at a time when perhaps the greatest need is to understand other countries and other cultures—at just this time, high schools everywhere concentrate heavily on the teaching of American history, civics, and literature! Not only this, but, all too often, emphasis on the study of things American has wrong motives and wrong objectives. The motives are chauvinistic; the objectives, parochial. The young do not need more nationalism, but less. They do not need less study of Greece and Rome, of Britain, of Canada and South America, and of France, but more. The young do not need to be confirmed in their instinctive belief that fifty years of American literature is worth a cycle of English or French, nor do they need to have their enthusiasm for something called vaguely "the American system" whipped up artificially. There is no reason to suppose that the compulsory study of American history in the elementary school and again in the high school necessarily makes good citizens. And we might keep in mind the sobering fact that the great men who won our independence and laid the foundations for our Republic—Washington, Jefferson, Adams, Hamilton, Madison, Mason, and others—were trained on the histories of Greece and Rome.

Fifth, I doubt that educators have adjusted themselves to the significance of the most elementary educational statistics. In 1890, when our population was 63,000,000, our college population was 157,000. Since then, the population has increased almost threefold; the college and university population, some 20 times! Add to this the fact that something like 25,000,000 Americans participate in some adult-education programs, and the conclusion is inescapable that the high school is no longer our educational terminal. Within a single generation a revolution has occurred: the college today occupies pretty much the place which the high school occupied in 1912.

Of course, in a general way, we all know what is happening, but we still use the high schools as if they were, in a sense, our last chance. An ever increasing number of our young people will have three or four years in which to learn many of the things that high schools now try to inculcate. They are not under such heavy pressure as they were to learn manners and social dancing, to learn typewriting and driving, to enjoy competitive sports and adult social life, to learn the other non-academic subjects to which the schools gave, and give, their attention. Some of these things they can be expected to learn in college. Some they can be expected to learn from the many other agencies now engaged in assuring that the young are well adjusted. Now that most adults enjoy a 35- or 40-hour work week and now that labor-saving devices have shortened the hours devoted to housework, perhaps even parents can resume their traditional tasks of teaching their young some of the things they should know! It is a paradox that, just when technology has made it possible for parents to spend far more of their time in training their children than ever before, they should foist so much responsibility upon schools. There is more justification for using the crucial high-school years for training the mind than there was in the nineteenth or early twentieth century and less justification for not doing so.

There is an additional argument here for concentration on academic activities, and even on rather traditional academic interests. On the one hand, modern technology and automation have simplified the purely mechanical tasks of industry to the point where any reasonably intelligent young man or woman can learn what he needs to know in a week or so. On the other hand, the demands of the professions are so large and elaborate that, more and more, the professional schools prefer that the young learn special skills in college or in the professional school rather than in the high school. Industry, business, college, and professional schools unite in urging the desirability of thorough training in elementary skills in the high schools of today and tomorrow, and the key word here is "thorough."

Sixth, it is possible that abandonment of many of the extra-curriculum activities of the high school and a concentration on academic activities might hasten one badly needed change: the reduction by one year, or more, of the time ordinarily devoted to preparation for college or for industry or business. It was (characteristically) an American, John Fiske, who hit upon the important social law of the prolongation of infancy as one of the human habits that explains not only civilization but morality. Americans have, perhaps, carried the practice to excess. A rich nation can doubtless afford, financially, the prolongation of childhood and youth well into the twenties, but a sensible people will not permit the growing waste of years and of talents involved in our current educational practices.

It is (need I remind you?) an illusion that life is growing longer. It is, to be sure, growing longer at one end (for those who survive), but there is little evidence that the span of years available for work or for public service has lengthened appreciably since the eighteenth century. Men live longer but retire in their sixties. On the other hand, instead of plunging into their profession or into public service at twenty, they are not ready until they are thirty. The doctor, the lawyer, the school administrator, the psychiatrist, the scholar, the statesman—these are rarely able, in our system, to get under way until they are thirtyish. All of us are familiar with the growing habit of turning preparation for a career into a career and of regarding a writer, a scholar, or a statesman who is only forty as something of an infant prodigy!

We are, in a sense, prisoners of the nineteenth-century habit of thinking of education in terms of twelve years. I need not remind my readers that there is nothing sacred about twelve years, whether divided into eight and four or into six and three and three. Nor, for that matter, is there anything sacred about the additional four years we customarily devote to the university. Other societies have not allowed themselves to become bemused by this chronological arrangement and have not suffered for their independence. There is every reason now for speeding up the educational process and getting young men and women into production as rapidly as possible. Military service exacts one or two years of the lives of our young men; the demands of professional training are ever more time-consuming; the nation desperately needs the talents and the energy of the young; the costs that society has to pay for maintaining the young in school are immense; the young themselves, in revolt against the prolongation of infancy, are marrying and rearing families in their early twenties. How much longer can we go on accepting four years as the norm for secondary education?

As the high school is released, or releases itself, from responsibility for many of the extraneous duties placed upon it in the nineteenth century, it can devote more time to academic duties. As teachers are better trained, students better prepared, and new techniques for speeding up the teaching and learning processes developed and applied, the high schools may well be expected to do in three years, perhaps less, what they now do in four.

I suspect that, if they did, students who now go on to college would enter with more enthusiasm for learning than they now have and that many young persons who now find it necessary to go to work at eighteen would be able to enjoy one or two years of college —and maybe find the experience so delightful that they would somehow manage to stay on! I know that general conclusions cannot be drawn from special cases, but it is at least interesting that Jefferson graduated from William and Mary at nineteen, Gouverneur Morris from King's at sixteen, and Jay from King's at nineteen; Hancock from Harvard at seventeen; Samuel Adams from Harvard at eighteen; Emerson from Harvard at eighteen and Charles W. Eliot at nineteen, while the first president of the University of Chicago, William Rainey Harper, graduated from Muskingum College at sixteen and received his Ph.D. from Yale when he was nineteen!

Need for Redirection

Educators, then, must emancipate themselves from the notion that they are to reflect, rather than guide, the interests of society; that they must cater to community prejudices as well as to community interests; that they are somehow bound by the educational mechanics of the past. They should emancipate themselves, too, from one psychotic fear whose roots go back into the Old World— the fear of becoming financially involved with the national government.

The relation of the national government to education is a large and complex subject, and I cannot more than touch on it. For reasons familiar to all of us, our schools were, from the beginning, controlled by district, town, and state rather than by the nation. This was, and is, all to the good, for local control made it impossible for any government or any party to use the schools of the nation as a political instrument. We have assumed that local and state, or private, control cannot be retained if the national government helps foot the bill. This assumption is both illogical and pernicious. It is illogical because it flies in the face of our experience with national support to state universities and to agricultural experiment stations, and national support to a whole series of scholarly, scientific, and artistic enterprises, such as the Library of Congress, the National Archives, the National Gallery of Art, the U.S. Geological Survey, the Coast and Geodetic Survey, the Bureau of Standards, the Smithsonian Institution, and others—all of them largely dependent on federal money but happily free from federal control of their substantive activities. It is pernicious because it inevitably condemns large groups of our children—those who reside in poor states—to an education inferior to that enjoyed by children in rich states. Nor is this a matter that concerns the states alone. The vote of a badly educated young man or woman counts just as much as the vote of a well-educated young man or woman; both alike vote for congressmen and for President and therefore decide national questions of concern to everyone.

Fear of political interference in education is deep-seated and understandable. But so far as the record shows, the national government has not been more guilty than have local or state governments of interference with intellectual freedom; it has been less guilty. The task of educators is not to bewail the inadequacy of local funds and fight to the death against the threat of federal appropriations which may carry with them improper controls. Their task is to find whatever money is necessary to do the job of education as it should be done and to educate legislators and administrators, local and national alike, to the perils of improper interference. There is no evidence that this cannot be done. It has been done in Britain, in Denmark, in Sweden, in Holland, and elsewhere. It has not even been tried in our country, and it is time that American educators abandoned the unmanly practice of scaring themselves with buga-boos of national politics and addressed themselves to the task of educating and civilizing the political processes.

One final suggestion. In the generation after 1830 a large number of American educators—notably, Horace Mann, Henry Barnard, Calvin Stowe—streamed over to Germany and France to study educational practices there. They came home to apply the lessons that they had learned to conditions in this country, particularly to elementary education. Again, in the period from 1880 to 1900, American educators turned to Europe, this time to study higher education, and again they brought back much of value—and some things of little value. Today we have, I think, much to learn about secondary education, especially from the Scandinavian countries and from Switzerland and Holland—countries with democratic education systems closer to ours than are the systems of Britain or Germany or France, and countries, too, with social institutions much like ours. Perhaps some future Mann or Barnard, some future Eliot or Gilman, will bring to secondary education, as these did for the elementary and the advanced levels, the benefit of relevant European experience.

Writing in the 1830's, when Horace Mann and Henry Barnard, Thaddeus Stevens and John D. Pierce, Mary Lyon and Catherine Beecher were just beginning their great work and the high school was still an experiment, Alexis de Tocqueville said: "In that land the great experiment was to be made by civilized man, of the attempt to construct society upon a new basis, and it was there, for the first time, that theories hitherto unknown, or deemed impracticable, were to exhibit a spectacle for which the world had not been prepared by the history of the past."

And at almost the same time Horace Mann, commenting on the Old Deluder Satan Law of the Bay Colony, observed: "As a matter of *fact* it had no precedent in world history, and as a *theory* it could have been refuted and silenced by a more formidable array of argument and experience than was ever marshaled against any other institution of human origin. But time has ratified its soundness."

We, too, can say that time has ratified the soundness of the American experiment in mass education, even to our own time, and that nations whose leaders a century ago had only contempt for that experiment imitate it today. The experiment was successful because the men and the women who launched it and guided it consulted their hopes and not their fears. It was successful because they and their successors gambled on the intelligence and the virtue of the people. It was successful because, in the light of conditions which obtained in the nineteenth century, they were bold, generous, and imaginative.

As the high school enters a new era—an era in which most of its graduates will go on to advanced education, and an era in which its products will be citizens of the most influential of world powers— we should make sure that it is not too timid to challenge its own society, that it is not too conservative to break with its own habits, that it is not too wanting in faith to have confidence in the integrity of its own government.

An American Looks at European Education*

History shows that, except under conditions of duress brought about by external forces, schools and colleges have developed gradually in different parts of the world in response to a variety of different conditions. They are a product of the society they serve, and they also influence the future of this society. Reformers who have sought to change education have had to be content with minor alterations or else have had to devote a lifetime to their task.

It is clear that various educational devices have in the past been outmoded by social changes. The situation of Oxford and Cambridge during the first two-thirds of the nineteenth century is a case in point. For two generations many leaders of public opinion argued for the need of either establishing modern universities in England or reforming the two ancient seats of learning. Eventually both courses of action were followed; the modification of Oxford and Cambridge by successive royal commissions was so radical as to constitute the equivalent of a series of drastic biological mutations. By the end of the century English universities were once again well adapted to the tasks at hand.

To one interested in comparative education, it is fascinating to see how, today, many nations are struggling to solve the basic problems connected with their educational systems. To a student of comparative education, many questions about education in different countries are questions almost without meaning. Asking whether European schools are better than schools in the United States is like asking a comparative anatomist whether a whale is a better mammal than an elephant.

The comparative anatomist is interested in examining the similarities and differences to be found in animal or plant organs which carry out the same function; he is very cautious, however, about

* Copyright by James B. Conant.

20

proclaiming the virtues of a device found in one particular species over a device for a similar purpose found in another. Of course the anatomist knows that mammals are modified only slowly by changes in environment; unlike schools or colleges, no man-made decisions will radically alter the structure of the functioning organism he is examining.

Some will argue that this vitiates my analogy; they may claim that the essence of human organizations lies in the fact that conscious acts of men and women can change them, and, as history shows, overnight if need be. "But wait a moment," the student of the comparative anatomy of schools will say, "not overnight surely, except at the point of a bayonet or in our time under the shadow of armored vehicles and tanks." And such changes, he will argue, are the equivalent of pathological alterations.

Education for the Professions

First, I should like to examine in particular the way the future members of the professions are recruited, selected, and educated in certain European nations and the United States.

For a number of professions one phase of professional education—the final stage, so to speak—is essentially identical in all countries. There is little to be gained by noting the minor differences to be found in various nations. This is true of medicine, of engineering, and of the natural sciences; it is likewise true, to a lesser degree, of certain areas within the social sciences and the humanities. It is possible to pass judgment on the work of the medical faculty of a university, for example, almost without taking into account the traditions of the institutions or its surroundings. Considering the training of a medical man only from the standpoint of professional competency, it would not be too difficult to classify all the medical schools of Europe and America into groups according to their degree of excellence. The same would apply to the training of engineers and research scientists.

It is not so much professional education as the education provided *prior* to professional studies that varies from nation to nation. This is particularly true if one directs attention to the way the future members of the professions are recruited and selected. Nowhere on the European continent will one find the equivalent of the American four-year liberal arts college. The European youth, unlike his American contemporary, passes directly from a university-preparatory school to professional training.

Americans find it difficult to imagine an educational system without a college; Europeans find it hard to imagine what sort of an institution an American college can be. And the task of explaining the situation in the United States to a German, for example, is not made easier by the fact that there are more than fifteen hundred four-year colleges in our country (some, part of a university; some, not); their curriculums and criteria for admission and graduation vary enormously. The one thing they have in common is the right to award a Bachelor's degree—an academic symbol derived from the Middle Ages which has completely disappeared in German-speaking nations, though not in France.

One sometimes hears it said that the characteristic feature of American education is the proportion of our youth attending a university. So phrased, this is a completely misleading statement. What is characteristic is the very large proportion of our youth from eighteen to twenty years of age who are engaged in full-time studies; the fraction is something like a quarter to a third. In Great Britain, France, Germany, and Switzerland not more than a tenth of the youth are so engaged. Equally characteristic are the figures for school attendance at the age sixteen to seventeen. In America more than 75 per cent of those of this age are in school full-time; in European countries and Great Britain the corresponding figure is less than 20 per cent. Some Europeans have said that only a rich nation could afford to keep so many of its youth in school so long. But with the increase in automation, it is a question whether the withdrawal of a considerable fraction of youth from the labor force is a luxury. The type of training needed in the distributive industries more and more requires considerable "book learning."

At all events, when we consider the proportion of youth engaged in *professional* studies, the position of the United States is not so different from that of the rest of the world. Perhaps it is fair to compare the proportion of young men enrolled in the first year of a university in Europe or Great Britain to the proportion in the United States entering engineering, law, and medical schools and starting in the graduate schools of arts and sciences. Taking the figures for young men, the proportion in the United States seems to be something like 6 per cent; surprisingly small, many would say. But what is equally surprising is that similar figures represent the situation in all nations for which I have seen statistics. Therefore one could say that the proportion of youth studying *professionally* in a university is about the same in the United States as in other nations. What *is* different between America and Europe is the method by which this very small percentage is selected and educated prior to engaging in professional studies.

Selection of Students for Pre-professional Study

Today, unlike the situation of a hundred years ago, the education of members of the professions (particularly natural scientists and engineers) is a concern of statesmen; public opinion has an interest in hearing the answers to such questions as the following: Are we training enough professional people? Are we including in our education for the professions a large fraction of those who have the requisite ability, or are we overlooking many with high potentialities?

In a totalitarian state these questions lead directly to a control of the entire educational process; the capable are to be sorted out and educated for the different professions according to the nation's need for these professions. This is essentially the directive of the Party Executive Committee to those in charge of schools and universities in the Soviet Zone of Germany. In a free country the political situation is, thank God, very different, not only because of the impossibility of government's ordering youth into different educational channels but because of the freedom of parents to express their desires to school authorities and, if need be, to politicians.

National concern with the number and quality of scientists and engineers is clearly a result of the last phases of the Industrial Revolution, which started two hundred years ago. Parental concern with education as a way by which a son may better himself economically and socially is a consequence of the spread of that spirit of democracy of which Tocqueville wrote more than a century ago. It has taken time for the equalitarian doctrines of the French Revolution reinforced by American notions to affect European education; but there is no doubt that the problem of selecting future university students is becoming more, rather than less, difficult in England and a number of European states. The question of social prestige is becoming involved, as it has been involved with us in America for at least fifty years.

Let me give a few concrete examples. During the Second World War the British Parliament made certain changes in the English system of tax-supported schools. Among the objectives which the new legislation sought to achieve was the widening of opportunity for children of the less well to do; another was an elimination of the great difference in prestige that in the past had characterized one type of tax-supported school as compared with another. The traditional view of the content of a school program was, however, not modified. A long course was held to be necessary; and selection of those capable of entering those schools which provided this course was to be made at the age of eleven to twelve.

From the point of view of a parent with a low income and a talented child, the new arrangement must appear to be better than the old. But parents of medium income view the altered situation highly critically. In the past, the "grammar schools" had provided excellent roads to the universities open to those who could afford to pay a moderate fee. (For well-to-do families the usual road to the university is provided by the famous "public schools.") The new regulations abolished the fees and made the admission of *all* children subject to a competitive examination. And to make matters worse, so some parents have said, a new type of examination is employed— so-called psychological tests—that has no apparent relation to school work! As a result the whole subject of selection at age eleven-plus is a topic of heated discussion among educators and laymen.

In one county in England the experiment is being made of abolishing the examination in two selected geographic areas and sending all children from eleven to fifteen to one school and then providing grammar-school places for those whose parents are willing to keep them in school until at least sixteen. Presumably ability to handle the work in the grammar school will be the determining factor in deciding who goes on to the university. The article in the London *Observer* reviewing the experiment carries the heading "Eleven-plus Condemned." This caption corresponds to the sentiment expressed in a number of articles and letters to the editor that have been appearing in British journals and papers in the last few years.

On the European continent, too, difficulties have arisen in regard to the process of selecting those who are to attend the Gymnasium in preparation for a university education. Each one of eleven states in the Federal Republic of Germany has complete authority in educational matters; so too have the twenty-five cantons in Switzerland (with a few exceptions). A comparison of the roads to the university in each of these states is interesting; it shows how different local conditions have modified to a certain degree the European pattern. The points at issue are often the exact length of the pre-university school course and the methods by which pupils are selected for the special pre-university schools.

The parental pressure varies greatly from place to place and reflects differences in tradition and economic circumstances. Sometimes the selection can be made solely on the basis of advice given by teachers and accepted by parents. Sometimes examinations are required in order to decide who should start on the road to the professions. If so, parental protests frequently arise. In one German state I heard a mother complaining that the entrance tests for the Gymnasium were so foolish and arbitrary that many of her friends could not get their children admitted; as a consequence the parents were pressed into the expense of sending them to private schools. In France, where the road to the professions has been studded with stiff competitive examinations, anguish over the selection process has been particularly acute. The entrance examinations for the pre-university schools (lycées) have just been abolished, and the program in these schools lightened. Selection of the pupils who head for the university is now to be made on the basis of the primary-school record. In Switzerland the psychological effect on the child of failure in the pre-university school (in some cantons a half to two-thirds drop out) is giving concern to the school authorities.

In several German states, parents have brought suit against the government because a child had been barred from a pre-university school. The matter has even become a political issue. It is not the method of selection but the length of the pre-university school course that is in controversy. If the course is nine years, then selection must be made at the age of ten to eleven; this was the usual pattern in Germany, I judge, some years ago. But in the postwar years in some states the pre-university course was shortened, and the time of selection correspondingly postponed.

The arguments in favor of keeping all the children together in one school as long as possible are familiar to Americans; an additional (and for Europeans more weighty) argument for a shorter pre-university period of schooling is that it may be easier to select those suited for university work at twelve or thirteen rather than ten or eleven. The abbreviated course has been attacked, however, on the grounds that nine years is necessary if the pupil is to master the subjects required for later university work (particularly Latin). The differences of opinion on the matter seem to run along the usual lines of political cleavage in both Germany and Switzerland; in general, the moderate right favors the longer course, the moderate left the shorter.

In one state election in Germany the issue was of major importance. This is hard for Americans to understand, since the difference of opinion appears to be relatively slight and the educational question involved touches the schooling of not more than a fifth of the children. It is interesting to us as evidence of the intimate connection between school problems and sociological questions.

Requirements for Admission to University Studies

From what I have already reported, it is clear that the age at which selection is made and the time it is made is intimately associated with the content of the pre-university course of study. And here we meet the second major difference between the road to the professions in Europe and in the United States. In Europe the state determines the requirements which must be satisfactorily fulfilled in order to obtain, on finishing school, the necessary credentials which will enable the holder to enter a university. In Germany and Switzerland, for example, the certificate which a youth obtains after passing a set of final examinations in the last school year is an admission ticket to *any* university. The absence of any such uniform requirements in America astonishes and perplexes the European observer of our chaotic system.

Though each state in the Federal Republic of Germany is autonomous, the standards throughout are essentially the same. Certain variations in the subjects on which a student is examined are permitted, but one may say that the essential subjects are languages and mathematics. In the classical Gymnasium (in Germany called the humanistic school), Latin and Greek are obligatory; in most of the others, Latin and at least one modern foreign language; in a few schools, exposure to a heavy dose of modern languages, mathematics, and natural science is considered a substitute for Latin. A European university is *not* an American college, and language instruction is not one of its functions; scientists, lawyers, medical men, economists, and historians, therefore, have no opportunity for studying any language after they leave school. With this in mind, one realizes why a long school course is believed necessary for future university students. The central position occupied in the curriculums of pre-university schools by foreign languages is a reflection of the role played by both tradition and geography in educational matters. As far as future professional men are concerned, Europeans are convinced that the traditional education in languages, literature, mathematics, and European history comprises the best general education.

For the 75 or 80 per cent who have no ambition or no opportunity to head for a university, formal full-time education ends at fourteen or fifteen; further educational development in part-time courses will depend on the occupation of the young man or woman in question. The apprentice system together with continuation schools takes care of industrial workers, it may be said. For apprentices with special mechanical aptitude, technical schools are available. For the 10 per cent or so who must drop out of the pre-university schools, some special type of education with more emphasis on practical business affairs is needed. This the European would grant, but the idea of a general education for a large proportion of adolescents aged sixteen to twenty-one is unheard of on the continent of Europe.

American and European General Education Contrasted

"How is it at the end of the road?" one may ask. Are those Europeans who complete the hard journey and arrive at a university and later become professional men (some 6 per cent of the young men) better educated than the corresponding Americans? This is the type of question a student of comparative education refuses to answer;

for so much depends on your standard of judgment, on what basis you evaluate the non-professional knowledge, ability, and attitude of a professional man or woman.

One thing is certain: the average American medical man, lawyer, chemist, physicist, or engineer has acquired a quite different store of general knowledge from that of his European counterpart. If command of foreign languages is the test of a well-educated man or woman, relatively few Americans can claim to be well educated. If knowledge of European literature and art is taken as a measure, there again the average American professional man will fail in comparison with the Europeans. European pre-university education is in essence literary education; American college education can rarely be so described.

On the other hand, every American in school and in college will have sampled at least a bit of some of the social sciences. Indeed perhaps the majority of those whom we are here considering will have acquired a considerable knowledge of economics and political science; a large proportion will have studied psychology and sociology. With rare exceptions these disciplines are only available to a European in a university; and while the student enrolled under the law faculty may find time to listen to some lectures in these fields, the medical man and the natural scientist will not.

In other words, those Americans who complete at least three years of a four-year liberal arts college course will have had a kind of academic experience unknown on the continent of Europe. (A possible exception to this statement is the education provided for the future teachers in the pre-university schools who are educated in the famous École Normale in Paris and in the philosophical faculties of the German universities.)

But it is not only the content of the program which characterizes the American college. The whole atmosphere is different from either a European school or a European university. There is far more freedom for the student than in a school, of course, and there is far more personal instruction of the student by the professor than is possible in a university of the European type with its relatively small staff in proportion to the size of the student body. The American student is ready to express an opinion to anyone; discussion is encouraged at every turn. Student activities ranging from dramatics through debating and journalism stimulate student independence; there is no parallel to these expressions of student initiative in Europe. All of which, of course, reflects what Americans have come to believe are important aspects of college education.

Indeed one can sum up the comparison I have been making by saying that the leading citizens of Europe and the United States have quite different aims in mind when they talk about education as apart from professional training. And the difference reflects the different social histories on the two sides of the Atlantic.

Impact of Social Change on Education

As a first approximation, one may say that Europe adjusted its education to modern times nearly a hundred years ago. A period of rapid educational change on the Continent took place in the middle of the nineteenth century; this reflected the first impact of industrialization. The pattern thus established has persisted to the present with relatively few changes; it is obviously intimately associated with the apprentice system of training industrial workers and a relative lack of geographic and social mobility. It also reflects the powerful influence of the university faculties which were well intrenched when the educational changes were in progress, particularly the influence of the professors of the classics.

During the period of change in the United States in which we are still living, traditional academic forces have played a far less important role. But such social factors as the raising of the school-leaving age in the United States and the near disappearance of the European apprentice system were of more importance in determining the shape of the new educational system which is now emerging.

I have written "emerging" because it is clear that in this country we are still in process of adapting our schools, colleges, and universities to the current needs of our society (and trying to adapt to future needs as well). In England, too, a process of change has been, and still is, at work. In the nations of Western Europe, on the other hand (with the exception of Scandinavia), few alterations in the systems have been made in the last fifty years; though there are many educational problems similar to our own and England's, a period of reform has not yet begun.

An American observer cannot help wondering if such a period is not considerably overdue. It may well be that the more immediate political and social issues in France and the urgent task of reconstruction in post-war Germany have merely pushed aside consideration of educational changes. I seem to detect signs of dissatisfaction in the Federal Republic of Germany which may be the prelude to important actions. In parts of Switzerland the road to the professions is being resurveyed. In France a few important changes have just been made, and a bill providing for a drastic alteration in the French system has been introduced into parliament by the minister of education.

We here in the United States are still engaged in remaking our educational roads; the nature of the task varies considerably from state to state, from community to community. Pedagogic devices and plans for the organization of schools and universities are not always transferable across state lines; they are almost never exportable to foreign countries. But nonetheless the exchange of ideas and blueprints is always helpful because it stimulates and arouses discussion.

We may watch with interest, therefore, the new developments in those Western nations from which came originally our cultural traditions and our ideas about education. The free nations of the world in planning for their youth, as in many other matters, must be in constant communication; for, however diverse their methods, their fundamental aims remain the same: the preservation and extension of personal freedom.

The University and the High School—
Past and Future

Everyone, or almost everyone, is aware of the fact that the future of our free way of life depends upon an educated citizenry; and over the last half-century, as the percentage of young people attending the public high school has jumped from roughly 10 to well over 90, our public interest began to center in secondary-school education. We all realize that there has been an enormous amount of criticism of the high school in recent years, and, while some of it has been uninformed and irresponsible, some also has been informed and telling. I should like in this paper to try to make a fresh start upon the problem from the only vantage point that I possess, namely, that of a philosopher by training turned administrator by profession.

Whenever we talk about education, we base our statements, consciously or unconsciously, upon certain very fundamental philosophical ideas. Philosophy has been said to be the science of bewildering one's self methodically, and there is something in this definition. Philosophy really is bewildering, and this is the reason so few people are able and willing to reveal the fundamental philosophical presuppositions that direct their educational judgments. What knowledge is and how one acquires it are the problems of that branch of philosophy referred to by the fancy name of "epistemology"; and epistemology, in turn, is based upon certain even more fundamental ideas about the nature of man, the universe, and man's relation to the universe, collected under the name of "metaphysics." Incidentally, the word "metaphysics," the most fundamental of all the philosophical disciplines, really means nothing at all. When the works of Aristotle were assembled, there was a great deal of material for which no previously known category could be found, so it was put in a book which followed his statements on physics, and hence the word "metaphysics" or "after the physics."

31

Dewey and Progressive Education

The metaphysican and epistemologist who has played the greatest role in the determination of the methods and objectives of contemporary elementary and secondary education is Professor John Dewey, who, by the way, was a professor of philosophy at the University of Chicago from 1894 to 1904 and one of the founders of our Laboratory School. Mr. Dewey had the misfortune of being widely misunderstood and so, unwittingly, has served as the great philosophical instigator and prophet for what has come to be called "progressive education." It seems clear that he had little realization of what he had wrought until his later years, when he made several efforts to correct the misunderstanding that had occurred.

Now I happen to believe that Mr. Dewey was a pretty good philosopher and that, correctly understood, what he really had to say has relevance to the educational enterprise. Dewey was concerned with the problem of how we think, and this was the title of one of his earliest and best books. To express his conclusions in the jargon of the philosophers, all thinking originates in a problematic situation and is brought to a conclusion within a context which shapes the thinking and determines the relevance and, indeed, the truth of the conclusion. Let me illustrate his meaning with an example. Robinson Crusoe finds himself upon a desert island which he believes to be deserted. One day while walking on the beach he sees a footprint, and this datum, as Dewey calls it, constitutes the problematic situation. "Who made the footprint? Is he friendly or unfriendly? And, if I assume the latter, what ought I to do about it?" We all know the rest of the story. Robinson Crusoe decided that the footprint was made by a cannibal and took steps to defend himself; and he did, in fact, successfully defend himself later against an attack. This is what Dewey is saying in essence, and there is nothing very earth-shaking about it. We think when we have a problem to think about. The way we think is determined by a complex context involving certain partial information and certain desired conclusions, for example, in the case of Robinson Crusoe, saving his own life. It is understandable, therefore, that Dewey emerged with a somewhat new definition of knowledge and of truth. Knowledge is what we seek in trying to solve a problem, and truth is the answer that satisfactorily solves the problem.

There is one other fundamental idea about Dewey's philosophy, developed in his later work, namely, the concept of value or the end of human life. The object of living, according to Dewey, is growth, and all he really means by this is that we must go right on having problems if we are to realize the full richness of life. I think we all know from our own experience what he is talking about. Too many minds become frozen at a certain point: they possess all the answers. Thinking ceases, according to Dewey, when all one's values become fixed and there are no live, interesting, and new things to think about. The essential principles, then, of Mr. Dewey's philosophy are that the learning process occurs within a context of concern and challenge, and life takes on values as long as this continues as an active process.

But look what happened when certain persuasive teachers of teachers began to explain what Dewey meant. Thinking begins, says Mr. Dewey, in an interest or a concern. Therefore, said the educator, our problem is to interest students; and this interpretation passed over easily into the distortion of amusing and entertaining them. Dewey certainly did not mean anything like this. I suppose it is true to say that one way of interesting the child in mathematics is to play games which involve the use of arithmetic, but another way of getting him interested is to require him to learn enough mathematics so that he becomes aware of problems that had not previously existed for him. It is a valuable thing, of course, to interest a child in learning to read, but this does not mean keeping the child amused and entertained whether or not he learns to read. Still another kind of unfortunate misunderstanding occurred as to Dewey's theory of truth. For Dewey, truth is the solution, the particular set of facts and hypotheses that actually work to solve a problem. Now this became translated into some kind of inverted "adjustment to the environment," a phrase which Dewey himself often uses. Dewey is really saying that thinking begins in maladjustment to the environment and continues as an active, tough, and difficult process, whereby we solve the problems that occur within our experience. This was misunderstood by certain professional educators, whose influence exceeded their wisdom, to mean that the end of the educational process is the adjustment of our youngsters to their environment with no particular concern or activity on their part. For example, marks were eliminated so that the young person might not suffer the frustration of feeling inferior to others. Students were promoted in both the elementary and the secondary schools whether they deserved it or not in order that they might have no sense of maladjustment. This enormous sensitivity and tenderness for the sense of security and adaptation of the child is a frightful travesty upon Dewey's thinking. His was really a rigorous mind, believing that the adjustments that we make to the problems arising in our experience occur only through hard and active thinking, and if the adjustments are made for us, nothing of any educational significance occurs.

And a final grievous error is made in the interpretation of Dewey's theory of value. He did say that value was growth, meaning by that that the good life is being endlessly challenged and endlessly dissatisfied with the limitations of the present. This is how we grow and stay alive, said Dewey, but this principle was translated by certain thoughtless progressives into a complete lack of discipline for youth. Let them express themselves, it was said, and give them complete and unrestrained freedom of action and speech, of manners and lack of manners; only then will they grow. This is a curious kind of confusion of the philosopher John Dewey with the Frenchman Jean Jacques Rousseau. Rousseau really did believe in the noble savage, as he expressed it, and he honestly felt that, if all human minds could only completely and fully express themselves, the millennium would come. But Dewey entertained no such idea. Growth, for him, was a thoroughly disciplined kind of concept, in terms of which the human mind was constantly beaten back and forth between brute fact and the flights of human hope and aspiration. John Dewey was one of the most significant philosophers of our time, and the serious misunderstanding of him—unlike most philosophical misunderstandings—has affected millions of lives.

Teacher Education and the University

I am greatly troubled when I turn, as a university administrator, to consider this serious philosophical and educational misunderstanding. I believe that universities have been in large part responsible for it by separating themselves from high-school education and the training of high-school teachers. I fear that this separation has resulted not only in a distortion of the philosophy upon which much of our secondary education rests but also in a watering-down of the subject matter taught in many of the classrooms. Let me try to state some of the origins and causes of this separation and make some suggestions about the need of directing the attention of the entire university toward the problems of the American high school.

For reasons that I do not altogether understand, the field of education spelled with a capital *E* came into disrepute at the universities. The professional educator was looked down upon by his colleagues within the university community until a professor hesitated to admit that he was a member of the school of education. It has been the habit of oppressed minorities through the centuries to band themselves closely together for common defense and, even though separated from the main part of the community, to play a powerful role in its life. And this is precisely what happened in the schools of education at the great American universities. Sneered at by their colleagues as second-class citizens, the educators withdrew from the general life of the university but proceeded through active and strong lobbies in the state legislatures to set up requirements for the licensing of teachers that involved taking their courses and their degrees. Always apart from the universities there were the normal schools, established to train the teachers of the communities, and most of these became teachers' colleges. The schools of education of the universities began then to train these teachers of teachers for the teachers' colleges, thus cutting off the high school even further from the mainstream of the universities. As the schools of education, independent of the universities, became stronger, they developed their own courses, not in psychology but in educational psychology, not in physics but in how to teach physics, and not in history but in the techniques of presenting history to the student. With the combination of state licensing laws, schools of education, and teachers' colleges, the circle became complete. The American high school was cut off from the main body of the American university.

What is the solution to this problem? It is simple enough to state though not easy to realize. The universities must stop grousing about the education of our high-school students and get back into the business of training teachers. The schools of education must become a real part of the universities, and the universities must begin to relate themselves properly and effectively to the work of the schools of education. The philosophy of education must be taught by a member of the department of philosophy. The department of physics must stop regarding the Master's degree as being of no importance. The high-school teacher of mathematics or the teacher of teachers of mathematics in the school of education must receive his training in subject matter at the hands of a competent mathematician.

This does not mean that the school of education ceases to have a part to play in this educational program. It has been conspicuously successful over a number of years in the development of useful and valuable educational techniques. Because of the schools of education, a great deal is known about curriculum development, tests and testing, the techniques of counseling and vocational guidance, and school administration. These things are important and necessary to the teacher and to the school administrator. And, if Mr. Dewey is right that knowledge begins in interest and challenge, there are techniques of stimulating these among students. The school of education, moreover, is, and will remain, the real link between the university and the high school, translating out the theory and new discovery of the universities into the high-school classrooms. We are all too acutely aware of the enormous time lag that now occurs between new developments in any field of knowledge and the high-school classroom. Mathematics, for example, has made enormous progress within the last half-century, and yet the program of high-school mathematics has remained substantially unchanged over this same period. And, if it is the role of the school of education to stand between new knowledge and its applications, I should add that this bridge should support traffic going in two directions. It is of considerable importance that the universities know more than most of them now do about the real activities and problems of the classroom teacher. So much of the research in education seems sterile and irrelevant to the teacher because the research worker is unacquainted with what actually happens in the classroom.

We have long prided ourselves in America upon our ability as administrators. We are an efficient people, and our universities reflect this; upon the whole, they successfully accomplish the ends to which they are directed. But somehow we have failed with the high school, and we are paying a high price. We have allowed a part of the university to drift out of its proper relationship with other parts and to take over the entire problem of the secondary education of our youth. The school of education must be re-established as one of the important focal points within the university where the content fields converge. The school of education must give this content appropriate configurations for the high-school program and add the necessary techniques of presentation. The minds of our youth are the future of America, not to be intrusted to a single part of our educational enterprise. It is our responsibility as citizens, as teachers and administrators in high schools and universities, to insist that these minds receive the best that all of American education can provide.

The Commissioner of Education
Looks at the High School

We of the Office of Education engaged in several extensive preparatory conferences as a basis for the drafting of this paper. The ideas that I shall offer, in this look at the American high school, reflect common views in which my colleagues, some of the most creative thinkers and leaders in secondary education, have joined. I shall try to be a good spokesman for them as well as for myself.

Only 137 years have passed since that May morning in 1821 when some hundred children trooped into a new kind of school: the English High School in Boston. They had no idea that they were starting the most tremendous educational experiment in history and setting in motion forces which have helped to bring this country to the position of leadership it now holds in world affairs.

When those Boston youngsters met their first principal, Mr. George Barrell Emerson, the entire school and college population of the country was about three million. More than forty-three million are enrolled for the academic year 1957–58. Today one out of every four of our entire population is in school or college. Almost nine and a half million students are in Grades IX through XII in approximately thirty thousand high schools scattered across the nation—schools which vary from one-room establishments in remote rural areas to the modern high schools in the cities and their mushrooming suburbs.

An Amazing Achievement

The development of the high-school system in this country is a truly amazing achievement. Nothing like it has ever been seen in history. During the nineteenth century, thirty million immigrants, with varied languages and cultural backgrounds, came to these

38

shores. Despite language differences, fantastic growth in population, and a lack of national unity that led to the tragedy of the Civil War, despite the shattering effects of a depression and two world wars, we have succeeded in giving our millions of citizens the ability to communicate with one another in a common tongue—and this has led to a high degree of national unity and understanding.

Foreign visitors frequently see us with a sharper focus than we see ourselves. A British student of the American scene, Denis W. Brogan, makes the point that our schools are doing far more than instructing students; they are letting students instruct each other in how to live in America.[1] He also notes that our national student body is made up of many children of immigrants to whom English is still largely a foreign tongue, of children of migrants, and of children of rural-bred parents forced to adjust themselves to a new urban environment. In school they are succeeding in learning a common language, common habits, common tolerances, and a common political and national faith.

The development of this general level of literacy of the masses is in sharp contrast to conditions in many other countries, where an educated elite has very little opportunity for communication with the uneducated masses. We have become more aware of this contrast in the past few years through our contacts with other countries in the educational exchange programs. We have seen, at first hand, selective educational systems which produce a sort of "intellectual aristocracy." In these countries the well-educated minority hold jealously to their superiority over the less-educated majority. This results inevitably in restriction of job opportunity and loss of creative energy. A teacher who recently arrived here on an exchange program from one of the European countries told us that she had taken forty examinations over the past five years in order to win her professional status. To obtain the post she now holds, she had to compete against a thousand other applicants.

Here in the United States, where there is no monopoly on education, we have abundant job opportunities for the educated. Of course the reason is that in our system, which provides educational opportunity for all and moves all of our people onward and upward, trained manpower creates the demand for more trained manpower.

[1] Denis W. Brogan, *The American Character* (New York: A. A. Knopf, 1944).

Students and teachers from other lands come here in ever increasing numbers to study our way of life. They equate our prosperity with our effort to provide education for all the children of all the people. They marvel at the magnitude of the task we faced in the development of a new country and a new pattern of education at one and the same time. They marvel still more when they consider the vast geographical distances that have had to be covered and the varied cultural origins that have contributed to the rich mosaic of our American life. These students from other lands see the wisdom as well as the nobility of the American dream. They are spreading over the entire world our concept of the importance of every individual and of his right to develop his potential through education. They recognize this educational concept as the driving force of the American dynamo.

Our universal education has led to our outstanding achievements in this country in science, agriculture, and industry. Many of those responsible for significant contributions to science and technology would have been lost to society had they not been discovered, motivated, and sent on from high school. Yes, there is good reason for pride in the conduct of our public education program to date. But, in all things, appreciation of accomplishment is most wisely judged not by satisfaction with achievement but by the measure of what remains to be done. And today that is a very great deal.

The Challenge of a New Age

The past century, in relation to the history of the human race, has been no more than a split second. Yet, in that second, more has been compassed in technological achievement than in all previous history. In a tenth part of that second, a mere decade, we have seen the advent of television, the development of nuclear energy, the perfection of jet airplanes, electronic brains, and other wonders. And man is racing on to unfold new wonders at a speed as dizzying, it seems, as that of the missiles he can now hurl into outer space. The eerie "beep-beep" of sputnik on its man-made orbit through space dramatized anew that a galvanic program of education is needed to keep abreast of the needs of our increasingly complex society.

The pace of education in the days ahead is being set, in part, by forces outside the control of the education profession, and they are all accelerating forces. There is a constant acceleration of scientific development, a constant acceleration of the importance of our world position, and an acceleration of the sum total of knowledge.

Young people today face a new era of enormous promise and enormous challenge. Industry, government, and the professions are clamoring for an ever increasing level of literacy and technical skill. According to the United States Department of Labor, most of the routine jobs for American youth now require four years of high school. The Department estimates that the need for professional and technical personnel in our society will increase by almost 40 per cent by 1965, while the need for unskilled labor will drop. Yet 40 per cent of our young people are still selling their future short by dropping out of high school before graduation. And each year an estimated two hundred thousand of the most talented of our young people fail, for a variety of reasons, to carry their education beyond the high school.

Students today look to the high school for instruction, not only in how to live in America, but also how to live in other parts of a shrinking world. They may live and work all over the world, as some three and a half million Americans are doing at this very minute. Modern travel and modern communications have produced a society in which John Donne's "no man is an island" philosophy has reached a new dimension. Young people today need an education, not only to prepare them for possible work and travel abroad, but also to help them play an intelligent part here at home, in shaping national and international policy in an age which can no longer afford misunderstanding and unwise decisions.

Our interests as individuals and as a nation make it vital that we now work with all peoples to maintain the free and democratic way of life. The young people in school today must be cultural missionaries of this ideal we call democracy. They have a tough time ahead of them if they are to win out—as they must win out—against the conflicting ideology, communism, and all that it involves.

The going is made harder, not easier, for them by the very nature of our way of life today. The seeds of democracy, we must remember, were not scattered easily by our forefathers on ground ready to receive them. They had to be planted the hard way, by men and women brave enough to adventure an ocean and determined enough to track and clear a wilderness, to fight and die, to work as well as dream, to bring their precious ideal to full flowering.

In 1800 the average work week was eighty-four hours. In 1900 it was down to sixty. Today it is forty, and technology has galloped ahead at such a rate that this year's worker can produce six times as much as his grandfather could for every hour he stays on the job. More and more, man is using machines to do his work for him. More and more, brain-power rather than brawn-power counts, as the forty-hour work week is slipping into history and labor unions talk in terms of a work week of only four days. More and more, leisure rather than labor can become a problem.

The upcoming generation can expect to enjoy less physical work and more luxury in their everyday lives than any before them, and that without some of the catalysts that helped to spur earlier generations of Americans—the hard labor, the long hours, the struggle to acquire the niceties of living in the days before one could buy everything, from one's home to a new car every year, "on time."

In the past we depended on three institutions to nurture the values that make for the best in healthy individualism: the home, the church, and the school. And these forces were strengthened for the most part by life in a community where folks knew most of the other folks and had a feeling of "belonging."

How different it is for the youngsters of today! With both parents often working, many of them have very little home life in the old-time sense. Their community is a city or one of the towns burgeoning around the cities. And, in addition to the three traditional forces of influence, there is now a fourth: the force of mass media. Through radio and television, films, newspapers, and magazines, children are absorbing more and more of their education outside the classroom. Mass media literally deluge them with new ideas and emotions. They may not mature physically or emotionally at an earlier age than their parents did, but they assume elements of adult sophistication much earlier.

Overnight a popular entertainer on television can start them rocking and rolling from the Atlantic to the Pacific. Or a producer can stage a show which sends them to the library for books on Davy Crockett and to the drugstore for coon-skin caps. Because of mass media, young people travel around the world, visit with Columbus and Macbeth, and voyage by space ship to the moon itself. Their vocabularies seem to be more extensive than ever; their knowledge of life and the ways of life, in its best and worst forms, is confusing and sometimes most perturbing.

With so much competition for youthful enthusiasm, small wonder that teachers find it difficult to motivate youngsters to work hard in school to achieve long-term goals. The future has always seemed a never-never land to boys and girls, but they cannot live for today and neglect the future. They need to set long-range goals. In fact, our national survival in this century may well depend upon how successfully we, as educators, help them to plan for their future and realize their progress toward it.

How Can Schools Be Improved?

How, then, can high-school programs be improved to meet the needs of a nation and of youth who now face the unparalleled problems, not merely of their own world, but of space and the islands in space?

First, let us do a more resolute job of educating Americans, through every possible avenue of communication, on the wisdom of investing more of their dollars to wipe out the shortage of teachers and classrooms. This, the most prosperous country on earth, spends only 4.8 per cent of the national income on education—the commodity which made its prosperity. Soviet Russia, now openly dedicated to outstripping America in science and technology, is spending 10 per cent—or more.

To indicate some directions for this improvement is no mean assignment even for the collective brains of the United States Office of Education. Some of these recommendations will not be new to you. I venture to state them with the thought that, taken together, they may give us a grouping of bench marks to guide us as we look to the future.

1. The general and the specific roles of the secondary school, established more than a century ago, must be redefined in the light of realistic responsibilities and achievements of the elementary school and of the now widely available programs and opportunities for post-high-school education.

The role of the high school is the subject of much discussion in many communities and by numerous professional and interested citizen groups. Because the schools are both created and supported by local communities, public discussions of what the high schools should accomplish are healthy expressions of democracy and usually beneficial to education. These efforts will be greatly accelerated by the study completed under the auspices of the Russell Sage Foundation in co-operation with numerous professional associations, agencies, and individual educators.[2] This study presents an organized consensus of the expectations that citizens and educators hold for the American high school. I commend the timeliness of the study and its potential uses in evaluating and improving secondary education.

2. Agreements must be reached concerning the values, knowledges, and skills which can be, and must be, acquired at the most appropriate levels in our educational system with adequate attention to differences in individual aptitude, ability, and aspiration. With so much to be learned, time is at a premium in schools today, and critical evaluation of programs is needed if students are to get the maximum of useful learning out of their school day. Today confusion and uncertainty as to what youth should learn and how they can most effectively learn it beset most parents, school-board members, educators, and citizens.

This problem is particularly acute in our secondary schools, which now take all the products of the lower school and prepare them for increasingly higher employment standards, on the one hand, and college-entrance requirements, on the other. High-school education is today no longer terminal education for more than 50 per cent of the students.

3. The time is *now* for a reappraisal of the uses made of both professional personnel and facilities according to the most enlightened and rigorous administrative management standards available. The pressures of increasing enrolments have brought into sharp focus deficiencies in the supply of competent teachers and other school personnel as well as crowded and inadequate physical facilities for instruction. Ways must also be found in each local school

[2] Will French and Associates, *Behavioral Goals of General Education in High School* (New York: Russell Sage Foundation, 1957).

and school district to recruit, increase prestige for, and help to retain, our ablest teachers and school administrators.

All of us in this business of education must realize that it is a fast-growing business. We have to look ahead and plan ahead to keep pace with the swift growth of our economy and our society. We must be alert to all reasonable experiments which hold out promise of enabling us to get greater mileage out of our existing school facilities. The school day and the school year are all too short; schools and school equipment are costly; the process of learning grows more expensive per student per year. We have to make the most of every hour of every school day for every student. That may mean using school buildings and equipment more during evenings, during the summer, and on week ends. It may also mean making them available for more groups and varied uses.

4. We must find more effective ways of developing educational statesmanship in our school leaders. Several important and promising programs are now under way to improve the professional preparation of school administrators. The University of Chicago is one of the key centers in this effort. A superintendent of schools or a high-school principal does not have an easy life today. Most of these officials are conscientious and work hard to do an effective job. However, it is all too easy to lose one's central direction in the maze of "administrivia" or to succumb to the doing of those things one likes to do best. Buildings, budgets, and buses can, and often do, command too much of our time and attention at the expense of the improvement of curriculums, leadership in staff development, and the upgrading of instruction.

5. Teachers, parents, students, and citizens today are concerned with the efficiency of the educational enterprise, and the profession needs courage in accelerating its program of evaluation and appraisal. Programs, of necessity, have grown more complex and can be expected to grow still more complex in the era ahead. Flexibility and diversity of patterns should be encouraged, and increased emphasis placed upon the qualitative side of education. Greater attention needs to be given to quality control of the product, though obviously the schools' problem here is quite different from the problem of industry or business.

6. Educators and non-educators together must continue to share

the team spirit in the educational effort. Teamwork has been an American tradition since frontier days. The quality of education in the new space era is more significantly related to an intelligently informed citizenry than ever before.

Some promising developments are under way for the improvement of the content and the quality of what is taught in the basic areas of the arts, mathematics, science, and foreign languages, as well as the areas of human relations, education of exceptional children, education of the gifted, international understanding, vocational education, guidance, and counseling. And, as we all know, there is room always for improvement.

For example, how well are we teaching English? Robert C. Pooley has recently stated:

> A great number of elementary-school children are taught a large number of formal grammatical concepts, . . . these same materials are begun again in the junior high school and carried a little farther, and . . . the same materials are begun again in the ninth grade of senior high school, and are repeated year after year through the twelfth grade. The results do not in any way justify the time and effort apparently put forth in this endless repetition.[3]

There is a lot of controversy these days about better ways to teach Johnny to read. There is more for him to read and less time to do it. Advances in science, the mass appeals of advertising, the complexities of government, even the concise instructions on do-it-yourself kits—all require a high degree of reading ability. Educators will be interested in a new bulletin of the Office of Education called *Improving Reading in the Junior High School.*[4] The result of a conference of reading authorities called by the Office in December, 1956, this publication will, we believe, make important contributions in the areas of both developmental and remedial reading.

Language is the key to thinking, and an ability to live together in today's culture is placing greater demands upon all phases of the language arts. Television and radio test our ability to listen critically, and social and business situations call for improved competencies in speaking and writing.

There is a growing awareness, too, of the importance of the other

[3] Robert C. Pooley, *Teaching English Grammar* (New York: Appleton-Century-Crofts, Inc., 1957), pp. 52–53.

[4] Arno Jewett (ed.), *Improving Reading in the Junior High School* (United States Office of Education Bulletin 1957, No. 10 [Washington: Government Printing Office, 1957]).

languages. As a nation we are underdeveloped linguistically for our part in the modern world. Only 14 per cent of all our public high school students are studying a modern foreign language today, and then generally for only two years—far too short a time for substantial accomplishment. The modern languages commonly offered in the high schools are French and Spanish, although in a few places instruction is available in German, Italian, modern Hebrew, and a scattering of other European languages. We must remember, however, that 70 per cent of the world's population speaks other languages. In addition to strengthening the language programs already available, we need to consider ways of including at least the official languages of the United Nations in our high-school offerings. Members of the Office of Education staff, in co-operation with school officials and professional organizations, are now studying the problem of refashioning the high-school program in language to bring it in line with existing needs.

Because of the impact of science and technology, new attention is being given to the teaching of mathematics and science. The mathematics project at the University of Illinois and the Physical Science Study at the Massachusetts Institute of Technology are examples of the way in which private and public resources are being harnessed for the better formulation of learning procedures in these vital fields.

We are now appreciating, as never before, the contributions that basic research in education can make to man's advancement. The money spent on educational research is still infinitesimal when compared with the dollars being spent in this country on other forms of research. But many important programs are under way, including the Office of Education's co-operative research activities. By the end of September, 1957, 111 contracts had been signed, involving 92 projects in more than 60 colleges, universities, and state educational agencies around the nation. About half of the first year's projects deal with the problems of mentally retarded children. The remainder cover a range of other subjects which fall, generally speaking, into four areas: (1) development of special abilities, (2) retention of students in schools and colleges, (3) staffing and housing the nation's schools, and (4) educational aspects of juvenile delinquency.

The potentialities of these studies are truly exciting, and many bear directly on the work of the American high school. The results of these and other studies will help us find ways to adapt the school curriculum to meet better the needs of all boys and girls in our high schools, for, as one distinguished school administrator has said so well, "Gifts come in many sizes."

In making changes for the sake of progress, however, we must beware of equating change with progress. Many of the old-time "fundamentals" are eternal. We cannot turn the clock back, as some people are eager to have us do, but we can see to it that the clock goes on ticking strongly for the things that are as valid today as they have ever been. We would never want to lose, indeed we must increase the emphasis placed on, such values of achievement as hard work, thrift, and integrity. The three R's are as important as they ever were. Equally important, however, are three other R's we do not hear quite so much about—three R's that stand for resourcefulness, reliabiliy, and righteousness. Moral values and spiritual ideals must permeate and guide all activities of the school day. Let us never lose sight of the fact that it is the sum total of the integrity in each individual that adds to the well-being of all humanity.

The problems in education today are matched in scope only by the possibilities that their solution can offer to children in the high schools of today and tomorrow. These children will have miraculous "mechanical brains" to solve many of their problems, amazing new sources of power to work for them. But there can never be a substitute for man's unique gift of original thinking. And push buttons cannot develop a sound moral and mental outlook. Without these things, our civilization will assuredly suffer the fate that has befallen earlier civilizations in the history of this planet.

One hundred and thirty-seven years ago the men and women who fought for the opening of the school which pioneered the high-school movement in this country knew this. Theirs was an era of steamships. Ours is an era of atomic submarines and space satellites. Their report noted: "Though the present system of public education, and the munificence with which it is supported, are highly beneficial and honorable to the town; yet, in the opinion of the Committee, it is susceptible to a greater degree of perfection and usefulness."[5] Let us hold fast to that opinion.

[5] "*Minutes* of the Boston School Committee, 1821" (copied by E. E. Brown) in Ellwood P. Cubberley, *Readings in Public Education in the United States* (Boston: Houghton Mifflin Co., 1934), p. 229.

II

*New Conditions Arising from Science and Technology
Are Analyzed for Educational Implications*

The Emerging American Scene

My title, "The Emerging American Scene," certainly takes in much territory and gives me great latitude, but I have no intention of listing every trend that seems likely to emerge over the next decade or two. I will, however, indicate a few things that illustrate the pace at which the scene is changing.

As a means of simplification, let us divide the emerging scene into three parts. First, let us scan briefly some of the new tangible products of our present knowledge and the harvest of current research. Many of these physical changes will be soon upon us and can be foreseen distinctly. Next, let us consider what seem to be the dominant social changes emerging as a consequence of the new physical aspects of our way of living. These changes will be much slower and less predictable than the physical changes. Third, it seems appropriate to recall some of the fundamentals—the things that will remain unchanged. Finally, I will try to relate all three parts of the scene to the challenge confronting the American high school.

Physical Changes

Turning first to the physical aspect of the scene, what are the outstanding tangible changes? And what is remarkable about them? Of course it is true that man forever lives at the edge of the unknown and moves past surroundings that change. But a backward look of only fifty years reminds us how recent are some of the major changes and how explosive are the changes now in process. The remarkable feature of modern technological development is its rate of acceleration.

While I still wonder at transcontinental telephones and radio, to say nothing of their boisterous child, television, many of my readers were born to some of these things and are much closer than I to the growing edge. I followed the newspaper account of the Wright

51

Brothers' development of the airplane, but the younger members of my audience begin their inventory of changes with nuclear power, the wonders of man-made fibers, and the electronic microscope.

Certainly I cannot unveil any secrets about the physical aspects of our culture beyond the present date. I can, however, point out a few landmarks and leave to your reason and imagination the details of the landscape.

The modern laboratory is one such landmark. Applied science is developing an evergrowing catalogue of new materials and devices for our use and enjoyment. Synthetic substances often outperform the products of nature. Automatic machines outperform the human eye and hand. These creations of the laboratory are accelerating the pursuit of two conspicuous goals. One is communication—man's conquest of distance, time, and isolation. The second is the pursuit of abundance—man's desire for more things and for their reciprocal, leisure; man's wish for sufficient things with less expenditure of effort.

Let us take a look at the direction of these two pursuits and gauge their speed as they sweep us along ever faster. Recalling a few events of the last fifty years in the field of communication will give us sufficient bearings to get a reliable estimate of our course. In 1907 there were 7 million telephones in the United States and 8.5 million throughout the world. Now the world has a total of 114 million, of which 62 million are in the United States. A few ships were experimenting in 1907 with radio, but it did not reach the knowledge of the general public until a man named Sarnoff, still young in vision today, played a famous part as a wireless operator in 1912 when the "Titanic" sank. It was the 1924 deadlock in the Democratic convention that opened the minds of thousands to the possibilities of radio broadcasting. Even though they had only crystal sets, a lot of people heard Alabama cast 24 votes for Underwood. Today there are 135 million radios in this country and 44.5 million television screens. Last year 225 million phonograph records were sold, whereas in 1907 His Master's Voice was just emerging from a wax cylinder and the motion-picture industry had not yet been born.

Every change in techniques of communication leaves its imprint on the agencies and media of mass communication. Printing was the prototype five hundred years ago. The telegraph and the telephone came next. Think what has been added in the past fifty years —cinema, phonograph, radio, television, tape recorder. Think of the growing network of transmission facilities opened up by coaxial cables and microwaves. Think of the burgeoning application of electronics to the storage and sorting of all kinds of information.

Certain other developments arising out of improved communication should be noted because of their influence upon our lives. These include, for example, great advances in accounting, economic statistics, credit and banking, and widely recognized standards of purity, size, and quality. These are just a few of the many less dramatic changes which we have developed for sharing information in order to accomplish our purposes.

But time and space are conquered not only in the transmission of pictures and messages. Transporting people and things are equally important. Here the changes are less dramatic, but I suspect equally influential. A half-century ago Fords and Oldsmobiles were on the roads—though not always in motion. They already had assumed the general form from which evolved our present vehicles. The airplane is a different matter; new materials, new engines, and the whole science of aerodynamics joined in creating something revolutionary. London is now closer to Chicago than New York was fifty years ago.

In fifty years we have shrunk the world to a tenth of its former size. We have multiplied our ability to see and hear each other many thousandfold; we have expanded by a large factor our markets, our raw materials, and our products. The magic of printing from type to diffuse information has been extended to the even greater magic of our new media for diffusing information, entertainment, and music on a mass scale, and the pace is accelerating.

So much for the changes that are occurring in the pursuit of communication. The pursuit of material abundance is just as exciting. Let me give you a few brief examples.

In 1907 the average work week in the United States was fifty-two hours. The factory worker had neither automobile nor telephone nor radio nor leisure. Today he has a multitude of comforts and conveniences, while his average work week has dropped below forty hours. His wife, thanks to the revolution in the kitchen, has leisure also. In 1907 she often took in washing for others. Now she has an electric refrigerator, frozen and factory-prepared foods, a washing machine, a vacuum cleaner, and all the servants of Aladdin's lamp.

What has happened to the individual and the family is mirrored in the business, manufacturing, and merchandising world. Labor-saving devices appear everywhere. Machine tools multiply the output of the worker. As his production grows, new jobs are thereby created in order to assure that the work flow may be smooth and the process neatly programed.

Automation in factory and in office is one of the factors in saving labor and increasing productivity. The growing complexity of our assembly-line society is made possible, and endurable, by the help of machines which perform with fantastic speed a thousand slavish tasks too dull and repetitious to be tolerated by a high-school graduate.

There is a distinction between mechanization and automation which is important to discussions on the American high school. Mechanization comes from an earlier period when the emphasis was upon substituting power for brawn. In a certain sense, men and machines used to be interchangeable. A hundred years ago, animals (human and domestic) were responsible for 13 per cent of our energy. Today less than 1 per cent of our energy is supplied by men and animals. The machine furnishes most of the power. But, in the multiplication of output, the jobs frequently became more monotonous; machine-tenders took the place of craftsmen.

Automation, which is the more recent development, seeks to replace not merely the exercise of muscles but of eyes and memory as well. Its object is not the introduction of more power but the reduction of monotony, so that intelligent people can be free to do things more equal to their capabilities. Electronic automatons can now be made to perform those tasks of observation and control in which accuracy, consistency, and unquestioning obedience are paramount and personal opinion is intolerable.

The further results of mechanization and automation can be summed up in one sentence. The Bureau of Labor Statistics estimates that, while the labor force will grow by 21 millions in the next two decades, professional and technical occupations will have the largest increase (up 75 per cent), and the only decreases will be in the occupations of laborers and farmers and farm workers (down 23 per cent).

This country has had a long history of increasing productivity on the part of the individual. It now seems to be compounding at the rate of 3 per cent or 3.5 per cent a year, which is more rapid than the average rate of increase experienced over the last half-century. As a result the hourly production of an individual may more than double in twenty years, and thus in 1977 the average family may consume more than twice as many goods and services as it now consumes or may take some of the gain in the form of leisure.

We are living in an age of accelerating technical progress because technology is propelled by research at a scale hitherto unknown. Ten years ago, only two and a half billion dollars were spent annually on research by business, government, and educational institutions, while in 1957 the expenditure was close to seven billion dollars. The appropriation of thirty-seven billion dollars in the past decade to research is a colossal investment in the future. The age of erratic progress dependent on the luck of the solitary creator is being replaced by organized and planned co-operative efforts. This research is the seed corn for a harvest we can confidently expect. It is the basis for our belief in our expanding economy.

We are too much inclined to think of careers and opportunities as if the oncoming generations were growing up to fill the jobs that are now held by their seniors. This is not true. Our young people will fill many jobs that do not now exist. They will invent products that will need new skills. Old-fashioned mercantilism and the nineteenth-century theory, in which one man's gain was another man's loss, are being replaced by a dynamism in which the new ideas of a lot of people become the gains for many, many more.

These new developments carry us, willy-nilly, toward cheaper forms of energy, jet propulsion, new plastics, new jobs, and new skills. What is perhaps more important, progress in basic science seems to be keeping pace with technology. On the exciting new frontiers, the reproduction of the cell and the origin of life itself may yield to man's relentless curiosity, armed as it now is with such analytical tools as the tracer isotopes. I could point out many other fascinating directions in which knowledge and mastery of nature are going forward, but these visions are as familiar to you as to me, and I would end up by losing the direction of my talk in a haze of crystal-gazing.

I have given enough examples to show the direction of the substantial changes in our physical way of life—a world that is shrinking in virtual size and growing in material abundance. The rapidity of change in the past fifty years and its increasing rate literally suggest that we are moving toward an explosive climax where our ingenuity will outrun our wisdom. For a second time, man may have partaken of the apple of the tree of knowledge before God had prepared him for it.

Social Changes

Fortunately man changes his habits more slowly than he changes his artifacts. Thus our group behavior in the next two decades will not be so different from what it has been in the recent past. It will change, however, and that brings me to the second part of my talk—the relatively slower emergence of some social changes. What are the emerging patterns of living for the next two decades? They will be derived from many sources, two of which I have already recounted: the pervasive impact of mass communications and the growing abundance of things or of leisure, as we may choose.

It will be enough for my purpose here to point out one major cultural change whose consequences are irresistible. In 1907, 37 per cent of our population lived on farms. Today the per cent is only 13. The other 24 per cent have become clustered in towns, cities, and suburbs. The consequences of industrialization and urbanization are tremendous. Here I will mention only a few of them.

The individual becomes part of an intricate process over which he has no personal control. The willing and competent worker in a factory making steam locomotives suffers technological unemployment. Unless he can find a job in a factory making diesel locomotives or in some other expanding enterprise, his family will suffer, through no fault of his own. Even the farmer, until recently the symbol of rugged individualism, cannot raise his crop without machinery from Detroit, oil from Texas, and fertilizers from Florida. In an earlier age the individual was a Jack-of-many-trades, and, by and large, his family ate as well as it could farm.

This nation is pressing forward with enormous ingenuity to the plenty of the semi-automatic factory, but the price tag on this abundance is the responsibility of society for the welfare of the individuals who are, from time to time, dislocated. Government is becoming an increasingly important factor in our lives, and it will more and more perform many functions of adjustment and alleviation which are not clearly the responsibility of any one of us.

The crowded living in this urban society also enforces many conformities. Besides the physical and social pressures of the city, other homogenizing factors are at work. Mass communication can elevate and stimulate, but it can also influence toward common denominators. The cultural impact of television, national magazines, and syndicated columnists is felt in rural, no less than in urban, homes.

Thus Americans all stand in danger of losing individuality by drifting into the well-marked standards of group behavior. Many of these standards and conformities will be unavoidable. An increasingly important task will be to retain, in as full measure as possible, freedom of self-expression and encouragement of originality in thought and attitude.

Interdependence, with all its political and social implications, will surely continue to grow in the next few decades. If we Americans had only ourselves to consider, we might cope with the factor of interdependence in a fairly predictable way. But it is hard to predict what will happen as industrialization filters into hitherto agrarian nations. The unbalance between our plenty and their scarcity will recede, and the comparative advantages of our skills and resources will decline. One thing is certain: just as the erstwhile farm family must react to the facts of the industrial process, just so must our national objectives be modified by the growing prosperity and influence of other countries. This impending development is of great importance.

Let me amplify another consequence of our growing industrial efficiency which will surely continue. I have spoken already of the shortening work week and the growth of leisure. These march hand in hand with the further division of labor, the proliferation of new skills, and the diversification of goods and services offered to the consumer.

Technicians man the new machines; engineers design them; specialists program the work; experts market the product. Each new machine or tool or instrument or procedure must have its votaries. The United States Employment Service has classified forty-two thousand titles of present-day occupations; a handful of generic job titles and extensive knacks, such as "carpenter," "steam fitter," and "clerk," sufficed in an earlier time. Even the artist who used to starve in a garret or eat the unsavory bread of patronage is now an integral part of the modern industrial process, and artists are becoming specialized, too. The buyer of mass-produced goods can now afford to look for more than serviceability. He can add taste to his specifications, and the manufacturer who ignores this trend will soon be out of business.

The leisure to enjoy the daily contributions of the arts and sciences will stem from four changes in our lives: fewer hours per day, fewer days per week, and fewer weeks per year of work; and a marked increase in the life-span. What a gift is now within the reach of mankind! Our factories have manufactured time! The family can be together more. Though we live in the town, we can readily enjoy the country. We can choose our recreations and have time to enjoy them. We can afford more time for formal schooling and enjoy self-cultivation in the adult years. There will be time to learn from the culture of the past how to enrich the present and to assure the future. We have the time for all these things—but can we, and will we, grasp them?

There are those who fear that our leisure has arrived before we are fully prepared to use it. Paradoxical as it may seem, leisure and abundance are not unmixed blessings. They create unfamiliar, and perhaps serious, problems—new problems with which man has never had to deal on a national scale. Let me suggest a few of these problems, only enough to stimulate your imagination. In an earlier and simpler time we had fresh air, sparkling streams, and restful landscapes. Now we have to spend money to secure a measure of unpolluted air out of the smog of our cities where most of us now live. We must tax the city dweller in order to provide green parks, which are a poor imitation of the charms of a simpler rural landscape. Even the fish are too smart to start families in our rivers.

There is no doubt that our fine roads and automobiles give us great mobility, but we have to patrol our highways to keep the annual fatalities close to the toll of World War I. The consequence of our greater mobility is often more acquaintances and fewer friends. The consequence of our mass-produced entertainment is often satiety and not enjoyment. We have more impressions and fewer thoughts. We have less knowledge about more things. Such are the growing problems of abundance. Leisure is not a passive state like rest or sleep. It is not time to be filled in. It is time re- leased to our choosing. The problem of finding rewarding uses for spare time is illustrated by an interesting derivative of the shortened work week. Enough people are taking second jobs in preference to enjoying their leisure to cause comment in employer and labor- union circles.

Holding a second job is called "moonlighting." According to recent estimates, about 5 per cent of the labor force are "moon- lighters," and the proportion seems to be growing. This practice has long been commonplace among school teachers, firemen, and policemen. Now it is spreading. For example, in Akron, where the regular work week is thirty-six hours, almost half the rubber workers hold a second job.

If moonlighting were more widespread, it could be serious. Even now, it is at least significant. The consequences of moonlighting may be an exhausted wage-earner and an absentee parent, who has no time to enjoy the fruits of the labor-saving devices which his inge- nuity has created. To be sure, he may be able to buy more things, but the correlation between things and enjoyment declines rapidly. As yet, we cannot be sure whether moonlighting is only attractive as a means to more income or whether it reflects an unconscious decision to fill time for which there is no other use.

This much is certain: the employment of leisure is a social prob- lem which we shall have to face much more seriously in the decades ahead. Americans have become experts at consuming goods. Now they must learn to consume leisure. They have instinctively sought meaning and inner rewards from within their work. Now they must seek equivalent satisfaction outside their work.

Our productivity is constantly increasing. We have achieved in this country mass consumption, mass leisure, mass communication, and mass access to education. This is a new way—a never-before- experienced way—to live on a national scale. The success of the experiment will depend on our capacity to meet the difficulties that follow in the wake of these developments.

To me there is no avoidance of the three major problems that I have referred to: first, our expanding economic activity with its demands for new skills; second, the conflict between individuality and the conformities demanded by our organized, urban, interdependent, intercommunicated way of living; and, third, the use of our leisure and the associated dilemmas of abundance.

The solution of all these problems lies in our ability to educate the young people in the years ahead. Does it not seem clear that, as the number of required skills multiply, the more necessary it is to build up a firm general foundation? Why take precious time to train for proficiencies which may disappear or be modified? Many skills can be taught on the job. We need to learn those things which will be useful to any career: how to relate to our surroundings, how to read critically, how to be honest with ourselves, how to reach rational conclusions, how to master our emotions, how to enjoy the accumulated wealth of things and ideas which we have inherited, and how to leave a richer heritage behind us.

Unchanging Aspects of the Scene

Fortunately for those who will guide education in the years ahead, there are some brakes upon our ever-faster-moving trends, and that brings me to the last of the three aspects of the emerging American scene—the unchanged part. Simply stated, the constant element is human nature. Man himself, in his innermost qualities, has remained unchanged as far back as we have any record of his existence. The same fundamental desires, aspirations, noble qualities, and frailties are as evident today as they were five thousand years ago.

To be sure, we have learned that we cannot live together without self-restraint. We have refined our beliefs. We have developed ethical systems. All these were necessary parts of the emerging of an increasingly complicated civilization. But this, I think, is true: man himself has not changed.

Thus the changes created by man's ingenuity reflect back on his constant nature and create new patterns of behavior. The culture of the days ahead will result from the interaction between the influences I have enumerated and man's fundamental attributes.

The mind and emotions of man will have the same capacities as always. Courage, envy, generosity, brutality appear each century in slightly different costumes. The capacity to learn is no greater now than in was five millennia ago. Besides things of the spirit, the bodily aspects also remain the same. The periods of childhood, adolescence, maturity, and senility each have their share of the journey from birth to death, and each have characteristics which the educator can understand and make the best of. These then—spirit and body—are the fixed foundations amid change.

Implications for Education

Our difficulties are not insuperable. The world has always been emerging. From time immemorial we have been saying, "What will young people come to?" We have worried about juvenile delinquency, students who wouldn't learn, and how little time there was to teach all that they should know. The decades ahead will not, then, present an utterly new and different challenge. With a single exception, the challenge will be the same as it has always been: how to give to youth's unchanging mind and nature the foundation upon which can be built the capacity to learn new jobs, adjust to changing social patterns, and make the best of increasing abundance.

But, as I have said, one exception should perhaps be noted: one new challenge arising from leisure. Leisure must not be allowed to become a mere escape from work, an opiate, for want of learning how best to use it. Abundant goods may confer satisfaction as an integral part of their purchase and use, but this is not so of leisure. True enjoyment of leisure is entirely subjective and requires initiative. We have new-found time. How dread is the sound of that expression "killing time."

Turn now from problems to opportunities in the emerging decades. Never has education had a more important role. At the base stands our formal system. The young are propelled forward by encouragement, cajolerie, and pressure. They pass through the conventional stages. The goal is not a parchment but self-cultivation.

Never in our history have we stood in such need of self-cultivation, and never has the opportunity appeared more rewarding. Unless there is instilled in each young person a resolve to develop himself to his full capacity, he will be left behind. But if we all learn to continue our own enlightenment throughout our lives, we not only shall survive amid the proliferating complications of organized society but shall have richer and happier lives for ourselves and our children and for the community in which we live.

With each addition to the sciences and the technologies, new needs for education and training come into view, and new pressures are added to the curriculum. How can we encompass all we may have to know in the fast-changing decades ahead?

The danger in our learning process will be, as always, the temptation to develop the skill for a particular job before we have established a foundation of character and education. John Stuart Mill pointed this out almost a hundred years ago in his inaugural address at the University of St. Andrews: "Men are men before they are lawyers, physicians, or manufacturers and if you make them capable and sensible men they will make themselves capable and sensible lawyers or physicians."

Within limits, the crisis in education is not so much the shortage of teachers as it is how capable they are, just as the important matter of communication is not how rapidly a report is sent but what is communicated. It is not how fast we are going that counts but where. It is not what we manufacture but how we use the product. It is not the time we save but what we do with the extra hours.

We are swept along on a broad current of known direction and unknown destination. We can make no progress directly against it. The forces are powerful but not quite overwhelming. We are able to maneuver a little bit. This small freedom of maneuver we are proud to express in nobler terms—independence, self-determination, personal accountability, and moral purpose. These will prove enough, because our spiritual beliefs give us the vision and systematic education will show the way.

The Changing Dimensions of the World Community

A commonly heard observation during the five decades since the American high school assumed its present form is that the world is getting smaller. Another is that the world is getting more complex. Still another is that the physical world has changed little, while societies have changed radically.

From the fact and myth that are compounded in these statements we can suggest some of the basic changes that are taking place in the dimensions of the world community. These changes promise to continue at an accelerated rate. And that prospect, in view of the apparent state of teaching about them, is one of which our high-school students may be unaware.

Knowledge Available to Students in a Shrinking World

Without doubt the earth is getting smaller in terms of travel time. In 1900 only parts of the United States and Canada were accessible from Chicago in three days' travel by commercial passenger transport. In 1957 more than half of the urban areas of the earth are so accessible. The prospect is that this area will be expanded and that the area accessible within one day's travel will be tremendously enlarged as new aircraft and trucks come into use. We all recognize these and other technological facts and see at once their implications for a view of the world as being, in terms of transportation, a closely linked neighborhood.

During the same period the views which students develop of the world through the use of maps have become more nearly accurate. No map in two dimensions ever can faithfully represent the three-dimensional world. The literal globe remains a basic teaching device, but flat maps for showing a spherical world have improved.

63

The Mercator projection, with its navigators' willingness to distort area and shape in the interest of direction, has yielded place in textbooks to projections which are true in area. The equal-area view is an illuminating one, particularly when used to show the volume of population and resources concentrated in any area. In some books an equal-area map of population has replaced the traditional Mercator map of political units.

Orientation of maps also is changing. The United Nations has graphically suggested that North America may not be the center for all purposes. The International Geophysical Year has reminded us that 90° latitude may be a pole of interest as well as the limit of "our" hemisphere. One has only to examine the textbooks of other populous continents to recognize the ethnocentrism of much of our map-teaching.

On the whole, cartographic representation has improved tremendously. It is more balanced, accurate, and unbiased than it was five decades ago. And the day may not be far off when an American railroad company will have the courage to publish a timetable map in which its line is not shown as the shortest available route between two points.

Students' Needs for New Ways of Thinking about Geographic Relations

One might hope that, with the dramatically contracting transport times and with increasingly accurate representations of the world, the high-school graduate would emerge sensitive to the character of the world which now is at his doorstep. The contrary appears to be the case.

Benjamin Fine several years ago made it painfully clear that the American college student, while entirely capable of making seasonal migrations across the Atlantic on a shoestring, is quite unaware of simple facts of location.[1] Fine showed, you may recall, that there was fuzziness about major locations in the United States and rank ignorance about overseas areas. Perhaps the perfect but sad example of this illiteracy was cited by Jesse H. Wheeler, who found at the peak of the Korean War that 46 per cent of a representative

[1] Benjamin Fine, "U.S. College Students Flunk in Knowledge of Geography," *Journal of Geography*, L (November, 1951), 334–41.

group of university students did not know the whereabouts of Korea.[2] If any of you have any doubt about this, ask a group of high-school graduates to enter on an outline map of the world the places named on the front page of a large metropolitan newspaper for that day.

Having noted this deficiency, I shall maintain that it is not in itself important. Any reasonably intelligent person can go to an atlas and find Algeria, Little Rock, or Moscow. May all the map-publishers preserve us from teaching, as some textbooks did in the early part of the century, the countries that bounded Austria and the capitals of the states! That is no more modern-day geography than rote recital of grammatical rules is literature.

I do maintain, however, that this illiteracy as to place is symptomatic of a truly alarming ignorance about spatial relations and ways of thinking about them. Two common attitudes which I have observed among American high-school graduates illustrate the point. One is the attitude that all foreign areas are uniform in character within their boundaries and are much alike, one to another. This is perhaps forgivable in a country where slang, gasoline stations, malted milks, and textbooks are nearly the same from coast to coast. It encourages easy and unwarranted generalizations about other parts of the world. Indeed the tacit response to a question about Indonesia, Iraq, and Iran is that probably all are much the same wherever they are and that it doesn't make too much difference where they are because they are all much the same.

A second attitude is that man has done a good job of conquering nature for his own benefit in the United States and that, if other peoples had enough energy and know-how to turn to and handle their own resources similarly, the obstacles to improving human welfare would be largely removed. The United States, it is true, has had as many natural resources per capita as any other major nation except perhaps Canada. The United States is using up its resources at a higher rate than any other nation. This present circumstance makes it difficult to recognize the combinations of factors that in fact impede or foster economic growth in other countries and that attach to the earth's capacity to support its growing popu-

[2] Jesse H. Wheeler, Jr., "The Role of Geography in General Education," in *A Half-Century of Geography—What Next?* (Chicago: Department of Geography, University of Chicago, 1955), pp. 25–34.

lation. It also impedes the understanding of the impending necessity to husband resources more carefully both at home and abroad. Technology is in fact changing the face, as well as the space, of the earth. Since 1900 the vegetable cover has been destroyed or modified over large areas, the courses and flows of rivers have been changed radically, mineral deposits have been exhausted, and urban settlement has stretched out and coalesced over the rural landscape at a rapid rate.[3] But it is gravely misleading to believe that conditions for applying technology are everywhere the same or everywhere favorable. Man the conqueror must also be seen as man the cautious adjuster and man the destroyer.

If students are to be expected to deal intelligently with the perplexing and frustrating diversity of the world of which they are a part, they will need to be given a clear view of its true dimensions. Among these dimensions I will suggest only two that cry out for literate understanding at the high-school level. One is the dimension of areal organization. The other is the dimension of capacity to support population.

By "areal organization" I mean the arrangement of various social functions on the earth's surface. For example, each small town serves as the focus for retail trade in the surrounding area. In similar fashion a larger town may be the center for religious organizations in its area. We may recognize the world's surface as covered with an intricate network of such activities—some related, some independent of others—arranged in various hierarchies of concentration. In the Chicago region, distinct hierarchies of urban places are familiar to us, and similar arrangements may be found elsewhere.[4] The shifts that are taking place seem to be in the direction of greater concentration and complexity. Whole zones of primitive agriculture, which were largely independent in their functional organization in 1900, are now linked by movements of goods, people, and ideas to the rest of the world. The world political organization is increasingly complex, not only through the increase in number of political

[3] These changes are reviewed in William L. Thomas, Jr. (ed.), *Man's Role in Changing the Face of the Earth* (Chicago: Published for the Wenner-Gren Foundation for Anthropological Research and the National Science Foundation by the University of Chicago Press, 1956).

[4] Allen K. Philbrick, "Principles of Areal Functional Organization in Regional Human Geography," *Economic Geography*, XXXIII (October, 1957), 299–336.

units, but through the increase in the international functions. The area with which any one group of people has functional relations has been immensely expanded. Students need a framework of thought in which these multiplying contacts and relations of this expanding world may find a meaningful place.

Areas of the earth differ from one another in their capacity to support people as well as in their relations to one another (see map on page 68). Probably much of the public discussion of the dangers of overpopulation has been emotional and distorted, but the underlying situation which it reflects is profoundly serious. At least four hard facts stand out and cannot be ignored. (1) World population is exploding at an increasing rate. (2) In some areas, such as the uplands of Latin America and the grazing lands of the Eastern Mediterranean, resource destruction is accelerating. (3) While technology has brought greater productivity and halted resource destruction in certain areas, its rate of acceptance is so slow in other high-density areas, such as India, that it barely keeps up with population growth. (4) The present relation of population to resources in some areas is such that, although increases in the level of living may be expected, the differential between the level in those areas and the level in the United States probably will increase rather than decrease.

To the dilemma of rising population and fixed resources, many solutions, ranging from resource development through population control, suggest themselves. The dilemma is not insoluble. Most of the solutions assume widespread improvement in education affecting technical skills, marketing, family organization, and social goals. Even if we assume a magnificent deployment of educational effort for these purposes across the earth, there remains for us in the United States and in a few other countries a challenge of a very special sort. How do we prepare our young people to take their places in a world in which large numbers in other countries are struggling for economic and cultural survival, while our own country progressively widens the economic gap between itself and the others?

Let me sum up my argument thus far. The world into which the next generation of high-school students will move seems likely to be one that will have more intense and complex confrontation of

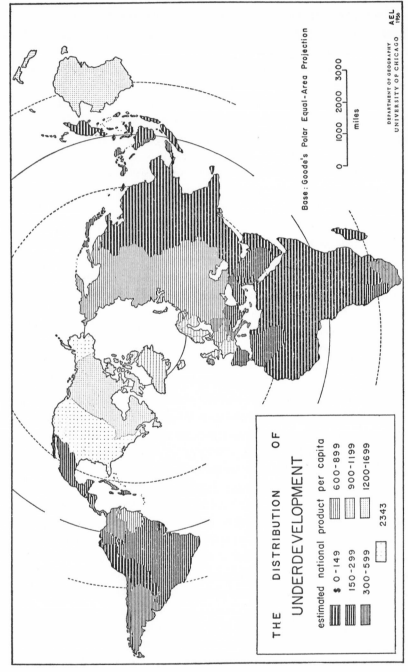

THE DISTRIBUTION OF UNDERDEVELOPMENT

estimated national product per capita

$ 0-149
150-299
300-599
600-899
900-1199
1200-1699
2343

Base: Goode's Polar Equal-Area Projection

0 1000 2000 3000
miles

DEPARTMENT OF GEOGRAPHY
UNIVERSITY OF CHICAGO

AEL
1956

From N. S. Ginsburg, "National Resources and Economic Development, *Annals of the Association of American Geographers*, XLVII (October, 1957).

cultures than ours; that will struggle with a more severe pressure of population upon physical resources; and that will maintain, and even deepen, over a long time the present inequalities in levels of living. While the dimensions of time in the movement of ideas and men and goods continue to shrink, the dimensions of organization promise to expand.

Understanding these changing dimensions thus will be a more difficult task than it is now. Clearly it is a far more important one. We may hope for students who will see the world, in its areal differences and similarities, with perspective and sensitivity and who will have begun to think about the reasons for these patterns.

Ways of Cultivating Understanding

Just as we have only begun to view education as a comparative study, recognizing the strengths and weaknesses of different methods to serve differing aims of societies, we have only begun to explore ways of cultivating understanding of the world's dimensions. Literature and history, natural science and geography—all offer opportunities largely unexplored. What are the effective ways of teaching critical respect for the literatures of other cultures without sacrificing our own tradition? What are the means of developing an appreciation of our own short history in relation to the broad panorama of world history? How can the science studies aid in seeing the possibilities and frustrations of adjusting resource use to multiplying human needs? What are the fruitful means of teaching the geography of the changing earth?

Many partial answers are already at hand. To assess our experience to date with these efforts and to explore the challenges ahead, it may help to offer one general observation and to illustrate the observation with one concrete venture in teaching.

An apparent dilemma arising in any effort to sharpen understanding of world dimensions is that covering the earth in our teaching is at the cost of superficiality. If the United States becomes conscious of a politically emergent Africa, the tendency is to call for a unit on Africa somewhere among the social studies or to include a few Bantu legends in a book of graded readings. Such a response is attractive because it is direct and relatively easy, but, taken alone, it is distressing. The addition of new subject matter is hopeless in terms of its rapidly growing volume, and it is likely to be confusing. The solution does not lie in the direction of more units of study covering more parts of the world or more of its interrelated aspects. It lies in focusing upon a few of the basic modes of thought that will help in illuminating the new and continually changing facts about the world.

For example, one of the elementary ideas in geography is that of regional association of phenomena on the earth's surface—the recognition that the distributions of climate, soils, vegetation, minerals, and population occur in distinctive combinations and that a change in one element in the complex may bring profound changes in the others.[5] This concept, if understood by the student, helps him to see related physical phenomena in a unified framework. Perhaps more important, it helps him to recognize that any familiar or new part of the earth has its own distinctive combination and is likely to respond in its own unique way to changes. So-called underdeveloped countries are then seen to be radically different from one another in their conditions of economic growth and in their response to new technology or social organization. With this idea the student begins to recognize that meeting the world's food needs is not a simple matter of generously spreading American know-how wherever it is lacking. And he is prepared to find that a spread in democratic forms of government will not necessarily prevent a deterioration in a country's soil resources. This concept of regional association of phenomena can be taught in high schools. It requires preliminary work on more elementary ideas of earth features. Once mastered for one area, the concept becomes applicable to any area, and students no longer can regard a little-known region as being as uniform as the color shading on a political map.

The teaching of such a concept at the high-school level may well begin in the school's back yard with local complexes and be carried far enough afield to show its meaning for distant places. Thus, at the University of Chicago High School the work in geography starts with the port of Chicago and the functions it performs for the city and for faraway places. It asks what will be the effect of the opening

[5] For a clear review of basic geographic ideas, see Edith Putnam Parker, "Developing the Science of Teaching Geography," in *The Teaching of Geography* (Thirty-second Yearbook of the National Society for the Study of Education [Chicago: Distributed by the University of Chicago Press, 1933]), pp. 73–177.

of the St. Lawrence Seaway in 1959 upon those services and upon the life of the city and of neighboring areas. In that fashion the student builds upon elementary ideas of space and resources to appraise one area and to see it in relation to other areas near and far.

This kind of thinking is encouraged in some social studies and in geography. I have the impression that it fares less well in the combined social studies and that the tendency is for students to emerge from such studies with a certain familiarity with social problems rather than with a discipline of thinking about them. Both historical and geographical modes of thought seem to have lost precision and strength from being merged in the broader approach of social studies.[6] There are distinct and refined teaching techniques that apply to geographical ideas alone, and some are being lost rather than refined.[7]

Challenge to the School

In our earnest concern to prepare young people to live in an increasingly complex world, we are in danger of trying to teach them so many facts about the world as it was last year that we shall teach them little of the ways of thinking about the world that is becoming. The challenges that lie ahead in the changing dimensions of the world community are to fit people to think about the immense diversity of that spatially contracting community and to recognize the sobering inequality of conditions that figure in our united efforts to advance the welfare of its two and a half billion members.

[6] C. F. Kohn (ed.), *Geographic Approaches to Social Education* (Nineteenth Yearbook of the National Council for the Social Studies, Prepared with the co-operation of the National Council of Geography Teachers, Association of American Geographers, American Society for Professional Geographers [Washington: National Council for the Social Studies, 1948]).

[7] See (a) Edith Putnam Parker, *op. cit.*; (b) Joe Russell Whitaker, *Geography in School and College: Talks on Values and Problems* (Nashville, Tennessee: George Peabody College for Teachers, 1948).

ALEXANDER J. STODDARD

The Communications Revolution and the High School

Civilization rides forward on the expanding ability of men to communicate with one another; or, as man becomes more civilized, he multiplies the scope and effectiveness of his power to communicate, as an important accomplishment of his civilization. Probably these are the two sides of the same coin.

Telling Was Difficult

The first forms of communication used by man were, of course, simple and crude. Their potentiality for transferring concepts and ideas from one person to another was limited. The making of simple movements and the production of elemental sounds preceded, by vast stretches of time, the development of elementary forms of sign language. Elementary sign language was followed in turn, during the passing centuries, by the transmission of ideas through various types of pictures.

Many times in the long history of communication, vast changes have occurred in the extent and the form of man's ability to impart his thoughts to his fellow man. Sometimes these changes may have evolved slowly, through many years or centuries. In other situations the changes may have come so suddenly and violently as to have constituted revolutionary departures from the traditional methods.

The development of alphabets, words, parts of speech, forms of writing, and other similar changes must have represented revolutionary departures from the past. Certainly the invention of movable type was no insignificant development of a casual and simple next step in the marvelous ability of one mind to transfer ideas to another. It crashed the gates of the future with the force of revolution. Life was never the same, after movable type was harnessed as a way and means of communication, as it had forever been before.

72

After movable type came, man went on for centuries, adding step by step to his ability to use it. More and better forms of printing and writing and making pictures were developed through the years. They were used by human beings as forms of communication always had been used: to make impressions on the senses of one another. These impressions or sensations were interpreted through common understanding of their meaning by sender and receiver. This evolutionary process of improvement in communication went on for a long time after its revolutionary beginning deep in the past.

Then Came Television

Then a few years ago, almost yesterday, another revolution, greater than any before, took place. Whereas pictures had been static, they now took on motion, as in life itself. A method was discovered to transmit sound over enormous distances. In fact, a new device made possible the union of sound and moving pictures so as to stimulate the actuality and reality of happenings and experience. And then came the climax in this revolution. Instead of putting what was to be communicated on a film or a disk for later use, a method was devised for transmitting directly and actually, as they occurred, the live impulses of sight and sound as they were united naturally. *This is television.*

The inventions of motion pictures, (silent and sound), of radio, and of television were not merely next steps beyond what man had already developed as his means and methods of communication. These represent vast steps forward, occurring in a relatively short space of time. They constitute a revolution. They involve such a change from all that ever was before in the field of human communications as to stagger the imagination. They dare our utmost ingenuity in harnessing their vast potentialities in many fields. This is especially so in education.

Consider for a moment how extensively television has become a part of modern life and how rapidly it has done so. There were practically no television receiving sets ten years ago. Now, more than half of the homes of America have TV sets. For every hour in school, boys and girls of school age spend, on the average, another hour before TV sets. Television is revolutionizing life on the farms, in hospitals, and in living rooms throughout the land. Old age has become enriched because of it. Common learnings and a common culture have now become realities to an extent surpassing imagination.

A President speaks to fifty million citizens at one time, and they see him as he does it! Vast numbers watch a ball game and hear the bat hit the ball, hundreds of miles away. But, already, many are beginning to take their television casually as part of modern living. The miracle that television represents is already losing its startling significance in this day of man-made moons probing the age-old mysteries of space beyond our little world.

But let us educators not forget that we are now in the midst of probably the greatest revolution that has yet taken place in the art and science of communication. Ours is the challenge of understanding the significance of that revolution and taking advantage of its potential contributions to push forward our processes of civilization, consistent with the needs of our day. To be specific, what can we do now to adapt television to help meet some of the baffling problems of our high schools?

This discussion will concentrate on a few problems that seem to be most related to this new and powerful means of communication, television. Much of what is said can apply also to motion pictures and radio, which are a part of the revolution and can have their respective and unique functions to perform in an expanding program of education.

It must be understood, from a communication standpoint, that radio deals only with the transmission of sensations of sound and that the sound motion picture does not involve reality as to the time of the experience it conveys. It is likely also that television will prove to be more flexible and practical for use in the schools than it now is. But sound motion pictures, radio, and television are not competitive means of communication. Each has its unique usage, its advantages and disadvantages, values and limitations.

The High School Is in Trouble

The American high school plays a powerful role in the life of our people and in effecting the purposes of our country. It is a vastly different school from the secondary schools of most of the other countries of the world. While in the beginning it was patterned after the Old-World attitude of higher education for the few, it has gradually and persistently grown in the direction of providing an educational program for *all* American youth, varied in its content to fit individual needs as far as practicable. The comprehensive high school is distinctly an American institution, designed to serve and promote the unique functions of American democracy.

All over the land, a re-examination and reappraisal of our high school is being undertaken to determine whether it is going in the direction it should go, what its strengths and weaknesses are, and what are its resources and limitations in realizing its purposes. A restlessness and a widespread concern about the high school and its future are evident, in a time of deep and violent change in our economic, political, and social relationships at home and abroad.

Particularly, the question is raised whether the high school does and, if not, whether it should, provide the dynamic program of educational service that will equip our young people to meet the challenge of this emerging new day. One point of view must dominate what we say or do: the American high-school program must serve the needs of *all,* and not just a part, of the youth of America, according to their varying abilities. When we consider opportunities for some of our youth, because of insistent pressures to do so, the needs of others must not be neglected. The present emphasis on the gifted or on such phases of the curriculum as science and mathematics must not lessen our determination to meet, equally effectively, the needs of all young people of high-school age.

Numbers Outstrip Facilities

Many serious problems now threaten the American high school. Several of them relate specially to the subject of this paper. The first has to do with sheer numbers. There are now more than nine million youth in our secondary schools. The number may be twelve million by 1965. Will the money be available to buy the personnel facilities necessary to service this number of young people, on the basis it has been done in the past?

There is already a growing shortage in personnel and facilities. The shortage in personnel may be reflected in an actual lack of teachers for classes or in the more insidious form of deterioration in quality of service rendered by substandard and inadequately trained teachers. Lack of facilities may be reflected in half-day sessions or in overcrowded or poorly equipped buildings. But merely multiplying outmoded buildings on the assumption that our educational program is static is not the answer. A shortage will not be met by perpetuating, for generations to come, the inadequacies of so many of our present high-school plants.

It is possible that the answer may lie in the direction of utilizing more effectively the resources we now have or can reasonably expect to have in the future. Maybe the personnel available can be redeployed in such a manner as to meet the needs of more students than could be cared for on the traditional basis and, at the same time, preserve or raise the total quality of education. It might be desirable also to change somewhat our concept of staff service from the highly individual to a team basis. There are undoubtedly many services, as in the fields of counseling and mental health, for example, that should be, and are not now, provided in the modern high school.

Similar economies might be effected in building and equipment facilities. Many high schools have large spaces that are used for only a small percentage of available time. It might be possible to assemble larger groups or classes in some of the subject areas and utilize these hitherto vacant spaces more fully. Fewer classrooms might be needed. Or some larger classrooms might be built at considerable saving in cost. The general practice of having classrooms of a uniform size, of assigning thirty pupils per teacher regardless of subject, may need re-examination.

Quality Must Be Stressed

Not only does the high school face the problems incident to rapidly *increasing numbers* to be educated, but the situation is further complicated by the fact that the *quantity and the quality* of education must also be increased materially if our schools are to do their share in preparing boys and girls to live successfully in the highly complex world ahead.

We live in a world of gadgets. How to train people to operate these contrivances safely and successfully imposes a rapidly increasing burden on education. Witness the impact on the school curriculum of driver education alone. But there is not only the area of physical things about which we must be educated. There are also intangible areas—politics, morals, economics, human relations, and many others—that throw increasing obligations on the schools to step up their program to meet the complexity of modern life.

Education depends to a large extent on processes of communication. Learning consists fundamentally of two phases: first, *perception*, which consists of gathering sensations through the five senses; and, second, *thinking*, which involves doing something with the sensations to turn them into knowledge and wisdom. The schools endeavor to raise the quantity and the quality of both phases. Communication must, and does, play an essential part in this process.

That television is a powerful means of communication no one doubts or denies. It can bring anything, even personality and human reaction, very close to those who listen and view. The camera can bring us nearer to what happens than we can be from our usually remote vantage points. The speaker or the teacher can look each of us in the eye over TV. Can television be utilized by the American high school to help meet its problems of numbers of students, amount of and complexity of the educational content? The answer to this question is yet to be determined, but the question must be met with an open mind and an intense willingness to explore the potentialities earnestly, thoroughly, and fully through study and experimentation.

Much has already been done experimentally in the use of television in direct teaching, especially at the college level. But not so much has been done relatively at the school level. The following preliminary tentative conclusions can be drawn from such experimentation thus far:

1. Television can be used profitably to supplement and enrich the instructional program.
2. Television can be used effectively to bring to the school live experiences of educational significance.
3. Television can be a powerful resource in teaching, overcoming the limitations of other resources, in many fields of the curriculum.
4. Television can be used directly to teach small classes in high schools not large enough to offer certain subjects.
5. Competent teachers from regular school staffs can be found and trained to present subject-matter effectively over television.
6. Television may make possible the teaching of large classes through utilizing the medium as a powerful resource for the teacher with the class.

Experimentation Is a Must

In order to secure further evidence on the last four of the tentative conclusions listed above, which might, if positive, serve as the basis for the general acceptance of the conclusions, an extensive experiment, designated as the National Program in the Use of Television in the Public Schools, has been set up. Included in this experiment are the school systems of nine large cities, one large county unit, nineteen medium-sized cities, and more than a hundred small communities in two states. More than fifty thousand pupils are involved in the total experiment. It covers elementary-school, junior high school, and senior high school levels and a wide range and many types of subject matter.

The experimental program is supported jointly by the participating school systems and the Fund for the Advancement of Education. The total budget is nearly two and a half million dollars for the year July 1, 1957, to June 30, 1958. It is considered a possibility, even a probability, that the experiment may be extended for one or two additional years.

While details of the projects in the different participating units vary considerably, the one common element, in all cases except the two state projects, is the teaching of large classes, varying in size from about 75 to 350. Both open- and closed-circuit facilities are used in the telecasting. Teachers at the studios and with the classes, as well as all other personnel, are selected and trained locally. An elaborate and thorough evaluation program has been planned, and preliminary tests have been given to both experimental and control groups.

From the standpoint of some of the problems confronting the high schools, this experiment should provide valuable evidence on such questions as the following:

1. Can large classes be taught as effectively, less effectively, or more effectively by using television as a valuable resource in comparison with teaching regular-sized classes with or without TV as a resource?
2. If large classes can be taught successfully, using TV as a resource, what savings can be effected in regular teaching positions, time, and building space and facilities?
3. What special problems are involved in teaching large classes in school, both procedural and technical? Can these problems be met readily without undue cost or impractical or other undesirable considerations?

4. Can the schools discover and develop satisfactory teaching talent, both for telecasting and for classroom service in teaching large classes?
5. Can the schools discover and develop subject-matter content to be involved in the TV presentations that will exploit the unique potentialities of this powerful means of communication to such an extent as to justify the necessary installation, development, and use of TV in education programs generally?
6. Will the teaching of large classes through the use of television as a resource raise the quantity and the quality of learning so as to contribute constructively to the sum total of the services rendered by the schools?
7. How can give-and-take discussions and the asking of questions be carried on with large classes? To what extent will these procedures be less or more necessary when TV is used as a resource in the teaching process?
8. What are the relative roles and relationships of the television studio and classroom teachers?
9. Can the teachers of large classes know their students intimately enough to provide proper and necessary remedial work?
10. Will television turn education from an active participation by the learner in an educational experience to a passive sitting before a TV set, merely looking and listening to vicarious experiences ready made for the purpose?

These are only part of the many questions on which this large National Program should furnish some evidence. Many other significant experiments are being conducted that bear directly or indirectly on the relation of television to the high-school crisis. Some of the most important of these are described briefly below.

University of Alabama.—With the idea of eventually establishing state-wide classroom instruction by open-circuit television, selected experimental classes in French, Spanish, reading, social science, physical science, mathematics, art, and music are being taught by using TV as a resource. The televised lecture-demonstrations are supplemented by classroom teacher instruction. Results will be compared with ordinary school operations.

Chicago Public Schools.—An open-circuit television program of junior-college education (significant in many ways for high schools) has been developed, so that by 1959 a full, two-year program of general education by television will be available at the junior-college level. In addition, there was offered in February, 1957, and continuing through the summer, a full-year course in high-school physics in twenty high schools of Chicago.

Evanston Township High School.—In 1956–57 this school tested the practicality of using closed-circuit TV and teaching assistants in courses in English, speech, and beginning typewriting, and it expanded the areas involved for 1957–58.

Snyder (Texas) Public Schools.—In Snyder, closed-circuit television was used during 1956–57 in the teaching of biology and general science. Such use was continued in 1957–58 and was expanded on a pilot basis to other areas of the curriculum at both junior and senior high school levels.

Pittsburgh Public Schools.—In 1955–56 Pittsburgh conducted an experiment using open-circuit television as a resource for classroom teachers with elementary-school subjects and high-school physics. In the school year 1956–57 the actual telecasts of the whole year of physics lessons were filmed (not kinescoped) both in color and in black and white. They are on sale and available for general use in the teaching of regular high-school physics either directly by television or as a TV resource to be used by the classroom teacher.

St. Louis Public Schools.—In 1955–56 selected experimental high schools and elementary schools in St. Louis offered open-circuit, direct television instruction to large classes, especially in ninth-grade English composition and ninth-grade general science. No supplementary classroom instruction was offered; that is, the telecasts were self-contained and were not accompanied by additional teaching in the classrooms.

Schenectady Public Schools.—In order to test the advisability of installing closed-circuit television on a school-wide basis, classes in mathematics, chemistry, English composition, and French were taught by specially selected teachers. Pupil monitors, cadet teachers, and teacher aides assisted the TV teachers in following up their work and in supervising pupils and in performing non-professional duties.

Washington County (Maryland) Public Schools.—Washington County is conducting the largest closed-circuit television experiment in the country. A whole school system, of considerable size, is involved. In addition to the extensive closed-circuit phases of the experiment, various sizes of classes are involved, particularly at the high-school level, and a wide range of subject matter is included. One of the stated objectives is the raising of instructional quality, through the improvement and redeployment of teaching service. While part of the cost of the experiment is provided by the Board of Education and the Fund for the Advancement of Education, the Radio-Electronics-Television Manufacturers Association has provided the equipment, and the Chesapeake and Potomac Telephone Company has provided and installed the retransmission setup between the schools. The experiment began in the fall of 1956 and is to continue for five years.

In addition to the experimentation indicated above, a number of schools and more than two dozen colleges and universities are conducting formal experimentation in the educational television field. All types of TV usage are involved. It is heartening to note the number of school systems and higher institutions that are willing to experiment in this important field. Within a short time the relation of the communications revolution, especially television, to the high school and its implications for the high-school program will have been fairly well determined, one way or another, and on a sound and defensible basis.

The Real Questions and Their Answers

Reference is now made again to the major problems confronting the high school and the potential of television in meeting these problems. Can television be utilized in connection with the educational program in such manner as to lessen the number of teaching positions needed under the usual school conditions? The answer hinges on how successfully large classes can be taught effectively by using TV as an instructional resource. In several of the experiments now under way, the answer to that question may be determined, because the organization of the teaching patterns involves many fewer teaching positions. It may be found possible to meet the practical difficulties inherent in large classes, but the acid test of quality of learning must also be met. There are always two possible results from experimentation—one positive, the other negative.

Of course the problem of growing numbers of students may be met by finding somehow the necessary economic and human resources to teach them on the traditional average of about one teacher to thirty students. But if this ratio can be increased practically and without learning loss, would it not be desirable to do so and to divert the saving in economic and human resources to supplying many of the other services so badly needed in the present high school?

Three illustrations come to mind. First, it may be that some of the subject matter should be taught in much smaller classes than it is at present. For instance, this may become apparent as mathematics and science courses are modernized to include much more complicated and difficult areas of these subjects at the high-school level. Second, large dividends might accrue from multiplying the amount and the quality of our counseling service. Doing so might play a dynamic role in reducing youth delinquency. It might be worth trying, anyhow. Third, there might be added to the high-school team a much more thorough health service, especially in the case of mental health. The specialists in this field state that many forms of ill health, including mental, have their origin long before adult life. Possibly no other area of high-school service offers a greater potential for big returns on the money spent than does the field of health.

But the final question is whether television offers the possibility of meeting the problem of providing more education, and education with a more highly complex substance, which the future undoubtedly will demand. The boundaries of the school curriculum are determined fundamentally by the limitation of the means of communication. Will television make possible the breaking of the shackles on the curriculum imposed by the relatively limited means of communication that we had in the past?

There is strong reason to believe that television can break these shackles if it is properly applied and exploited. Our experience thus far with television generally leads to the conclusion that both the breadth and the depth of sensations and their relationships can be increased, with this means of communication, beyond anything in the past. It does not substitute for what was in the past, but it adds new dimensions to what we have had and can continue to hold. The high-school curriculum may be far richer in scope and quality of content if we can extend the breadth and the depth of the perceptions on which it depends.

The Real Payoff

There is still the problem whether the second step in the learning process, *thinking*, or doing something about the sensation received, can or will take place when classes are large even though television is used as a resource. Much of the experimentation described above is pointed toward finding the answer to that fundamental question.

It may be that television, as its use grows in effectiveness, may be so powerful in its communication process that the importance of some of the "doing-something-about" part may be lessened. Possibly there will not need to be so many questions, so much discussion, and so large an amount of remedial work as are incident to, and necessary with, the teaching that takes place under traditional conditions. This, too, the experimentation now under way and that to come will help to decide.

The direction and the place of the American high school in our country's destiny are uncertain as we look toward a highly precarious future. But there is no doubt that the communications revolution is real and certain. Possibly it has come at an opportune moment in our history. What part this revolution may play in the future high school and its service will depend on our ability to capture and harness the powerful forces unleashed by this revolution, especially television. These forces must be applied so as to help build a high-school program that will prepare our youth to live in their times. Of one thing we can be sure: those times will be far different from ours. Give us schools to match those times.

Science in American Life
and in the Schools

No country enjoys a richer harvest of the fruits of science than the United States. Yet the nature of science itself is not understood. A television comedian recently quipped, "The Russians got the satellite up first because American scientists are busy testing tooth paste and administering hypodermic injections to fountain pens." This attempt to be funny is a perfect example of the prevailing misconception that labels as science a wide variety of activities ranging all the way from large-scale technology to tricky "gadgeteering." The advertising industry not only spuriously identifies the scientist with a host of commercial products but often succeeds, in the process, in making him something of a figure of fun. Thus we have the paradox in which science, which figures so prominently in our daily lives and contributes so much to our standard of living, is only imperfectly understood and not fully appreciated. On the other hand, in Europe, including the Union of Soviet Socialist Republics, where the material benefits of science are much less widely enjoyed, science and, indeed, all learning are held in far greater respect and esteem.

If we are to realize the full potentialities of science in American life, we must recognize the need to educate the public to a more perfect understanding of the true nature of science and how it is fostered. It is my purpose to touch upon the relation of society and certain phases of science where weaknesses are apparent and to suggest ways in which we can correct those weaknesses. I refer specifically to our relative neglect of basic research; to deficiencies in the teaching of science and mathematics, particularly at the secondary-school level; and to the need for the United States to play a larger role in international science activities.

At the outset I think I should mention the subject that has been

84

on everyone's mind—Russia's success in launching the sputnik. I doubt that there has been a scientific gathering, since news of the launching on October 4, in which the Russian satellite has not been an active subject of discussion. Individually and collectively, we have certainly asked ourselves, "What is the significance of the sputnik for the American people, both now and in the future?" We must acknowledge at the outset that it was, first of all, a major scientific achievement—one which commanded the respect and admiration of scientists throughout the world. I need not remind you that the launching of an earth-circling satellite for the purpose of studying the ionosphere is one of the major objectives of the International Geophysical Year. As early as July, 1955, the United States announced its intention of launching such a satellite during the International Geophysical Year. Later the Russians also gave notice of such an intention. Naturally, the fact that the Russians succeeded in accomplishing a launching before we did is a disappointment to American scientists, but our scientists were, nonetheless, the first to congratulate the Russians, and they shared in the general satisfaction of scientists that a new scientific tool is now available with which to study the earth from outside the earth's enveloping atmosphere.

The sputnik captured the imagination of people everywhere; from the propaganda viewpoint we lost prestige, initially. The loss is more than offset, however, by what we can gain provided we know how to profit by the lesson. With his characteristic forthrightness, Vannevar Bush, when questioned about the sputnik, commented, "If it wakes us up, I'm damn glad the Russians shot their satellite. We are altogether too smug in this country."[1]

My own reaction is that the Russian satellite furnishes us an invaluable object lesson of the ultimate reward of what was, in the beginning, extremely abstract research. One of our difficulties in obtaining adequate support for basic research has been the problem of making clear to the average citizen the relation between fundamental research, such as that carried on in university laboratories, and the end products of applied research and development, which may emerge only years, and sometimes decades, later. The Russian sat-

[1] "Dr. Vannevar Bush Talks Plain Talk about U.S. and Soviet Science," *Newsweek*, October 21, 1957, p. 30.

ellite focused the attention of the world upon the importance of science and technology more dramatically and more effectively than thousands of words. It also emphasized what is required in order to apply the results of basic research to the solution of a highly complex and difficult problem. As the *New York Times* commented editorially:

> It isn't as though the Russians have suddenly stumbled upon a magic formula that must remain unknown to the rest of the world. What the Russians have done has been to concentrate manpower, knowledge, skills, and resources on the advancement of a specific program, in presumably much the same way as we did a decade and a half ago on the atomic bomb.[2]

In other words, the sputnik accomplished, in one bold stroke, what many of us have been trying slowly and laboriously to accomplish for a number of years, namely, to create in the minds of the American people an awareness of the tremendous importance of science and technology in the world today, as well as an awareness of what we must be prepared to do if the United States is to maintain a leading position.

Basic Research

Take the matter of basic research, for example. We realize that the scholarly type of pure research not only is necessary to the continual expansion of the frontiers of knowledge but is also a fundamental element in the training of scientists. It is true that in 1950 Congress recognized the need for a specific agency to foster and encourage the support of basic research and training in the sciences, but public recognition of the need lags behind official action. Thus we find that, out of an estimated total of five and a half billion dollars spent in this country for research and development in 1953, less than a half-billion, or 9 per cent, was spent for basic research in the sciences. When we realize that this sum represents less than one-tenth of one per cent of the gross national product, we can appreciate what a really small portion of our total national effort goes for research at the frontiers of knowledge. This neglect is very much of a grass-roots problem; for a really adequate effort in basic research can only come as the result of an informed body of public opinion, which demands that adequate support be provided out of public as well as private funds.

[2] *New York Times*, October 16, 1957, p. 34.

It is becoming increasingly obvious that the proper support of basic research is indeed a public responsibility. Investigators who are pursuing research unconnected with specific problems or unrelated to the missions of specific agencies find it more and more difficult to obtain support for such research. Often the time and energy of able research scientists are consumed in the difficult and distasteful task of seeking funds to enable them to continue their research. Such a situation not only is wasteful of valuable talent but is generally unproductive. To suppose that industry can make up the deficit by extending greater support to basic research is unrealistic. Industry is already being called upon to contribute to general education, and to add the demands of basic research is, in effect, to compete with general education for the same dollars. Even if industry doubled its present research support to universities, this would be merely a drop in the bucket.

Then, too, we must face the fact that the tools required for modern research are more and more beyond the resources of private enterprise. The costs of such instruments as nuclear reactors, nuclear accelerators, large-scale telescopes (both optical and radio telescopes), electronic computers, and other research equipment are beyond the means of a university or even groups of universities. For this reason the National Science Foundation has undertaken to support, within the limits of its resources, the new radio astronomy observatory, which is being built and operated at Green Bank, West Virginia, by Associated Universities, Incorporated; the National Astronomical Observatory, to be located somewhere in the southwestern United States; and has helped to finance computers, accelerators, and reactors for use in basic research and training. I believe we must accept the fact that this constitutes the pattern for the future and that tools of modern research will increasingly require the support, not only of one government, but, as in the case of atomic energy for peaceful purposes, the pooled resources of several governments.

To sum up, then, we may say that basic research in the United States is apparently unrecognized by a great number of the rank and file of the American people and is imperfectly understood by the rest. If our national research effort is to have the support that it requires, there must be a concentrated effort to educate the public to an understanding and appreciation of basic research and the need for its support on a much broader scale. We must also reconcile ourselves to the fact that an adequate effort in basic research requires, and will continue to require, substantial support from the federal government.

Deficiencies in Education

Turning now to the question of education, I shall address myself specifically to some of the problems that have arisen in connection with the training of adequate numbers of scientists and engineers, for these matters are of immediate concern to us in the National Science Foundation.

The whole matter of scientific manpower has been much more widely publicized than have the problems of basic research. This has resulted in greater public understanding, and hence action has been taken in some quarters. The reason for this difference lies perhaps not so much in any organized attempt at publicizing the problem as in the natural functioning of the law of supply and demand. The widespread needs for engineers, mathematicians, physicists, and other technically trained persons and the elaborate advertising campaigns springing from these needs have served to inform the public of acute shortages in certain fields.

The National Science Foundation received its first operational budget in 1951, and our initial effort was to launch, as quickly as possible, the fellowship program in the sciences which our basic legislation directed us to provide. Such a program went into effect for the academic year 1951–52 and has continued ever since, with expansion in certain areas.

It became apparent to us very early, however, that a fundamental problem lay in the inadequate preparation of students in secondary schools. As the reader is well aware, we cannot train scientists and engineers in a vacuum; we must have a strong educational system with adequate facilities and competent teachers in all subjects from the elementary grades on up. Nor have we lost sight of the fact, in our special concern for the training of scientists, that our society has great need for well-trained people in all fields. Our aim is not to create a so-called "technological society" but rather to insure that in an increasingly complex society there shall be competent leaders in every field. One of our problems is to insure that, in the process of

producing skilled scientists and engineers, we also produce cultivated and well-rounded individuals with breadth of outlook as well
as special competence. If we are to achieve these highly-to-be-de-
sired ends, we must direct our attention to the whole system and
begin at once to repair the damages resulting from neglect and in-
difference.

Persons from urban areas, where our public school system enjoys
comparatively strong financial support and where both teaching and
facilities are of reasonably high standard, need to take account of
the greater problem of the thousands of schools in rural areas. There
sincere, hard-working teachers and administrators faithfully strive
to provide good education without adequate facilities, without adequate preparation on the part of teachers, and without funds to attend educational meetings.

By way of illustration, I have in mind a small community in
which the National Science Foundation is active at the moment,
where the meagerness of the school facilities is in sharp contrast to
the sincerity and devotion of the staff. I was told that an effort to
float a bond issue for the benefit of the school was greeted by the
community with bitterness and recrimination, even on the part of
those who had children of school age. I do not think we have examined our consciences sufficiently on this point; we must ask ourselves why a nation which enjoys the highest standard of living on
earth and spends millions each year on automobiles, liquor, cosmet-
ics, and cigarettes, cannot manage to provide adequate schools or to
pay its teachers properly.

During the past half-century, teaching has slipped from the
highly esteemed position it once held in the United States. Now
teachers are accorded neither the prestige that they deserve nor the
salaries they should be receiving. The inevitable result has been that
teaching is no longer so attractive a profession as it once was and
the deficit in the number of young people going into teaching is
serious indeed.

Federal Action To Strengthen Teaching of
Science and Mathematics

From the viewpoint of science, one of the critical factors in the
present situation is the great shortage of adequately trained teachers
of science and mathematics in the secondary schools. Congress has

recognized this problem and for two successive years has earmarked certain of the National Science Foundation funds for the improvement of the teaching of science and mathematics in the nation's secondary schools.

The Foundation has met this mandate in various ways, but chiefly through the expansion of its summer-institute program, begun on an experimental basis in the summer of 1953. Through this program, high-school and college teachers of science and mathematics are given from six to eight weeks of intensive study in the fields which they are required to teach.

One of the unhappy facts revealed as we developed this program was that large numbers of teachers are required to teach various fields of science without any prior training whatsoever in those fields. We found home-economics majors teaching general science, biology teachers teaching astronomy, and a few unhappy souls teaching physics who had never studied the subject. The Foundation's summer institutes are administered by colleges and universities and are operated by the appropriate science department. Considerable effort is expended in obtaining distinguished scientists to bring to these teachers some of the newest developments in their fields. Thus the program at its best tends to be stimulating and inspirational as well as factual. The program has been gradually expanded since 1953 and has included both high-school and college teachers; and last year two academic-year institutes were set up, also on an experimental basis. These institutes gave selected teachers the opportunity to return to graduate school for a full year of work in their own and relevant fields.

In 1957, in response to the encouragement of Congress, the summer-institutes program was enlarged to include ninety-six such institutes, and the academic-year institutes number sixteen. Since Congress has made the same stipulation with respect to this year's funds, both the summer institutes and the academic-year institutes will continue at about the same level in 1957–58.

The National Science Foundation prescribes a pattern for these institutes in only the most general terms, and each host institution sets up the institute along the lines it thinks best. There is, accordingly, considerable diversity among them, and teachers are afforded a good deal of choice in selecting the kind of institute that will best suit their needs. Once a year the Foundation holds a conference of institute directors in order that each may be fully acquainted with what the others are doing.

As might be expected in any program of such magnitude and diversity, there is some unevenness of quality and effectiveness, but the overwhelming consensus among the participating teachers is one of great enthusiasm as well as appreciation for the opportunity thus afforded. It is still too early, of course, for any assessment of the effects of these programs on the quality of teaching, but it seems safe to predict that the results will more than justify both the money and the effort that have been expended.

We have supplemented the summer-institutes program with a variety of other activities, including a visiting-lecturers program; a Traveling Science Library program, in co-operation with the American Association for the Advancement of Science; a demonstration-lectures program, in co-operation with the Oak Ridge Institute for Nuclear Studies; and a science-clubs program, in co-operation with Science Service.

These various efforts illustrate one way in which the federal government, through the National Science Foundation, is helping to strengthen the teaching of science and mathematics, particularly at the high-school level.

Obviously, however, the several agencies of the federal government operating in the field of education cannot do the whole job, and I am sure that you would agree that such a situation would not be desirable in any case. It should be a matter of local concern that the high schools are well staffed and equipped. Science cannot be adequately taught without good laboratories, equipped with appropriate materials, including those needed for demonstration lectures. The teaching of mathematics as well as the sciences is considerably enhanced by the use of the colorful and attractive teaching aids that are now available for this purpose. The school library should be well stocked and run by a competent librarian. The accessibility of correlated reading can be an important factor in the progress of high-school students.

In order to attract and hold the kinds of teachers it should have, each community should be prepared to pay good salaries in terms of the current cost of living, to reward good teaching by periodic promotions, and to restore to the teaching profession the prestige and respect it once was accorded. These are clearly matters of local responsibility. Each community should examine critically its own school facilities and its own teacher-salary scales and, where these are below standard, take prompt remedial action. Federal aid should be sought only when local resources have been fully tapped and proved inadequate to the need. The federal government may properly exert leadership, however, and, where local interest lags or is lacking altogether, take steps to arouse the public to the gravity of the situation and the extent of the need.

A group with special responsibility in this area is the President's Committee on Scientists and Engineers, for which the National Science Foundation provides funds and secretariat. Appointed by the President in April, 1956, the committee is essentially a citizens' action group. It was directed to assist the federal government in identifying the problems associated with the development of more highly qualified scientists and engineers and to enlist the co-operation of interested individuals and groups in developing programs to meet these problems. The committee operates largely through the organizations represented in its membership.

Recapitulating for a moment, we see that two significant weaknesses are hampering the full effectiveness of science in American life: (1) lack of appreciation and full support of the importance of basic research and (2) deficiencies in our school system which keep us from realizing our full potential, not only in science, but in other fields as well.

Role of U.S. in International Science

I turn now to international science, the third area where there is clearly need for improvement with respect to our own role. In science, especially, are the words of John Donne true:

> No man is an *Iland* intire of it selfe;
> every man is a peece of the *Continent*,
> a part of the *maine*.[3]

Despite the sensation created by the Russian sputnik, 1957–58 may still be remembered as the International Geophysical Year and

[3] John Donne, "Devotions upon Emergent Occasions," XVII, *Complete Poetry and Selected Prose*, ed. John Hayward (New York: Random House, 1929), p. 538.

not solely as the date that marked the first appearance of an earth-circling satellite. The I.G.Y. constitutes a truly inspirational example of international co-operation in science at its best. For a period of six years before its inception, scientists representing the majority of the nations of the earth were planning and working together toward a common objective. In the Antarctic alone, twelve nations have established stations, collaborating wherever necessary and sharing, as often as needed, meteorological and other data of interest to all.

I mention the I.G.Y., which is an exciting topic in itself, to illustrate the kinds of ends that can be accomplished through effective co-operation. Geophysical research, by its very nature, often demands widely scattered synoptic observations; and, without the complete co-operation of many nations, it would have been impossible even to attempt studies of the kind included in the I.G.Y.

Effective international co-operation in science depends upon the free exchange of scientific information; interchange of scientific personnel through scientific meetings and congresses, individual visits, and student and teacher exchanges; and upon adequate scientific representation abroad. At the present time the role of the United States in each of these three situations leaves something to be desired.

During World War II, free interchange of scientific information between ourselves and the Allied nations was one of the decisive factors in the winning of the war. Since the war, exchanges of both information and personnel have been on a far less satisfactory basis. Visa restrictions, for example, have hampered the entry of foreign scientists into the United States to the point where international scientific groups shun the United States as a place in which to hold their meetings. For example, the International Congress on Genetics recommended, in 1953, that its international meetings not be held in any country where "scientists would be refused permission to enter on grounds of race, nationality, place of birth, or political association, past or present." The United States has also been niggardly in its financial support of such gatherings, and such a combination of circumstances is injurious to the prestige of the United States in international scientific circles.

Exchange of scientific information through journals, reports, and similar media is absolutely essential to scientific progress. Nevertheless we find that the free exchange of non-classified scientific journals and reports has been hampered by cumbersome United States regulations surrounding the export of certain types of non-classified technical material. Other countries cannot understand why it should be necessary to place restrictions upon the flow of unclassified information, and in some cases their reaction has been to place similar restrictions on their own material. As a result the United States is failing to receive important scientific and technical data that it should be receiving on a reciprocal basis.

We can only guess at what may be our net loss in terms of inadequate participation in international science because of lack of full representation in science in the principal capitals of the world. In 1950 a major report, entitled *Science and Foreign Relations*,[4] was presented to the State Department. This report, the work of specialists in a number of fields, summarized the numerous areas in which science impinges upon our foreign policy. One of its major recommendations was the appointment of a science adviser to the State Department and the designation of science attachés in the principal capitals of the world. These recommendations were put into effect and for several years gave ample demonstration of their soundness. It is now proposed that the science program be revived with the appointment of a new science adviser and with the appointment, once again, of science attachés in at least some of the capitals where we were so represented before.

Without touching upon the number of detailed ways in which the participation of the United States in world science might profitably be strengthened, I have nevertheless called attention to certain broad areas in which improvement can be brought about only through informed public opinion. The government in Washington must always be responsive to the will of the people, and major reforms affecting the free interchange of scientific information and personnel and adequate U.S. representation in science abroad can be brought about if the people as a whole clearly understand the

[4] United States Department of State, International Science Policy Survey Group, *Science and Foreign Relations* (Department of State Publication 3860, General Foreign Policy Series 30 [Washington: Division of Publications, Office of Public Affairs, Department of State, May, 1950]).

issues and express their wishes through their elected representatives.

Fortunately a good many of these problems have received considerable notice in the press and otherwise, with the result that we have tended to look at some of them in a wholesomely critical way. The fact that the British Prime Minister discussed with President Eisenhower a renewal of the interchange of scientific and technical information between ourselves and the British raises the hope that we shall view all these problems in clearer perspective.

The withdrawal of the fingerprint requirement for visitors is another heartening sign. Some progress, too, has been made in easing the visa regulations, so that distinguished foreign visitors can come to this country with greater ease than has been possible in recent years.

The number of areas in which science touches upon public policy is growing every day. This is one reason why informed leaders of the scientific community have spoken out vigorously against excessive secrecy in science. Actually there can be no secrets in pure science; history has proved again and again that scientific problems which can be solved by one nation can also, in time, be solved by other nations. Scientists know that knowledge of the secrets of nature, once discovered, cannot be indefinitely concealed. On the other hand, technological know-how, involving applications, processes, and techniques, are properly subject to secrecy, especially when they involve new weapons or other military equipment and devices. But discoveries relating to the fundamental facts of nature should be freely published for all to read, and the restrictions applied to scientific information should be held to the minimum consonant with national security; for our national security depends, in a larger sense, upon an informed citizenry which is able to vote intelligently upon issues affecting the national safety and welfare.

I have endeavored here to recall to your attention factors which limit our full realization of the scientific potential available to us. I have omitted those details that are the responsibility of the scientific community, or science administrators, or the federal government. I have mentioned issues in which every thinking, voting citizen can have a part. These issues are too important to be neglected, particularly at this critical juncture in history. The understanding and support of basic research, the strengthening and improvement of our educational system, and the maintenance of United States prestige in international science are matters which deserve full consideration by all our people.

In presenting the Atoms for Peace Award to Dr. Niels Bohr, President Eisenhower said: "The whole world can gain through support and respect for basic research, for education and for learning. Science today is a priceless heritage from the past. We, as trustees of that inheritance, have an obligation to increase it for the benefit of posterity."[5]

[5] *New York Times,* October 25, 1957, p. 12.

The Emerging Economic Scene and Its
Relation to High-School Education

In a first draft of this paper, I began by considering whether the people of the United States can afford our very expensive educational system. I dropped this question, however, because any attempt to treat this issue directly gets one nowhere. It leads only to *ad hoc* dicta, because I know of no established standards that I can use in placing a value on this education.

What I am doing, instead, is much more indirect but, I trust, more meaningful. I begin by asking: Why do the costs of education rise more than the cost of living? I then bring together what a number of new studies in economics seem to tell us about the contributions of education to economic growth and national income. I close with some reflections on the implications of all this for the high school.

Why Costs of Education Rise More
than the Cost of Living

Education has become increasingly expensive. There is much more than inflation that is increasing the cost of education. What is generally overlooked is the fact that one of the basic characteristics of our economic growth has been that the cost of education per student per year rises more than the cost of living and that this differential is a consequence of the rise in real wages in the economy. Let me put it in figures. Consumer prices have risen about 95 per cent since 1940; we ascribe this rise to inflation. Meanwhile the cost of education per student appears to have increased upward of 40 per cent more than the rise in the index of consumer prices. By "cost of education" I mean the total value per student of all the resources used for education, that is, the human effort, the materials and their services (whether paid for on public or private account) employed in our educational system. Moreover, this cost of education will have to go up substantially more above the rise in cost of living before it strikes a balance with real wages that now prevail in the economy. And all this takes no account of the fact that, as a people, we really want to improve the quality of education and that carrying out this desire surely will make education still more expensive.

The economy establishes the prices and wages that rule, and it is up to the educational system to adjust itself to whatever basic changes in prices and wages occur. This truth has been a hard lesson for many of those who manage our educational system. Many would like to believe that competition characteristic of the market place, with its prices and wages, is a thing apart; that education is not dependent upon these factors; and that it can and should isolate itself. The inflation and the remarkable rise in real wages since 1940 have, however, thoroughly shaken this mistaken belief. We now know that the cost of education is closely related to changes in salaries, wages, and the prices of materials throughout the economy. There is, nevertheless, much confusion about the nature of the changes that have been occurring and how they alter the cost of education. Our economic development since 1940 has had two important effects upon the costs of education. I shall call these (1) the inflation effects and (2) the rise-in-real-wages effects.

1. *Inflation effects.*—Inflation since 1940 has come close to doubling the index of consumer prices.[1] The rise in these prices, moreover, has been uneven. Food, apparel, and most consumer durables were the first to rise in price as a consequence of the inflation. Other prices have lagged, for example, those represented by transportation, rent, medical care, and notably education.

The school boards and administrators responsible for the budgets for education were slow to increase them in line with the inflation. The old school buildings were there for education as before; and, as for teachers who had committed themselves to education, they would not, it was said, leave the classroom for other occupations, where wages were being adjusted upward because of the inflation. This erroneous view of the consequences of the inflation was dis-

[1] When 1947–49 prices = 100, this price index rose from 59.9 in 1940 to 116.1 in 1956, representing a rise of 94 per cent.

carded after a few years, but not until a lot of damage had been done. Those responsible for the budgets for education were then surprised to find that the costs of education rose much more than the cost of living.[2]

2. *Rise-in-real-wages effects.*—One of the fundamental characteristics of our kind of economic growth has been the rise in wages relative to consumer prices. This characteristic has been very prominent since 1940. Between 1940 and 1956 wages trebled, rising from $0.66 to $1.98 per hour, and real wages per hour, accordingly, rose about 55 per cent.[3] Weekly wages rose almost 64 per cent in real terms.[4]

Although there has been a considerable lag, it is clear that the salaries of teachers have not been set in isolation, that competition has been making itself felt, and that the big rise in real wages in industry has been transmitted, in substantial part, to teachers. From 1940 to 1956 real salaries of workers in public education rose about 36 per cent.[5] This is, of course, a good deal less than the increase enjoyed by workers in industry. I shall argue below that there has been an appreciable loss in the quality of the personnel available to our schools as a consequence of the more favorable earning opportunities in many occupations other than teaching.

Let me add three brief notes on related issues.

a) Suppose we leave inflation aside and assume that the quality of education is not being changed. Why is it that under these con-

---

[2] New construction costs, for example, rose from an index of 52 in 1940 to 138 in 1956, representing a rise of 165 per cent compared with a rise of 94 per cent in the case of the consumer price index.

[3] When 1940 wages and prices = 100, the consumer price index stood at 194 in 1956 and average hourly earnings in all manufacturing at 300 in 1956.

[4] Average weekly wages rose somewhat more than this—from $25.20 in 1940 to $80.13 in 1956—thus rising to an index of 318, or 64 per cent in *real terms*.

[5] The following estimates of earnings are per full-time employee during 1940 and 1956:

	All Industry	Public Education
1940...................	$1,306	$1,436
1956...................	4,021	3,786
Rise with 1940 = 100.....	308	264

Real earnings per full-time employee in public education rose about 36 per cent (264 ÷ 194), compared to about 59 per cent (308 ÷ 194) for all industries.

It should be noted that under the circumstances that prevailed in 1940, with its vast unemployment, the salaries of teachers may have been higher relative to wages than would be normal under conditions of full employment.

ditions the index of consumer prices could stay constant but the cost of education per student could not, while real wages rose? One at once thinks of advances in technology and of the increase in the stock of capital and the resulting rise in productivity per worker. What this comes down to is simply that there are many fewer possibilities of substituting capital for human effort and of introducing labor-saving technology in education than in the economy generally.[6]

b) Workers demand more leisure as their earnings rise, and teachers are no exception. This development is strictly an income effect, and the income elasticity of the demand for leisure (free time) is positive. While I know of no studies of the changes that have occurred in the amount of leisure of teachers, I doubt that it has kept pace with the rest of the economy. If I am right in this assessment, teachers have lost ground on this score relative to workers in industry, and appropriate adjustments in classroom, office, and homework schedules must be made to hold and attract teachers against the over-all competitions set by the economy. The cost implication of such an adjustment is clear: education will cost even more when this adjustment has been made.

c) A third consequence of the rapid rise in real wages is that in all likelihood the quality of personnel serving education has suffered in the process of adjusting salaries to the rises in real wages. The lag in making these adjustments has been, and continues to be, substantial. For example, as noted above, real wages were 55–64 per cent higher in 1956 than in 1940, whereas teachers' real salaries were up only 36 per cent. The score, so it appears, has also been running against teaching in adjusting work schedules to satisfy the increasing demand for leisure. In our society, with its values and with the mobility of our workers, we get the quality of personnel that we are prepared to pay for. Education is no exception.

[6] Nor, so it would appear, has there been as much of an incentive to substitute along these lines in education, because real salaries for teachers have not risen as much as have real wages in industry. For example, since both the salaries of teachers and the cost of new construction have risen about the same—one from an index of 100 in 1940 to 265, and the other to 264 in 1956—no incentive has been created to substitute one for the other.

Contributions of Education to Economic Growth and National Income

This topic takes me onto very difficult terrain; the hill we climb may hide the mountain we would like to scale. There are the usual vague claims for education. But these tell us little about what it is that our high schools contribute to economic growth. The claims are not convincing because they are not based on analysis that rests on hypotheses that can be put to test. Marshall, Pigou, and other distinguished economists clearly perceived that education is, on the one hand, something to be acquired for its cultural value and, on the other hand, also represents, in many circumstances, a form of capital that increases production. But there the matter has rested, except for a study or two that estimated the cost of the instruction, training, and time required to become a highly skilled professional worker, for example, a doctor of medicine, and estimated the returns on that investment.

During the last few years several studies have been under way in economics that are beginning to throw some light on this issue. In these brief remarks I cannot consider the many difficult theoretical and estimating problems that arise. However, at the risk of greatly oversimplifying the analysis, I shall try to summarize what appears to be emerging from these studies.

1. *Only about half of our economic growth has been coming from increases in the labor force and in the stock of conventional capital.* —This statement is based on net national product as a measure of economic growth. It does not credit the economy with the large additional amount of leisure that it has made possible. The labor force is measured in man-hours and capital. This capital covers a large part of our tangible wealth, but not consumer equipment, military assets, and land and subsoil assets.

I shall draw on only two studies for estimates on which the above statement rests. Abramovitz[7] puts the rate of increase of the United States net national product since 1870 at 3.5 per cent per annum, and the increase of labor and capital combined at 1.7 per cent per

[7] Moses Abramovitz, *Resource and Output Trends in the United States since 1870* ("Occasional Paper 52" [New York: National Bureau of Economic Research, 1956]).

annum. These estimates leave 1.8 per cent per annum, or about half of the increase in real income, that is unexplained by man-hours and traditional capital. A study by Kendrick,[8] restricted to the private domestic economy for the period between 1899 and 1953, puts the rise in real product at 3.3 per cent per annum and the increase in inputs of labor and capital at 1.6 per cent per annum, thus leaving 1.7 per cent per annum unaccounted for.

2. *Only a small part of the very large increase in real product per man-hour is attributable to increases in conventional capital.*—What is this "very large increase in real product"? Let me state it, first, in per capita terms. The average rate of increase per capita has been 1.9 per cent per annum. To acquire some feel of what this means, I cannot do better than to quote Fabricant, who, in his 1954 report to the directors of the National Bureau of Economic Research, said:

> The average family in the United States had an income of somewhat over $5,000 in 1953. If we progress at as high and consistent a rate in the next eighty years as in the last, our grandchildren and great-grandchildren will have average family incomes of about $25,000 of 1953 purchasing power—a level now attained only by the top 1 per cent or so of the nation's families.[9]

To return now to Statement 2 above. I introduced it because of the widespread belief that so much of our economic growth represents a cashing-in on increases in the stock of conventional capital. I do not want to belittle the role of savings and capital formation; I want only to put its role into a perspective that is consistent with such estimates as are available. On this point, then, I turn to Solow,[10] who finds that in the United States gross output per man-hour approximately doubled between 1909 and 1949 and that only one-eighth of this increase is attributable to increased use of capital.

[8] John W. Kendrick, *Productivity Trends: Capital and Labor* ("Occasional Paper 53" [New York: National Bureau of Economic Research, 1956]).

[9] Solomon Fabricant, "Economic Progress and Economic Change," in *34th Annual Report* (New York: National Bureau of Economic Research, Inc., 1954), p. 5.

[10] Robert Solow, "Technical Change and the Aggregate Production Function," *Review of Economics and Statistics*, XXXIX (August, 1957), 312–20.
Solow also reports that his measured shifts of the aggregate production function netted out to be approximately neutral; that is, the shifts were pure scale changes, leaving marginal rates of substitution unchanged at given capital-labor ratios. It is this result which permits us to do the arithmetic appearing under Statement 1 above.

The other seven-eighths is, accordingly, not attributable to the increases in the stock of conventional capital.

If it is true, as these estimates show, that only half of the increases in net national product is attributable to more man-hours and conventional capital and that only one-eighth of the rise in gross income per man-hour is from additional capital, where did the rest of the income come from? Did it simply fall gently upon us like manna from heaven? Or is it perhaps some new twist of the invisible hand? One hypothesis would be that we have been gaining income from a great deal of increasing returns to scale from greater division of labor and specialization as the economy has increased in size.

3. *Although this hypothesis should not be rejected, such evidence as we now have suggests that in general there have been some persistent diminishing returns to scale.*—Again I turn to Solow, who reports that, for the United States between 1909 and 1949, the aggregate production function gives a distinct impression of persistent diminishing returns.

4. *There is a growing body of evidence that supports another hypothesis:* that there have been improvements in the *quality* of resources and that it is these improvements that account primarily for the large unexplained increases in income reviewed under Statements 1 and 2 above.

There is, first, an inference from plain economics: that, if returns to scale are constant, and if the marginal rate of substitution between labor and capital is unchanged, and if under these circumstances more output is forthcoming, it is the production function that has been altered; that is, production has risen relative to inputs of labor and capital as conceived and measured. We can, however, transpose any gains in output under these conditions back to the input account and embody them in the labor and capital as improvements in quality. This, then, permits us to treat the production function as unchanged and to represent the increases in output as a measure of the improvements in the quality of labor and capital.

We observe all manner of improvements that are of this general class. Better health and much of our education may be represented as improvements in the human agent. Additions to our stock of useful knowledge, which is a broader concept than "techniques of production" or "technology," are in substantial part embodied into the physical capital that we use in production. A bushel of hybrid seed corn and a bushel of open pollinated seed corn are both bits of physical capital, differing, however, greatly in quality. Young men and women as they enter the labor force also differ substantially in quality depending on whether they have had a high-school or only an elementary-school education.

But we must ask: Are the additional investments that improve the quality of our resources, both human and non-human, large enough, and are the returns that we realize on these investments high enough, to give us the kind of increases in income that we reviewed under Statements 1 and 2? (Conceivably the amount so invested could be so large that, even with rates of return below that realized on conventional capital, it could account for the extra income. If this were true, one inference could be that too much was being invested in "quality" relative to conventional "quantity" of labor and capital.)

There are many signs that the income contributions of many new techniques of production are far in excess of what it could possibly have cost to have "discovered" and developed such new techniques. Griliches' studies of hybrid corn[11] are the first I know of, however, where an attempt is made to estimate the rate of return on this type of investment; they show that the rate of return has been more than a hundred times as large as the ordinary rate of return on conventional capital.

But what about education? Zeman's study of "White and Non-white Income Differentials in the United States"[12] is a careful and critical analysis of 1940 data to isolate the effects of color, region, sex, age, city size, and education upon wages and salaries of male urban workers. I shall restrict myself to only one part of this important study, namely, to the mean wage and salary income of white urban males in 1940. This part shows that, of these males, those who had completed 12 years of school earned about 30 per

[11 a) Zvi Griliches, "Hybrid Corn: An Exploration in Economics of Technological Change," *Econometrica*, XXV (October, 1957), 501–22.

b) Zvi Griliches, "Research Costs and Social Returns: Hybrid Corn with Comparisons," *Journal of Political Economy* (forthcoming).

12 Morton Zeman, "White and Non-white Income Differentials in the United States" (unpublished Doctor's dissertation, University of Chicago, 1955), Table 25.

cent more than those who had completed 7–8 years of school, for the ages 25–29, regardless of city size; for ages 30–34, between 34 and 43 per cent more, depending on city size; and for ages 35–44, between 37 and 57 per cent more, again depending on city size.

The implications are that our economy in 1940 found it profitable to pay substantially higher wages and salaries to those white urban males in these age groups who had completed the equivalent of a high-school education, compared with those who had completed only 7–8 years of school. How the vast unemployment of 1940 affects these wages and salaries, we do not know. Data for 1950, unfortunately, do not lend themselves to the same treatment. How large a rate of return these higher wages and salaries may have represented on the private and public investment in this additional education has not as yet been estimated.

One may treat the resources used in education as a measure of the capital that is formed in this way. I have attempted to estimate the gross capital formation represented by the four high-school years (the ninth, tenth, eleventh, and twelfth years of school) and also that represented by education beyond the twelfth year of school. Both private and public resources used for these purposes were taken into account. My tentative estimates for 1920 and 1956 along with estimates of conventional capital are shown in Table 1. When we look upon this education as improving the quality of the human agent and treat it as capital formation, one finds that the gross figures have risen much more since 1920 than has the gross capital formation of the conventional types. Also, the totals for education are far from being unimportant, for they were already 7 per cent as large as that of conventional capital in 1920 and have risen to 28 per cent of that of conventional capital in 1956.

My efforts to get at net capital formation are less complete because of difficulties in obtaining data. But what is clear is that capital embodied in humans has acquired over a period of time a somewhat longer average life, whereas capital in physical forms (non-human) has moved in the other direction; its average life has been declining. Accordingly, the increases in net capital formation have been even more favorable to education relative to conventional capital than that shown above for gross capital formation.

There are, however, many unknowns. All that I want to say is:

if the rate of return on this and on other capital used to improve the quality of human agents is high, as it seems to be, then the increases in this form of capital may account for a substantial part of the unexplained economic growth considered under Statements 1 and 2 above.

Let me close this part by calling attention to some new data which permit one to compare the use of manpower for education in Great Britain and the United States. Students of economic history

TABLE 1

ESTIMATED GROSS CAPITAL FORMATION REPRESENTED BY THE FOUR HIGH-SCHOOL YEARS AND BY EDUCATION BEYOND THE TWELFTH YEAR OF SCHOOL IN 1920 AND 1956 IN THE UNITED STATES

	GROSS CAPITAL FORMATION (IN BILLIONS OF DOLLARS AT CURRENT PRICES)	
	1920	1956
1. High-school years....................	1.0	12.4
2. Education beyond the twelfth year of school............................	.6	10.3
3. Total for this education (1+2)........	1.6	22.7
4. Total conventional capital............	23.1	80.6
Per cent that gross capital formation in this education is of gross capital formation of conventional type (3÷4×100)........................	7	28

have been hard put to explain why the economy of Great Britain has been falling behind that of the United States in economic growth and in output per man-hour. May it not be that a basic underlying factor has been the relatively small investment on the part of Great Britain in its secondary schools and in its colleges and universities? The Abramovitz-Eliasberg data[13] are not inconsistent with the hypothesis implied in this question.

In 1900 in the United States, 1.8 per cent of the labor force was employed in state and local schools, whereas in 1901 in Great Britain, the per cent was only 0.9. In 1950 this figure for the United

[13] Moses Abramovitz and Vera Eliasberg, *The Growth of Public Employment in Great Britain* (Princeton, New Jersey: Princeton University Press, 1957).

States had risen to 2.4 per cent and that for Great Britain to 1.4 per cent. A better figure is the per cent of the population of school ages enrolled in all regular schools. For 1950 we have the figures shown in Table 2.

Some Implications and Reflections

I now cast caution overboard and enter the dangerous shoals of beliefs and values. The course I take is, in large part, based on what I see and believe as a citizen.

1. Additions to the stock of useful knowledge and improvements

TABLE 2

PER CENT OF POPULATION OF VARIOUS
AGES ENROLLED IN SCHOOLS IN GREAT
BRITAIN AND THE UNITED STATES IN
1950

AGE GROUP	PER CENT ENROLLED	
	Great Britain	United States
5–14............	94	91
15–18............	12	76
19–22............	4*	30*

* Based on total enrolment in college and university (thus not restricted to the ages 19–22) as a per cent of the number of individuals in the population of ages 19–22.

in the quality of a people, viewed narrowly (if one so wishes) as human effort and its contributions to production, have been exceedingly important in achieving our economic growth.

2. Our secondary schools and our colleges and universities have played a major role in making it possible to accumulate this stock of useful knowledge and to achieve these improvements in the quality of our human resources.

3. It is my impression that a number of the leading countries of Western Europe have done fully as well as we have in their elementary education for "all children," and as well or better in education for those few highly competent students who enter a university. We have done much more, however, in education for the rank and file of students in the high-school age group and have served more students in the college and university age group.

4. Our high schools and colleges and universities have contributed importantly in making our people less tradition-bound, less tied to particular occupations, and more mobile in taking jobs and in migrating to where there are good jobs than would otherwise have been the case. These changes in outlook are one of the basic preconditions of our kind of economic growth and development, where people are essentially free agents in entering upon jobs.

5. Our high schools and colleges and universities have also contributed much in bringing to the surface a wide variety of talents that would otherwise have remained undiscovered and dormant. The economy, I am convinced, has gained measurably from these additional talents that have been found and realized.

6. Yet it is precisely in the process of discovering and developing students of varying talents that our high schools and colleges and universities have fallen far short of making the most of the possibilities open to us. Many students who have better-than-average talents, especially many of those who have unusually fine talents, have not been served satisfactorily by our education.

7. Neither our high schools nor our colleges and universities are employing anywhere near enough resources to instruct and train students to do difficult intellectual work. Many students, I feel sure, are capable of doing vastly more difficult intellectual work than they are now being instructed to do. In this respect we are, therefore, under-investing in education, and thus the quality of the human resources made available to the economy is substantially less than it could be, and economic growth is to this extent retarded.

8. What the schools can do in discovering and developing talents, much more fully than they now do, affects the supply side of our human resources as seen by an economist. A word or two about the demand side is also in order. There is market discrimination against some human resources because of their color, religion, and education,[14] especially against Negroes who have completed high school, and even more so in the case of those who have a college or university education.[15] Then, too, a strong case could be made to show that there is much misuse of the better talents in the labor force on

[14] Gary S. Becker, *The Economics of Discrimination* (Chicago: University of Chicago Press, 1957).

[15] Morton Zeman, *op. cit.*

the part of both the private and the public sectors of the economy. Individuals who are qualified to do difficult intellectual work are, it would seem, all too frequently induced to take jobs which fall far short in using these talents efficiently. Conventional salaries are often the key to this kind of misallocation of the more talented in the labor force.

9. These problems, whether one looks at the demand or the supply of our human resources, are beset with difficulties that go deep into our cultural values and into our fundamental attitudes toward those among us who, with adequate instruction and training, are capable of doing the tough intellectual work that must be done if we are to achieve as is our wont. Our schools, all along the line, can do much in bringing about the kind of re-examination of our cultural values that will be necessary if we are to succeed in making the required changes on this score. That our schools have not been bringing these values under critical review, long before this, is a measure of mistaken belief as to what should be given priority. That so many talented students in our high schools who strive to develop their fine talents should find themselves on the defensive, as is now so often the case, because of the hostile attitudes of fellow students, is not only to be deplored but is basically, as I see it, one of the strange fruits of our educational system. If I am right, the system must assume a large measure of responsibility for this awesome development in attitudes on the part of many students.

10. Finally, there is the question whether a very general or a less general education is the better way of achieving the ends implicit in what I have been arguing for. I find that an unsettled issue. The tentative lesson that I draw from our experiences is that it can be done either way, provided we are agreed and clear on such basic matters as have been introduced in this paper.

III

Concepts, Values, and Criteria Are Offered for the Redirection of American Secondary Education

REUBEN G. GUSTAVSON

Maintaining Balance between Science and the Humanities

The purpose of education is to make available to man the facts and tools that are necessary to an understanding of his physical, biological, and social environment. This includes understanding man himself and his relations with his fellow human beings. A relatively new tool in this great adventure is basic science. This tool has revealed a consistent universe; if nature is asked a question by way of experiment at two different times and the conditions of the experiment are the same, nature will give identical answers on both occasions.

Preconceptions in Science and Art

Professor Niels Bohr, distinguished atomic physicist of Denmark, has said that our knowledge of basic science resulted from techniques that have enabled man to place limiting values on his preconceptions. In basic science the great stimulus is curiosity—the desire to know for the sake of knowing. Aristotle's conviction that the velocity of falling bodies depends upon their weight seems common sense, and his idea was accepted for thousands of years. It was Galileo's idea that bodies might fall with velocity independent of their weight. This did not seem like common sense. Galileo carried out a visual demonstration, according to tradition at least, by dropping bodies of different weights from the top of the leaning tower of Pisa so the students and professors of the university could see them fall side by side. The difference between Galileo and Aristotle was not primarily a difference in the significance of their convictions, because, if either conviction had led to the simple experiment of falling bodies, the true nature of the velocity of falling bodies would have been discovered. It is the technique which is important.

113

Let us contrast this with a conception of art, which may be defined as a body of accomplishment obtained by realizing preconceptions. If you would paint a portrait of Abraham Lincoln, you must first develop within your own mind a conception of the painting. You decide whether you are painting the rail-splitter, the Indian fighter, the weary war President. You examine paintings, photographs, and various pieces of art representing the Great Emancipator, and then you start to work with brush and paint and canvas. But there is nothing in the painting process that tells you whether you are right or wrong, and your success as a painter depends upon how clearly the final product represents the preconceptions that you started with.

Science and Invention

Science leads to invention—the building of contrivances or instruments or the development of new methods serving some desired purpose and based upon the information discovered as a result of curiosity. Inventions today are taken over by the engineer, who makes the invention available to large numbers of people by developing mass-production methods. Let us examine a few examples from history to illustrate our problem.

Diabetes is a very old disease. For thousands of years man has recognized a disease in which the urine contains sugar and which causes the sufferers to become weak and die. Shortly before 1890 two scientists, von Mering and Minkowski, with no thought of diabetes, tried to find out what part the pancreas, an organ which pours its juices into the intestine, plays in the digestive process. They removed the pancreas from dogs. Nothing very much happened as far as the digestion of food was concerned. But, according to tradition, the animal caretaker observed that bees coming in through the laboratory windows congregated on the urine of these animals. This was reported to von Mering and Minkowski, who quickly proved that the urine contained sugar. They had established experimental diabetes. Following the clue of this fundamental science discovery, a group of Canadians, under the leadership of Dr. F. G. Banting, succeeded in isolating, in impure form, the substance from the pancreas which we call insulin and which, when injected into the animal with experimental diabetes or the human being with spontaneous diabetes, enables him to burn his sugar. The disease is controlled. This is the development based upon the basic science of von Mering and Minkowski. Somewhat later this substance was isolated in pure form by Dr. John J. Abel, of Johns Hopkins University. In the meantime engineers had taken over. Methods of large-scale production were used, and insulin was produced in such quantities that diabetic patients anywhere in the world could be relieved of their diabetic difficulty.

Another example is supplied by cellulose, the basic substance of plant life which makes up paper, linen, wood fiber, and so on. This substance is highly insoluble. Every student of elementary chemistry recognizes this when he pours his many kinds of solutions over a piece of filter paper. A chemist by the name of Schweitzer became curious about this fact and, as a result of experimentation, discovered that the highly insoluble cellulose would dissolve in a solution made up of copper hydroxide and ammonia. This was a basic science discovery. Some years later a French worker by the name of Chardonnet saw the possibility of dissolving cellulose, then forcing it through a tiny orifice into an acid, causing the cellulose to separate out in very fine threads. This is the basic invention of rayon. The engineer has mass-produced this form of rayon along with others, and now it is available in immense quantities to mankind. Nylon has a similar history. The result has been increasing use of these synthetic fibers to clothe man.

A group of scientists—Enrico Fermi in Rome, Joliot in France, Otto Hahn in Germany—learned to split the atom and to liberate tremendous quantities of energy as well as tremendous quantities of radioactive substances. The inventions growing out of this discovery included the atomic bomb and the hydrogen bomb (great destructive agents). But it also showed the possibility of great new sources of power, which can, potentially at least, raise the level of the standard of living of men all over the world; of the production of isotopes leading to techniques for understanding disease and for creating new varieties of plants with greater food yields. At the same time the possibility of doing genetic damage to generations yet unborn is real.

The basic scientific discoveries of Faraday and the fundamental theoretical work of Maxwell in electromagnetic-wave theory, coupled with the basic work of many investigators on vacuum tubes, have given us radio and television. Industry has mass-produced these inventions so that it is now difficult to find any place on the globe that is not equipped with one or both of these great inventions. Woodrow Wilson was not able to reach many more people with his voice than was Lincoln or Demosthenes. Today millions can see and hear President Eisenhower. These inventions, capable of such great educational contributions, have also made possible the sale of huge quantities of medicines of questionable efficacy and have increased the consumption of certain food products through the transmission of advertising statements so cleverly produced that it takes careful study to see that they have no real meaning for the purchaser.

Need for Value Judgments

I am sure most of you working in education are struggling with basic problems. You want science to add to human happiness and welfare. You would protect mankind from harm by education; by increasing his allegiance to that which is good; by establishing better government, local, national, and world-wide, to make possible a better world. You are now making value judgments. These judgments constitute a part of what we have come to know as the humanities. They are based on our conceptions of right and wrong, of justice and injustice, of the place of mercy in human relations, of liberty, and of the worth and dignity of man.

Where shall we find help in making these most important value judgments on the basis of which we must act? Not in science, because science is not concerned with value judgments. In the humanities? Here is a better chance, because here over the centuries has been recorded man's experience with these value judgments.

We can get some help from Moses, who dealt with the problem of freedom and slavery in the clay pits of Egypt. We can get some help from the prophets of old, who compared the value of human life with every other value of the world. We can get some help from other great religious leaders, who based their teaching on the concept that all men are the sons of God.

We can get help from history—the record of the long struggle for the democratic conception of government. We can get some help from philosophers—from Immanuel Kant, for example, who told men to so act that their actions might become the standards of conduct. We can get some help from Steinmetz, who maintained that only that civilization can survive in which the great masses of the people participate in the benefits of the civilization.

We can get help from the world of great literature. Where will you find a finer presentation of the great human problem "how to do justice without doing an injustice" than in Shakespeare's *Hamlet?*

The Humanities in the Curriculum

Should the humanities have an important part in the high-school curriculum? I can speak only as a product of the public high school and as a teacher who has tried to carry on the educational process at the college and graduate level. Speaking of my own high-school education, I can say only that I prize most highly the great teacher who introduced me in my Junior year to the world of literature in a magnificent way through a study of Halleck's *History of English Literature* and to a book of selected readings from Chaucer to Arnold.

I can think of no better place to cultivate the habit of independent thinking than in the study of the humanities. Some years ago while I was a member of the Board of Visitors of the Naval Academy, the Senior students were asked what course of study they had enjoyed most while in the academy and why. The answers, obtained in a way that permitted the students to speak with complete sincerity and freedom, were most interesting. The great majority indicated that their favorite subject was literature, world literature. Their reasons, if I could quote them, would run something like this: "When we are studying naval subjects, there is always a Navy answer which is the acceptable one. When we study science, there is always the scientific answer which is the acceptable one and which we must try to meet. But in literature one can have one's own opinion, one's own analysis. One can differ with one's fellow students; one can even differ with the teacher."

A superfiicial review of history reveals the fact that the ability to solve basic problems in science and engineering and the ability to make fundamental judgments in the field of the humanities is limited to a relatively small percentage of mankind. However, nearly all men have the ability to understand these great contributions. It seems to me, therefore, that man's greatest chance of finding answers to his fundamental problems is to take advantage of the tremendous variability that exists among men, and to look with great concern upon any movement or any device which places limits on our freedom of thought in attempting to formulate value judgments. One of the great problems of our time, as someone has recently suggested, is to overcome the "rising tide of social entropy." Entropy is a scientific concept which deals with the leveling of energy. It has been defined as the condition of run-downness, and social entropy consequently would be the condition of run-downness in social judgments. It is the leveling-off, or the unifying, of man's thinking.

Mass communication today offers an unprecedented opportunity to raise the level of understanding among men and by men. It also offers one of the most powerful tools for placing limiting values on freedom of thought. It is the function of the humanities, through the study of philosophy, through the study of history, through the study of the world's great literature, to help man formulate increasingly sound and realistic judgments. These judgments will be useful in obtaining freedom and security, liberty within law, justice with less injustice. They will diminish the tendency of mass communications to cause social entropy and, by use of the same media, will increase the individual's concern for the kind of a world in which he lives. Let me quote from Gordon Keith Chalmers:

> The best we can say is that so far as human apprehension is concerned, here are two orders of reality and two methods of grasping reality: the order of matter and number, and the order of man and words. Emerson's familiar rhyme comes to mind:
>
> > There are two laws discrete
> > Not reconciled,—
> > Law for man, and law for thing;
> > The last builds town and fleet,
> > But it runs wild,
> > And doth the man unking.
>
> Justice, due process, and the universal applicability of law are principles expressing something in our nature as men. So is the root idea of democracy—which historically and in fact is a religious idea—that each individual is free and valuable, the idea of equality before the law having come historically and in present fact from the Christian, Jewish, and ancient re-

ligious idea of equality not of men among themselves, but of each man before God. These principles or ideas implicit in our nature are a part of the law for man. The law for thing includes, of course, the laws of thermodynamics, of gravitation, of surface tension, and so forth. When applied to man, as in dialectical materialism at Moscow, the law for thing *has* unkinged the man and will continue to do so. Unless we at home are thoroughly men, it will do the same to us.[1]

Or let us listen to Santayana when he bids us remember:

> [Nature] hath not made us like her other children,
> Merely for peopling of her spacious kingdoms,
> Beasts of the wild, or insects of summer,
> Breeding and dying,
> But also that we might, half knowing, worship
> The deathless beauty of her guiding vision,
> And learn to love, in all things mortal, only
> What is eternal.[2]

[1] Gordon Keith Chalmers, "The Academy and the 'Enquiry Squad,'" *American Scholar*, XXVI (Spring, 1957), 171.

[2] George Santayana, "Odes, II," *Sonnets and Other Verses* (New York: Stone & Kimball, 1894), p. 71.

Essential Qualifications of Teachers
for the New Era

None of us can doubt that we are living in an era of great change. We need only to cast our minds back over the span of our lives. Many of my readers can recall, as I can, the first automobile, the first airplane, the first radio, the first television set. Our generation has seen the tremendous shifting of balances among the nations in the wake of two world wars. And it seems certain that the changes we have witnessed are but the prelude to even more momentous new developments for mankind. Newspaper headlines make this more clear every day. The creation by human brains and hands of an earth satellite unveils prospects even more startling to the imagination than were uncovered to our forefathers by the discovery of the New World of the Americas through the voyages of European explorers a few centuries ago.

But who is able to make out just what the prospects are, just what the precise shape of things to come will be, and what are their precise implications for education? Are we to expect regularly scheduled rocket flights to points in outer space? Can we take seriously the predictions of an indefinite prolongation of human life? What, to be literally more mundane, does the future hold as an outcome of the ideological and political struggles of the cold war and of the titanic efforts of African and Asian peoples for an equal place in the sun of technology?

I cannot pretend to answer these and similar questions which will occur to all of us as we try to think what, assuming the imminence of great change, the new era will be like. I cannot, in short, give a preview of the new era. I am therefore unable, from my vantage point, to describe the kinds of teachers needed for the future.

120

Relation of Education to the Changes in Our Society

Let me try another and less pretentious approach to the problem. The great changes which have taken place in human affairs—our rapidly burgeoning science and technology, the development of new democratic political institutions, and the challenge offered to them by new totalitarian states, the great changes in our social life and institutions, the secularization of our outlook on life, the ascendancy of the empirical and scientific point of view—all these have been the result not of some play of natural or non-human forces but of human aims, ideas, and activities. There may be some question whether the human animal has not developed so unevenly, especially as regards his scientific achievements and his philosophic outlook and wisdom, as to threaten the future of the race. Certainly the greatest change in the outlook of man since my boyhood has been the loss of a sense of inevitable progress and the development instead of a sense of possible catastrophe for mankind. But in any case the changes which have taken place and those which may be imminent, for weal or woe, have been, and will be, humanly produced.

The great question, then, about the new era is not just what it will be like, because its form depends upon the unpredictables of human behavior, but how we shall be prepared to shape it rightly, to realize its possibilities for good, and to cope with the mistakes which may be made. In short, how may we by insight, forethought, and wisdom, avoid disaster and realize the immensely promising possibilities of mankind's future? The problem of education in the new era, consequently, is how to develop the capacity of human intelligence and thought.

What I have in mind may be suggested by reporting a recent conference with a group of Asian educators who had come to this country to study the American educational system. One of our Asian visitors opened the session by making two assertions and then asking a question. He said: "America has achieved such progress in the last 150 years as, in effect, to make the other peoples of the world relatively underprivileged. We in Asia think that America's achievements are in large part the result of your educational system. What is the secret of the American educational system?"

In the ensuing discussion some of us took the position that the secret of American education, if indeed it was a secret, was its commitment to universal education, to equal and full educational opportunities for all, though we confessed (what else could we do in view of Little Rock?) that we were far from having realized this ideal perfectly. Our commitment to universal education, we said, was not a result of general humanitarian notions or even merely of general democratic principles. We were committed to universal education out of a conviction that our strength as a people lay, not in our natural resources, but in our human resources, in the possibilities of the development of human intelligence. As a people we have been convinced that intelligence is not inherited, is not the possession of an aristocratic class, does not depend upon social or economic station or upon racial origins. We have been convinced, therefore, that, if we were to make the most of our greatest potential, the development of intelligence, of knowledge, of wisdom, we needed to make sure that every new member of our society, regardless of race and class, has the opportunities of education.

Factors Determining Kinds of Teachers Required

If we were right in our response to our Asian visitors about the past, then our best hope for realizing the promising possibilities that the new era holds out for mankind lies in attempting to develop the human intelligence to its fullest. To this task the American educational system must be dedicated. And teachers for the new era must be the kinds of persons with the kinds of preparation necessary to carry on this task successfully.

To describe the ideal teacher of the future, then, we need to consider two questions, for one of which I have already, in a general way, suggested an answer. The first question is: What shall be the purpose of our schools or, more specifically, of our high schools? For surely we cannot describe the teacher we need without a clear idea of the functions the teacher is to fulfil. The second question is: What, given a clear view of the purposes of the schools, should be their organization and method of operation? For surely we cannot describe the kinds of teachers we need and desire without knowing how they are to function and just what they are expected to do in order to achieve the results we hope for. Let me try to take up these two questions in at least enough detail to initiate discussion of the problem and perhaps to stimulate my readers to set up a sounder point of view.

Staffing Schools To Develop Capacity To Acquire Wisdom

The first question is: What conception of the functions of the schools should determine the kinds of teachers needed for them? The answer I have suggested—that the function of the schools is the fullest possible development of the intelligence—is no doubt too general for our purpose, except in one respect. If correct, it establishes a priority for attention to mental growth as compared with attention to social adjustment, to physical health, to merely vocational skills.

Such establishing of priority may be of no little importance. We have done much, as I see it, to confuse the schools and render them ineffective by loading them with many tasks without establishing any priorities among the assignments. There is current a strange perversion of the doctrine of "the whole child," which, having asserted the wholeness of the student, proceeds to segment him; to divide him into mental, physical, and social compartments; to divide him into citizen, producer, and consumer, and so on, and does this without making any distinctions or setting any priorities among these parts or aspects. As a result, physical education, social adjustment, consumer education, citizenship education, and general education seem all of equal importance. But if we are to consider the whole child, as indeed I believe we should, are we not obliged to consider the relationship of the various aspects of his behavior and responsibilities? And are we not obliged to try to determine what principle makes for wholeness? I suggest that, if we consider these questions, we shall conclude that, though physical health, emotional stability, and social skills are important, the central and governing principle of the wholeness of human beings is, or ought to be, intelligence. Without the development of this quality, physical health is mere animal strength. Without the guidance of intelligence, emotional life is an irresolvable conflict of passionate drives and will inevitably be ordered only by external power and authority. Without intelligence, social adjustment degenerates into mere conformism. Surely education, while recognizing the physical and non-rational aspects of human nature, must proceed on the assumption that these may be, and need to be, intelligently organized and directed.

With respect to the development of intelligence, three points may be worth considering. The first involves a recognition of the differences in capacity for intellectual development. In the past decade we have rightly become increasingly concerned about the problem of the gifted. The new concern about the gifted is a valuable development in American education, both in the interests of society, which needs the fullest possible development of the capacities of our ablest youth, and in the interests of the individual, who is, after all, the ultimate concern of a society which exists not to maintain its own group strength but to provide the fullest development of individual capacities.

Concern about the gifted should lead us to concern about teachers competent to insure the development of talent. This competence does not, fortunately, require teachers who are themselves geniuses. It does require teachers who are prepared to assist students to be better than themselves. Indeed one might lay it down as a fundamental principle that the task for education is constantly to make the next generation better than ourselves, to make students better than their teachers, for only in this way can we have any assurance of future progress.

The idea that teachers should be prepared to assist students to go far beyond themselves implies that the teacher must not be content simply to inform the student of the present state of knowledge or to confirm him in the present view of things but must stimulate him to independent endeavors to go beyond our present knowledge and our present conceptions.

Closely connected, too, with this conception of the teacher's role is the view that the teacher ought to be prepared to encourage uniqueness and difference rather than to require conformity. It is one of the most serious dangers of any highly organized society such as ours that it encourages, especially in times of stress, the development of the organization man, the social and intellectual conformist, the well-balanced and well-adjusted individual, and tends to discourage, if not to suppress, the unique, the different, the independent, the pioneer. We should do well not only to suffer, but to welcome, independence even when it seems troublesome, dissent even when it is annoying, individuality even when it seems to border on oddity. Only so can we hope to provide the climate in which new ideas can flourish and genius can flower.

Finally, free and independent intelligence may not only exhibit itself in unconventional forms but may cover a variety of abilities. It expresses itself in the development of technical know-how, in the development of scientific insight, in discriminating appreciation of the arts, and in the acquisition of philosophic insight and wisdom. I should like to plead that, in high-school and early college education, we put the emphasis upon the development of wisdom, the capacity to make sound and independent judgments about fundamental human problems—about the better and the worse in human associations, about the significance and ends of human life, about the nature of human responsibility.

What I have in mind may be suggested by the almost feverish discussions generated by the Russian production of a satellite. One would suppose from some of the talk about the satellite, even among educators, that America's failure to be first in the field was a result of the failure of our schools to train a sufficient number of able scientists. This seems to me to miss the point entirely. We certainly have as many good scientists as have the Russians, and, if we were not first in launching a satellite, it is not because our high schools and colleges over the past generation have failed to produce the men who could have planned, constructed, and launched a satellite into space. We did not produce the first satellite simply because we had not devoted our energies and resources to this task. Whether we should have done so, whether the decisions which lay behind our not doing so were sound are questions not of scientific, but of political, wisdom. If the political decision is to be challenged and if the decision can be traced to a failure of our schools, we should have to say that the schools had failed, not in teaching science, but in developing in our people and in our leaders the political wisdom required to reach a better conclusion.

In any case, the appearance of the satellite dramatized a fundamental problem—how mankind may achieve peace. This again is not a scientific problem. It cannot be solved by technicians or managed by the highest reaches of material know-how. It calls for wisdom about human beings and human society, their desires, their ways, their true purposes. Because problems of this kind are the most urgent problems of the next generation, our schools need to give highest priority to the development of wisdom about man and about human affairs.

We need, then, in providing the teachers for the new era, to be concerned above all with finding, enlisting, and properly preparing teachers who will be competent to assist students in the development of the capacity of youth to acquire wisdom, which I am democrat enough to believe is far beyond our usual expectations. For developing this capacity we shall need to enlist our best minds in teaching and to make sure that they receive as broad and as deep a liberal or general education as possible.

Now I know the objection which will be immediately raised to the proposal that schools give priority to the development of what I have called wisdom. It will be pointed out that students differ widely in ability and in interests and that it is therefore impossible to aim so high for all students. Let me hasten to reply that I am not talking about college-preparatory work, which may well be inappropriate for a portion of our high-school students who lack the ability or the interest or both to make college work profitable or desirable. And I certainly recognize that, if we attempt at least to lay the foundations for the development of wisdom about man and society in all students, we cannot use the same materials or the same methods, or sustain the same pace of learning for all. What we need to find (and this is one of the great challenges for the teachers of the new era) are appropriate though different means to develop some degree of wisdom about fundamental human concerns in students having different interests and capacities. The so-called slow learner and the inadequately motivated student may not study the same materials, or be guided by the same methods, or manage to maintain the same pace, as those who are gifted and well motivated. But I am convinced that, if we give our minds earnestly enough to the problem and experiment wisely and boldly enough, we shall be able to find the materials, the methods, and the pace that will enable all but the mentally defective to acquire some grasp and some insight into the questions with which as human beings and as citizens in a democratic society they will have to deal.

I do not see how we can otherwise avoid giving up our confidence in democracy, which depends on the assumption that the judgments of the majority will, in the long run, be trustworthy. We give up that confidence, it seems to me, if we assume that only a fraction of our young people are capable of acquiring what I have called wisdom and that others can be given only vocational skills, can become only the equivalent in a technological society of the hewers of wood and the drawers of water.

The finding of appropriate ways to develop the intelligence of young people, with full recognition of the differences in their native ability, so that they can make wise choices concerning the purposes and ordering of their individual lives and the ends and the ordering of society and government is, I am convinced, the great problem of the modern American high school and will certainly be the great problem of the high school of the new era. Ideally, the high school of the future must be "comprehensive" in a somewhat different sense from that now ordinarily given to the term. It needs to be comprehensive, not by providing in one institutional arrangement for college-preparatory, terminal, and vocational education, but comprehensive in providing a range of programs and in employing appropriately different materials, methods, and pace, for developing in all students (up to the limits of their capacity) the knowledge of, the insight into, and the ability to think independently about, mankind's individual and collective concerns—thinking that deserves the designation of wisdom.

Organization of Schools Determines Kinds of Teachers Required

A second set of considerations with respect to the teacher of the future arises from the question of how the schools of the future are to be organized and to operate. It is all too easy to suppose that our present modes of deploying teaching resources are not merely contrivances to handle, more or less effectively, the task of educating the young but that they are somehow natural and inevitable. It seems to me that our present utilization of teachers is hopelessly inadequate to the task of education that we as a people have set for ourselves. We have rightly committed ourselves to universal education. This year more than forty million students are enrolled in our schools and colleges. Yet our arrangements for relating teachers to students are, so to speak, in a horse-and-buggy stage.

The sheer pressure of numbers will force us to reconsider them. The biggest school in the biggest city is, in effect, simply a collection of little red schoolhouses. In a kind of egg-crate arrangement, we provide one teacher for every thirty students, requiring that teacher to perform all the chores of the teacher in the little red schoolhouse except attending a potbellied stove. Probably little more than half a teacher's time in our elementary schools is spent in tasks requiring professional competence. The teacher takes off rubbers and puts them on, collects the milk money, polices the playground and lunchroom, does a good deal of mere clerical work. The teaching profession is the only profession that has not participated in the revolution of the past fifty years, in which technicians and aides relieve the professionally competent person of non-professional chores so as to enable him to concentrate his time and professional activities and to make his competence available to larger numbers. Surely in the schools of the future, teachers will be provided various aids to enlarge the scope of their professional effectiveness. Otherwise, it would seem impossible to staff our schools with enough able people. Already the shortages at all levels have reached alarming, if not crisis, proportions.

We shall be driven also to draw into service in the schools, on some part-time basis, large numbers of college-bred people in the community who have not prepared to make a career of teaching. Dr. Henry Chauncey, of the Educational Testing Service, pointed out some years ago that, paradoxically, we find ourselves unable to provide enough teachers to read enough English papers to enable students to learn to write well, while at the same time there are in many communities college-bred women who have majored in English and who, with some orientation for the task, could read more papers than the students need to write. Something like the same situation obtains with respect to foreign languages. We are forced to employ for instruction in foreign languages many teachers who are inadequately prepared to teach French or German or Spanish well. And in these same communities, college-bred women who have majored in a foreign language could be recruited for part-time service in the high schools.

We have only begun to realize the possibilities that the powerful new medium of communication in our day, television, has as an educational instrument. Television could be as important in spreading the benefits of education and raising the quality of education as was the first great visual aid, the printed book. It would enable us to make the best teachers in the land available in every far corner. It would enable us to bring events all over the world into every classroom. With it, we could command for the classrooms in every hamlet the resources of our finest museums, orchestras, and dramatic companies.

The co-ordination of these new elements in education would open an enlarged and, I believe, enticing prospect for the career teachers whose task it would be to see that these elements were properly related and directed to achieve the highest quality of education and who might themselves serve that essential and critical function, long ago described by Socrates, of the midwife assisting the birth of knowledge in individual minds.

All this need not necessarily make education more mechanical. It need not give it an assembly-line form. I should hope, indeed, that even the largest schools of the future might follow the lead of some contemporary high schools in organizing themselves in groups of three or four hundred students with a number of faculty members regularly assigned to them—groups small enough so that teachers and students might learn to know each other well individually, groups that could be different enough to take care adequately of students having different abilities and, at the same time, could allow the faculty greater initiative in devising educational programs than a large monolithic school makes possible. Under such an arrangement, teachers might work in teams, each devoting himself to his special interests and competences.

What I am saying would imply that teachers for the high school of the new era would not, in ability, preparation, or function, be cast in one mold. The staff of the high school would include many members of the community not now drawn into its service. It would include aides to take care of much of the clerical work and of the non-professional chores now through necessity performed by full-time, professionally prepared teachers. It would draw upon the part-time services of many specialists in the community, for such things as the reading of English papers and for instruction in foreign languages. It would draw upon the part-time services of men in business and industry—accountants to assist in the teaching of mathematics, for example, and laboratory men in industry for assistance in the teaching of science. It would draw upon businessmen and lawyers for assistance in the social studies. It would depend upon full-time, career teachers for the co-ordination and effective direction of these resources. It would make use of persons having the collection of abilities required for effective teaching over television.

The increasing proportion of college graduates in our population and the prospect of increasing leisure in our society should make these plans feasible and practical. In short, our prospects justify us in assuming that we shall be in a position to command the time, or a significant part of the time, of large numbers of our population for the purposes of education.

A New View of Universal Education

I should like here to repeat a suggestion I have made elsewhere: that we take a new and larger view of our national commitment to universal education. We have come to see, in the last decade, that our commitment to universal education means that education must become everybody's business, in the sense that citizens need to interest themselves in our schools, need to be informed about their problems and requirements, and need to give them their financial and moral support. The work of the National Citizens Council for Better Schools over the past six or seven years has dramatically demonstrated the growing awareness in this country of the need for citizen participation in the solution of school problems.

I am suggesting that there is another sense in which, if we are to have universal education of high quality, virtually everyone must be involved, namely, through widespread participation in the educational work of our schools. Young people as they acquire knowledge should begin to assist in the education of those less mature, and our technological developments will make it possible to enlist an increasingly large number of competent adults for work of various kinds in our educational system. Indeed, as the proportion of adults who have graduated from college increases, these resources should be increasingly valuable.

We should turn to them, not as a move of desperation to man our schools at the expense of educational quality, but as a consequence of a fuller and richer conception of the responsibility of all our people for the education of all our youth and as a means for improving our educational system. We should discover in them, furthermore, a new and potent instrument of adult education, for, as many of us have discovered from experience, one learns most, not as a pupil, but as a teacher.

We should be required, if we took this view of universal education, to think of the school, not as a building within the walls of which a separate professional class of society takes care of the instruction of youth, but as an institution which through its professional staff co-ordinates the educational efforts of the community, drawing upon all the community's resources to lay the foundations for lifelong learning—and teaching—in the community's young people.

Teacher-training insitutions would need to enlarge their ideas and practices so that, instead of providing a single road into teaching marked by required courses in professional education and leading simply to one kind of teaching certificate, they would direct and co-ordinate a wide range of programs along appropriately different paths for preparing many persons to make a wide range of useful contributions to education. They would need, first, to extend, broaden, and deepen the education of those who propose to enter immediately on a full-time career in teaching so as to prepare them adequately for the larger and more important role they would need to take in co-ordinating and leading the educational work of local communities. They would need also to provide short courses for teachers' aides, develop special programs for preparing older college graduates in the community to do effectively a variety of educational work in the schools, work out programs (perhaps combinations of summer conferences and independent-reading plans) for enlisting and preparing people in industry, business, government, and the professions to do part-time work in our schools, and contrive programs for preparing people as they approach retirement to make substantial contributions to our educational system. It need hardly be said that, since teaching is a demanding art, these programs would need to be carefully developed and tested.

These measures would rest on a conception of universal education as involving not merely an extensive period of schooling for all young people but as coextensive with the life of each individual, so that learning and, as soon as possible, teaching, would begin in youth and proceed throughout life. It would involve the conception of education as not merely a means to an end (that is, to the maintenance and development of our technical know-how, or to the strengthening of our society against the threats of totalitarian states, or as a means for increasing the occupational competence and the career success of individuals) but as itself among the very highest ends of life.

Views of this sort and the practices flowing from them would add a new dimension or, it would be better to say, a new foundation, to the conception we hold of America as a dynamic society. We should think of our society as dynamic, not merely in material productivity, but in intellectual and spiritual power, one in which education—including schooling, self-education, and education through teaching—was a major concern of all its members throughout their lives. Then we might indeed have good reason to hope that the bold experiment in the democratic way of life initiated by our Founding Fathers would long endure, that the society flowing from it would grow in wisdom, strength, and promise, and that increasingly it would realize its fundamental purpose—the fullest and richest possible development of each individual person in it.

The Increasing Concern for Effective
Teacher Utilization

Using teachers more effectively is but one of several proposals for assuring that our students will be well guided in their learning. Virtually all these proposals are predicated upon the assumption that the demand for qualified teachers will far outstrip the supply unless those available are used more imaginatively than they are at present. Several of these proposals are enjoying such acclaim that, however closely they may approximate their potentialities, the results will be disappointing. Quietly and little heeded, meanwhile, a soft voice in the background keeps persistently reminding us that the utilization of teachers or even of teaching talent is not the first question. The central problem is learners learning and not teachers teaching. Actually, then, the title of my paper properly should be "Using Teaching Resources for Effective Student Learning."

The Need To Establish Priorities

There are forces at work seeking to prevent cruelty to teachers. There are, likewise, forces at work seeking to use teachers in the most efficient manner. Then, there are forces at work extolling teaching as a profession and teachers as professionals. This is all to the good. But one laments the frequent emphasis upon the privileges rather than the responsibilities, upon the form rather than the substance. All these forces derive from the assumption that teachers are necessary. Should it ever be generally concluded that teachers are not essential to the ends of education, these forces suddenly would be without purpose. Professional organizations, teachers' unions, supervisors, administrators—and, of course, teachers—would disappear or, worse, would while away the time until death idly reminiscing battles won and lost.

It is most improbable that we shall ever conclude that teachers are unnecessary. But the generally accepted conclusion that teachers are necessary in their own right has led frequently to the further conclusion that teachers should be utilized in line with factors derived from studying teachers and what they do and, ultimately, to the conclusion that the proper study of education is teachers. The danger in this line of thinking is an ultimate equation of teaching with the educative process. If the educative process cannot yet be described as a unitary phenomenon, at least some ordering of the relative factors must be attempted. Our central concern thus becomes the learning of students. Only by viewing learners learning can we come to see the appropriate roles of teachers in the educative process.

It is abundantly apparent that such appropriate priorities are not clearly established in the minds of some educational practitioners. For example, recently a group of high-school teachers engaged seriously in the planning of a curriculum for a new school. They gave attention to the purposes of this school, to the kinds of activities that should go on in it, to the way the program should be organized, and to like significant questions. They agreed, after extensive analysis of the social studies and the language arts, that some combinations of these fields would be in the best interest of the learners. They then turned to the planning of daily schedules, and the order of priorities suddenly shifted. Teachers are most comfortable teaching in a single subject of specialization, some said. Teacher time is used most effectively, said others, when each uses the same lesson preparation as frequently as possible. Thus a teacher should teach both a single grade level and a single subject area. Clearly we have now moved down from the question of advancing learning to that of advancing the comfort of teachers. We are now on the road to deciding that twenty-five young people are enough for any teacher to handle. By relating these conclusions, we describe the classroom setting within which American secondary education is largely being conducted: a single teacher working very much on his own with a group of from twenty-five to forty adolescents in a single subject area and at a specific grade level.

Crystallization of such a setting for instruction set in very quickly after the Quincy Grammar School in Boston—a graded school and a landmark in the emergence of lock step in school organization—opened the doors of its new, specially designed school building in 1848. By the end of the century the curriculum was a chopped salad, prepared by cutting content vertically into grades and horizontally into subjects. Textbooks prepackaged these curricular goods, presumably for easier pupil consumption, and teachers prepared themselves with a keen eye to grade level, subject field, and prescribed textbooks.

However, the interlocking pieces in the graded school were only beginning to settle comfortably into place when thoughtful educators were observing that overemphasis on order was hobbling creativity. Consequently for several decades, spanning the old age of one century and the childhood of another, experiments like the Gary Plan, Pueblo Plan, Winnetka Plan, and others chipped away, with some temporary success, at the tightly meshed machinery that grew steadily more ponderous. But educators grew increasingly reluctant, apparently, to tamper with any part of the machinery for fear of stripping the gears. Since the thirties, when advocates of the core curriculum stirred up a little excitement, we have contented ourselves with shifting our eyes elsewhere or with applying a little oil here and adjusting a valve there, perhaps in the fond hope that, unseen and unheard, the monster would just shuffle off on synchronized treads.

Ghosts of past failure stand guard over our mechanized legacy. The various experiments of several decades ago are now but dimly understood. It is easy to say that they did not get at the heart of the educational problem, that they were but manipulative devices seeking to get more wear out of buildings and teachers. In part, such criticisms are valid, but most of the explorations having at least temporary influence went much deeper. They made some attempt to analyze the learning process. The Winnetka Plan, for example, recognized different types of learning, even if superficially when judged from today's analyses. Too often, unfortunately, it was the form that spread, and innovations became increasingly mechanistic in proportion to the number of models separating each new version from the original. Thus many so-called core programs today are little more than the teaching of two subjects (usually English and social studies) by a single teacher in a double-length period. The exciting initial insights dissipated themselves against the protective wall of well-established mass procedures. A poor corruption of the form remains, but the substance is largely gone.

It is now so easy and, sometimes, so convenient to equate the insights of new proposals with the forms of the old and to predict dismally, "These things too shall pass away." The suggestion that teams of teachers work for various purposes with groups of varying sizes is casually dismissed as an attempt to revive the monitorial system. While previously inadequate approaches to old problems are not likely to be successful if merely dressed in modern garb, at least we must be willing to study the past dispassionately in recognition of the possibility that previous timing may have been poor or previous analyses imperfect.

Pressures Requiring Consideration of Effective Utilization of Teachers

We can ill afford to be chilled into immobility by ghosts rising up from the past. Tangible dangers threaten us. Hordes of pupils rampaging through our elementary schools are about to come clambering at the doors of our high schools. We could cheerfully say that the situation is temporary and that the high school will survive, as did the elementary school. But the situation is not temporary. Children already born—20,000,000 of them not yet in school—will tax our schools for twenty years to come, and the birthrate, although stabilizing, shows little sign of slackening significantly. And when the postwar baby crop begins to harvest its own babies, a still further upsurge in school enrolment is almost certain. Furthermore, we cannot truthfully say either that the elementary school has found a solution for greater pupil absorption or that it is coming through its ordeal unscathed. It has merely sought to adjust. For example, the plan of action of the Association for Childhood Education International calling for elementary-school classes of twenty-five pupils appears anachronistic in an educational environment where enrolments up to 100 per cent higher are the rule rather than the exception.

The elementary school entered into its period of crisis under certain favorable circumstances. The Bachelor's degree as a minimum credential and equal pay with high-school teachers were in process of establishment for its personnel. The wholehearted embracing of in-service programs focusing upon the child and his learning created a gratifying *esprit de corps* among some schools of every state. Critics boring in on inadequacies, real and imagined, came away licking wounds inflicted by irate parents, who believed in their schools and who then intensified their efforts to make the schools better. Initial cracks caused by the impact of the first few waves of increased enrolments were quickly shored up, but the cracks are broader and deeper today. Some teachers have resigned themselves to perpetual baby-sitting and, in many quarters, require special inducements for participation in programs of in-service education. When asked about their problems, teachers list topics that have more and more to do with managing large classes and less and less to do with educational function and curriculum theory. It is unlikely that the elementary school would have fared even this well had its house been in somewhat greater disarray.

In my judgment, the secondary school will adjust less well. In fact, the American secondary school as we know it today may not withstand its various impending crises. Structure that managed to expand and contract during a hundred years of generally expansive movement now threatens to collapse completely under pressures inadequately planned for. This unit of our public school system faces grave ideological, as well as crushing physical, burdens. From above and below and from all sides it is being caught in a squeeze that may well strangle it. The nature of these pressures is analyzed elsewhere in this volume, and I need only summarize several that most concern us here.

From below come millions of youngsters educated in a school unit espousing a philosophy of taking children from where they are and doing with them the best it can. Elementary-school policies of acceleration, retardation, or both do not materially reduce the increasing variability in pupil achievement with which teachers must deal. Consequently the secondary school either must anticipate great variability and plan accordingly or must set minimum standards that will doom a considerable portion of our population to six, seven, or eight years in the high school. From above, in these times of increasing college enrolments, comes the cry that the high schools are not adequately preparing their graduates for college. From

"Take them from where they are" to "Bring them up to rigorous standards" lies a mighty gulf! But from the elementary school to college extends a brief span of years for bridging it.

From all sides is heard a clamor of voices. We are losing our technological race with Russia; prepare our young people in the sciences. Men cannot live by bread alone; teach them the meaning of life. Cultivate the gifted; develop remedial programs for the laggards. Education is for those who can profit from it; weed out those who cannot. Determine pupil potentialities early; set up academic programs for the college-bound and vocational programs for the remainder. Most assuredly, the American people are not giving today's secondary school clear-cut directives as to function.

Toward such a school the hordes advance. To predict for it an unchanged future would, indeed, be unrealistic. We look at the statistics and conclude that one of every two college graduates, rather than the present one in every four or five, must be attracted into teaching if current pupil-teacher ratios are to be maintained. Realizing that there is little likelihood of such a marked shift, we conclude that teachers must be utilized more effectively. But again we hear the soft voice reminding us of first questions, and we ask: Utilizing teachers more effectively for what? A hierarchy of questions now spins out before us:

Who shall be educated in the high school and for what?

What is the nature of the process in which these learners shall engage and how shall the school be organized for carrying out the process?

Who and what shall assist in this process and how shall these teaching resources be most effectively used?

How shall the human resources be prepared for, and inducted into, these various tasks?

When the tumult and the shouting shall have faded into the somewhat softer sounds of a social institution doing well what it knows to do, an important reaffirmation will have been made: a vigorous, self-appraising society demands an educated citizenry. Furthermore, the American people will be much closer to conceiving an educated citizenry as one that devotes serious thought both to its central problems and to the directions that intelligent social action should take. Education, in large measure through the secondary school, must serve both to extend the view of reality held in common by larger and larger numbers of people and to expose for analysis those views that markedly differ. We must not be deluded into the beguiling notion that a significant portion of our people shall be excluded from such an education simply because they appear to lack either the appetite or the capacity for it.

The definition of common kinds of behaviors for our educated citizenry and the identification of a range of possible educational experiences conducive to their attainment does not mean that the school shall indorse, willy-nilly, participation in whatever strikes the learner's fancy. Each specific educational activity indorsed must be seen as both pertinent to envisioned goals and more pertinent than other alternatives. Nor does this mean that prescribed blocks of content are to be "covered" by all in uniformly prescribed periods of time. Learning, as we shall define it, cannot be equated with covering anything. Nor does it mean that learners of widely varying abilities shall proceed over any given route at the same rate. Such a proposition is inane.

Broad Basis for Teacher Utilization

Several broad bases for using teaching resources now move into position. While resources will be committed to at least a common core of ends, they will not necessarily be committed to common means. Furthermore, while diversity in learner interests and abilities frequently will be the prime determinant of diversity in means, unique approaches will be designed also to provide excitingly fresh ways of viewing the same phenomenon or of developing the same skills in alternative settings. Dewey turned the energies of his pupils toward the school shop, for example, not because he wished to substitute vocational for intellectual ends, but because new materials offered a fresh challenge to the processes of inquiry he deemed paramount.

The foregoing paragraphs suggest, also, that creative utilization of resources will facilitate widely varying levels of insight or skill as outcomes of the learning process even though a given group of learners may be engaged in an outwardly common learning experience. (By definition of "experience," of course, there exists no truly common learning experience.)

Finally and more important, development of an educated citizenry will demand utilization and organization of teaching resources in such a fashion that differing cultural groups will share the associations essential to greater cultural unification. The "blue-stocking" child, the labor child, and all the others learn to communicate with their own kind whether or not they learn to read and write. But they will not readily acquire the communication systems of other than their own kind—and hence membership in the widest possible range of groups—unless they associate some of the time with other than their own kind. When education is viewed as serving only to foster and refine tool skills such as reading and writing, preparing teachers for instructing learners grouped for long periods of time on criteria of likeness seems quite appropriate. But such a practice runs counter to the broader view of education indorsed here. Regrettably, there are, in our society, persons who advocate various kinds of long-term educational segregation because they hold a narrow view of education, and there are also persons who recognize only too well that such a practice will safeguard the advantages which they acquired automatically through initial membership in a favored sealed-off group.

We must recognize that the final roosting place of all learnings—and the only place where they can be properly understood—is in the lonely self of just one individual, standing alone and trying to live with his aloneness as best he can. There is nothing sacred, then, about the group or any particular size of group for learning in general. There may be, however, something extremely significant about both the size and the character of a group for a particular learning. For example, if a considerable portion of a school population has relatively little insight into the fact that where and when one lives profoundly influence the character of human living, then grouping these young people to view a skilfully prepared film of persons living in other times and other places may be quite appropriate for at least introducing them to the concepts involved. If, on the other hand, the purpose is to explore the relation of social, political, and economic factors in England to the development of social institutions in America, then an appropriate group may perhaps include only twenty learners whose time and space concepts are well advanced. But, within this small group, a few students will be motivated to dig deeply into the relationship between cultural transmission and communication systems. These few will require access to books, pictures, tapes, and records, perhaps to specialized human talent, and to peers who are exploring related phenomena. Some learning is in no way hindered even when a given stimulus is placed before hunderds of learners simultaneously. Other learning proceeds best in a small group carefully constituted on a basis of specific criteria. And learning sometimes is blocked when the group is larger than one person.

Any stimulus for learning (and, therefore, the structure for conveying that stimulus) must take into account the present attainment floor and attainment ceiling of the group for whom the stimulus is intended. Gross data such as intelligence-test scores, for example, constitute inadequate bases for establishing groups for a variety of learnings. Furthermore, the distance between attainment floor and attainment ceiling to be spanned by a single stimulus probably can be greater in one area (language arts) than in another (mathematics). Consequently, in contemplating expanded group size—for economical reasons, say—we must be cognizant of the extent to which such expansion threatens to destroy the capacity of appropriate stimuli for spanning any increased distance between attainment floors and attainment ceilings.

But individual and group readiness for certain learning involves much more than either general ability or specific attainment. Increasingly, we are seeing that anxiety-producing situations in school or elsewhere inhibit learning, even when the student's general ability level and certain specific attainment levels are high. A generalized state of anxiety, not causally related to the present learning situation, may block the experience hoped for although the stimulus appears to be well suited to other aspects of pupil readiness. Perhaps, then, each secondary-school student should spend a portion of the day with a group of his peers and a teacher skilled in group-guidance procedures. This might well be the group, constituted on criteria of diversity rather than similarity, in which the important, culture-unifying processes would be refined. Research must tell us how large such groups should be, how frequently and for how long they should meet, and what kind of diversity in membership is best suited to the functions to be served.

Suggestion for Effective
Teacher Utilization

Even the brief analysis of learning presented here challenges the desirability of promoting all learnings through a group of thirty learners assigned to a single teacher for a given subject, at a given grade level, and for an arbitrary time period. Present group, grade, and subject patterns may have come into being on the basis of at least some conception of learners learning, but they have been perpetuated, apparently, for reasons of a quite different sort.

So far, I have implied suggestions for identifying and utilizing teaching resources but have not attempted to make them explicit. The film picturing other times and other places need not be prepared by teachers or with the objectives of secondary education in mind. But an educator must decide its appropriateness for a particular segment of high-school youth. The large-group stimulus might as readily be a distinguished philosopher, poet, or humanitarian appearing on closed-circuit television. Again, however, someone close to the particular learners involved must determine the timing of the specific stimulus. Similarly, the variety of small-group situations requires a variety of resources, human and otherwise. The group seeking to deepen a given mathematical concept often requires the clear exposition of a person who sees the concept in all its ramifications. It may be possible to observe the initial presentation on film and to test its application through textbook problems; but direct human help, probably providing talents differing from those of the film demonstrator, frequently will be important to the learner as he struggles with his successes and failures.

In view of the variety of learnings to be carried on and of the situations and resources appropriate for their pursuit, it becomes clear that the variety of teaching talents desired cannot be found in one person. Nor is there any good reason for seeking this variety of teaching talents only among those now classified as teachers. Communications experts, under the guidance of curriculum specialists, appear to be the logical persons both for developing educational films, filmstrips, tapes, and recordings and for planning the uses of television. Artists, scientists, engineers, and specialists of endless variety constitute a source of talent we have not yet learned to channel effectively. Many well-educated mothers who feel that a full-time teaching load would seriously endanger the conduct of their home responsibilities would be thrilled at the opportunity to come into the school on a part-time basis. Future teachers, frequently far from the scene of high-school activity until they engage in student teaching, would profit from participation as student aides throughout their preparation programs.

The central problem in utilizing this diverse array of potential teaching talent is, of course, an organizational problem, and it is viewed here as belonging in the hands of professional career teachers and administrators. This does not mean, however, that all career teachers would assume a kind of entrepreneur role, managing the enterprise as one manages a business. Let us, instead, visualize a team operation, which brings together a number of individuals representing talents appropriate to the tasks in which a designated group of learners probably would engage. A given team, perhaps organized with social-studies instruction in mind (although there is nothing inviolable about subjects as a basis for team organization), might include two experienced and highly qualified career teachers. The particular talent of one might be skill in presenting and clarifying central concepts; that of the other, identifying and moving toward the solution of group problems. Both would have a sound understanding of school function, learning, curriculum development, and other educational lore. Only part of their day, instead of the entire day as in conventional practice, would be spent in direct association with children. A significant portion of daily time would be devoted to curriculum planning—that essential but frequently neglected aspect of the educational enterprise. The remaining time would go to diverse aspects of team leadership. Other members of the team would be anything but robots. The team would include technically qualified but inexperienced teachers preparing for team leadership. Part-time lay persons, employed on a continuing relationship, would assist individuals and groups of learners, and highly specialized "guest teachers" would contribute in line with their talents and the requests made of them. All of these, with the possible exception of persons in the guest category, would meet regularly for the purpose of developing a reasonably common view of the over-all program, of the diversity of learning activities going on at given time, and of the potential contribution of each team member.

This description certainly does not exhaust team possibilities. Nor does it reveal the potential cross-team enterprises and the school-wide planning of the entire professional staff functioning as the very heart of the school organism. But it does suggest using teaching resources to further learning without doing violence to, or even slightly damaging, teacher selfhood.

The team concept in teaching already is under attack on the ground that it creates several classes of teacher-citizens. Different classes of citizens are, indeed, created when membership in a given class is restricted to present membership or when affiliation is denied on the basis of personal characteristics unrelated to group purpose. In the arrangement described, however, not only do the avenues to advancement remain open to all, but a greater number of avenues is created. Furthermore, the mother and part-time team member, who currently is under constant pressure to survive as a full-time teacher or not teach at all, simply because no other alternative is open, may elect to add some teaching to home responsibilities without harm to either set of obligations or to self.

The present lot of teachers promises to be materially improved through the identification of diverse teaching opportunities and the creation of teams directly related to the learning tasks to be promoted. At present, teaching frequently fails to attract and hold certain talented persons who could contribute to a team but who simply cannot see themselves indefinitely carrying on the demanding range of activities now required of teaching. The team-leadership role offers both continued challenge in teaching and the possibility of increasing remuneration, whereas top salaries are now available only through moving from teaching to administration. Currently, developing one's unique talents frequently leads to no increased opportunity to exercise those talents, let alone to being materially rewarded for them. It is difficult to see how a structure that creates greater opportunity for upward movement on the basis of professional competence, and broadens task selection on the basis of unique talents, is detrimental to a profession or its membership.

Attack on existing patterns of utilizing teacher talent is not likely to be productive (for education, for learners, or, in the long run, for professional teachers) until we are clear about who are to be educated and for what. Then the potential resources for teaching and the patterns for utilizing these resources effectively begin to move into view in almost endless variety. Obviously, then, the team concept suggested here and elsewhere is only one of the exciting new possibilities that more and more will become established in practice. This structure, like others that will prove useful, emerged from an analysis of learners learning rather than teachers teaching. Under the impact of such analyses, it is indeed unlikely that the American high school, now threatened by physical and ideological pressures that challenge us with new opportunities, will remain unchanged in the new era.

The Acquisition of Values
in School and Society

In two preceding papers, one dealing with the school[1] and the other with the library,[2] I attempted to present what might be called a conceptual framework for the study of values and, within this framework, to offer some views regarding the relationship between our American values and the education of our children. I argued that the central neglected issue facing the schools today is the problem of values. For whatever else the child may be expected to do in school, he is inevitably exposed, explicitly or implicitly, to *some* system of values. Indeed the nature of his self-identity—his answer to the question of who he is and where he belongs—depends on the nature of the values he interiorizes. Moreover, whether we will it or not—in fact, whether we know it or not—the choices that we educators and parents make with respect to educational objectives, curriculum, methods, personnel, and even the buildings we construct, are founded on some system of values, however subliminally these may be held in any particular case. In short, the specific forms that our child-rearing and educational practices take from among the almost infinite range of possibilities cannot be understood outside the context of our dominant values and the shifts and cleavages these values are presently undergoing.

My two preceding papers were, in the main, essays derived largely from the work of Lynd, Riesman, Spindler, and Naegele, among others. I suggested that what was needed in this area was some research capable of replication, some so-called empirical data, against which to test our concepts and impressions. Recently, with

[1] J. W. Getzels, "Changing Values Challenge the Schools," *School Review,* LXV (Spring, 1957), 92–102.

[2] J. W. Getzels, "The Child in the Changing Society: Implications for the Librarian," *Library Quarterly,* XXVII (October, 1957), 267–78.

the help of a grant from the Lilly Endowment, I have begun to collect some of the necessary data, and the work reported here may be regarded as a step, however preliminary and halting, toward the systematic study of the relations between values and education.

I shall direct attention in this paper to two major issues: (1) What is the nature of the dominant American value system and the shifts and cleavages that this system is currently undergoing?

(2) What is the nature of the available empirical data regarding the effects of these shifts and cleavages on the education of our children?

In considering the first issue, I shall be constrained to repeat a number of the formulations presented in the preceding papers. These repetitions are unavoidable, since a detailed consideration of the first issue serves as the essential context for a meaningful consideration of the second issue.

America's Sacred Values

The definition of the term "value," as I shall be using it throughout this paper, is borrowed from Clyde Kluckhohn: "A value is a conception, explicit or implicit, distinctive of an individual or characteristic of a group, of the *desirable* which influences the selection from available modes, means, and ends of action."[3]

As one looks at Americans from this point of view, we seem in many ways an enigma. As Kaspar Naegele points out, "At one time our values appear obvious and clear cut; at another they are elusive and complicated by many cleavages."[4] One oscillates between the conviction that there is a common value orientation and a common type of American, and the doubt as to what indeed is held in common by the Western farmer and the Eastern businessman, the member of the National Association for the Advancement of Colored People in Illinois and the supporter of the White Citizens Council

[3] C. Kluckhohn and Others, "Values and Value-Orientations in the Theory of Action," in Talcott Parsons and E. A. Shils (eds.), *Toward a General Theory of Action* (Cambridge, Massachusetts: Harvard University Press, 1952), p. 395.

[4] I am indebted for many of the formulations and sources in this section of the paper to an unpublished memorandum on selected studies of American values by Professor Kaspar Naegele, who very kindly permitted me to make use of the material. It is regrettable that this comprehensive and provocative research memorandum has not been published for general reference.

or some such in Alabama, the subscriber to *Fortune* and the reader of *True Romance*. The American foreground is full of contrasts, as well as similarities. Where do our values overlap? Where do they diverge?

Our values overlap, at the ideological level, in the American creed. For there is an American creed which has been variously enunciated since Jefferson first wrote it—and this creed constitutes our basic and undivorceable beliefs, our *sacred values*, as Naegele calls them. These we try to teach our children as our ultimate goals, "the things really worth fighting for." In order to understand our current value system in operation, it is necessary to examine, first, the main values supported by the creed and, second, the stresses and strains to which these values are subject.

1. *Democracy.*—As a general value, democracy implies that the experience of the many is more inclusive than the experience of the few, that what people want is what they need, and that the people are the best judges of their needs. It implies further the right to wrong opinions and the familiar freedoms of speech, press, assemblage, and organization. And yet, as de Tocqueville observed a hundred years ago, and Kluckhohn reiterated within the last ten, the contrast between the principles of democracy and its practice is nowhere as sharp as in certain aspects of our life.

2. *Individualism.*—As a general value, individualism implies that "the individual is the fountain source of energy, initiative, and responsibility in society and has a right to self-expression."[5] This has three major implications: politically, it means subservience of the government to the citizenry; economically, it means free enterprise based on individual risk; morally and religiously, it means that man is a free agent with a right to live his life in his own way. But again, we must remark on the gap between the dream and the deed. We value individualism but fear personal individuality. We value personal initiative but are given to "chasing the band wagon." We value individual responsibility but insist on social conformity.

3. *Equality.*—Alexis de Tocqueville, among other detached ob-

[5] E. W. Burgess, "Social Planning and the Mores," *Publication of the American Sociological Society*, XXIX (August, 1935), 1–18.

servers, emphasizes equality as perhaps the fundamental American value:

> In America, no one is degraded because he works, for everyone about him works also; nor is anyone humiliated by the notion of receiving pay, for the President of the United States also works for pay. He is paid for commanding, other men for obeying orders. In the United States professions are more or less laborious, more or less profitable; but they are never either high or low; every honest calling is honorable.[6]

This is, of course, an overstatement, but nonetheless equality is one of the values by which we would want to live. Yet as de Tocqueville himself notes, our democratic institutions awaken and foster a passion for equality they can never entirely satisfy in practice.[7] And so, believing in equality, we still exhibit a hypocrisy of luxury which Veblen, in his vivid phrase, called "conspicuous consumption."

4. *Human perfectibility.*—As Naegele states, "To be basically hopeful, because the future counts and the past can be forgotten, even rejected, is defiantly cherished by all of us." Yet this optimism must not be confused with gaiety. America is wryly humorous but fundamentally serious. Our genius is Mark Twain, both of the comic public figure and the bitter private beliefs, and Riesman's title for us, *The Lonely Crowd*, is not without point here. As Lynd remarks:

> The reverse side of the optimistic dream is woven of trouble. This is a thing we don't talk about. . . . A society as determined as ours to be optimistic imposes false faces on all of us. . . . To the greeting "How are you?" the answer must be a confident and hearty "Fine." . . . With us the simple admission of discouragement and a troubled mind is often withheld even from our closest friends. In a culture in which to be unsuccessful means automatically to be in some wise a failure, one tends perforce to struggle with one's black moods alone and unaided.[8]

These, then, despite the stresses and strains, are our sacred values: democracy, individualism, equality, and human perfectibility (or optimism). These are the values that all of us cherish and want our children to cherish—at least, we feel that we and they *ought* to cherish them. It is to these values that we appeal when we wish to legitimize significant action.

[6] Alexis de Tocqueville, *Democracy in America* (Cambridge, Massachusetts: Sever & Francis, 1864), II, 185–86.

[7] *Ibid.*, I, 255.

[8] R. S. Lynd in E. L. Koos, *Families in Trouble* (New York: King's Crown Press, 1946), pp. vii–viii.

America's Secular Values

But, in a sense, we stand in relation to these sacred values as we do to the Ten Commandments or the Golden Rule: at the moment when we may be departing from them most directly, we would maintain that we are supporting them most firmly. And just as it is impossible to understand our Judeo-Christian culture merely by reading the precepts of the Bible, so it is impossible to understand our American culture merely by knowing the creed or the sacred values. For in addition to these, there are a core of operating or down-to-earth beliefs which constitute our *secular* values. In effect, if I may overstate the case somewhat, we pay homage most frequently to the sacred values on Sundays and on state occasions, and in our day-to-day activity we behave in terms of the *secular* values.

Traditionally (and I want to emphasize the time dimension, for evidence is accumulating that we are rapidly departing from these traditional beliefs), the following have been our major secular values.[9]

1. *The work-success ethic.*—Values of achievement took precedence over values of being. Anyone could get to the top if he tried hard enough, and everyone had an obligation to try hard enough. To be sure, as Naegele points out, kindness, forbearance, charity, and compassion also had value, but, he adds, success could excuse one for having intermittently broken the Golden Rule.

2. *Future-time orientation.*—The future, not the past or even the present, was important. We must be (note the vernacular) "forward looking" and "on the go." For what was to come was always bigger and better than what was at the moment. Time, therefore, became a value in its own right and became equated with money (again note the vernacular, "Time is money"). The present was undervalued for the sake of the future, and immediate needs were denied satisfaction for greater satisfactions to come.

3. *Independence, or the autonomous self.*—The self was inviolable and, as such, of greater ultimate significance than the group. The independence of the self must be guarded from authority and

[9] The classification and analysis of *traditional* and *emergent* values are based in part on G. D. Spindler, "Education in a Transforming American Culture," *Harvard Educational Review*, XXV (Summer, 1955), 145–53.

from bureaucratic interference. Self-determination, self-activity, self-perfection were the criteria of personal worth.

4. *Puritan morality.*—Respectability, thrift, self-denial, hard work —these were the marks of common decency.[10] Personal virtue was measured by the seriousness of the ethical commitment. To be sure, there was the holiday, the time to "have fun" and "be sociable." But, as Naegele says, this was kept outside the values of everyday living. Indeed for many of us even now, vacation must be rationalized as the replenishment of energy—a good investment, as it were—for the serious and therefore significant things of life. Sociability for the sake of sociability was held to be akin to sloth—and sloth was a sin second only to idolatry.

Changes in Our Values

The sacred values have remained relatively stable. This is not to say that they have not been under stress and strain. Despite these stresses and strains, however, democracy, equality, individualism, and human perfectibility as values remain sacred. They are celebrated as *ideals* for ourselves and our children no less today than they were 150 years ago.

The traditional operating or *secular* values, however—the work-success ethic, future-time orientation, personal independence, and Puritan morality—have undergone, and are undergoing, crucial transformation as a function of change in our technology and cleavage in our social structure.

The shifts and diversities of the American scene have been remarked upon frequently enough, and the image of America as a melting pot is well known. I should like to suggest, however, that today a more appropriate image than the melting pot is that of the mosaic. There are *regional* differences, and when we go from Maine to Southern California or from New York to Arkansas, we are moving, not only from one place to another, but also, in large measure, from one way of life to another. There have always been *rural-urban* differences. Although these differences are diminishing because of the mass-communications media, we now have in their place newly sprung differences between the urban, the suburban,

[10] *Ibid.*, p. 149.

and the so-called ex-urban cultures. For such observers as Lloyd
Warner and Allison Davis, *social stratification* is the major source
of diversity; they would argue that any understanding of our values
must take into account the critical differences in attitudes and goals
produced by differences in social-class membership.

Now, without in any way minimizing the preceding well-known
sources of cleavage in our value system, I would suggest that the
most significant source of cleavage at this time resides in the rapid
and crucial transformation that the dominant secular values themselves are undergoing. Riesman called our attention to this in his
trenchant distinction between our former *inner-directed* values and
our prevailing *other-directed* values.[11] And more recently Spindler
in a brilliant paper remarked upon the transformation as a change
from *traditional* to *emergent* values:[12]

From the work-success ethic to sociability.—Instead of the work-
success ethic, there is an overriding value of sociability and friction-
less interpersonal relations. As someone remarked, the hard-working, self-determined Horatio Alger hero as a national model is giving
way to the affable young man in the gray flannel suit. Let me cite
just one relevant study. Two hundred Seniors in twenty colleges
and universities were asked to describe their personal aspirations
and life goals.[13] Typically, the Seniors talked more about social and
personal gratification than about career achievement. They explicitly rejected the "push" of their fathers and aspired to suburbia
as their goal. As one Senior said, "Dad was a lone wolf, and I
wouldn't have the brass." And another remarked, "I'm not really interested in one of those big executive jobs. None of this ulcer and
breakdown stuff for me—just making money doesn't stack up with
keeping your health." A Midwestern university Senior summed up
his point of view as follows—and note the emphasis on the affable
as against the ambitious values:

I'm not money-mad by any means, but I'd like enough to buy a house,
and have transportation, and of course good clothes for the family. Plus
entertainment: I'd like to be able to see the good plays and movies. And

[11] David Riesman, *The Lonely Crowd* (New Haven, Connecticut: Yale University Press, 1950).

[12] G. D. Spindler, *op. cit.*

[13] "None of This Ulcer Stuff," *Fortune*, LIV (October, 1956), 155.

I suppose I'd want a trip every year: visit around in the big urban areas, you know, Berlin, Paris, Rome. I can't set any exact amount I'd like to make, so long as it's enough for the *necessities* of life.

From future-time orientation to present-time orientation.—Instead of future-time orientation and consequent self-denial, there is a hedonistic present-time orientation. "A penny saved is a penny earned" is giving way to the more modern slogan, "No down payment necessary," and our wealth is measured more by how much we owe than how much we own. As a recent article in *Harper's Bazaar* points out: "The people principally responsible for our twenty-nine billion dollar instalment debt on consumer goods are married couples under thirty; two-thirds of these young families are in debt."[14]

From personal independence to group conformity.—Instead of independence and the autonomous self, there is compliance and conformity to the group. As Riesman has observed, we are replacing our inner gyroscope with a built-in radar that alerts us to the feelings of others. The goal of behavior is not personal rectitude but group consensus, not originality but adjustment. There are numerous signs of this transformation: the values advocated in some books that are best sellers, as in the stereotyped interpretations of events in the mass media, in the explicit exhortations of such things as the *McCall's* "togetherness" advertisements, to mention only the more obvious instances. William H. Whyte, Jr., the editor of *Fortune*, studied this transformation in industry. He points out that there are now master-profiles of personal characteristics for various occupational groups and that the closer a man fits the group profile, the more likely he is to be accepted. The three common denominators of these profiles are: extraversion, disinterest in the creative arts, and cheerful acceptance of the status quo. If you are being evaluated for a job, Whyte urges that you would be wise to take the following two pieces of advice:

1. When asked for word associations or comments about the world, give the most conventional, run-of-the-mill, pedestrian answer possible.

2. When in doubt about the most beneficial answer to any question, repeat to yourself:

I loved my mother and my father, but my father a little bit more.

[14] Caroline Bird, "Born 1930: The Unlost Generation," *Harper's Bazaar*, XC (February, 1957), 106.

I like things pretty well as they are.
I never worry much about anything.
I don't care for books or music much.
I love my wife and children.
I don't let them get in the way of company work.[15]

Individual stimulation has given way to group tranquillity—the switch in the medicine cabinet has been from Benzedrine to Miltown.

From Puritan morality to moral relativism.—Finally, instead of Puritan morality, or at least moral commitment, as a value, there are relativistic moral attitudes without strong personal commitments. Absolutes in right and wrong are questionable. In a sense, morality has become a statistical, rather than an ethical, concept: morality is what the group thinks is moral.

These conflicting values, these values in flux, are held in various degrees by the different persons in our society and in our schools. As Spindler points out, the younger teachers are more likely to be emergent in their values than the older teachers, the superintendents and principals more emergent than the parents and public they serve, the parents and public more emergent than the school-board members they select.[16] So we have side by side, in the community and in the educational institutions, a kaleidoscope of shifting and confusing, if not absolutely contradictory, assumptions about life and the values that are really ours. For example, to use Lynd's list, competing for the child's attention, we may have the following inconsistencies, or, as we shall call them, *value dilemmas:*

1. Individualism, or "survival of the fittest" is the secret of American greatness, and restrictions on individual freedom are un-American and kill initiative. *But:* No man should live for himself alone; for people ought to stand together and work for common causes.

2. Religion and the "finer things of life" are our ultimate values and the things all of us are really working for. *But:* A man owes it to himself and to his family to make as much money as he can.

3. Poverty is deplorable and should be abolished. *But:* There never has been enough to go around, and the Bible tells us that "the poor you have always with you."

15 William H. Whyte, Jr., "Beware of Your Personality," *Encounter*, VII (August, 1956), 17.

16 G. D. Spindler, *op. cit.*, p. 151.

4. Everyone should try to be successful. *But:* The kind of a person you are is more important than how successful you are.

5. Education is a fine thing. *But:* It is the practical man who gets things done.[17]

Current ambiguities and uncertainties in the nature of our educational objectives, our curriculum, methods, teaching and administrative personnel may be understood in the context of our changing values and our value dilemmas. And while we are worrying about motivating our children to acquire an appropriate set of values, the children may properly be asking the prior question: *"What* values?"

Effects of Changing Values on Education

With this framework in mind, I shall now consider five relevant research studies in the area of values and education. I shall try to do this systematically by posing a number of significant questions and examining the answers offered by the research. Four of the studies were carried on in the Department of Education at the University of Chicago under a grant from the Lilly Endowment. They were done specifically within the framework just described. The fifth I have adapted from data previously reported by others.

1. We may turn first to the most general and, in a sense, the preliminary question: Is there evidence that our values have indeed changed along the dimensions I have postulated and that, accordingly, the cleavages suggested have appeared among various age groups? It may be useful to examine briefly a specific study in this area.

In 1923 the Pressey X-O Test was given to 955 undergraduate students at Ohio State University. The test contains a series of 125 items, such as "immodest," "extravagance," "flirting," and so on, and the respondent is required to cross out the items he considers objectionable or wrong (that is, the behaviors that outrage his value standards). In 1953 the same test was given to 842 students at the same institution and to 408 adults ranging in age from the twenties to the sixties. The responses given by the Juniors and Seniors in 1923 and in 1953, and in 1953 by the adults over fifty years of age,

[17] R. S. Lynd, *Knowledge for What?* (Princeton, N.J.: Princeton University Press, 1946), 60–62.

provide some illuminating data regarding changes in what is considered right and wrong over a thirty-year span.[18]

Here is a sampling of results. The item "extravagance" was held to be wrong in 1923 by 61 per cent of the male Juniors and Seniors; in 1953 by only 25 per cent. But 65 per cent of the 1953 sample of fifty-year-olds held this to be wrong. Note the similarity of the older group to the Juniors and Seniors of 1923 and the difference from the Juniors and Seniors of their own time. "Immodesty" was held to be wrong in 1923 by 70 per cent of the Juniors and Seniors; in 1953 by only 40 per cent. But 86 per cent of the 1953 sample of fifty-year-olds held this to be wrong. Again the older group of 1953 is more similar to the younger group of 1923 than to the younger group of their own time. And so on for a number of other items.

2. Are similar cleavages in values to be found among teachers, specifically, high-school teachers, of different ages? To answer this question, Richard Prince, the principal of Chicago Christian High School, constructed a forced-choice values questionnaire containing sixty-four pairs of items, one item in each pair representing a traditional value, and the other an emergent value.[19] Here are some sample pairs:

27A. Say what I think is right about things.

27B. Think of the effect on others before I speak.

30A. Feel that the most important thing in school is to gain knowledge useful to me in the future.

30B. Feel that the most important thing in school is to learn to get along well with people.

34A. Go to school affairs to enjoy myself being with people.

34B. Go to school affairs because it is my duty to be loyal to my school.

62A. Choose to work with people I like in a job I don't like.

62B. Choose to work with people I don't like in a job I like.

Prince administered the instrument to ninety-eight teachers varying in age from the twenties to the sixties. Consistently the results

[18] S. L. Pressey and A. W. Jones, "1923–1953 and 20–60 Age Changes in Moral Codes, Anxieties, and Interests," *Journal of Psychology*, XXXIX (April, 1955), 485–502.

[19] Richard Prince, "A Study of the Relationships between Individual Values and Administrative Effectiveness in the School Situation." Unpublished Doctor's dissertation, University of Chicago, December, 1957.

showed that, the younger the teacher, the more frequently he tended to choose the emergent value as desirable; the older the teacher, the more frequently he tended to choose the traditional value as desirable. The same thing was true of school principals. Prince compared the responses of ten principals under forty-seven years of age with the responses of ten principals over forty-seven years of age. He found a statistically significant difference at the .01 level of confidence, with the younger principals consistently more emergent in their values than the older principals.

3. We may now raise a question about the children themselves: Are the values held by children related to their performance in school? Prince gave the values instrument just described to superior students and inferior students at the Freshman and Senior levels in sixteen public high schools and in four parochial high schools. The results were striking. In each type of school and for each social class within the schools, the superior students were significantly higher in traditional values, the inferior students in emergent values. That is, the superior students tended to emphasize the work-success ethic, personal independence, future-time orientation, and moral commitment, while the inferior students tended to emphasize sociability, group conformity, present-time orientation, and moral relativism.

4. A second related question we may raise about children of high-school age is: What is the effect of differential values on career choice? Shelley Stone, a research assistant working with me in the Department of Education at Chicago, in a pilot investigation, administered the values instrument to sixty Senior students at a metropolitan high school. He also asked them a number of questions regarding their career and life goals. He found that fully 64 per cent of those high in traditional values and none of those high in emergent values indicated a desire to enter the professions. Similarly, 64 per cent of those high in traditional values, compared with only 21 per cent of those high in emergent values, said they planned to enter college.

Two other differences in the career and life goals of students high in traditional values and students high in emergent values are noteworthy. We asked the following question from the Cornell Values Survey:

Here are three different jobs. If you had your choice, which would you pick? (1) A job that pays a moderate income but which you were sure of keeping? (2) A job which pays a good income but which you have a 50–50 chance of losing? (3) A job which pays an extremely good income if you make the grade but in which you lose almost everything if you don't make it?

To a significant degree, those high in traditional values tended to choose the third job, and those high in emergent values tended to choose the first. Finally, we asked:

Different people have different ideas about what things are most important to them. Here are some things that you may have thought about. Rank them according to how important each one of them is to you: (1) being well thought of by my teachers, (2) living up to my own ideals and beliefs, (3) being well thought of by my friends, (4) pleasing my parents, (5) taking part in school activities, (6) learning as much as possible in school.

Forty-three per cent of those high in traditional values gave first rank to "Living up to my own ideals and beliefs," while only 8 per cent of those high in emergent values gave first rank to this item.

5. It is clear that the values held by children make a difference in the things they do in school and the things they plan to do as adults. I should like now to pose my last, and in many ways the most crucial, question within the present context: If the matter of values is so critical both in what children achieve in school and in what they propose to achieve as adults, is the present high school having any systematic effect on the nature of the values they acquire? The research design for answering this question was straightforward. Prince administered the values instrument to Freshmen and to Seniors in sixteen public high schools, four religious high schools, and two private high schools. The results were unequivocal. Differences in values were found *among* the different types of schools, showing that the instrument did indeed discriminate among groups. But *within* each type of school, whatever the type of school, *there were no significant differences between the values held by Freshmen and the values held by Seniors.*

If we may briefly turn to some actual figures, the mean traditional value score of private-school Freshmen was 31 (that is, on the average, private-school Freshmen chose 31 of the possible 64 traditional value items); the mean value score of public school Freshmen was 32; and of parochial-school Freshmen 37. Now, the mean score for private-school Seniors was 30, no significant change from the Freshmen's 31; for public school Seniors 34, again no significant change from the Freshmen's 32; for parochial-school Seniors 37, absolutely no change from the Freshmen's 37. Although the differences among the types of schools were statistically reliable at at least the .05 probability level (with the single exception of private-school and public-school Freshmen), none of the differences between Freshmen and Seniors for any of the types of schools even approaches statistical significance.

This result seemed quite remarkable. Accordingly, we repeated the experiment, this time using three carefully selected public high schools (two from an industrial city near Chicago and one from a residential suburb of Chicago). Although we found a difference in the values of the industrial and the suburban schools, there were again only negligible differences between the Freshmen and the Seniors in either the industrial or the suburban schools.

In short, on the average, whatever values a child brought with him when he entered a particular high school he also took away with him when he left the high school—nothing gained, nothing lost, nothing changed, at least for the types of values represented in the instrument used.[20] And neither the private school nor the parochial school nor the public school is better or, for that matter, worse, than any other in this respect.

Why Schools Have Difficulty in Influencing Values

I have already emphasized the preliminary nature of the data and of the analyses I have presented. Nevertheless the general findings are strongly corroborated by other recent studies using other aspects and dimensions of the value concept. By way of conclusion I should like to consider with you some possible reasons for the difficulties that the schools are having in influencing values.

The human organism is not born into the world with a ready-made set of culturally adaptive behavior and values. Instead he must inevitably learn to put the question to himself: "May I yield to the impulse within me, or shall I, by doing so, imperil the highest

---

[20] There is, of course, no implication that other types of values, for example, appreciation of the arts, may not have changed during this period.

values of my society?" He must learn, on the one hand, to suppress or to modify certain of his drives. He must learn, on the other hand, to acquire certain culturally adaptive attitudes and values. Indeed one of the functions of the school is to help the child do just this.

But the word "learning" or "schooling" is something of a euphemism here, for it is not the same kind of learning as, say, memorizing the multiplication tables, or the capitals of the several states, or the pledge of allegiance. The child's learning, or perhaps better here "interiorizing," of social values is a much more intimate and complex process. Learning, imitation, conscious emulation play a part, to be sure. But the fundamental mechanism by which we interiorize values, in school as elsewhere, is *identification*.[21] As the child struggles to integrate and to maintain a stable self-image from among his piecemeal perceptions of who he is and where he fits, he is led to view himself as at one with another person. The parents are the child's earliest objects of identification. Later he may add older siblings, favorite neighbors, community heroes, and, of course, school personnel. In making these identifications, the child not only assumes the outward manners and expressive movements of his "significant figures" but attempts also to incorporate their values and attitudes.

It is in this context that the school situation can acquire an eminence second only to the home perhaps—an eminence that it certainly does not have now. To be sure, many aspects of the child's values and personality are already formed by the time he enters school. But the way in which these aspects are developed and modified depends on the character of the educational institution of which he becomes a part. The teachers become, or at least can become, significant figures for the child.[22] And where values are concerned, it is not so much what people *say* the child should do that matters as the kinds of models the significant figures provide that is important. One cannot so much *teach* values as *offer appropriate models for identification*.

[21] *a*) D. R. Miller and M. L. Hutt, "Value Interiorization and Personality Development," *Journal of Social Issues*, V, No. 4 (1949), 2–30.

b) See also Erik H. Erikson, *Childhood and Society* (New York: W. W. Norton &. Co., Inc., 1950).

[22] M. L. Hutt and D. L. Miller, "Value Interiorization and Democratic Education," *Journal of Social Issues*, V, No. 4 (1949), 31–43.

When we find ourselves in a period of rapidly changing values, such as we are undergoing now, the various significant figures in the school and in the community provide inconsistent and contradictory models for the child. In such situations, identification, if it occurs at all, results in conflict and anxiety. The child obtains no answer to his inquiry: "*What* values?" For to incorporate one model means to reject another: to incorporate the parent's values as a model may mean to reject the teacher's values; to accept the teacher's values may mean to reject the community hero's values; to accept the community hero's values may mean to reject the religious leader's values; and so on.

As a result the child faces an extraordinarily difficult problem in adaptation. The solution may be either inflexible incorporation of one model or renunciation of all models. In one case we have *over-identification* and consequent restriction and inflexibility; in the other we have *under-identification* and consequent rebellion and delinquency. Both represent a serious inadequacy in personal development—an inadequacy that inhibits any further change in the acquisition of values.

Let me say again that the research data I have presented are preliminary and in need of replication, especially with greater control of the intelligence variable and in longitudinal rather than cross-sectional studies. Nevertheless I would hope that the over-all conceptual framework and impressions as well as the research findings will be of some service—if only as a point of departure—when making plans for the high school of the future. Surely it is a truism that education is not merely the dissemination of facts but a preparation for life. And preparation for life, as life itself, requires not only the technological wisdom of *how* to do, that is, the wisdom of means, but also the greater wisdom of *what* to do, that is, the wisdom of ends and of values.

Freedom and Discipline
in the High School

This is a discourse on the rod and the reed—the unsparing rod and the thinking reed. It does not deal with methods of keeping school or controlling the teen-age population. It is not concerned with the horsemanship necessary to ride a principal's or a superintendent's chair. I cannot pretend to be able to tell you when to give a free rein to the foibles and fancies of youth and when to rear back in the saddle and say "Whoa!" By "freedom" I shall not mean permissiveness, and by "discipline" I shall not mean restraint.

In taking this negative approach, I am not trying to cut myself off from communication with the profession, nor am I trying to cut a semantic fandango. I have long been under the impression that as a profession we communicate too much, and talk too much, and probably hold too many conferences, and meet too often in conventions. The most ingenious and efficient means of communication invented is the international Morse code, which is an orthodoxy of set symbols. I think that educators are in some danger of inventing a similar set of stereotypes if they find it necessary, as they apparently do, to remain in such constant communication with each other. My mission is not communication but confusion. The easiest and dullest thing to do in education today is to converse. And in thousands of committees all over the country, conversation is taking place. It is possible to spend years in educational conversation, and not much of it requires thought. Once you have a reasonable acquaintance with the stereotypes of the language, or the signals, or the symbols, and know how to push them around glibly, you can almost pass for an expert in almost any field. I could speak for hours or even weeks delivering myself of commonplace thoughts on freedom and discipline in the high school, and so could many of you. Anyone with sufficient energy and sufficient lack of imagination could readily turn to the writing of a book on the subject. Thus is immortality, or at least promotion, achieved. And a lot of poor writing and low-wattage cerebration it has taken for people to get places. But I am a teacher, and as a teacher I ask questions—always questions—and I sometimes speak in parables. The object of my teaching is not to give answers or to edify audiences or even to delight them but to make them think, to make students wish to inquire with me and never to be content with the stereotype, the half-truth, or the easy conclusion.

Freedom and Discipline of the Mind

I think that the words "freedom" and "discipline" applied to secondary education are more significantly applied to the mind than to the will. I have watched the band wagons of citizenship education go by, and I am still unimpressed with all the noise and fury about the school's responsibility to teach manners and courtesy and a decent respect for one's fellow human beings. This is primarily the job of the home, although a good school will always do it, too, and do it well. But the good school never will do it directly, never by indoctrination, never by deep-breathing exercises in the rituals of citizenship, nor, I hope, by emotional and sentimental appeal. You cannot turn out good citizens by state worship or flag worship or memorization of constitutions. The practice of democratic citizenship is a moral habit, and its roots are in reason and not emotion. The first commitment which a school must make, for both its teachers and its students, is the commitent to the training of the mind to reason.

If this is an acceptable basic proposition, the relevant question then becomes: What freedoms and what disciplines may be called upon to release the mind to the far-ranging and penetrating insights of rational thought? But before we can begin to answer that question, we must first decide whether the two terms "freedom" and "discipline" are antipodal or only antiphonal. Are these two polarities and is this a true duality—freedom and discipline? Or are these terms merely the names of reciprocal phases of the development of mind and reason? Is freedom a means to freedom and, therefore, both means and end? Is discipline a means to freedom, and never an end in itself? Is freedom to know without purpose unless it is more than a release from bondage of not knowing? Unless, in other words, it is a commitment to know and to inquire—a commitment which can find its fulfilment only through disciplined, rational inquiry?

Let us dissect the terms "freedom" and "discipline" in the context of the intellectual tasks of the school. I am, of course, conscious of the bad psychology of this narrow approach. One should educate the whole child wholly the whole time, but I still press for the isolation and the identification of the quality of reason in the mind of man. Perhaps it cannot be dissected out of its relation to the ductless glands and the rest of the nervous system, but, if the schools are to remain, or perhaps become, institutions of learning with a primary emphasis upon intellectual matters, and not super social service stations or emotional herbariums for the cultivation of the flowers of sentiment, we must make the raw assumption that it is the mind of the student with which the school is most concerned.

What then of the unspared rod and the thinking reed? I quote from Pascal:

Man is but a reed, the most feeble thing in Nature; but he is a thinking reed. The entire universe need not arm itself to crush him. A vapor, a drop of water suffices to kill him. But if the universe were to crush him, man would still be more noble than that which killed him because he knows that he dies and the advantage which the universe has over him; the universe knows nothing of this.

All our dignity consists then in thought. By it we must elevate ourselves and not by space and time which we cannot fill. Let us endeavor then to think well; this is the principle of morality.[1]

If it is true that only man can know himself and comprehend the world, the voice of this great seventeenth-century French humanist speaks the clear moral duty of schools and schoolmasters to the end of man's history as man. Sir Richard Livingstone has been often quoted, and few modern writers on education more richly deserve to be. It was Livingstone who said, "The good schoolmaster is known by the number of valuable subjects that he declines to teach."[2]

---

[1] *Pascal* ("Great Books of the Western World," Vol. XXXIII [Chicago: Encyclopaedia Britannica, 1952]), pp. 233–34.

[2] Sir Richard Livingstone, *On Education* (Cambridge, England: At the University Press [New York: Macmillan Co.], 1944), p. 28.

Freedom and Discipline in the Curriculum

How free and wide ranging should your curriculum be in the content of education in the high school? Not nearly as free and loose as it has become under the pressures of a consumer approach to public education. The schools are not in business to teach anything to anyone or everything to everyone. They are not to be confused—although sometimes they may be by their architecture—with shopping centers. We do not, I hope, put signs in our school corridors: "What you don't see, ask for." If we have them up, I hope we take down the signs which say: "The customer is always right."

American education's great concern with its social tasks has, I think, made a shibboleth of the phrase "holding power." Before this graven image we have proliferated offerings and poured dilute libations of intellectual content. We have given our students great freedom of choice of courses, in almost super-market variety at times. But the customers are still leaving with baskets full of credits and craniums full of nothing—or at least some people say so. I realize that the awful orthodoxy which once surrounded the pedagogic priesthood of permissiveness is rather "old hat" by this time, and fewer sins in education are committed against freedom in freedom's name. Perhaps what we need is not a new orthodoxy or a neo-classical revival, but an embracing of the wholesome negativism of Sir Richard Livingstone's suggestion regarding subjects we might decline to teach no matter how valuable we are told they are. If the training of the mind is not only the peculiar, but the prior, task of the school, there must be a priority of goods, or a priority of disciplines by which the task is achieved. It cannot be true that all subjects are created equal or that any method of teaching is as good as any other method. One is further impressed by the necessity of priorities when one considers the extreme shortness of time allowed in the span of secondary-school education. We have only four years of the most impressionable period of a student's life. The circumstances of human development give a relatively long, long period for the growth of the human brain compared with the leap to adulthood in the rest of the animal kingdom. But in terms of the enormous complexities of our culture, time is very short and must be wisely spent.

So far as our freedoms and disciplines are concerned, as we attempt to learn, and to teach our youth, something about themselves and their world and ours, there are disciplines which make us men and disciplines which merely prevent us from reverting to the brute, and there are freedoms which we enjoy as men and freedoms which we have forsworn as men. We have forsworn the freedom of the jungle and have accepted the freedom of society under law. The discipline of the will and of desire we have accepted in order to remain human. But the disciplines of mind which have made us men and the freedoms we have won by our reason and imagination should be the substantial content of the education of the young.

We have won our place in creation by the discipline of memory and by graceful submission to the tyranny of fact. We have trained our minds to remember, and, by remembering, we have made analogies, sorted out facts, and put together conclusions about the nature of the world and the nature of man. "Memory," says Pascal, "is necessary for all the operations of reason."[3] It is an inescapable discipline of education, then, that that which is known be remembered as known, that knowledge be held as clay for the shaping reason or passed to the hands of that primitive potterer, man's transcendent imagination. There is a grammar of thought, a basic language of logic and of proof, a fundamental body of knowledge which must be mastered before one is ready for speculative philosophy, flights of fancy, or even political debate. Few consequences of an undisciplined education are more pathetic than the educated, or at least diplomaed, man whose conversation on political or social matters crackles with clichés, stereotypes, and slogans, like the shelling of dry pods of dead ideas. You cannot turn out a thinker with any less effort than you turn out a musician or an artist, or even an athlete. The discipline of hard and patient effort is inescapable. While permissiveness may lead to a charming whimsicality, it can never lead to wisdom.

Regarding wisdom, Alfred North Whitehead writes:

Now wisdom is the way in which knowledge is held. It concerns the handling of knowledge, its selection for the determination of relevant issues, its employment to add value to our immediate experience. This mastery of knowledge, which is wisdom, is the most intimate freedom

[3] *Op. cit.*, p. 236.

obtainable. . . . But the only avenue towards knowledge is by discipline in the acquirement of ordered fact. . . .

Accordingly, it should be the aim of an ideally constructed education that the discipline should be the voluntary issue of free choice, and that the freedom should gain an enrichment of possibility as the issue of discipline.[4]

Those of you who have read Whitehead's *The Aims of Education* know that his third chapter, "The Rhythmic Claims of Freedom and Discipline," is the substantial argument which I am now adorning with a tinsel of commentary. The dilemma of teaching, as Whitehead points out, is the necessity of encouraging both initiative and training, and training or a rigorous attention to the needful things to know is apt to kill initiative. I think every teacher has had to face this dilemma. He knows that he must inculcate the habit of inquiry at the same time that he is attempting to generate spontaneity. He knows that he must stand for ordered knowledge and yet not fence in with barbed logic the antic imagination. He must restrain and discipline the mind. He must make a careful balance, in his teaching, between those things which demand conformity on the part of the student and much restraint and discipline of study, and those things which may develop the student's capacities for creativity, for aesthetic appreciation, and independence of view. The school life, like all life in a civilized society, must instruct in rules and regulations which surround every civilized person's life and press to a necessary and lawful conformity. And yet we recognize, at least in our free society, that it is always necessary also to give as free play as is consonant with the principles of law, duty, and good habit to the development of the individual.

The teacher always must recognize the importance of routine and the threat of routine, the importance of encouraging and demanding regular habits of study and inquiry, and the balancing importance of having students feel that part of their time can and must be used in free inquiry and creation. Every teacher, I am sure, recognizes the damaging effect of anxieties which block a student's learning, but he must also recognize the need of anxieties to spur education. I think everyone who has ever tried to teach realizes that there is a sharp dichotomy between the conceptual structure of the intellec-

[4] Alfred North Whitehead, *The Aims of Education and Other Essays* (New York: Macmillan Co., 1929), pp. 46–47.

tual disciplines and the chaotic, large, insistent, social, and emotional concerns of life. One of our great problems has been, and will remain, how to relate and reconcile and, if possible, harmonize the conceptual structure and intellectual content of education and the emotional and social demands of life surrounding students in school.

Freedom and Discipline as Paradox

It is at the high-school level, of course, that the paradoxes of the teacher's task are most perturbing. Youth is reaching for at least a presumed maturity and freedom of adulthood at the very time when it is most necessary for him to be subjecting his mind to the greatest rigors of precise knowledge. It is in the high school, above all, where he must receive the instruments of thought, of reason, of expression and inquiry. These are methods and tools not to be casually handled, and the teacher's conception of this task in the high school must be very clearly and sharply defined. Quoting Whitehead again:

A certain ruthless definiteness is essential in education. I am sure that one secret of a successful teacher is that he has formulated quite clearly in his mind what the pupil has got to know in precise fashion. He will then cease from half-hearted attempts to worry his pupils with memorizing a lot of irrelevant stuff of inferior importance. The secret of success is pace, and the secret of pace is concentration. But, in respect to precise knowledge the watchword is pace, pace, pace. Get your knowledge quickly, and then use it. If you can use it, you will retain it.[5]

There is need for the discipline of memory, the discipline of habit (which is to say the reconcilement to effort), the discipline of clarity on the part of the teacher, and, finally, the discipline of pace to achieve a dynamic mastery of knowledge that the ends of wisdom may be served. There are three qualities of a fine teacher: a quiet zeal, unending patience, and clarity. And I think the greatest of these is clarity. For if a teacher is a clear master of what he teaches, he cannot fail to teach with zeal as well as pace. And if he teaches with zeal, he perhaps will not need endless resources of patience.

But the clarity of the teaching is always directed not so much to the acquisition of exact knowledge as to the well-paced exercise of that knowledge, to the enrichment of mind, the grasp of first principles, the achievement of wise purposes, and the service of great causes. For the achievement of these great ends, only the disciplined

[5] *Ibid.*, p. 57.

mind is free. There is no harsher bondage than the half-emanci-
pated mind. Chained to a middling conformity, nibbling fragments
of truth, it flies in dreams, wakes to the tether of the half-effort, and
walks its wisely-consuming, life-adjusted round. Untutored ignorance is happier than this, since it at least can enjoy a childlike illusion of freedom. The freest man I know has the freest mind because
his profound learning has made freedom and discipline indistin-
guishable to him in his way of life. And he has won his freedom,
not as a last gasp on a serene peak, but through the exciting rigors
of the climb. To him, the way of discipline is the way of freedom,
and his life, like those of scholars and wise men like him, is a witness to the illimitable humanity of man. This is a freedom which
cannot be hawked in the streets or advertised or conferred or
bought and sold. Yet it is the only freedom which is worth a man's
seeking or a school's teaching, because it is the only freedom which
cannot be diminished, corrupted, or destroyed by either blandish-
ment or terror.

"Man is a reed, but a thinking reed," says Pascal. His frail mor-
tality is sustained by an iron core—his free and disciplined mind.
This is the unique gift of man and the moral and human center of
him, and it is to this center that we must reach.

New Criteria for Curriculum Content and Method

A thoughtful observer of the American high school is impressed by two important facts. On the one hand, in the brief period in which it has been in existence, the high school has contributed tremendously to the "American dream." On the other hand, the rapid social changes, particularly those that have taken place since the second World War, are calling on it for still greater achievements.

In one generation the high school has made tremendous advances. It enrols more than three-fourths of all the young people of high-school age. Most of its students like the school and like the work they are doing there. Many of the school activities appeal to the students as vital and meaningful. The interpersonal relations, particularly the relations between teachers and pupils, are informal and warm. Student personnel services are becoming increasingly common and more widely developed. High-school graduates demonstrate that they have learned many significant things. Compared with those not graduating, the graduates are more effective in their occupations, they do more reading of newspapers and magazines, they have more information about public affairs, and they are more concerned about the education of their children. On the whole, the American high school has changed the cultural level of the adult population in this country.

But there are still critical inadequacies in the high school when its achievements are compared with the current demands made on it and with its own aspirations and ideals. Many of these shortcomings are found in the curriculum, this term being used in the broad sense to include the objectives sought in the educational program; the learning experiences provided; the way in which the learning experiences are organized into courses, sequences, and the like; and the means used for appraising the progress that students are making.

170

This broad definition of the curriculum is commonly used today because of the close interrelatedness of these several components of the educational program.

Deficiencies in the High-School Curriculum

To illustrate the fact that important improvements are still needed in the high-school curriculum in spite of the tremendous progress already achieved, I shall mention six current deficiencies.

Although almost all youth of high-school age are in school, they do not have equal educational opportunity. Success in most high-school courses requires a fairly high level of verbal facility and a background of middle-class experience with books and language. Those youth who do not have this background usually find it difficult to pursue the normal high-school program. This situation should be a challenge to the school to work out ways of helping young people with different backgrounds to achieve the basic objectives of secondary education, but the more common tendency is to guide these students into vocational or other non-verbal programs, not as a means of attaining the liberal objectives of the high school, but as a substitute for these objectives. Probably there has never been a time when it was so important for all citizens to understand science, mathematics, the social sciences, literature, art, and so on, and this need is not met by shifting some students into programs that emphasize technical skills and manual facility at the expense of broader understanding. Even though it is difficult to reach students whose backgrounds have been limited, this responsibility the school cannot cast aside.

A second deficiency is the failure to enlarge and extend the intellectual and aesthetic interests of many students. Their liking for the school arises from doing in school what they already enjoy rather than from developing new and more mature interests. With the great increase in the average length of life, individual happiness and effectiveness are closely related to the significance and breadth of individual interests. Narrow and immature interests can quickly lead to boredom in the long hours available for leisure and the many years ahead for living. It is important for the school to help young people acquire new and more mature interests rather than simply to continue with their present ones.

A third deficiency is related to the second. Development in the high school of an understanding and appreciation of intellectual and aesthetic values has not kept pace with the understanding and satisfactions which young people have in the extra curriculum activities of the school. I have examined a great many results from various types of city-wide and state-wide testing programs. It is common to find that high-school students who score in the upper half of the distribution make little progress after the tenth grade on tests of understanding and ability to apply concepts and principles. Their scores level off to a plateau. Interviews with samples of these students indicate that they turn increasingly to the extra curriculum activities because these have proved more stimulating and meaningful to them than their courses in the eleventh and twelfth grades. They have therefore become more deeply involved in the extra-curriculum than in their courses and have put into it a great deal of effort that could have been devoted to the development of understanding and appreciation of intellectual and aesthetic values.

A fourth deficiency is the failure to extend the informal social contacts existing between students and teachers into cordial relations that will help vitalize classroom learning. The students usually view the teacher as a "good guy," and he, in turn, likes most of them. Rarely, however, do we find a recognition by either teacher or students that all are companions engaged in an intellectual quest, seeking to understand and to apply what they are learning. The warmth of social relationships makes the high school a pleasant place in which to work, but the great value of this comradeship is not utilized effectively in the important educational work of the school.

A fifth deficiency is found in many high schools where the student personnel services are viewed as ends in themselves and not as aids to learning. Some school personnel officers consider that helping John with a personal problem, providing vocational counseling, helping Sally get a part-time job are the ultimate purposes of the personnel services, when they should see these services as ways of helping students to direct their attention and energy more effectively in the educational program. Hence an important force in making education effective in the American high school is not adequately utilized.

As a final illustration of improvements still to be made in the high-school curriculum, we may note that, although many students learn a great deal from their high-school experience, there are still important educational areas which they touch only lightly and experience inadequately. Often a limited experience in an area closes, rather than opens, doors for the students. Mathematics, for example, is often treated so superficially that many students believe they cannot learn mathematics and develop a distaste for it. Many boys report a similar reaction to literature and language. Many girls feel the same about science. It is probably safe to say that most high schools attempt so much that many students do not reach the level of achievement required for self-direction and continued lifelong learning.

Criteria To Guide Improvement Programs

Although these deficiences in the high-school curriculum are serious, they should be seen in relation to the many positive features. The purpose of mentioning deficiencies here is not to find fault but to suggest opportunities for improvement in the years ahead. Many constructive improvements in the high-school curriculum can be made by giving careful attention to criteria of five sorts.

1. *Emphasize tasks appropriate for the school.*—Let us first consider the selection of the major educational tasks of the high school. The tasks emphasized should be those particularly appropriate for the school in contrast to those that are best carried on by other educative agencies. The school is not the only institution through which young people learn. The home, the church, the youth organizations, the mass media of communication—television, radio, magazines, and newspapers—are illustrations of other agencies that influence student learning. Because the school can provide trained teaching personnel and special types of equipment and because it can organize learning experiences over a considerable period of time, the school can perform certain important tasks more effectively than can other agencies. Emphasis should be placed on these things rather than on activities which others can do as well.

There are several kinds of educational tasks which are particularly appropriate for the school. One of these is the learning of complex and difficult things that require organization of experience and distribution of practice over rather long periods of time. A number of illustrations will quickly come to mind. To develop a high level of skill and understanding in reading, for example, requires carefully organized experience, in which the young person starts out with easy materials involving limited vocabulary and simple sentence structure and moves gradually into reading materials that involve a wider range of vocabulary and more complex sentence structure. As the student moves on, the high school uses materials of increasing complexity, with varied purposes and with different modes of presentation, to organize the reading experience in such a way that the student can acquire greater and greater skill and understanding. Mathematics is another illustration of a complex and difficult kind of learning which requires organization of experience and distribution of practice over considerable periods of time. The basic mathematical concepts and the simpler skills are begun in the early years of the elementary school, and, by using carefully organized experiences through the high school, it is possible to carry the student to a high level of understanding and competence in this field. Similar illustrations are easily found in other fields, like science, social studies, literature, and the arts.

It is appropriate for the school to provide learning opportunities in cases in which the essential factors are not obvious to one observing the phenomenon and the principles, concepts, and meanings must be specially brought to the attention of the learner. Thus the scientific concepts and principles which explain the growth and development of plants are not obvious to the observer of plants or even to an uneducated farm hand. The school can more effectively provide for this learning than can the home or the job.

It is appropriate for the school to provide learning experiences that cannot be provided directly in the ordinary activities of daily life. Geography and history are excellent illustrations of fields where daily life experience alone is not likely to provide sufficient insight into historic matters and affairs relating to places far removed. If young people are to develop an understanding of history, it will require the attention of a specialized agency able to provide materials serving to give vicarious experiences and to organize them effectively. The same is true for geography. We cannot depend entirely upon the informal experiences of daily life to provide these kinds of learning.

A kind of learning particularly appropriate for the school is that which requires more "purified" experience than is commonly available in life outside the school. Students may learn something of art, music, literature, or human relations from the examples commonly found in the community, but when these fall far short of the best the students have no chance to set high standards for themselves. The school can provide examples for study and enjoyment which represent the best available.

Another kind of learning particularly appropriate to the school is that in which re-examination and interpretation of experience are essential. Our basic ethical values are commonly involved in the daily experiences of youth. Questions of justice, fairness, goodness arise again and again on the playground, in the market place, and elsewhere. It is not likely, however, that sheer contact with these ideas will be enough to help youth to develop for themselves values that are clearly understood and effectively utilized. The school can provide opportunity from time to time to recall these experiences, to examine them and seek to interpret them, and thus to clarify the meanings of values as well as to help students to appreciate them more adequately. In the realm of ethical values this type of responsibility will be shared by the home, the church, and youth organizations. In the realm of aesthetic values, however, only the school is likely to provide this opportunity systematically.

The five kinds of learning which are peculiarly appropriate to the school ought to be strongly emphasized in the school program in contrast to other learnings which can be provided as well or better by other agencies. Unfortunately, various groups in the community exert pressure to bring the school to undertake activities which do not require the specialized competence of the school staff and can be done by other agencies. Some types of physical-education programs, driver education, some recreation programs, some occupational training which can be learned on the job are illustrations of types of learnings that are good in themselves but do not require the particular conditions provided by the school. Hence, when the school undertakes such programs, it must either neglect other important things or attempt more than it can do well. In the latter case it spreads itself too thin and does not achieve as effective educational results as it should.

2. *Utilize scholarly contributions as vital means of learning.*—In improving the high-school curriculum, we should see to it that the contributions of science, scholarship, and the arts are utilized as vital means of learning, not as dead items to recall. Commonly the current arguments over the high-school curriculum are posed as either-or arguments. Will the school emphasize textbook memorization or direct experience with the problems of life? Will it deal with subject matter or with life? These arguments indicate a failure of curriculum makers to identify the constructive role of the fields of science, scholarship, and the arts. Properly understood, the subject matter of these fields is not dead but provides a variety of understandings, values, abilities, and the like which can aid the student in living more effectively and more happily. The school is able to draw upon these resources to enrich the lives of the students. Our effort should be not to make the classroom more like life outside the school but to make life outside the school more in harmony with the values, purposes, and knowledge gained from the classroom.

All of us can think of illustrations of the way in which each of the major fields of science and scholarship can provide things that open up avenues for living rather than being dead items for recall. In science, for example, the kinds of problems with which scientists deal in seeking to understand natural phenomena and to gain some control over them, the methods that scientists use for studying problems, the concepts they have developed for helping to understand the phenomena with which they deal, the data they are obtaining about various natural phenomena, and the generalizations which they have developed for relating factors and for explaining phenomena—all give us tools for understanding our natural world and for seeking to gain more control over it. They also give the student a basis for continuing his own study and learning about natural phenomena long after high school.

In history, to take another example, we find bases for understanding developments which take place over periods of time. History gives us methods for studying problems which involve the time dimension and the interrelations of political, economic, social, and intellectual life. History gives us concepts with which to think about, and to understand, developments of our own time. It gives us data and some generalizations. It can help the high-school student to be at home in a world of change and development and to take an active, understanding role in this world.

The other subject fields can furnish similar examples of problems, methods, concepts, and generalizations that are important in finding meaning and effectiveness in life. In building the high-school curriculum, the fields of science, scholarship, and the arts need to be treated as vital means of learning and examined carefully for their possible contributions rather than viewed as matters of rote memorization.

3. *Seek equal educational opportunity for all.*—The improvement of the high-school curriculum requires that we seek more intelligently and energetically than we have in the past to achieve the ideal of equality of educational opportunity for all. Accomplishment of this ideal requires different means for students with varied backgrounds, but it does not mean the denial of opportunity to learn to think, feel, and act as adequately as possible on the aspects of life that matter. To learn to run a lathe, helpful as that is for earning a living, is no substitute for understanding what life is about and how science, social studies, art, literature, and other fields can help us understand our world and gain greater command over it. The essential educational values are important for all youth; they are not different for different social classes or for youth of different abilities. Whether or not I go to college, whether or not I take a job immediately after high school, whether or not I am bright or a slow learner, the school has a responsibility to help me attain as much as I can of these values that are basic in living a human and humane life. Of course the attainment of this criterion is not easy. We are relatively effective in teaching youngsters who have high verbal facility and come from backgrounds like our own. We are less effective in teaching others; here we have much to learn. A major task for the high school in the next twenty years is to solve the problem of how to reach all children and how to help them learn important things.

4. *Apply our knowledge of laws of learning.*—The improvement of the high-school curriculum requires better understanding and more imaginative application of what is known about the conditions

for effective learning. Over the years, psychologists, other social scientists, and educational practitioners have learned a great deal about the conditions required for effective learning to take place. Various listings of these conditions can be made, but most of the lists contain similar elements. Although these conditions are known to leaders and to many teachers, they are not usually applied with understanding and imagination. It is still commonly assumed that a teacher interacts with twenty to forty children in a classroom and that this kind of interaction provides the basic condition for learning to take place. Actually, learning takes place in various places, with or without teachers, and in groups of varying sizes. What is essential is that the necessary conditions for effective learning be provided.

One necessary condition is student motivation. The learner learns what he is thinking, feeling, or doing. Hence learning is not possible except as the learner himself is involved in it. This fact makes motivation, that is, the impelling force for his own active involvement, a most important condition.

A second condition for effective learning is that the learner finds his previous ways of reacting unsatisfactory, so that he is stimulated to try new ways of reacting. As long as the learner does not recognize that his earlier modes of behavior are inappropriate, he will keep on doing what he has been doing and will not really learn anything new. Hence it is important that the learner discover the inadequacy of his previous behavior so that he will not continue to repeat it.

A third condition is that the learner have some guidance of the new behavior which he tries in seeking to overcome the inadequacy of previous reactions. If he simply tries new behavior by trial and error, learning is very slow and he is often discouraged and gives up. Some means of indicating to him more promising reactions serve to guide him. Many ways are used to guide the learner. Questions may be asked which lead him to scrutinize various factors that he may previously have overlooked in his search for meaningful relationships. He may be aided in learning a skill by direct demonstration. These are but two illustrations of the many common methods used in guiding behavior in learning.

A fourth condition for learning is for the learner to have appropriate materials to work on. If he is to learn to solve problems, he has to have problems to attempt to solve. If he is to gain skills, he must have tasks which give him opportunity to practice those skills. If he is to gain appreciation, he must have materials that he can listen to, see, or respond to in other appreciative ways.

A fifth condition for effective learning is that the learner have time to carry on the behavior, to keep practicing it. We may refer to this as having study time. Often schools assume that the student is spending time in study outside the classroom when observation or interview will uncover the student's notion that, if he comes to class, he learns all that is required. A more effective provision of study time is important for high-level learning to be reached.

A sixth essential condition for learning is for the learner to get satisfaction from the desired behavior. As the learner interacts in the various learning situations, the reactions which give him satisfaction are continued; those which do not give satisfaction are dropped from his repertoire of behavior. Teachers are in a position to help learners derive satisfaction from desired behavior. If the learner wants very much to acquire a certain skill, the actual satisfaction of getting the skill is sufficient. On the other hand, some kinds of learning require a long time. It is not easy, for example, to become competent in a foreign language so that one can read stories or articles in the foreign tongue. During the long learning period the teacher may exercise a considerable influence by complimenting the student on his progress, by helping to get group approval, by providing tests or other means for him to perceive that he is progressing toward his goal.

A seventh essential condition for learning is opportunity for sequential practice of the desired behavior. Sequential practice means that each subsequent practice goes more broadly or more deeply into the subject than did the previous practice. Sheer repetition quickly becomes boring to the learner and thus has little or no further effect. Only as each new practice requires the learner to give attention to it because of its new elements does it serve adequately as a basis for effective learning.

An eighth condition is that the learner set high standards of performance for himself. One of the common difficulties in high school, particularly with the gifted, is that the student becomes satisfied with mediocre performance and no longer puts forth effort to learn. It is often necessary to help the student acquire standards of performance that for him are high but attainable and that lead him on continually to seek greater excellence.

The ninth condition is related to the eighth. To continue learning when a teacher is no longer available, the learner must have means of judging his performance, of discovering how well he is doing. Without such knowledge, his standards are useless.

The purpose of outlining these conditions for effective learning in this sketchy fashion is to demonstrate that the stimulation and the guidance of learning are not defined by a particular arrangement of teachers and students. The student is learning as the necessary conditions are met for him. Some conditions may be met within, and some outside, the classroom. For example, in some schools the attitude of the student body, more than the steps taken by individual teachers, largely influences motivation. As one visits high schools over the country, one is impressed by the different attitudes toward classroom learning. Among some student bodies there is widespread concern for classroom learning, and the teacher needs to do very little, in addition, to motivate his students. In other schools the reverse is true. As with motivation, so with each of the other conditions, there are various ways of meeting them. Imaginative teachers and curriculum makers should be encouraged to devise new and better ways to provide students with conditions for effective learning. As each educational objective is examined, efforts should be directed toward suggestions for motivating this learning, for helping the student see where his present behavior is inadequate, for guiding his new behavior, for providing materials and situations on which he can work, for providing "study time," for obtaining satisfactions from the desired behavior, for getting sequential practice, for setting high standards, and for devising ways by which he can judge his performance. This encouragement should lead to varied arrangements of teachers and students, to promising utilization of audio-visual aids and other new materials and modes of instruction. Not only may it lead to a revolution in teaching-learning arrangements, but it should also enable us to do an effective teaching job in the difficult years ahead.

5. *Provide administrative leadership.*—Improving the high-school

curriculum requires active administrative leadership. Rarely is curriculum development effective when the school administration is not involved. Unfortunately, however, many school administrators now devote their primary attention to matters not directly related to the educational program, such as public relations, school buildings, finance, and the like. Of course these matters are functions of educational administration, but they should not become the exclusive preoccupation of the administration, for then the leadership required to improve the high-school curriculum is lacking. Constructive efforts require the intelligent concern of the administrator. The high-school faculty is stimulated and aided, when the administrator discusses curriculum issues with the staff in an intelligent, understanding fashion; gives recognition to teachers for their accomplishments in teaching and curriculum planning; and encourages research and study of the effectiveness of learning in the high school. It is easy for teachers to shift their attention from matters of curriculum planning and instruction to extra-curriculum activities or to school politics or to the community social life. The extent to which teachers deeply involve themselves in the improvement of the curriculum is greatly influenced by the attitude shown by the administration and the intelligent steps taken to help and to reward the teachers' efforts. Hence the type of administrative leadership is one of the critical criteria for the improvement of curriculum.

The High School and the Current Social Scene

This presentation should be related to other papers presented here, which point out the dynamic nature of the American economy and the rapid changes taking place in the demands for various occupations. The per cent of the population employed in farm labor, unskilled labor, and skilled labor is dropping rapidly, while the per cents in science, technology, health services, educational services, social services, entertainment services, and administrative services are going up at a rapid rate. Our civilization is setting educational requirements that are new in history. Persons who are able only to learn unskilled tasks will have little or no opportunity for employment, and our developing economy will require a much larger portion of educated people than ever before. The high school will have to encourage an interest in learning more effectively than it has ever done before. Failures and drop-outs from the school will be more clearly recognized as serious losses to society as well as to the persons involved. With increasing concentration of population, and with rapidly changing conditions in the industrial, social, economical, and political fields, the abilities to learn new skills, to acquire new knowledge, and to deal with new problems will become even more important. This is the task which the high-school curriculum must be designed to accomplish.

Making the High School a Place
for Study and Learning

The accomplishments of the high school are woven into the fabric of American life and add to its strength, suppleness, and luster. It is not my purpose to praise the high school, or to defend it, or to heap upon it the shortcomings of the virile but uneven culture which it both mirrors and shapes. Many of us today share a common belief that what happens to, and in, the American high school will influence deeply what happens in, and to, our nation; and we hold a common conviction that our schools can be, and should be, improved.

Dissatisfaction and criticism are necessary preludes to any fundamental redirection of our efforts in education. These we have, and in abundance. Now it is time to face the much tougher task of bringing forth acceptable concepts of what high schools should be in the latter part of the twentieth century and to begin the process of enlightening the public as to the measures through which such schools may be achieved.

In seeking approaches to needed improvements, we must, of course, take stock of factors that make it difficult for our schools to become effective centers of learning. In doing this, it is not profitable or practical to try to fix the blame for shortcomings which have been imbedded through a long process of development, unless we wish to indict the whole of American society.

Our present system of education is a mass-production system, an assembly-line operation or lock step which can be broken only by the valiant efforts of unusually competent teachers and administrators. It operates on the curious notion that learning can be compartmentalized in interchangeable time units, which, added together to the number of sixteen, satisfy the requirements for secondary

183

education. Add to this an insistence that every child must be assured entrance to the high school and the corollary that no achievement standards should be set that are not attainable by the majority, and you have set the stage for mechanizing the process of learning and for elevating mediocrity.

The vitality having been removed from learning, the schools found it expedient to introduce a wide array of extra-curriculum activities in order to find outlets for the adolescent enthusiasm, initiative, and energy repressed by the weight of inert ideas in the curriculum. Thus it has come about that, except for the classes and schools presided over by teachers and administrators of unusual skill and insight, students can hardly be said to be given much incentive or opportunity to pursue with zest the study of mathematics and science, to enter deeply into the delights of great literature, or to exercise their creative talents in any direction. These are harsh words, and I specifically exempt from them all situations where creative and insightful teachers are at work under administrators who encourage them to exercise professional responsibility and ingenuity. The fact remains that the weight of the system is too much for even the most competent administrators and teachers to drag along without sapping their energy and diminishing their effectiveness.

Even with due allowance for many schools with unusually wise leadership and unusually competent teachers, we do not have in American society sufficient provision for the intellectual development of the adolescent or sufficient incentive to independent study. This leads me to ask whether there is a place in the American school system for a school, or a unit within a school, which caters to the needs of adolescents who are capable of self-motivated, sustained study. If so, how would it differ from existing provisions, and how would it be fitted into the existing structure and related to other units which it is thought desirable to retain in the system?

Why Our High Schools Must Change

As you have detected, back of these questions there are assumptions which I should perhaps make explicit before proceeding to elaborate on some of the characteristics that may be found in many schools in the future.

One of the basic premises that underlies my thinking is that we have reached the stage when we need to provide for the many a quality of education at least as good as that offered to a small elite in the most advanced nations of the world. I think it is not necessary to review the facts or the process of reasoning through which I arrived at this conclusion. I would like, however, to relate it to certain articles of the American faith.

Although we have not fully realized our aspirations, we are committed to a belief that the full development of the individual is one of the primary obligations upon society and the best means through which a society may secure its own well-being. An equally basic tenet of the American faith is that the way to fullest development of the individual is to give him freedom to choose and to hold him responsible for the consequences of his choice. Closely allied with this is the doctrine that public policy should be fashioned through the uncoerced decisions of individual citizens.

The shrinking of the earth through the fantastic speeding-up of communication and transportation makes it more important than ever that decisions be informed and responsible. This is true not only of the decisions of highly placed men but also of the many in less conspicuous places. The ill-considered decision of a Governor Faubus can disturb our domestic tranquillity and threaten the objectives of our foreign policy. Similar effects can be produced by the nameless members of a mob in Chicago who choose violence to express their prejudice against colored neighbors.

Thus the importance of wise decisions is heightened at the same time that the complexity of interacting factors is making the choice between alternative courses increasingly difficult. This situation places upon the schools a heavy burden for developing among the people generally a high degree of ability to select and analyze relevant data so as to predict the consequences of choice. It calls as well for inculcation of the disposition to choose higher over lower values and to identify personal interests with the long-range welfare of mankind. Now more than ever the price of our freedoms is a genuinely liberating education for all the children in every group in every part of the country.

The American definition of full development for the individual also includes development for, and through, productive work in some significant field of human endeavor. This does not mean that the schools must accept responsibility for teaching specific work skills, but it does mean that they must provide the basis for entry into some occupation and cultivate the habits and skills which make learning on the job possible. One of the more striking aspects of our technological civilization is the constant increase in the level of literacy and technical skill required for effective work in industry, government, and the professions. The advance of the American economy is punctuated by the continuing destruction of low-skilled jobs and their replacement by jobs requiring highly developed technical or managerial skills. This process is now being accelerated so that industry will be demanding fewer and fewer routine operators and ever larger numbers of men with the skills to design, build, instal, repair, and control machinery.[1] A high proportion of the new jobs being created require basic understandings and skills in mathematics, science, and the arts of communication. Heavier demands are being made, too, on the ability to plan, to co-ordinate operations, and to exercise independent judgment. These industrial demands for highly literate workers are paralleled in government and the military services. Our scientific and professional occupations now employ more than 5,000,000 persons as compared with just over 1,200,000 in 1900, and the demand is still rising.

We have discussed but two of the factors which call for improvements in education for all citizens. Many other factors might be cited to support the contention that the conditions of modern life have produced a set of demands so complex and exacting as to require even the most literate nations to undertake a major upgrading of their schools. Our high schools must change because the inescapable conditions of our day demand a quality of education for the many which the schools as now constituted are unable to provide. It is as simple as that. Yet to bring about the needed changes in our schools will not be easy, not only because of the well-advertised shortage of teachers and classrooms, but for other reasons, which require examination in order to determine the direction of change.

Guides to the Redirection of Secondary Education

Schools are established in human society for many reasons and address themselves to many objectives. But, in a society which holds

[1] Cf. Peter F. Drucker, "America's Next Twenty Years," *Harper's Magazine,* CCX (April, 1955), 39–44.

that its own well-being demands the fullest possible development and freedom of choice for the individuals in it, schools must provide experiences designed:

To enable man to perceive new meaning and richness in nature, in art, and in human institutions and relationships;

To equip him to learn from the experiences and thoughts of others, particularly those removed in time and place;

To free him from slavery to circumstance, environment, and personal whim by giving him an increased measure of ability to make rational choices and to put the choices into effect;

To enable him to play a significant part in the advancement of mankind and the improvement of human institutions.

Man is not only a thinking animal but one that is able to project himself beyond what is perceivable through the physical senses. He has a need and an ability to look beyond what is to what may be, to reach out for wholeness and perfection, for beauty of form and quality. He is an aspiring animal that can conceive of goals transcending human achievement and incorporate these goals into his own purposes. He is capable of making value judgments and rational choices and is able, therefore, to choose future good over immediate satisfactions. Although he tends to be a pragmatist and a relativist, judging ideas and acts by their observed or predicted consequences or relationships, he often is at the same time an idealist or a transcendentalist, judging ideas and acts in a deeper sense by their harmony with an imagined (or revealed) perfection. Most men apply these dual criteria to judgments, sometimes emphasizing one, sometimes the other, although some men have a strong emotional attachment to one or the other as a basis for judging human behavior.

Schools should incorporate both kinds of criteria and use the motivational power of both ideal goals and pragmatic sanctions. Excellence itself is an ideal, a metaphysical term not susceptible of exact definition or measurement; yet it is a standard which can be given pragmatic meanings within the context of education. Our high schools apply it to football and band performance. Why not to mathematics, literature, and other spheres where reason and imagination find expression?

Among man's most powerful drives is a need to understand himself and his environment and to relate himself in meaningful ways to the universe. Learning is a process of groping through doubt, following gleams which lead occasionally to truths bright enough to light up a portion of the unknown and create a sense of arrival; but learning continues only as this sense of achievement or adjustment gives way, in turn, to the need to explore the shadows at the edges of the illumination. Adjustment is the sleep of learning, or at best a pause in which the powers are gathered for new learning. The schools should work with the young in such a way as to preserve the sense of wonder and to encourage learning through self-motivated inquiry, but they should give sufficient guidance to assure that the learner makes a real effort to assimilate significant portions of the vast storehouse of knowledge that has been accumulated and systematized in the course of human history. At the same time the schools must refrain from deadening learning by dealing in inert ideas which Whitehead has defined as "ideas that are merely received into the mind without being utilized, or tested, or thrown into fresh combinations."[2]

Many schools ignore these views and are organized and operated in acordance with no longer tenable assumptions as to how human beings learn. Moreover, much of the content of instruction in our schools is a result of historical accidents, philosophical aberrations, and personal whims rather than of any well-thought-out effort to abstract from our vast cultural heritage those elements most useful in enlarging the horizons and extending the powers of the young. It may be observed also that the quality of teaching and the values underlying school administration too often are not conducive to sustained intellectual effort.

Ways must be found to overcome the apparent purposelessness and lack of standards which characterize so many of the programs in our schools. Something also must be done to shield the schools from the anti-intellectualism which so often perverts the values of our society. If teachers and school administrators are to perform effectively in their essential roles, there must be a reduction of the enormous energy consumed in providing custodial care and exercising police functions. There must somewhere be an answer to the deplorable situation which arises from the fact that, for many chil-

[2] Alfred North Whitehead, *The Aims of Education and Other Essays* (2d ed.; London: Williams & Norgate, Ltd., 1950), pp. 1–2.

dren, schools, instead of representing a coveted opportunity, stand for a sentence to be served to the end of the compulsory attendance age.

I have stated some of the basic assumptions that must guide us in the redirection of secondary education. It may be well to state here some of the corollaries that follow from these propositions when related to the present state of psychological knowledge and certain value judgments which find support in the American tradition:

1. The development of the individual, with special reference to the intellectual powers, is a primary function of education.
2. The content of instruction should serve both to transmit the cultural heritage and to provide suitable material on which the learner can exercise and extend his powers.
3. The learner has powerful drives and needs, one of the most important of which is to understand himself and his environment.
4. The school should take account of the inherent purposiveness of the learner and feed his need to know with experiences which will whet his appetite for more vital and precise knowledge.
5. Such abilities as those involved in analyzing problems, making rational choices among alternatives, and assuming responsibility for one's acts can be cultivated in the schools.
6. School practices—such as the ways in which classes are organized and taught, the criteria used to evaluate learning, the kinds of achievement which are recognized and rewarded, the bases for teacher selection and assignment—have important effects on the learning that takes place in the school.
7. The development of the powers of the individual is most likely to come from tasks which can be related to the learner's purposes but which require the exercise of his highest powers and the invoking of powers not yet fully developed.

Some Thoughts on a New School Unit

As I think about the implications for secondary education of the kinds of views that I have been expressing and of the new and exacting demands that will be made on education in the latter part of the twentieth century, I cannot help wondering whether the times are not ripe for the creation of essentially new types of schools. As already indicated, my thoughts have been running more and more strongly to the idea of a school unit or division to which one must earn admission by exhibiting a capacity for self-motivated effort and sustained study. The mere presence of such a division within our system would offer incentives toward intellectual achievement and responsible behavior in all parts of the system. It would free the teachers from their present custodial and police functions and permit them to assist students in setting appropriate goals at various stages of their development, in planning experiences to test and extend their capacities, in discovering new sources of knowledge, and in learning ways of systematizing inquiry.

I visualize a school unit or division open only to those who have acquired certain fundamental tools of learning and have demonstrated a capacity for study. Admission might occur anywhere between ages eleven and fifteen; the mode probably would be about age thirteen. Although, as the new value and incentive systems begin to work and schools consequently become more effective, the mode might well drop to age twelve. It should be noted that admission is not based primarily on intelligence or abstract ability, except as these are reflected in the ability to read, write, use numbers, and engage in sustained study without the necessity for external discipline. It is assumed, therefore, that the school will make provision for those who will learn best through direct experiences in the laboratories and shops as well as through language symbols.

Such a school or division would not need to lay out all learning tasks in units of so many minutes per day for a period of a year or to use the Carnegie unit of credit as the basic means of recording progress. Instead, learning progress could be described with reference to specified skills or the understanding of particular bodies of organized knowledge. Students would be grouped on the basis of ability to profit from a particular bit of instruction, and the time assigned to any learning task would vary according to the nature of the task and the capacity of the individuals engaged in it.

There would be no need of policed study halls. Students would spend the time not scheduled for group instruction in the library, a laboratory, or a shop; in a booth practicing speech or music skills or studying from a film, a talking book, or other communication device; or in a small room or nook participating in small-group discussions.

We should remember, too, that the technological progress, which has created new problems for schools, has also provided devices that may be used to facilitate learning. For example, closed-circuit television would enable our schools to have exhibit rooms and individual cubicles where films and kinescopes may be shown when needed; talking books and manuals could be provided from which the individual learner might seek information or guidance to satisfy his own need; tape-recording devices might be used to permit him to check his own progress in language and other fields. These and many other devices have genuine educational value if used as means of freeing the teacher from the laborious and often ineffective attempt to communicate information through lectures, thus permitting him to use his time in motivating, guiding, and resolving the perplexities of students. In the high school of the future such devices will, if intelligently used, permit a much greater individualization of instruction than is possible under existing conditions. They can also be used to increase the amount of self-directed study and thus hasten the development of habits of independent inquiry. No one should imagine, however, that the tough, persistent problems of education will be solved by the introduction of electronic and mechanical marvels into the schoolroom.

The school will need to be staffed by teachers with a variety of specialized abilities. First, it will need a core of counselors, or homeroom teachers, whose functions will include (1) gaining as full as possible an understanding of the needs and the present stage of development of each student as well as insights into his undeveloped capacities; (2) helping each child plan a schedule of study which will advance the redirection of his own purposes as well as the acquisition of significant knowledge and the extension of his powers; (3) evaluating continuously the progress of the child toward his own goals and in the development of socially desirable abilities; and (4) bringing to the attention of other teachers special needs of a particular student and seeking assistance in diagnosis, evaluation, or remediation as indicated.

Second, there will be need for a core of librarians, who will assist students in discovering and using the resources found in books, documents, recordings, films, and other records of human experience, natural phenomena, and technological processes.

Third, there will be need for specialists in mathematics, the sciences, and the humanities who have unusual skill in introducing the young to these fields and helping them to assimilate important portions of the cultural heritage. These will be persons of broad scholarship who know how to awaken enthusiasm for their particular fields of knowledge and how to induct the student into methods of inquiry which will enable him to share in the riches to be found in each area.

Fourth, there will be staff members particularly gifted in awakening creative impulses and in nurturing aesthetic taste. Such persons will be found in charge of the shops, craft rooms, the art studios, the music rooms, and the like.

And, fifth, there will be technicians, who will help put at the disposal of teachers and students the mechanical, visual, and electronic devices in such a way as to make them means to the achievement of valid educational objectives rather than determiners of what is to be taught.

For those not ready for the type of high school which I have been describing, there should be an intermediate school or division following the primary school, the normal expectation being that the child would stay in the primary school to age twelve and then enter either the intermediate school or the upper division. The intermediate school (or junior high school, if you like) would devote itself not only to discovering and remedying deficiences in the command of the tools of learning but to bringing its pupils along toward maturity and the ability to engage in independent study.

Its primary goal would be to prepare its charges for entrance into the upper division. Now I know this notion will shock those sentimental souls who insist on regarding each school as an end in itself and seem deeply distressed that anything should be regarded as preparatory for anything else. But, if I am right, this very notion is one of the things that has interfered with the exercise by schools of the maturing influence that should characterize genuine education. The intermediate school, therefore, should be staffed with teachers who have unusual skill in diagnosis, in calling forth the latent powers of young people, in removing blocks to emotional and intellectual maturation. Its programs should be carefully fitted to the special needs of its charges, because it must arouse dormant purposes, reawaken the sense of wonder where it has been dulled, and develop powers of independent study.

Some of those attending the intermediate school, instead of transferring to the higher school, might go into gainful employment, where opportunities for continued education would be made available, or perhaps be transferred to specialized vocational schools. In any case, it will be necessary to make provision for a continuance of general education under the conditions most useful to the learner.

Would, or should, the type of institution which I have been discussing replace the present high school? Or should the two types of institutions coexist? The answer will have to come from a variety of attempts to achieve the substance of what has been described. In large centers of population the new type of school might, in some cases, be organized separately as a supplement to existing schools. In other situations and in smaller communities generally, it might emerge as a school within a school. In any case it will require great ingenuity to overcome the tough problems of organization, administration, and staffing; but American inventiveness should be equal to the task.

Another aspect requiring careful attention is the replacing of the passing mark and the unit of credit with continuous evaluation throughout the student's career and thorough appraisals at the time of departure from the school as well as at intervals during the stay. Such appraisals should provide explicit statements of the degree of ability achieved by the student to express himself orally and in writing, his ability in using numbers and in understanding the theory of mathematics, his level of competence in the use of the scientific method as well as in the mastery of certain bodies of scientific knowledge, and his understanding of the development and functioning of human institutions and of their effects on individual freedom and happiness.

We live in a fearful and wonderful world. Mankind, perched precariously on the abyss of self-destruction, yet can perceive a narrow path leading up to unimaginable splendors—a path that can be traveled by men equipped with a genuinely liberalizing education. Let us take counsel not of our fears but of man's insatiable sense of wonder, his need to explore, and his ability to contrive rational solutions to his dilemmas. Let us see if we can build a program of education that will make the slide into destruction less likely and the application of rational solutions more probable.

IV

*Current Innovations in High-School Practice
Are Described and Some Proposals
for the Future Are Presented*

Innovations in the High-School Curriculum

Because an analysis of educational materials already published could not provide an up-to-date account of curriculum practices throughout the country, I wrote, in preparation for this paper, to a number of professors of secondary education, asking them to indicate significant, forward-looking experiments of promising practices. They responded generously and suggested sixty-one school systems to which I might write for descriptions of forward-looking practices. In selecting the practices upon which to report, I have tried to keep in mind the fact that our secondary schools should reflect what is known about the learning process and about the developmental needs of adolescents.

Effective Learning in the Classroom

Courses of study, curriculum-organization plans, and discussions on curriculum may never have an impact on the learning of pupils. The experiences of boys and girls in the classroom are of primary importance in any consideration of the curriculum. Here promising classroom practices are discussed first to emphasize their importance.

Defining Objectives That Go beyond Subject-Matter Acquisition and Evaluating Their Attainment

Some schools are beginning to recognize that there must be school-wide objectives toward which every teacher is striving if the secondary school is to serve its role effectively. The University School at Ohio State University has identified sixteen continuous curriculum experiences which are directly related to, or implied by, democratic values and which it tries to emphasize throughout the school environment.[1] These "threads of continuity" or all-school outcomes give direction to the selection and evaluation of learning experiences in all areas of the program.

[1] Faculty of the University School, "A Description of Curricular Experiences, Grades 7–12" (Columbus, Ohio: Ohio State University, 1956), pp. 2–4.

197

In its evaluation program the University School emphasizes the importance of these continuous experiences. Written progress reports instead of marks are given to parents. At graduation each student receives a letter rather than a diploma. The evaluations do not stop with reporting on subject-matter achievement. The skills, attitudes, understandings, and behavior of the student are evaluated and reported.

Many other schools described their efforts to define school-wide objectives and their attempts to set up environments in which these goals can be achieved. The Phoenix Union High School emphasizes mental health as a goal in all subject fields. The University of Illinois is working with several high schools in Illinois to improve the teaching of critical thinking.[2] Evanston, Niles, and New Trier are three of the high schools engaged in this project. The aim is to develop critical thinking through instruction in logic, semantics, and scientific method in connection with four of the subject-matter areas.

International understanding as an objective is receiving increased attention. Student bodies in many high schools, for example, Scotts Bluff (Nebraska) and Clayton and University City (Missouri), raise funds for support of exchange students. Students from other countries enrolled in these schools make it possible for American-born students to learn at first hand of the customs and the problems of other countries. Many organizations invite high schools to cooperate with them in planning trips to other lands in the summer.

Changes in the emphasis in tests also indicate more attention to objectives which go beyond subject-matter acquisition. For example, a recent letter to educators from the Educational Testing Service announces a new test designed to measure school progress in terms of what students can *do* with their learning rather than what they learn. This viewpoint is reflected in many of the nationwide testing programs, and the tests themselves are likely to influence both curriculum making and teaching practices.

Perhaps the most significant and far-reaching development which will eventually affect learning experiences in the high-school classroom is the Study of Behavioral Outcomes of General Education in High School. This project, financed by the Russell Sage Foundation,

[2] "Project for the Improvement of Thinking: Rationale and Design" (Urbana, Illinois: College of Education, University of Illinois, n.d. [mimeographed]).

is being conducted by the Educational Testing Service, with the advisory assistance of the United States Office of Education, the American Association of School Administrators, the Association for Supervision and Curriculum Development, and the National Association of Secondary-School Principals. A resulting publication describes the end products of secondary education in behavioral terms.[3]

Making Curriculum Content
More Consistent with Objectives

Several promising practices in the various subject fields suggest ways in which curriculum content may be more effectively organized for achieving avowed objectives. I shall cite illustrations in only a few of the subject areas.

Increased attention to science and mathematics reflects the country's growing concern about the shortage of scientists and about the role which science is playing in modern life. Many schools and some national organizations and agencies are making concentrated efforts to improve the curriculum in these areas. The science program of the Evanston (Illinois) Township High School illustrates the efforts of a number of major high schools.

Science at Evanston Township High School is for everyone—the most strongly academic student and the pupil of low ability. . . .
To provide for students planning a career in science or engineering, ETHS offers strong mathematics and science curriculums. Mathematics courses and science courses through college-level physics, analytical geometry and differential and integral calculus, opportunity for original study and research in a science seminar, and rigorous laboratory experience—all contribute toward giving students an excellent opportunity to prepare for subsequent work in any college program but especially for a major in science.
To provide for the non-college bound and low-ability pupil, whose only formal study of science will be that in high school, ETHS offers nonlaboratory courses which emphasize practical aspects of science, aim to acquaint pupils with the "method of science," develop skills that may prove useful, and provide general cultural and educational values. . . .
Science enrolment at ETHS is on the increase.[4]

A physical-science study project sponsored by the National Science Foundation has definite implications for the science curricu-

---

[3] Will French and Associates, *Behavioral Goals of General Education in High School* (New York: Russell Sage Foundation, 1957).

[4] "Science Is for Everyone" in *Excerpts from the Annual Report, 1956–57* (Evanston, Illinois: Evanston Township High School, 1957), p. 4.

lum. Under a grant from the Foundation, the Massachusetts Institute of Technology has undertaken a project to improve the teaching of physics in secondary schools. A Physical Science Study Committee, made up of scientists from colleges and universities and industrial laboratories as well as of high-school teachers and educators, is directing the project. The purpose of the project is expressed in the following quotation:

[The committee's] point of view is expressed in three fundamental and interrelated aims: (1) to plan a course of study in which the major developments of physics, up to the present time, are presented as a logical and an integrated whole; (2) to present physics as an intellectual and cultural pursuit which is part of present-day human activity and achievement; and (3) to assist existing physics teachers, by means of various teaching aids, to carry out the proposed program.[5]

As a first step, the committee will prepare a physics course for high-school Juniors and Seniors, including the fundamental chemistry that enters naturally. In presenting their plans, the committee goes on to say:

The new physics course will not be aimed specifically at preparing students for college physics, nor does the committee expect that all high-school students will take it. At present about one-quarter of them take physical science, and the new course will address itself to the same fraction. From this group come most of our lawyers, businessmen, statesmen, and other professionals who will not take science in college. The committee hopes that the new course will build a sound scientific background in this section of the population; that the resulting greater interest in science and better teaching methods will encourage more children to take science in high school and more young people with scientific aptitudes to elect science as their career.[6]

Many educators are also observing with interest a project to strengthen high-school mathematics which is being sponsored by the University of Illinois. At that institution the Colleges of Education, Engineering, and Liberal Arts and Sciences have been collaborating for a number of years in efforts to improve the teaching of high-school mathematics. The Illinois project aims, among other things, to achieve these objectives:

[5] Physical Science Study Committee, "General Report, March 25, 1957" (Cambridge, Massachusetts: Massachusetts Institute of Technology, 1957 [processed]), pp. 1–2.

[6] Ibid., pp. 6–7.

1. To vitalize the high-school mathematics curriculum by giving the student opportunities to approach his mathematics from the creative point of view of the contemporary mathematician and by including certain topics which are new to the high-school curriculum.

2. To develop student and teacher materials which present mathematics as an integrated subject rather than as a group of isolated courses.

3. To enable teachers to teach the program's mathematics by providing classroom text materials, by demonstrating teaching techniques for the teachers in their own classrooms, by writing guides to accompany student materials, by holding training conferences, and by bringing experienced teachers and teacher trainers to the University of Illinois Campus for a year of study.[7]

There seem also to be fundamental and far-reaching changes in the thinking of English teachers concerning the program of language arts in the high school. Leaders in the National Council of English Teachers are recommending that the English curriculum must give every student the opportunity to develop essential communications skills and help him see the relations between the rapidly expanding fields of knowledge.[8] The teaching of spelling, handwriting, and grammar is being approached from a functional standpoint.

The teaching of modern foreign languages in the high school is receiving attention. The United States Office of Education held a three-day conference in May, 1957, to consider how modern foreign-language programs in the high school can be redesigned to serve the national need. The conferees were drawn from broadly representative groups, including superintendents, principals, and teachers. The conference approved unanimously a statement, already indorsed by fifteen national and regional language associations, which is based on these principles of language learning "in the new key":

1. The elementary language course, at whatever level, should concentrate at the beginning upon the learner's *hearing and speaking* the foreign tongue. Throughout later stages, the student should have considerable practice in maintaining his hearing and speaking skills.

2. Learning to *read* a foreign language, the third phase of the hearing-

[7] "University of Illinois Committee on School Mathematics Project for the Improvement of Secondary School Mathematics" (Urbana, Illinois: University of Illinois, June, 1957 [mimeographed leaflet]).

[8] Commission on the English Curriculum of the National Council of Teachers of English, *The English Language Arts* (New York: Appleton-Century-Crofts, Inc., 1952), pp. vii–ix.

speaking-reading-writing progression in the acquiring of language skills, should aim at the ability to grasp the meaning directly, without translating. Translation, to be used only in rare instances as a device for teaching reading, comes later as a meaningful literary or linguistic exercise.[9]

In addition to revising the content of existing subject fields, many high schools are incorporating into their offerings new subjects or entirely new units of existing subjects.

Modifying Teaching Methods and Utilizing Aids to Learning

More effective learning occurs as teachers discover teaching methods consistent with learning processes and adolescent development. Several practices along this line deserve mention.

Many secondary-school classrooms are becoming laboratories which encourage particular kinds of learning. A social-studies laboratory in the Kokomo (Indiana) High School, as an illustration, contains conference tables and chairs, work tables and chairs, maps of all types, reference books, and parliamentary equipment.

A phase of the Massachusetts Institute of Technology program sponsored by the National Science Foundation is concerned with the development of simple, readily available equipment for physical-science courses. Baling wire, razor blades, and copper foil are examples of the cheap and available materials that are proposed for use by students. According to Director Jerrold Zacharias, such materials are used "to inspire students to devise equipment, just as working scientists do. Instead of merely reading about past discoveries—often in outmoded textbooks—they will to some extent participate in making those discoveries for themselves, and thereby learn how it feels to work on the frontier of science."[10]

The possibility of using television to enrich classroom learning is now the subject of much discussion and study. More than twenty educational television stations are now in operation. It seems clear that television, used in an intelligent manner, can improve classroom teaching. The camera's ability to enlarge subjects to any size can give every student a closer and clearer view in science demonstra-

[9] Marjorie Johnston, "Modern Foreign Languages in the High School," *School Life*, XXXIX (June, 1957), 8.

[10] "Razors at the Frontier," *Time*, LXX (July 29, 1957).

tions. In fact, the relationship between the viewer and the person who is speaking on television seems to take on a certain intimacy.

An example of the use of television to supplement classroom instruction is the use of the physics film recently produced by Encyclopaedia Britannica Films, in which Dr. Harvey White, of the University of California, presents a complete course in introductory physics on 162 separate films. Nebraska is carrying on a state program of education by television, financed by the Fund for the Advancement of Education. Supervised correspondence study is correlated with the educational programs on television. The program enriches the curriculum of schools unable to employ qualified teachers for the subjects.

Significant developments are occurring in the use of community resources to enrich the high-school curriculum. These practices include bringing persons from the community into school classrooms and taking pupils out into the community for experiences which cannot be provided in the classroom. In Tulsa, Oklahoma, a committee of the Chamber of Commerce and of school administrators have worked out a plan in which several kinds of help have been made available to science teachers in junior and senior high schools. Personnel from industry speak to classes on various topics and conduct individual conferences for guidance purposes. Teachers and pupils are invited to community meetings where the subject under discussion is of interest to them. Technical literature, bulletins, magazines, films, filmstrips, and exhibits, if relatively free of advertising, are made available to schools. Tours of industrial laboratories and plants are arranged. Science teachers are employed in summer jobs related to their teaching fields. More than twenty firms have already volunteered to take part in the project, and a "Thirty Hour Club," composed of engineers, geologists, geophysicists, mathematicians, chemists, physicists, and other research personnel, has been formed. Each member has agreed to give a total of thirty hours a year to school service.

Work-experience programs in which adolescents have an opportunity to perform significant work under good supervision is a promising practice. Many co-operative work programs are designed to lead directly into vocations, and a few school systems have programs which are integral parts of the general-education program.

The program of the Santa Barbara County high schools, with an annual participation of approximately five hundred Senior students, is outstanding.[11]

Provision of Team Teaching and Integrated Courses

Teachers often find that working with colleagues in joint projects helps them do more effective teaching. In some instances the provision of a longer block of time and the opportunity to use an approach in which the subject matter of more than one field is utilized represents a promising area for experimentation. The Tulsa (Oklahoma) senior high schools use a block program which includes English, social studies, and science. The same students are scheduled to the three teachers of these areas, and these three teachers are scheduled together daily in a joint planning period. Through co-operative planning, units of work in the three areas are correlated; strengths, weaknesses, and common needs of the classes are determined; individual students with problems are identified; and a concerted effort is made to meet individual and common needs that have been discovered.

In the Evanston (Illinois) Township High School, team teaching is being used to give the student more individualized attention. In a plan designed to increase student learning through more effective use of teacher effort, five teachers on a team work closely together to direct the operation of a project. The student is a member of his "own" class, a member of at least one "skills laboratory," and a member of a "community class." He attends skill laboratories and community classes as his needs and special conditions dictate. The classroom grouping consists of a large central community room surrounded by four smaller classrooms. This physical setup makes it possible for the teachers to meet the students' needs. On designated days the rooms serve as reading, writing, speaking, and grammar laboratories, where concentrated help can be offered. There is also a "make-up laboratory" for students who have missed work.

The project involves eight regular classes in Senior English, four classroom teachers, one reading consultant, and a half-time clerk. These classes meet as regular classes for over half of the sessions

[11] Frank Cameron, "Work Is Good for Kids," *Saturday Evening Post*, CCXXVIII (June 2, 1956), 42.

during the year. At other times the classes are broken down by "needs," and the student attends a skills laboratory. On other planned days the students attend the community classes to hear guest speakers, see movies, listen to lectures, enjoy plays, and so on.

In Univerity City (Missouri) High School, an art teacher, a history teacher, a mechanical-drawing teacher, and a French teacher have teamed up to show students the relationships among their subjects. Making use of preparation periods, a teacher plans to work closely with another class utilizing his particular specialty through demonstration, lecture, or discussion. Art, history, and French classes come together to view a film or a demonstration, with each class making a contribution to the discussion.

A Senior seminar has been developed for gifted students in one San Francisco high school. In this program several teachers handle instruction and discussion, and the program is co-ordinated by the school's curriculum assistant. One teacher works with the group on anthropology for six weeks, another handles philosophy for the same period of time, and a third works with the group on comparative literature. Not only does this plan stimulate gifted students and provide them with an opportunity to work together in certain fields which the high-school program might not otherwise open to them, but the students themselves are particularly appreciative after they have gone to college for the orientation provided in these subjects and for the experience of working in a seminar situation.

Examples of integrated courses are provided by Whittier (California) High School and by the Edsel Ford High School of Dearborn, Michigan. A course offered at the Whittier High School is the equivalent of the second year of algebra, and the regular course in college-preparatory physics, plus theory and practice in an advanced shop-type course in electronics. The mathematics taught is related both to the general physics field and to the electronic field.

The Edsel Ford High School offers an integrated humanities course which covers various cultures of the world. The course is under the supervision of a regular teacher who acts as a co-ordinator, working with a music teacher, an art teacher, and a teacher of literature. Also, the staff in the same school has written its own textbooks for a course entitled "High-School Social Science," which presents an integrated approach to the social-science field, covering the broad fields of history, philosophy, anthropology, economics, and civics.

The "Common Learnings Program" at Lakeview High School in Decatur, Illinois, is an integrated course in political, social, economic, and personal problems. Required of every student, it aims to prepare young people to live effectively by teaching them varied methods of solving problems in a changing world. The content cuts across subject-matter lines, but the units of work are exclusive to the "Common Learnings Program." The problem areas around which units have been developed are (1) Freshman: "Understanding the World about Us," (2) Sophomore: "Exploring the Individual's Potential," (3) Junior: "Meeting the Challenge of Democracy," (4) Senior: "Preparing for Adult Living."

School Organizations That Facilitate and Enhance Learning

Good classroom teaching is, of course, the major area in which any improvement of the high-school curriculum must take place. It is obvious, however, that the manner in which the school is administered can do much to affect the learning which goes on in an individual classroom.

Guidance Programs

Educators recognize that every pupil deserves to be known intimately by someone on the school staff and also that the student should be thoroughly informed about the offerings of the school in relation to his own purposes and needs. If these goals are to be accomplished, then the whole faculty must be involved in the guidance program. Well-trained individuals must co-ordinate the program and give it leadership. Certainly there will need to be team play in which the various specialists in pupil personnel and guidance services work closely together with each other and also with the teachers throughout the school.

In the Tulsa (Oklahoma) high schools the teacher assumes a strong, positive role in guidance, because it is believed that the teacher has a closer, more intimate association with the student than anyone else. This function is assumed more effectively because of a block schedule. Thirty-four persons are employed in the five high schools, in addition to the principal and the assistant principal, to participate in the counseling program. These specialists spend from one-sixth to five-sixths of their time in guidance activities.

Some high schools are emphasizing the importance of counseling gifted students. In San Francisco, high-school counselors are alerted to spot gifted pupils. The counselors help these students to plan in terms of their ability, to tailor their individual programs, and to supplement their formal education with broadening and developmental experiences outside the school.

Some high schools are emphasizing the importance of group guidance as a part of the total guidance program. At the Marshfield High School at Coos Bay, Oregon, a group-guidance syllabus has been developed covering fifty topics. It provides guides for discussing everything from administrative procedures to "Your Philosophy of Life." In the Lincoln (Nebraska) High School every student must register in group guidance each semester of his Junior and Senior years. The group-guidance classes meet twice a week, and the counselors assigned to each grade have an average of about fourteen periods a week for individual and small-group conferences on problems facing individuals.

Organizing Larger Schools into "Little Schools" or Small Units

A number of larger schools are being divided into "little schools," "houses," or small units. This arrangement is an attempt to provide an organization in which the student does not lose his identity in the mass. Each student in his unit becomes a personality rather than a name and yet has the many advantages that can be offered only by a large school. The Royal Oak (Michigan) Kimball High School has organized little schools within the large school. The school building has been constructed to allow for the "division" type of organization. Each division contains the counselor's office, conference rooms, study hall, locker lounge, and academic classrooms for teachers assigned to that particular division. The Syosset (New York) High School is a series of four "little schools," each consisting of ten classrooms, a unit library, several work areas, and a curriculum workroom, all surrounding a large open "project area." Each little school houses from three to four hundred students and is connected with the other three similar areas and with the common service areas—cafeteria, shops, homemaking rooms, the auditorium, and others.

Teacher and Citizen Participation in Curriculum Development

New practices to secure teacher and citizen participation in curriculum development probably have the most fundamental implications for the future of the American high school of any of the areas upon which I have reported. There is a growing tendency to recognize teachers as key persons in curriculum development rather than merely the recipients of the curriculum thinking that others do. There is also more general acceptance of the fact that citizens in the community must participate in curriculum development if they are to be intelligent about electing members to the board of education and about making decisions concerning the financing of the schools and other educational matters. In other words, citizens must have an opportunity to clarify their own thinking about the importance of education and some of the characteristics which a good educational program should possess. Then, too, educators are beginning to appreciate more and more that citizen participation in curriculum development will strengthen the educational program of the school.

Provision for Teachers To Work on Curriculum Problems

The 1957 Yearbook of the National Society for the Study of Education emphasizes the point that the only kind of curriculum-development work which is lasting and fundamental is that which affects the behavior of a teacher,[12] and the 1957 Yearbook of the Association for Supervision and Curriculum Development attempts to spell out specific ways in which classroom teachers can be part of the research effort which is carried on to improve education.[13] The Illinois

[12] *In-Service Education for Teachers, Supervisors, and Administrators* (Fifty-sixth Yearbook of the National Society for the Study of Education, Part I [Chicago: Distributed by the University of Chicago Press, 1957]).

[13] *Research for Curriculum Improvement* (Yearbook of the Association for Supervision and Curriculum Development [Washington: Association for Supervision and Curriculum Development, 1957]).

Curriculum Program is now engaged in a project which assumes that teachers can be researchers.[14]

Wider participation of teachers in curriculum development, coupled with their use of the best available research techniques in solving instructional problems, has great promise; for the research emphasis will mean that available knowledge on learning, on adolescent development, and on the needs of our society will become increasingly influential in the solution of curriculum problems. Specific reference to the curriculum-development programs of a few school systems will indicate the trends.

The St. Paul public schools are trying to avoid setting up a too prominent administrative superstructure in curriculum development. Curriculum steering committees at the elementary-school, junior high school, and senior high school levels are the chief bodies which deliberate on curriculum development. The principal outgrowth of their work is felt in in-service training activities. Some in-service courses or workshops are held in subject areas, but most are focused on "problems" (report cards, slow readers, unit construction, and others). The de-emphasis on subject-area curriculum committees is compensated for by the encouragement of local divisions of the state and national professional associations. The latter also provide an outlet for teacher leadership and recognition of professional growth, as do workshops, in many of which teachers serve as leaders or resource persons.

In the teacher appraisal program of the University City (Missouri) public schools, each teacher sets up goals for the year and then evaluates his practices in relation to the degree to which these goals are attained. This program provides a basis for the curriculum activities and the instructional-improvement programs in which teachers engage. Each teacher is encouraged to identify the problems upon which he proposes to work during a given year, based upon the evaluation made in the appraisal program. All teachers are expected to be involved in some professional-growth activities at all times, such as individual study on classroom problems, building projects, system-wide workshops, or attendance at university and college classes during the regular year in the late afternoon and Sat-

[14] Fred P. Barnes and Eric H. Johnson, "Curriculum Research," *Educational Leadership,* XIV (April, 1957), 445–47.

urdays or during the summer. Work on curriculum committees is considered an integral part of the program, since often the problems which teachers identify in their appraisal relate to the need for curriculum revision.

Perhaps the most far-reaching practice which provides for sound curriculum development is the twelve-month contract. Teachers then have adequate time to work on curriculum development outside the school year. Rochester, Minnesota, has such a plan. There teachers may choose ten-month contracts, or they may contract to work for twelve months with a vacation. During the summer some of those on twelve-month contracts are engaged in summer-school teaching or in supervision of recreation activities. Some teachers receive permission to go to summer schools for work on higher-degree programs. Requests to travel are approved for some. Many of the teachers are engaged in local workshop activities to improve their instructional techniques, while others are busy on curriculum-development activities.

Utilizing State, College, Lay, and Professional Groups

State and county departments of education, institutions of higher learning, the federal government, and many non-governmental organizations have programs in which resources are made available to local school systems. Lay and professional leadership from the local communities is often called upon in developing these programs. In many instances the state department or the teacher-education institution acts primarily as a co-ordinating agency in order that local school systems can team together to pool their efforts and to capitalize on the resources from the state and national level.

The Illinois Curriculum Program is an outstanding illustration of efforts at a state level.[15] Several fundamental principles underlie the program. For example, the policies governing the program should derive from a continuing advisory body made up of representatives of all state-wide organizations, both lay and professional, whose interests are touched by the program. The program should be basically a grass-roots program; it should recognize that *only* the local

---

[15] "Purposes and Activities of the Illinois Curriculum Program: A Report to the Steering Committee" (Springfield, Illinois: State Superintendent of Public Instruction, April 28, 1956 [processed]).

school staff, the local patrons, and the local students can effectively and durably improve the local school. The results of this project are too numerous to mention here. Numerous publications concerned with the various aspects of curriculum development have been issued and are available from the State Superintendent of Public Instruction, Springfield, Illinois.

An illustration of the leadership role of a state department of education is provided by the California social-studies project. The state superintendent appointed a Central Committee on Social Studies. Educators, in consultation with scholars in the several social-science areas, formulated a composite of key concepts in the social sciences, as well as a compilation of pupil characteristics and needs at various age levels. Using these two complementary lists, the committee plans to move ahead toward the development of the social-studies program. Further development of the project is taking place through summer workshops attended by teachers who teach social studies.

Nebraska University, in co-operation with the Nebraska Department of Education, the Nebraska State Education Association, and the Carnegie Corporation, is sponsoring the Nebraska community-education project in four schools in the state (Sidney, Syracuse, York, and Mullen). The experiment is designed to help the communities improve themselves, gather data on the process involved in community improvement, and find ways to help the school fulfil its role in community improvement while still teaching essentials. Six areas have been investigated by citizens: economics, culture, improved appearance, health, recreation, and education. The committees on education have been studying such topics as expanded opportunities for adult education; analysis of school facilities; analysis of goals of education; the means, other than the school plants, provided to meet the needs; and the school curriculum.

A Look Ahead

In this paper I have tried to indicate some of the innovations that are taking place in the high-school curriculum. They are only illustrations of the many efforts which are being made to meet the needs of youth in a swiftly changing social order. I should like to close by suggesting some of the directions which I think curriculum planning will take in the years ahead.

1. Teachers will be involved in curriculum development. They will be employed on an annual basis, and time will be set aside for curriculum work. Local leadership, supplemented by specialists from outside the local school system, will assist teachers in working out answers to problems which are of mutual concern. Laymen will participate. Communication with everyone affected by the educational program will be recognized as essential and the best techniques available will be utilized. Knowledge of adolescent development, of learning processes, and of society needs will be the bases upon which a sound program must be built.

2. The goals of a high school will be clearly defined in terms of the behavior, attitudes, values, skills, knowledge, and overt actions which are important for effective citizenship in a democracy. The program of the school will be appraised strictly in relation to the degree to which these goals are being attained.

3. Laymen and teachers will recognize that education, broadly conceived, is a total community responsibility—that the high school, the home, the church, business and industry, and youth-serving agencies must all assume their appropriate responsibilities.

The high school exists primarily for citizenship education. Since the ability to think is essential in a democracy, intellectual development is the central task of the high school. Values, problem-solving ability, skills, and knowledge become important outcomes—all developed in proper relationship to one another and to the over-all goal of intellectual development. The high school has a team responsibility to assume in the areas of vocational preparation, health, leisure living, and home and family living.

4. Every student and his parents will be known well by at least one faculty member. These faculty members, together with trained guidance specialists, will identify the specific needs of the students, and these needs will be respected as determinants of the curriculum.

5. Each student will be a member of a basic instructional group taught by the teacher who knows him well. Thus group guidance can most effectively take place, and students can be helped to sense the relationships among their various school experiences, their total experiences, and their goals. This teacher will be responsible for developing, with his students, learning units in areas which have been identified as fundamental to American citizenship now and in the

years immediately ahead. He will be responsible for planning and supervising curriculum experiences that take place in the community. He will work with each student in clarifying his goals and will help the learner plan his schedule. The basic teacher will then be in a position to supervise the student's self-evaluation and make valid judgments concerning the degree to which the youth is achieving to the maximum of his ability.

6. With close co-operation between home and school and with the basic teacher helping students to recognize why they are in high school and stimulating them to want to take advantage of the resources of the school, the high-school environment will take on an atmosphere of learning. Teachers can then become more nearly directors of learning and less dispensers of prescribed courses in which students sometimes only satisfy mark and credit requirements.

7. The high-school faculty, in addition to the basic teachers, will include specialists in the various subjects. Their classrooms will be laboratories equipped with appropriate aids for learning. The size of a class and the length of the period will be determined by the purpose to be achieved. The high school will utilize community resources whenever firsthand experience seems to offer greater promise for learning than does simulated experience on the school campus.

Some Approaches to the Better
Use of the Teaching Staff

This presentation describes some experiments currently being sponsored by the Commission on the Experimental Study of the Utilization of the Staff in the Secondary School, set up by the National Association of Secondary-School Principals and supported by financial grants from the Fund for the Advancement of Education, an agency of the Ford Foundation. For describing approaches to the better use of the teaching staff, the writer used an outline of nine categories presented in a brochure, *New Horizons for Secondary-School Teachers*,[1] but in this paper discussion will be devoted chiefly to two of these categories, namely, utilization of teaching assistants and material aids to instruction.

Use of Assistants to the Teacher

Teaching Assistants

Time-study data for high-school teachers published by the Central Michigan College Cooperative Study for the Better Utilization of Teacher Competencies,[2] as well as those assembled by Jones[3] in a doctoral dissertation at the University of Denver concerning junior high school teachers, indicate that upwards of 25 per cent of teacher time is consumed in doing things which non-professional or paraprofessional workers might do effectively. The use of teaching as-

[1] J. Lloyd Trump, *New Horizons for Secondary-School Teachers* (Urbana, Illinois: Commission on the Experimental Study of the Staff in the Secondary School, National Association of Secondary-School Principals [200 Gregory Hall], 1957). Copies of this brochure are available without charge by writing the commission.

[2] "A Cooperative Study for the Better Utilization of Teacher Competencies: Third Report" (Mount Pleasant, Michigan: Central Michigan College, June, 1957).

[3] Harold Dwight Jones, "Techniques for Analyzing the Job of the Junior High School Academic Teacher." Unpublished Doctor's dissertation, University of Denver, August, 1957.

214

sistants of various types, working under the supervision of, or in co-operation with, professionally certificated, experienced, competent teachers is being studied in several school systems.

Richwood, West Virginia, last year tested the hypothesis that the use of laboratory assistants in driver education would enable more students to take the course without seriously jeopardizing the effectiveness of the instruction. The laboratory assistant, a bus driver, would not merely do some of the clerical and other non-professional tasks of the teacher but would also assume responsibility for supervising students engaged in laboratory experiences—in this case, behind-the-wheel training.

Carefully conceived criteria for the selection of the bus-driver assistant were approved by the West Virginia State Board of Education. The bus driver must be a high-school graduate and be recommended by the local superintendent of schools as possessing these personal qualities: moral character, dependability, co-operativeness, and skill in the control of young people. He was required to attend a course in driver education given by a recognized university, pass specified tests on safety and driver knowledge, and work closely with the regular teacher of driver education. During the experiment all the classwork was conducted by the certificated teacher, and all the behind-the-wheel training was given by the bus-driver assistant. The two conferred frequently about general student progress and about problems of individual students. The driver-education teacher devoted two periods a day to driver education, and the balance of his time was spent in teaching business-education subjects, for which he was qualified.

To evaluate results, two equated groups located in neighboring school districts, which appeared to be similar in many respects, were compared. To keep the training as similar as possible, class procedures, materials, and training were defined and followed consistently in both groups. At the conclusion of the study, retests covering driver knowledge and attitudes were administered. A standard check list was utilized in giving the final driver-skill test. The evaluation was directed by two professors of West Virginia University and two West Virginia state policemen. An official of the State Department of Education of West Virginia, as well as local school administrators, supervised the study.

The Richwood study justified a number of conclusions and inferences. The objective data from the driver-skill test administered by the State Department of Public Safety indicated that, in driver skills, the experimental group (taught by a certificated teacher and the bus-driver assistant) gained more than the control group (taught entirely by a certificated teacher). So far as driver knowledge was concerned, there was no difference between the two groups. The driver-reaction inventory indicated that the control group gained slightly more in driver attitudes than did the experimental group. The cost per pupil per day was less for the experimental group than for the control group when success in the driver-skill tests was compared; the cost of the program with the assistant was $1,401 less for training a larger number of students than the cost in the previous year in the same school with the full-time teacher of driver education. The administrative problem of arranging student schedules was lessened with the use of the laboratory assistant, and more students could take advantage of the driver-education course. Responses of students and parents to questions concerning the use of the bus-driver as an assistant revealed that they indorsed the program and wanted it to be continued.

An experiment similar in some respects involves the use of non-certificated assistants in science laboratories in the Alexander Ramsey High School in Roseville, Minnesota, a suburb of St. Paul. With increasing enrolments in science and fewer facilities per pupil, the school faced the problem of how to provide more opportunities for students to follow science interests and engage in individual experimentation without overtaxing the regular teachers. To make facilities available for students to do science-project work on a voluntary basis, a decision was made to open the laboratories at activities periods during the school day, as well as after school and on Saturday mornings. The school employed non-certificated laboratory assistants to supervise the laboratories. Two sources of such personnel were available: Seniors and graduate students in colleges and universities in the area and science personnel in a number of industries in the locality. Four questions were posed for the study:

1. What benefits may be derived from additional laboratory experiences under the supervision of project assistants (non-certificated personnel)?
2. How can maximum use be made of the science facilities available?

3. Who will benefit most from the extended experiences: the gifted, the average, or the less-than-average student?

4. If classes are supplemented with extra time in the laboratories for volunteer work on projects related to classroom work, is it possible to have larger classes and still have a desirable learning situation?

At this writing, the study is in its second year. So far, there is relatively little evidence to commend or reject the project as conducted. Beginning and end-of-year tests in general science appear to show that the achievement of students who took advantage of the extra laboratory experiences tended to be higher than that of students who did not do supplemental laboratory work, even though some of the highest achievers in nine sections of general science were not in the extra-period program. In the chemistry classes the high achievers on two forms of the Anderson Chemistry Test were in the group who worked in the laboratory outside of regular school hours. Probably the most dramatic result of the extra laboratory period was the greatly increased interest and success of students in the Minnesota Academy of Science Fair. Modifications in the program are being made as experience is gained. More assistants are being employed during the second year of the project. In general, teachers and assistants, as well as students and their parents, are enthusiastic about the program.

Contract correcting of English themes in the Newton (Massachusetts) High School provides another example of the use of teacher assistants. During the summer of 1957 nineteen women from Newton and neighboring communities attended a workshop in reading and grading written compositions. They understood that a maximum of six persons would be chosen for the year's work. An instructor from the staff of the Harvard Graduate School of Education was assisted by a Newton High School teacher of English. Each of the six readers chosen for contract correcting was offered 200 hours of work for the school year, 160 to be spent in actual theme-correcting and 40 in conferences with teachers and students. All workshop members seemed well qualified for the work. Six readers have been employed for the high school and two for Newton Junior College.

In order to evaluate the program, teachers and classes involved are matched with control groups of teachers and classes of the same year and curriculum. In addition to pretesting and end-of-year testing, uniform written assignments are spotted throughout the year.

Each teacher who works with a reader teaches a comparable class without a reader. One teacher with three comparable classes will read all the papers written by one class, half of those written by the second class, and very few of those written by the third class. What is learned in this experiment doubtless will have implications for broader use, not only in the English classes of the school, but in other subject-matter fields as well.

Another type of teaching assistant is the college student who is preparing to teach. At Evanston, Illinois, in a closed-circuit television experiment, cadet teachers from Northwestern University supervised two classrooms of students receiving instruction by television while the regular teacher instructed a third class. In St. Paul, Minnesota, as part of a general experiment in teacher recruitment and training, teacher trainees will serve as assistants to teachers for two hours a week during their Freshman year up to fifteen hours a week during the final year of their college program.

Clerical Assistance

The provision of clerical assistance to teachers is increasing in many places. In Snyder, Texas, one of the questions raised in the staff-utilization study was: Does relieving teachers from petty chores by providing secretarial assistance for purely clerical duties contribute to efficient teaching? In the beginning of the study, clerical assistants were provided teachers to the extent of one clerk for each five teachers. Continuous experimentation is being carried on to discover which teaching tasks are appropriate for clerks and which clerical tasks should be performed by teachers.

In a small high school at Beecher, Illinois, a program involving the use of high-school students as clerical assistants was developed beyond that typically found in small schools. The purposes of the program were (1) to provide students with experiences that would help develop responsibility, personality, clerical skills, better work habits, and better pupil-teacher relationships and (2) to relieve teachers of clerical duties so that their time might be used in more professional ways.

General requirements for student clerks were set up by the faculty. The teachers described available student jobs, and announcements were made in a specially created "want-ad" section in the school newspaper. The students were not paid in money but were awarded points to be added to the extra-curriculum activity point system. An adviser was appointed to help with any employer-employee problems that might arise, to check on progress, and to organize the evaluation of the clerical program. Almost one-twelfth of the student body was involved in this program. Both students and faculty members want the program to be continued as a permanent feature of the school. In the first year, all but one teacher felt that the student helpers saved teacher time. Students felt that clerical jobs did not interfere with their extra-class activities or with their marks.

Need for Further Knowledge

We need to know more than we now do about what phases of the teaching responsibility should be done by professionally trained, certificated teachers and what phases of the teaching operation may be done effectively by specialists, para-professionals, clerks, general aides, community consultants, and other types of teaching assistants. We also need to know more about the selection and training of such assistants, how they may work co-operatively with teachers, and how the effectiveness of their services may be evaluated. This does not mean that all teachers should become specialists; doubtless both specialists and general practitioners will continue to be used in the teaching profession.

Material Aids to Instruction

The availability of television, films and slides, radio, recordings, flannel boards, mock-ups, and other visual, electronic, and mechanical aids; laboratories and libraries; and community resources is potentially changing the role of the teacher in instruction and may result in changing our ideas with respect to staff utilization. In a brief presentation it is impossible to describe all the studies in this area that are now being undertaken in secondary schools. Moreover, not all such techniques are known to any one person. Some illustrative studies will suffice.

Experiments with Television

An interesting study involving the use of closed-circuit television was carried on in 1956–57 in the Evanston Township High School.

Two courses, beginning typewriting and a tenth-grade course in English, were taught completely by television. The equipment was also used in numerous other areas of the total school program. All the units of instruction in typewriting included in a well-known and widely used first-year textbook, from learning the keyboard to producing difficult typewritten materials, were taught by an instructor who had a normal-sized class in the same room with him, while an additional normal-sized class, supervised by an adult clerical assistant, watched the lesson in a viewing room. Students in the two classrooms were similar to students in other typewriting classes and represented almost a cross-section of the student body. Three Sophomore sections in English speech, each numbering between twenty and twenty-five students, met in three adjoining rooms. Two of the sections were supervised by Senior cadet teachers from Northwestern University, while the third group met with the head teacher in the originating room equipped with cameras, extra lights, and a control room. The three groups rotated in such a way that each student was with the head teacher in the originating room every third day. All phases of the language arts—reading, writing, speaking, and listening—were included. In the receiving rooms a talk-back system enabled students in each viewing room to ask questions whenever they wished. Television cameras were operated by specially trained students.

On the whole, the school was pleased with the results of the use of television. Student achievement was generally satisfactory, and the conditions for learning were good. The use of television apparently did not interfere with the school's high standards of teaching and of achievement. Some gains were made in the effective use of teacher time. Attitudes toward the use of new instruments were favorable. Teachers found personal satisfaction in their experiences as television teachers even though some insecurity was felt.

The purchase of electronic equipment was costly, and plans had to be made for writing off the expenditures over a period of time. More than thirty thousand dollars were spent in equipping twenty-three classrooms for the Evanston project. This cost reflects equipment of both originating and viewing rooms. Additional viewing rooms can now be added for much less than the original cost.

Time does not permit detailed analysis of the results, which were appraised by a competent evaluating staff. The aspects of the situation which were unchanged, those that presented some difficulties, and those that were affected advantageously are listed below:

Factors Unchanged by Television Teaching

Transmission of information
Interest
Acceptance
Quality of teaching

Group rapport
Achievement
Individual activity

Difficulties Encountered in Television Teaching

Lessening of opportunities for participation for some students
More difficult for students to ask questions
Limited opportunities for group discussion

More focus on a few students
More formal activity
Reduced communication between students and teacher
Loss of color in black-and-white television

Advantages of Television Teaching

Ability to show films without lowering shades or taking students to another room and without using a projector
Opportunity for more students to view lessons, thus providing broader base of common experiences
Improved visibility
Increase in use of non-professional personnel

More uniform explanations
Economy of time for specialists on school staff
Dramatic presentation of materials
Better-planned lessons
Less repetition
More student independence
Greater emphasis on evaluation techniques

Many other television experiments have been undertaken. Mention should be made especially of the large-scale experimentation now under way in Washington County, Maryland, where both open-circuit and closed-circuit television are being used. Many excellent educational programs are being telecast daily for students at all grade levels in many parts of the United States.

Films, Tapes, and Other Devices

Related to television is an experiment in the use of films, which is currently under way in Utah. Like many other states, Utah is woefully short of trained teachers in the field of science. A survey of 61 physics teachers showed that 41 per cent had less than a minor of college training in the subject. A decision was made to experiment with the use of 162 kinescope films representing an entire course in physics taught by Professor Harvey E. White. The purpose of the project is to determine the extent of the mastery of physics resulting from the use of these films in actual classroom situations, the extent to which the films influence students in selecting science as a vocational career, and the way in which the films may assist teachers to master the subject matter for teaching purposes. The films are being used in schools in three categories: (1) schools in which physics has not been previously taught and teachers are not formally trained in the area of physics; (2) schools in which physics has been taught but teachers lack formal training in physics and equipment is meager; and (3) schools with well-trained teachers and adequate facilities in which a good job of teaching physics has been done. A careful program of evaluation, involving representatives of higher institutions and the State Department of Education, has been developed.

Effects of the use of locally prepared teaching tapes is being studied in the Westside Junior-Senior High School in Omaha, Nebraska. Three basic questions were set as a basis of the study: (1) Can spelling be taught to one hundred or more junior high school students at one time by specially prepared tapes as effectively as it can be taught to separate groups of thirty students each with a teacher? (2) Can classroom teachers in Grade VII teach modern languages with tapes even though the teachers do not know the language? (3) Can savings be made in teacher effort and fatigue, in teacher salaries, and in costs of books and use of classrooms if tapes can be designed that actually teach? Careful statistical analysis indicates that, on the basis of the first year of experimentation, all three questions apparently can be answered in the affirmative.

Many other types of electronic and mechanical aids are being used to meet needs developing in the studies of staff utilization. For example, when larger groups of students are assembled in a room, it becomes necessary to use some device to improve visibility and communication for students as well as to improve the quality of presentations. In Newton, Massachusetts, where groups of five hundred or more are assembled on occasion and groups of one hundred to three hundred are frequently taught together, the overhead projector and the 35mm slide projector are widely used. With the help of a teacher of art, half of whose time was freed for this purpose, teachers made more than five hundred transparencies—charts, diagrams, illustrations, exercises, and textual matter—for use in the presentations. Many of these were enhanced by color, and three to six overlays were not uncommon. Many 35mm slides also were locally made to supplement presentations. In Snyder, Texas, closed-circuit television was used primarily for purposes of magnification in science and other classes. Students in the rear of the room could see as well as, or even better than, those in the front rows.

The foregoing are only a few illustrations of the potential represented in a wide variety of material aids to instruction. Imaginative teachers are bound to discover much more about these and other material aids. Nothing has been said here about improved use of community resources, laboratories, workshops, and libraries. Released from habits and prejudices concerning teacher-dominated learning situations, creative teachers will be able, in the future, to make much greater use of these and other resources.

Relationships of Various Methods of Staff Utilization

The use of teaching assistants, material aids to instruction, and many other approaches have contributions to make, but none, by themselves, will provide completely satisfactory answers to the problem of how best to utilize the staff. In the final analysis, the secondary school of the future will find a place for all these approaches and for others which have not yet been discovered. What is needed now is a willingness on the part of school systems to take advantage of all that has been learned tentatively in the current studies and incorporate these approaches and others into a co-ordinated attack on the utilization problem.

The school using these aids and others to come will, of course, be quite different in many respects from the traditional junior and senior high school in the United States. It is interesting and stimulating to speculate about this school of the future. Whether it becomes a reality will depend upon creative imagination, administrative insights, and the ability to interpret to the lay constituencies the changes that are considered desirable and workable by the professional staffs of the school. Those who wish to maintain the status quo, or even retreat to an earlier day, will find vulnerable spots in the research on staff utilization. Those reasonable persons who are continuously seeking better ways of doing things will profit from the approaches described and from others that are being undertaken in many school systems and will carry forward their own approaches and experimentation, to the end that the professional competencies of teachers will be more fully utilized. Certainly it is evident in the approaches now under way that teachers are growing in service as they seek better use of their time and energies. Out of experimentation should come higher professional standards and high-school programs better even than those now in operation.

LLOYD S. MICHAEL

Innovations in the Organization
of the High School

To achieve the purposes of the high school of tomorrow in the most effective manner, greater attention must be given to the question: How shall high schools be organized? At the outset it should be said that a concept of dynamic organization emphasizes the fact that the structure of education is a facilitating agency through which the purposes of the school may be more effectively achieved and that there is no final validity either in the mechanics or in the form of organization. Structure is a means and not an end in the fulfilment of the objectives of the modern high school. It is essential that this concept of a functional and dynamic organization guide our thinking about, and our planning of innovations in, the structure of the high school of the future.

No rule of thumb can be applied in reaching a decision on an organizational pattern for a high school. There is no valid reason for accepting any existing type of organization merely because it has proved reasonably successful in certain communities. The best decision may be expected to emerge if attention is focused on the needs of youth and on the kinds of experiences that the school wants to provide for them.

This paper is concerned with three types of innovations: (1) those related to grade organization, (2) those related to the program design for general and specialized education, and (3) those related to the internal organization of the school.

Grade Organization

The grouping of students by grades has characterized school organization for a long time. How we arranged these grades into larger groups for administrative purposes has varied greatly with the times and in various communities. The simplest solution was to group the twelve grades into one school. Consequently we find six-year-old children and eighteen-year-old youth sharing many of the same facilities as members of one student body and under the guidance of the same school staff. This type of school is not passing from the American scene; it continues to flourish, particularly under the stimulus of consolidation of small rural and remote schools into regional and centralized school districts.

The four-year high school is still typical of a large portion of our rural communities, as well as of many urban centers. This organization, which was almost the only type of organization found in American secondary education until our century, is the pattern today in over ten thousand high schools, or 43 per cent of all public secondary schools.[1]

The great increase in enrolments in our secondary schools and the awareness of the high school as a non-selective institution with broader responsibilities were the primary reasons for the reorganization of secondary education. In 1952 there were more than 8,500 public junior-senior high schools; this represented 36 per cent of our public secondary schools. There were also some 1,800 senior high schools.[2] It is a most significant fact that from 1946 to 1952, a short period of six years, there was an increase of 3,253 in the number of reorganized high schools with an accompanying decrease of 3,629 in the number of regular high schools. For the first time in our history the total number of traditionally organized four-year high schools dropped below half of the total number of public secondary schools in the United States. National enrolment statistics also show that in 1952 only 25 per cent of the pupils attending the graded public schools were enrolled in regular four-year high schools.[3] One might safely predict that this striking shift in the grade structure of the high school will continue in the years ahead, probably at a declining rate, but certainly with the development of new organizational patterns.

A challenging proposal has recently attracted much public and professional interest. This plan, advocated by Paul Woodring, al-

---

[1] United States Office of Education, *Statistics of Public Secondary Day Schools, 1951–52*, Table I, p. 23, in *Biennial Survey of Education in the United States, 1950–52*, chap. v (Washington: Government Printing Office, 1954).

[2] *Loc. cit.*   [3] *Ibid.*, Table J, p. 23.

lows for increased flexibility in the admission and promotion of children and youth to the various levels of the educational ladder and bases progress more on readiness for subject-matter acquisition than on the length of time in school or the social and emotional maturity of the student. The early admission of gifted children to higher education and the Advanced Placement Program sponsored by the College Entrance Examination Board are other examples of innovations that change the common grade-organization plan.

These trends among our four major organizational types of high schools have frequently reflected sound educational philosophy and good practice. However, in too many instances the grade groupings resulted from rigid statutory requirements, financial and building needs, and numerous administrative expediencies rather than being evolved from an educational design or belief justified by careful planning related to basic principles of effective organization. Future innovations should be based upon a critical analysis of many factors, including the accepted purposes of the school, the requirements of the curriculum, the maturity level and needs of pupils, community needs and resources, and consolidation and reorganization of attendance units.

Although certain types of organization may seem to be preferable, American high schools should be encouraged to continue the diversity of organization that has been one of their characteristics and a source of their strength and growth. Innovations in structure that provide greater flexibility and diversity will stimulate, rather than retard, the development of adequate educational programs and services. No one organizational structure will be predominant, although provision for the thirteenth and fourteenth grades will become more common as communities continue to establish community colleges. The comprehensive high school, varying in grade structure and serving all the educational needs of all youth of a community, will prove itself the best instrumentality in the realization of the purposes of the secondary school. The internal organization within a particular school will follow no common design; it will be adaptable and functional as it serves pupils.

Any realistic approach to innovations in the organization of the high school must be concerned with the future role and emerging program of the comprehensive school. The Commission on Reorganization of Secondary Education redefined the goals of the secondary school and advocated the comprehensive high school, combining all curriculums in one unified organization, as the standard type of secondary school in the United States. Since that influential commission made its pronouncements some four decades ago, our schools have been offering broader and more extensive programs as they have tried to meet the educational needs of an increasing per cent of the youth of their communities. Gradually the multi-purpose secondary school has emerged as the agency most capable of serving all youth and of extending common-school education upward.

A number of specialized high schools exist in large cities and in certain other communities, usually those dominated by one trade or industry. Many of these special-purpose schools—vocational, trade, and technical—are strong schools and are making significant contributions to youth education. They appear to have served a useful purpose in broadening and extending the educational opportunities for some youth, but the present trend seems to be against expanding them.

Looking ahead in secondary education points to the comprehensive high school as the institution best qualified to meet the challenging demands of our modern society and the educational needs of a rapidly increasing youth population. The institution in the future that will provide the demanding and challenging education needed for all youth will be the comprehensive secondary school. This school will serve the many purposes of society and youth, including the common purpose of integrating education to insure social stability and balance and the several purposes of individual pupils—realization of their vocational, educational, and avocational goals.

Program Design for General and Specialized Education

General Education

A well-balanced program of secondary education should include, as one of its two main ingredients, a unified curriculum to meet the needs of all youth and of society. Persistent problems and common interests of pupils are guides to essential learning experiences for all youth. Because youth from all segments of American life attend our schools, provision must be made for the development of social competencies and attitudes. There are many issues and problems in our adult society that each citizen must face, understand, and attempt to solve. As a vital part of the process of growing into the role of responsible citizenship, youth should learn to understand and to deal effectively with these problems. These are recognized bases for a program of general education.

The conventional curriculum organization for general education is based upon separate subjects, each taught independently. This is still the program design in more than 90 per cent of the high schools. In 1956, in a study of 1,000 schools, Bossing found that 9 per cent of the undivided and junior-senior high schools, 6 per cent of the regular high schools, and 7 per cent of the senior high schools were using some form of core curriculum.[4] The Carnegie unit is still the measuring instrument of acceptability and respectability in the organization of common studies. Course offerings in English, American history, first-year mathematics, general science or biology, and physical education and health are the usual requirements. Approximately half of the usual sixteen units required for graduation are in this grouping. These prescriptions and others that may be added in local schools constitute the program of general education in most high schools. Some of the so-called undeveloped areas of general education, such as social-civic education, economic education, and home and family education, are coming to be included within the content of required subjects as short units on a sequential basis, particularly in Grades VII through X.

Another organizational plan is to develop different "tracks," or parallel courses in various common subjects to meet the varying abilities of pupils. Other program designs which deviate from conventional practice in curriculum organization include (1) informal and systematic correlation of subjects, (2) fused and unified fields of knowledge, and (3) core organization.

All these unconventional plans of organization appear to urge that instruction be oriented to problems and concerns of youth. Priority is placed on the obligation of the school to develop in youth

---

[4] Nelson L. Bossing, "Development of the Core Curriculum in the Senior High School," *School Review*, LXIV (May, 1956), 224.

a competence to deal with the practical and persistent problems they will face in everyday affairs now and in the future. These innovating practices in curriculum organization merit more widespread use in our high schools to determine their effectiveness in realizing the goals of general education.

A recently completed project[5] presents for the first time an organized consensus of the expectations that citizens and educators hold for the American high school. This study sought to determine the kind and level of behavior, stated as outcomes of general education, which may reasonably be expected from a well-matured high-school graduate. The report of this project should prove most useful to local schools in an evaluation of their present design and program of general education. It may reveal that there is no established pattern of common studies that contributes to these outcomes for all youth and that certain courses and experiences may possess high potential while others contribute little. The influences of home, church, and community may have greater educative value in developing these behavioral outcomes than schools generally recognize. It is no exaggeration to state that schools generally are neither effective nor consistent in their present programs of general education. A difficult task faces the high school as it attempts to reorganize and construct a challenging and functional program of general education.

Specialized Education

A well-balanced program not only should provide for general education which gives our society stability and balance but also should provide broad offerings of specialized education which gives youth an opportunity to develop any serviceable special abilities and talents they possess. The specialized offerings in the high school are roughly of two types: (1) courses organized into a defined sequence of work in preparation for a vocational field or for entrance into an institution for further study and (2) flexible courses that satisfy avocational or personal interests.

The scope and extent of the school's program of specialized education should be as great as the needs and interests of the students.

[5] Will French and Associates, *Behavioral Goals of General Education in High School* (New York: Russell Sage Foundation, 1957).

The students should have opportunity to elect courses in which they have a special interest or for which they have a particular need. Students preparing for college need to meet college-entrance requirements. For them the school curriculum should include advanced courses in academic fields not included in the general-education program. Today approximately 50 per cent of the high-school graduates are entering institutions for further study. Few schools have adjusted their thinking or their program to this new responsibility of college preparation; they are still trying to escape the assumed domination of the colleges. New demands and changing college-entrance requirements call for many innovations in the organization of so-called college-preparatory programs, including the introduction of honors courses and college-level offerings in schools that can justifiably present such programs.

Students planning to go from high school into employment need special courses which may include initial training and background experiences for an occupation. Students who have demonstrated real ability in one or more subject fields should have the opportunity to take advanced courses at the upper-school levels. A wide variety of possibilities should be open so that they may explore special interests for leisure use and other individual needs. An expanded and reorganized program of specialized education will insure, to a greater degree than is now done by most high schools, diversified experiences and educational services that will meet the unique educational needs of each youth.

Varying methods and procedures in subject organization, marking standards, and election of subjects, as well as greater flexibility in scheduling, must characterize the differentiating, specialized part of the curriculum. Recognized need, individual interest, and desire to achieve should establish requirements and standards different from, and usually higher than, those expected in required programs of general education.

A Crucial Problem in Secondary Education

The most crucial and pressing problem facing the American high school, then, is that of program organization—the need for the development of a new design of general and specialized education. With the increased acceptance of the need for the organization of the program of the high school into general education and specialized education and with clearer and more specific definition of the purposes and tasks of the schools, there is reason to be optimistic about the innovations that may be forthcoming in the structure of the high-school curriculum.

Internal Organization of the School

The size of the school is another aspect of high-school organization that deserves consideration. Because of our concern for the individual student and his welfare and because of our awareness of the need for personal identification and close relationship between teacher and student, many parents, teachers, and administrators have a sincere distrust of a large high school. As a principal of a school enrolling more than three thousand students, I speak from personal acquaintance with this feeling. It is thought that many of the unique advantages of the small school are lost in schools enrolling more than two or three hundred students unless the large schools are so organized as to protect individual interests and needs. There is much discussion on the optimum size of a good high school. On the other hand, there is equally strong belief that there are definite disadvantages in a small school. The limitations of a high school with fewer than three hundred students have been listed by educational planners as follows:

1. Many important subjects either cannot be offered at all or must be offered to extremely small classes.
2. The cost of maintaining a staff of good teachers is extremely high.
3. It is usually necessary for teachers to teach several subjects without being qualified in each subject taught.
4. Teachers who have prepared themselves in specialized areas usually seek a position in a larger school where they can spend their time in their field of specialization.
5. It is difficult and expensive to provide high-quality administrative and supervisory personnel.
6. Costly special facilities, such as shops, laboratories, and vocational units, often cannot be used throughout the day.
7. Important instructional services, such as visiting teachers, instruction for exceptional children, specialized guidance services, and vocational education, often cannot be offered.
8. Available monies will not provide as much high-quality education per student and per dollar.
9. Because of program limitations, accrediting agencies are often reluctant to approve the small high school.

The magnitude of the problem imposed by the elements of small-ness and bigness is revealed in statistics about the size of high schools.[6] In 1952 there were 824 high schools which had enrolments of fewer than 25 students. The term "small," when applied to high schools, refers to a school of fewer than 200 students. In 1952 that enrolment group included 13,142 schools, well over half of all the high schools in the United States. The element of bigness is emphasized in the fact that, while only 7 per cent of the high schools in 1952 had enrolments of 1,000 or more, these schools enrolled a sizable proportion of all youth attending school.

The quality of a high school is frequently thought of in terms of its size. Some educators will claim excellence for their school on the sole criterion of numbers in the student body. On the other hand, there is the interesting paradox that small schools are hopeful of attaining better status by becoming large schools, while large schools are organizing into several units to attain the advantages peculiar to small schools. Our task is to introduce those innovations which will increase the advantages associated with either a large or a small school and which will diminish the disadvantages attributed to them.

Internal Organization in Small Schools

A few small schools have adopted some promising practices to improve and extend their educational opportunities for youth. The Upper Catskill Area Project in small-school design is one outstanding development. This is a shared project undertaken by twenty-one central school districts in three counties in New York State and financed in part by the Fund for the Advancement of Education. The enrolments of these twenty-one schools range from 41 to 175 students. The project is attempting to increase both the quantity and the quality of their educational services to youth through the development of shared services in both equipment and personnel, the use of correspondence instruction, the greater utilization of community resources and technology; and the organization of multiple and ungraded classes in foreign languages and in other fields where the enrolments are very small.

[6] United States Office of Education, *Statistics of Public Secondary Day Schools, 1951–52*, Table 1, p. 42, in *Biennial Survey of Education in the United States, 1950–52*, chap. v (Washington: Government Printing Office, 1954).

Another study, somewhat similar to the Upper Catskill Project, is the Rocky Mountain Project. Seven small schools in Colorado are engaged in many of the practices developed in New York, but it is their intent to develop a more varied attack on the restrictions of a small school. In 1958–59 five additional schools will be a part of the program, and a year later some forty schools will be working co-operatively on the problems of organization.

A most successful approach to the problem of the extremely small high school has been made in the Death Valley High School in Shoshone, California. The school is staffed by three teachers, one of whom acts as district superintendent. The twenty-one students live within a radius of sixty-five miles and are transported to school in a bus each morning. This small community was challenged to offer to these twenty-one youth educational opportunities equal to those of a large city while operating within the limitations of a restricted budget. The students are receiving a complete high-school program, inclusive of college-preparatory courses, in a school building that was designed to provide convertible classrooms with adjoining alcoves for specialized offerings. This adaptable school plant is also being used extensively by the community. Creative thinking and planning in organization and facilities can surmount many of the restrictions of small high schools.

Internal Organization in Large Schools

Many of our large high schools show a real concern for the individual student and his identification with the school and its program. Some of the accepted advantages of smallness are lost in these schools unless they are so organized as to insure proper regard for the individual pupil. One of the significant trends among a few high schools has been the effort to group students into smaller units within a large institution. This practice is generally referred to as "schools within a school."

This concept in organization seeks to combine the advantages of the small high school (attention to the individual and his varying abilities, interests, and needs) with the advantages of the large high school (broad, multi-purpose curriculum and a staff of well-trained, experienced teachers). Specifically, present practices in the development of this concept of schools within a school seem to emphasize three objectives: (1) to eliminate the anonymity of large groups, (2) to effect administrative economy and efficiency, and (3) to make space more deployable. Illustrations of several of these innovations in organization will show how schools use the organizational structure of the school to obtain the advantages claimed for small schools.

The Citrus Union High School at Azusa, California, with an enrolment of two thousand students, has organized four small schools on a grade basis. Each unit has its separate physical facilities—classrooms, a multi-purpose building housing an administrative unit, faculty lounge, student lounge, and a shop building. Each has its own unit administrator and counselor. The student has many contacts in his unit office instead of going to an office serving the entire school. Since all a student's classes, except music and physical education, are scheduled in his unit, there is no need for large numbers of students to travel from one building to another. Each unit administrator is in charge of one high-school grade. He holds weekly staff meetings, supervises his teachers, helps build the curriculum, and does all those things which a principal would do for a small school of 400–600 students. The school believes that pupils are better served by a small-school atmosphere, where they are treated as individuals, and not as a number in a large student body. The parents and the community registered their approval by voting a second high school to be developed on the same philosophy and plan.

The Andrew Warde High School in Fairfield, Connecticut, consists of four self-contained "schools." Its twelve hundred pupils are enrolled in four separate "houses," each administered by a faculty housemaster and his assistants. Each house enrols about three hundred pupils. While the pupils remain identified with the houses to which they are assigned, they share in over-all facilities, such as special laboratories, the gymnasium, the auditorium, and the library. Each house has its own administrative and guidance facilities and an activities center known as "the commons room." Seventeen to nineteen teachers are assigned to each house. They have four basic tasks: instruction, supervision, guidance, and administration. The headmaster has stated that among other advantages the house plan helped to restore the classroom teacher to the "position of key person in the school."

Evanston Township High School nearly a quarter-century ago established a system of large home rooms, comprising 250 pupils each. These large units have been utilized chiefly for administrative and guidance purposes, although one unit, The New School, was for many years an experimental school, where the core program of studies was developed. In general, the experience with the large home room has been good, for the school sought personal understanding and attention for each student in a "small high school" while utilizing fully the advantages of specialization and diversity possible only in a large high school. By extending this relationship to staff and parents as well as to students, the school is now trying to enhance the value of the organization and further enrich the oportunities afforded to students.

The new subunit organization includes four divisions within the school. Each will have one-fourth of the students from each of the four high-school grades. On the basis of estimated peak enrolments, each would enrol approximately 900 students. Each would have its own parent-teachers' organization. Approximately one-fourth of the teaching staff would be affiliated with each division. Each would have an appropriate administrative, counseling, and clerical staff. Each would have, as its home base of operation, one quadrant of the building area, including three of the twelve large rooms.

It is believed that four divisions of 800–900 students would have numerous advantages over 10–15 units of 200–250. Among the major advantages are improvements in (1) the extent to which the total program can focus attention on the needs of students; (2) opportunities for student participation in socializing activities; (3) functional relationships among guidance, curriculum, and instruction; and (4) efficient organization and effective utilization of staff.

Each division will have the equivalent of four full-time counselors. Each counselor will serve, throughout the high-school career of four years, the pupils of one of each of the four classes in the division. Each division would have approximately one-fourth of the teaching staff of each instructional or service department as teacher associates. Teachers of required subjects will probably teach only those students enrolled in his division; other teachers may have pupils from all the divisions. Staff organization is based on the general assumption that, insofar as possible, two basic attachments should be provided in the assignment of each staff member: one in terms of the area of his special field, and the other oriented, through the division and the school as a whole, to common membership concerned with co-operatively understanding and serving the total educational needs of all students.

The Syossett (New York) Junior-Senior High School has "project areas" surrounded by ten classrooms, within which the general educational program of about 250 pupils, including social activities, counseling, and similar services, are programed. The new Linton High School in Schenectady, New York, will make many significant contributions as a result of the building and program design worked out by the school staff and the architects, which breaks the big school into smaller units, emphasizing desirable personal and social relationships. A number of other high schools have developed organizational plans to make the individual student the focal point of interest and concern and yet maintain the advantages of a large school.

The Random Falls Idea, yet to be introduced in any high school, is illustrative of a curriculum approach which proposes drastic changes in both purpose and structure. In outline, the plan calls for schools of not more than three hundred students, each school to include all high-school age groups, enrolled for full-time work except for brief vacations, and each school to be staffed by a variety of teachers and co-ordinators. In large centers the schools may be grouped as schools within a school. One of the school's purposes is *development of the individual's resources,* chiefly at the school itself. *Citizenship development* is furthered through vocational and service contacts with employers. *Community service* is provided through the student's volunteer service on community projects and, in reverse, through consultation and advisory services from individuals and community groups. This approach may suggest other more novel and drastic innovations in the structure of the emerging high school.

The innovations in the organization of large high schools described here and others not mentioned seem to place major emphasis on the objectives of smallness, administrative economy and efficiency, plant utilization and flexibility, and improved services, particularly in guidance. The adverse influences of bigness and mass education may be partially removed by these changes in the structure of the large high school.

Certain other innovations, however, might prove to be even more effective in improving the educational program in our large high schools. Little attention has yet been given to objectives more directly related to the educational needs of youth. What experiences that are not in the usual program of the school do young people need most? How can smaller units be organized to recognize the many differences among students, in terms of their abilities and their presumed college and vocational choices? Are curriculum patterns sound bases for the organization of groups of pupils? In essence, how can the large school, through its organizational patterns, develop greater individual diversity and at the same time promote social unity among its many students?

Other Aspects of School Organization

There are many other organizational problems that determine the effectiveness of the high school in accomplishing its tasks. These include the structuring of the teaching staff into effective relationships for the improvement of the quality of instruction and for fulfilling the many responsibilities in which teachers are involved. There is the need for the more effective organization and assignment of administrative, supervisory, and other non-teaching personnel to increase the productivity of the teacher and the pupil. The reorganization of some administrative patterns may also add to the improvement of the high school. Traditional practices that might well be examined include the organization of the school year and of the school day, pupil programs, teacher programs and assignments, class size, and credit arrangements. These and many other problems will demand better solutions if the high school of the future is to meet its challenge.

Educational leadership is charged with great responsibility to see that the quantity and the quality of secondary education is extended so that all the abilities of all our youth are properly developed. According to the Educational Policies Commission: "To locate the differences between educational theory and practice, to arrange these differences according to their importance, to probe for their causes, to prescribe for their removal, and to appraise the results of the entire process—these are the persistent tasks of educational leadership."[7] Many achievements of the high school of the future are dependent upon educational leaders who will effect needed innovations in organizational patterns and procedures.

[7] Educational Policies Commission, *Policies for Education in American Democracy* (Washington: Educational Policies Commission of the National Education Association and the American Association of School Administrators, 1946), p. 277.

Housing the High School
of the Future

No firm prophecy can be made concerning the high school of the future, the age groups and the numbers of students that it will serve (regularly or intermittently), the learning experiences that will be provided, the numbers and kinds of teachers who will be employed, and the extent of the use of teaching aids. Nevertheless, we encounter the awesome fact that we have to act, have to build buildings, and that, by our acts, we shall ourselves be helping to shape the future.

We do know that the high school of the future will serve people. In planning to house this high school, we must, then, bring to bear all we know, or can discover, about people—their common human needs and characteristics. As one simple illustration, we need to recognize that the American of this generation is inches taller and pounds heavier than was his father. And we need to recognize that a seat on a log may be made endurable but not comfortable by the presence of Mark Hopkins at the other end. Perhaps we might even return to context this misquotation so often misused. When President Garfield spoke in New York to the Williams College alumni in 1871, he said, in the pertinent paragraph: "I am not willing that this discussion should close without mention of the value of a true teacher. Give me a log hut, with only a simple bench, Mark Hopkins on one end and I on the other, and you may have all the buildings, apparatus and libraries without him."

This leads me nicely to the next point about people: they learn best under the inspiration and guidance of people. Television, movies, books, study guides, exercise books, the whole paraphernalia of learning aids—old, new, and still to come—cannot replace, but only can enrich, that vital relationship of the student and teacher.

240

We know that people need to learn (and live) variously—singly, in twos and little groups, in larger groups, and even en masse. We know that there is something in physical environment called "atmosphere." One arrangement of surfaces, textures, and colors repels; another invites. One design says "Relax," another says "Work," and still another says "Cringe." I do not know anything about the how, but I occasionally recognize the effect.

We know, still in fairly broad limits, something about Mother Nature. It will rain; it will snow; it will be hot, warm, cool, cold, dry, humid; the winds will blow; the sun will rise and set, will climb high overhead or struggle wanly across our southern quadrant—all these and much more will happen in slow or rapid succession. When we put today's man (and how much more tomorrow's) in a natural environment, we have to get him up off the wet and cold, under a shield from the direct rays of the sun and the pelting of the rain, and put up some kind of a barrier for him against wind and bugs. Against the irascibility of nature we place a loose-fitting armor, which we call a building.

Tomorrow's school will certainly do far more than keep out the rain, but as a controlled environment it will be more flexible and effective in providing ways to meet the changing natural conditions while adjusting to the ever varying physical demands of its occupants. Who knows, the builders may even have found ways to adjust air flow and temperature to the comfort and needs of the occupants, whatever their number or level of physical activity!

Types of School Buildings

The direction of the thinking concerning the role of our secondary schools constrains me to speak about the high schools, rather than the high school, of the future. This should come as no surprise. Any intelligent observer looking at the high schools of America, with their great variety in enrolments, in building provisions, in philosophy, and in their community settings, would realize that there could be no single development for all high schools. I have selected three high schools to describe. If in the description I reveal any bias or prejudice, that, too, should be expected. I have my prejudices, which I call convictions, as you do. Without our values, our convictions, and perhaps even our prejudices, we cannot make the myriads of decisions and choices which will help us, in our particular community, to get the high school that meets our felt needs and aspirations—our high school of the future.

The Multiple-Track School

This high school is built on the assumption that the principal goal of secondary education is to build intellectual power; that there is a central series of disciplines, largely verbal and to be found in books, which, when seriously undertaken by all youth, will lead them to a kind of intellectual power varying from one person to another mostly in degree. This high school will have large entering classes and small graduating classes. It will have every possible aid to learning, many yet undreamed of, but it will have ultimately rejected the use of substitutes for good teachers. At its very heart will be a superior group of dedicated adults who are highly developed intellectually. It will have small classes, of the seminar nature, and large classes. It will have not three tracks of learning but multiple tracks, with constant opportunity for the slow developer to be reassigned as his speed of learning and aptitude increases or decreases.

This school will be housed principally in a loft-type building with completely flexible interior partitions. It will undoubtedly have several stories, although, because of circulation problems, it certainly will not be a cathedral or tower of learning. The central building will house the seminar and classrooms, which will be grouped floor by floor according to the subject matter or department of the staff. The second building will house a large library and self-guided learning center, with nooks and booths for viewing pictures, hearing tape recordings, for reading and research work. The laboratories will be housed in a third building as a matter of economy and because of the rather different physical characteristics which make it difficult to encompass them within the same building with the classrooms. Music and the arts will occupy another building, beautifully designed to stimulate and to develop appreciation for the great music of the past, the great drama, and the other noble achievements of mankind. Lastly, there will be a physical-education plant, with adequate playing fields and courts, wherein emphasis can be placed largely on the individual and small-team sports which will develop the sound body and lifetime game skills.

The classroom building is described as a single building, but it could be a series of smaller buildings if the faculty's convenience is even more consulted. Whether a single building or a series of buildings, the organization of classroom and learning facilities will be grouped around subject matters and around the convenience and comfort of the faculty. Obviously it is more economical and more convenient if all the classes studying foreign languages, for instance, meet in a compact area. This arrangement permits the reassignment of students from the rapid track to Track B, C, D, or E with the maximum scheduling ease. Similarly, the teachers can exchange ideas, and they will have immediate access to all the learning aids which are appropriate to their particular subject matter. In each cluster of rooms there will be provision for the necessarily small advanced classes and for small groups of the slowest learners, since the conscientious staff will insist on the closest of tutoring for students who need it most and for those who can profit most from it. The great middle group will meet in large classes with a thoroughly trained teacher and a number of semi-professional assistants. Their meeting rooms will seat between forty and one hundred. In the larger rooms, television screens will be provided for every three or four seats.

One would have to look outside of this public secondary school to find all the educational and vocational training centers for people of secondary-school age, since inevitably the social conscience of this community will not permit it to reject from public concern the many boys and girls for whom the academic program is ill fitted or, to put it the other way, who are ill fitted for this academic program. However, in this particular community the young adolescents not attending the high school will be found in vocational schools operated by the large corporations or in youth camps operated by the United States Department of Defense. Thus will Plato's Republic finally be brought to fruition, with the rulers, the warriors, and the commoners joining the adult citizenry through a self-selective, non-caste process.

If I have been sketchy in my description of the housing of the multi-track high school and partisan in characterizing the curriculum and arrangements, it is because I cannot really believe that this will be the high school of the future in many, if any, communities.

The Children's Village

My next high school of the future I should like to call the "Children's Village." It differs from the multiple-track school caricatured above in that it provides for all the children of high-school age. It, too, is a campus-type development. It, too, takes advantage of every possible aid to learning, mechanical and otherwise. It, too, speaks a real concern for human values and reflects the conviction that, when fine adults are selected and put into intimate human contact with young people under conditions skilfully devised to stimulate curiosity and learning, the optimum learning will take place.

This village is the outgrowth of the comprehensive high school. While capable of serving young people ranging widely in abilities and in total numbers, its top enrolment will be twelve to fifteen hundred. Except for the activities in the home and in the church and for the usual wide range of community recreation activities, all the needs of young people will be provided for in the Children's Village, largely within the confines of the campus.

Spotted about the campus, in clusters of ten or twelve, are the home rooms, small structures of residential size and of very simple construction. Each home room has some thirty pupil stations, two teachers' offices, and a library-resources room. (In one community these have been grouped into buildings of twelve to fifteen classrooms, with offices and other facilities. To their astonishment, the administrators found that the heavier construction and the circulation spaces that were required gave them no net saving but greatly reduced their ability to divide a given space into smaller or larger sections.) These home rooms are shared by two classes each for about half the day. They provide a home base for the students during their whole stay in the high school. Here the heritage subjects are acquired.

Paths lead from these home rooms to a series of larger buildings inside the circumference. One of these is a language laboratory, where large and small spaces are provided for classroom groups and where a well-stocked library of books (fiction and non-fiction), tape recordings, records, films, filmstrips, and other useful aids to learning may be found. Another building houses laboratories. These range in complexity, but all the large laboratories are non-specialized. This building is characterized especially by a fairly large number of very small laboratory spaces, which are assigned to individuals and small groups when they have earned the right to pursue their special abilities and interests. Another feature is a large resources-warehouse, from which can be drawn all the materials and specialized equipment to be used by teacher or students.

A series of vocational shops comes next along this sweep of buildings. Here are the radio, the television, the electronic, and the handicrafts shops. Close by is the graphic-arts building, with all the needed equipment. Provision for the performing arts is made in a large building which is nearly at the center of the campus. Several theaters, in which the stages are the principal feature, a number of television and radio studios, and other such opportunities are provided.

Then there is a large library or cultural-resources building. This has classrooms for all the groups studying history, geometry, geography, ecology, sociology—in short, all the story of man's relation to man. These spaces are clustered on one side of a large library, with its attached collection of films, tape recordings, and other such repositories of experience and wisdom. On the other side of the library is the literature and publications section. This is, of course, related to the library for obvious reasons.

Still another avenue of buildings, in the interior, houses the general administration, the student activities and administration headquarters, the transportation section, the convocation hall, and the recreation building. In one corner of the campus are the playing fields and fieldhouse for the strenuous big-team activities so natural and so desirable for many boys and girls. In another corner are the maintenance shops, and alongside them are the heavy machinery shops for vocational preparation. Down in the corner of this campus, by itself, is a little group of nursery schools, each housed in its own separate structure and each planned not only to serve the needs of little children but to provide educational and observational opportunities for boys and girls of high-school age.

The whole campus profited from the wisdom gained in the development of large suburban shopping centers. Service roads are below level; ample parking has been provided; and yet the whole effect is one of a green campus with beauty spots in unexpected turns. A fuller description of this Children's Village would take into account the basic concept that this is a community of young people in which all their community needs must be met.

High School Serving Community and Youth

The third high school of the future is a community-serving and youth-serving high school. For the sake of identification let me call it the Random Falls High School. Its physical appearance reflects its dual role. A major part of its facilities are found on one large campus, but other facilities operated as part of the high school are spotted all over the district. On the campus itself are to be found buildings primarily for the activities unique to boys and girls of secondary-school age but also facilities not provided elsewhere which will serve the community's need.

John Lyon Reid and I have described this program and its housing elsewhere.[1] I shall not try to recapitulate all that is contained in this proposal. It is one community's response to its understanding of the needs of young people, to its aspirations for the young people and for the community. It is an effort to provide for the needs of all the youth of the community without watering down or diluting the academic or intellectual development of any. Its organization is flexible enough so that young people can really learn at their own rate. Basically it is truly a transitional program—transitional from dependent childhood to independent adulthood. It is distinguished from the Children's Village program largely by two philosophically opposite premises. Children's Village assumes that mature, well-equipped, and well-functioning citizens will result best from a program in which adolescents are trained to function in the world of adolescence, but Random Falls assumes that adolescence is a period of orientation or induction, in which each young person must progressively assume more responsibility as a citizen in the community at large. Children's Village also represents the philosophy that the community is responsible for providing for its young people and that this responsibility is fulfilled through the secondary school. Random Falls apparently believes that the school must more directly serve all the people of the district and that its young people can be best served by increasing their identification with the community as a whole.

[1] Archibald B. Shaw and John Lyon Reid, "A New Look at Secondary Education," *School Executive*, XV (March, 1956), 47–86.

Basic Ideas Held in Common

These are three very different high schools and represent three widely divergent community decisions. However, from the standpoint of housing, they have a great deal in common.

First of all, the future high school will be housed in such a way as to preserve the harmony between man and his natural surroundings. There will be space for trees and grass and other natural beauties, and consequently the school is almost certain to be a campus-type development even on downtown city sites. Most of the great redevelopment plans for downtown areas as well as the large shopping centers and the suburban headquarters-office developments share this concern for a human-scale and a pedestrian, rather than a motorist or mechanical, culture.

Second, the high school of the future will be served by peripheral transportation facilities and sunken or underground service roads.

Third, the buildings themselves will be simple and have much of the temporary about them. As we grow more and more accustomed to the idea of change and to the need for buildings to respond to change, we discover that the smaller building with the less complex structural and mechanical skeleton lends itself most easily to expansion, to flexibility, and to adaptability. It may be that insulation against the weather will be installed over some very large area, within which building units can be spaced. At any rate, space around and between buildings will provide for the easiest possible expansion and contraction of the several facilities as needs change.

The high school of the future will provide opportunities for learning in small groups, medium-sized groups, and large groups. It will take into account the need for solitude and for mass stimulation. It will provide for the most advanced learning aids and for their use by large groups or by individuals.

Most of all, the plant of the high school of the future will be human, warm. It will be designed to meet human needs, to build emotional, as well as physical, comfort. It will reinforce an organization in which the first and greatest consideration will be the provision of opportunity for fine and even great teachers to touch closely the lives of young people. Finally, like the school itself, the plant for the high school of the future will be characterized by variety. It will recognize the variation in learning rates and in the fruitful approaches to learning among young people. It will be no more committed to books alone than to television alone or to projects alone. Rather it will provide for a large variety of activities, each designed to constitute a genuine learning experience. It will be a tool for learning, not a jewel to be admired; a liberating influence, not restraining; human-centered, not machine-centered. This I believe.

Preparing Teachers for the High School of the Future

Our combined secondary-school and college enrolment in 1900 totaled slightly less than one million. Put another way, the elementary schools of the United States enrolled 94 per cent of the total school and college enrolment. If, in truth, those were the good old days of proper classical education, they were enjoyed by only a tiny minority.

Beginning Teachers in 1916 and 1956

In September, 1916, a young and immature person started teaching in a small, four-year, high school. His assignment was to teach all English and Latin, involving eight separate lesson preparations daily. Of course this cannot be done—but it was, painfully and poorly.

First-year Latin enrolled all forty of the ninth-grade students. After a month the young teacher started all over again, under the delusion that all the students could learn Latin and all wanted to. Years later I had the good fortune to observe a Boston master teacher of Latin give a demonstration. Using two attractive six-year-old children as models, she had two Latin students in senior high school display the important Roman costumes, describing how they were made and when they were worn. The costuming was beautiful. Using advertisements from current magazines, the students next convinced the rather skeptical group of state high-school supervisors that, to understand the advertisements, they needed Latin.

For four years in my first teaching position, I struggled to teach Milton's "L'Allegro," "Il Penseroso," "Comus," and "Lycidas." I learned to forget the osteology of the poems; to restrict my "scholarly" analysis of each line; and, in general, to read, and have the students read, the poetry for its own sake. But it was unnecessarily

249

hard going for teacher and students. Almost any fragment of professional education would have been helpful, but I had none. At the end of the four years I was perhaps a passable English teacher and above average as a Latin teacher, but meanwhile many students suffered poor teaching.

Now let us go from my teaching in 1916 to a group of young liberal arts graduates who, after six weeks of special professional education at Temple University, in 1956 began to teach in the high schools of Pennsylvania. These beginning teachers had spent four years (144 weeks) in liberal arts colleges. Assuming that they spent the entire time in liberal arts courses, they had about 96 per cent subject matter and 4 per cent professional education when they started teaching.

Eliminate the six weeks, and we are back a generation to my poor start in teaching—a full turn from no teacher education in 1916 to no teacher education in 1956. Pendulums have a penchant for swinging too far.

These beginning teachers at Temple had been carefully selected. They were to have good supervision. During the three ensuing years they were to complete a Master's degree in teaching with further professional study. Once started, they had infinitely more assistance than I had. I indorse the Temple University experiment and others which attract to our teaching professiona able young men and women. New light on old problems, revival of forgotten good practices, the introduction of newer scientific aids to teaching—are all to the good. If we are to resolve the situation ahead of us, we shall need a variety of experimentation and effort, including experimentation on better ways to give needed instruction in professional education. A generation of experience has convinced me that such instruction is needed.

What professional education should I have had in 1916 prior to teaching English and Latin?

Well, I should have read Virgil. This was but one of my difficulties. An understanding relative with a good library furnished me with an excellent interlinear. My one student in the Virgil class was reasonably bright, and, with the help of the interlinear and the bright student, the young teacher survived.

Let us look at the matter a little more seriously. I had no concept of the past or the then current development of the American public school. I needed to understand the brand new high school in a small-town situation, where a bare half-dozen of the fathers and mothers were college graduates. I have enjoyed reading the biography of Charles Duncan McIver,[1] recently published. As founder of the Carolina College for Women he was in 1891 professor of the art, science, and history of teaching. I needed at least one course under such a professor.

I should have learned that all ninth-grade students should not be required, or expected, to master Latin. Those who demonstrate aptitude for language by mastering English may be encouraged, or even urged, to take Latin. Others may find it a pre-professional course of some value. The young teacher had no knowledge of these things.

I should have had some forewarning of what happens when you try to teach the approved classics to a heterogeneous mixture of high-school boys and girls. Even if it fractured the Carnegie unit, I should have known enough to start where the students were, instead of assuming that they were ready for Milton's minor poems.

I had no idea of grouping within a class so that I might concentrate for specific purposes on a relatively homogeneous group. Later I divided a beginning Latin class into two sections, assigning to one those who made A's and B's and who would study; to the other, those who had difficulties or had to be made to study. I spent considerable time with the entire group, but I often excused the brighter section to read additional Latin, to study, or to go to the library. The abler group put on plays for assembly, assuming responsibilities for Roman dress and staging and having the whole class join in a Latin chorus.

Observation and practice teaching under supervision would have been the best professional preparation. Some methodology of teaching high-school students and an elementary knowledge of adolescents in general and of high-school youth in particular would have been helpful. The one conclusion I draw is that I was not prepared to teach English and Latin. I do not want any teacher in the future to start as I did.

[1] Rose Howell Holder, *McIver of North Carolina* (Chapel Hill, North Carolina: University of North Carolina Press, 1957).

A Proposed Program of Teacher Education

The Council on Cooperation in Teacher Education held a conference in 1956 in Princeton and issued a good summary report.[2] *A Fourth of a Nation,* by Paul Woodring,[3] supplies helpful suggestions. There are innumerable other reports and studies on the state of schools and teaching in the United States. Although some changes in the American secondary school will come, I do not expect the highly selective college-preparatory school to replace the American comprehensive high school. The changes that do come will be best handled by teachers who retain the flexibility which goes with continued study and investigation and experiment.

Suppose liberal arts professors and professors of education were given the time and money needed to formulate a program of preparation for high-school teachers and to implement it. It would be a dastardly deed, of course, for professors, like the rest of us, enjoy complaining about things with which they are familiar.

Let us eliminate the extremists of the liberal arts crowd—those who believe that a good liberal arts education, uncontaminated with methodology of any kind, is desirable for beginning high-school teachers. They seem happiest flying backwards. Let us eliminate their opposite numbers among the educationists—those whose concern is to keep the present duplication of professional education courses or who would prefer to have more courses rather than fewer.

Now presumably there remain the reasonable professors on both sides—we good folk if we care to be unctuous about it. But, since I cannot speak for the liberal arts or the education professors, let me speak solely for myself.

1. I do not believe that liberal arts professors can, or will, work out a teacher-training program. I ask of them understanding, a sympathetic attitude, and a bit more encouragement of the good students to enter teaching. Only the rare liberal arts professors will visit high schools and tailor somewhat their courses for the benefit

[2] *The Preparation of Secondary School Teachers* (Report of a Conference Held at the Princeton Inn, Princeton, New Jersey, September 28–29, 1956 [Washington, D.C.: Council on Cooperation in Teacher Education, American Council on Education]).

[3] Paul Woodring, *A Fourth of a Nation* (New York: McGraw-Hill Book Co., Inc., 1957).

of future teachers. May the Lord bless those who do. I charge some liberal arts professors with sabotage. On account of these, many liberal arts graduates have enhanced their natural conceit and have learned to look down their Roman or Greek noses at the barbarians who teach professional education and at their students who are preparing to teach.

It *is* possible for a liberal arts professor to visit high schools. I recall a university professor of mathematics and his wife, a former high-school teacher of mathematics, who on an occasion years ago visited all the mathematics teachers in the junior and senior high schools in and about Lexington, Kentucky. They concluded that some mathematics teachers were poor despite their mathematics major (something that they had not realized quite so fully before) and that others were good regardless of how much mathematics they had studied in college. These severe but fair-minded critics became more enlightened and sympathetic.

I object to the kind of attitude exhibited recently by a young professor of chemistry in a liberal arts college. "You will never get good high-school science teachers," he said, "until you pay them more." This is essentially true. Then he added, "As long as you won't pay high-school teachers of science enough, you won't get them, and I can do nothing to help." This casual dismissal of a problem which all of us educationists have to live with is a disclaimer of responsibility, with an irritatingly virtuous attitude.

2. I believe that there is no quick magic or breakthrough which will give us a new and better program but that more imagination in a synthesis of the best we know, and can do, will achieve a reasonable facsimile.

As I have read the celebrated Flexner story of the reform of medical education,[4] I have been impressed with what was done: the quality of medical faculties and students was raised; modern laboratories and teaching hospitals for "practice doctoring" were constructed; and medical schools were made part of a larger university center of learning. The breakthrough was an idea of quality and the money necessary to achieve it.

[4] Abraham Flexner, *Medical Education in the United States and Canada* (A Report to the Carnegie Foundation for the Advancement of Teaching, Bulletin No. 4 [New York: The Foundation, 1910]).

The Vanderbilt University medical faculty resigned to permit the selection of a new faculty. That was radical enough to be designated as a breakthrough. I doubt if I could have persuaded any faculty with which I have worked to resign en masse.

Most of the ideas seem to have emanated from Johns Hopkins University, where a fortunate combination of brilliant men who could co-operate set the pattern. It was similar in general to the popular education development at Teachers College about 1905, when Strayer, Suzzallo, Bruce Ryburn Payne, and others were studying together, getting ready to start a new pattern of professional education.

3. I believe an analysis of the best we have achieved, or are now achieving, in teacher education is helpful. For example, laboratory schools have lost their glamor and lighthouse position. Do away with them then? No, that surely must be wrong, because it is too easy. When Harvard and Yale, for example, have slipped into decades of academic doldrums, the trustees, to recover their eminence, have not abolished the universities but have sought a new administration or new professors or more money. I propose that laboratory schools be restored to their lighthouse positions. But how, it may be asked.

First, pay 'em, as Al Capp says. Pay the teachers. A generation ago, a Peabody leader remarked that the Peabody Demonstration School teachers were the best in Tennessee, and he added, "They ought to be, for we pay every teacher a thousand dollars more than any other teacher in Tennessee." That is no longer true at Peabody or any other laboratory school that I know. Let us try ten or twelve thousand dollars annually, and see what happens. At least we would know speedily if money is the answer, and it would not take a superlative amount of money to find out.

Parenthetically, I recall an instance concerning a well-known basketball coach in an American university. The administration found what salaries were being paid basketball coaches and saw to it that he got five hundred dollars more than any of them. At the time this was not a very big amount. The distinction of being the highest-paid basketball coach in America may not appeal to you, but I dare say it appealed to the coach. A sum of money which would put some laboratory-school teachers approximately on a par with college faculties in the matter of salaries and training and prestige would be a worth-while experiment.

Second, convert these laboratory schools into attractive and interesting experimental centers, as resources for public school systems trying to build experimental programs of quality. Employ those who thrive on vision and productivity. Then, and then only, will visitors find their calls stimulating and even exciting, as was true in the 1920's when I first visited the Lincoln Experimental School.

Third, make the laboratory schools exemplars of the best in scientific aids. I have never trusted magic gadgets. I never believed that the beautiful girl in tights really floated through the air. But magic gadgets—and beautiful girls, for that matter—may be powerful aids to any enterprise. The proper use of television and other scientific aids is a handmaiden to the good teacher.

Fourth, let us get rid of our pedagogical fetish that we must select average or worse-than-average conditions for demonstration or experiment. We want also examples of what can be done under the best conditions, ideal and wonderful examples which challenge our imagination. To be sure, both prospective and experienced teachers need to observe average and below-average conditions.

4. A word about college preparation. Let us keep sharply in mind that four or even five years of college is simply an introduction to learning. What is learned in college must always be a tiny fraction of what is known, and the denominator of this fraction keeps increasing so that the learned man of 1921, had he stopped learning then, would be pretty ignorant in 1957.

Let us, then, eliminate the academic fetish that the high-school teachers of Latin or English or history must have nice fat majors of specialization, or at least little skinny minors. After a year of graduate Latin, I was prone to teach the exceptions too soon. Sound pedagogy says to concentrate on a few general principles until these are learned. Once we accept as a fact the impossibility of learning enough in four or five years to be a good teacher, we can eliminate some of our *non sequitur*'s in the preparation of teachers. So long as the head of the English department insists that, to teach English literature, one must study all the minor English writers, we shall not get what we need.

5. I would wish for the teacher in preparation the good, func-

tional, four-year college education that should be the lot of all contributing citizens. The emphasis would be on general education or liberal education modified to become more immediately cultural.

I would devote seven semesters to general education—"subject matter," if you prefer the term—and one semester to learning how to teach. I would start afresh and challenge the professor of education to determine what are a few important things for the prospective teacher to know, and see, and learn how to do. Let us eliminate from professional education things like children's literature, child development, and much of our music and art. These are, or ought to be, good general education for all.

Most needed is a sympathetic understanding of our unique and peculiarly American doctrine of free and universal education. The student is least likely to get this in a private liberal arts college. When the president of an Ivy League university advises parents to send their boys to preparatory schools and at the same time public high school graduates in his own Freshman and Sophomore classes make better records than do private-school graduates, then surely an appreciation of the American public high school must be bootlegged into that institution. It will be over or around his dead academic body. There are liberal arts colleges where both knowledge and appreciation of the American public high school are taught, but it seems to go as much against the grain as for a big-time coach to worry over average football players.

This one semester of professional education or its equivalent should emphasize the practicum: practice teaching or internship, visiting homes of children, examples of fifth-grade reading, and so on. The professional teacher is going to deal with mass America. He needs firsthand impressions of what is back of the thirty or forty ninth-graders in his class, who look a good bit alike. He should follow them home and see the other nine-tenths of their environment.

My list of knowledge needed by the prospective teacher would include also some of the applications of psychology and research which are immediately useful: that there is little relation between intelligence and superior spelling; that many persons are born and later die with no evidence of mathematical aptitude or achievement; that only those bright enough to observe small distinctions ever become language scholars; that, on the contrary, almost anyone can learn to speak a second language with enough skill to communicate; that demonstrations of science are excellent for some purposes and some persons and bad for others; that, to teach love or even tolerance of literature, we start where Johnny is; and so on. Make your own list. Go further. Teach the young candidate for teaching that he or she may live to refute some of these findings or theories.

After four years I would prefer a year or two of experience and a return for graduate work and further professional study. A young Englishman who had just completed the full year of preparation for teaching which is now required in England, in addition to three years of subject-matter study, stated in a letter to the *London Times* last summer that he approved the program but that it would be best offered after a year of actual teaching. He has a point. If the students can stand it, it's good.

How many courses, hours, credits? I would arrange these to suit the state department of education. I learned long ago to label high-school civics or problems in citizenship as one-half unit of political science. It got the student into college and made the registrar as happy as a registrar can be. The registrar is concerned with paper compliance; that is his job. Let's not tangle with the keeper of the records on any except real problems.

Why the Proposed Program Is Not Adopted

Why not do what I have suggested? Well, someone has said that, to achieve any really worth-while reform in the college curriculum, we need brand-new professors and deans. Some deans of education and some professors of education will take as dim a view of cutting down courses and offerings as the liberal arts professor does of adding them. Nor does this myopia belong solely to education professors. At one university I counted twenty-eight separate semester courses offered by one man, the head of the department of Latin and Greek. His department was gone but not from the catalogue. He took umbrage when I suggested the elimination of some of the window dressing, at least all the Greek courses, in which there had been no registrations during the past decade. Do I need to tell you that there was no change until he retired? Do I need to argue the case for compulsory retirement?

We used to require in a university college of education either three or six semester hours (depending on the influence of the professor of educational measurement) of tests and measurements as part of the requirements for graduation. Tests and measurements still have their place, but the part that is useful for most teachers can be gained as part of a seminar.

A generation ago professors of education who taught methods of teaching geography spent much of their time teaching geography. One of my colleagues now teaches methods of teaching mathematics, required for certification in some states, and the students complain that he teaches mathematics all the time. A professor of English may bootleg in a little methodology. An excellent liberal arts professor of English discovered that lesson plans which he insisted on for his English majors expecting to teach meant units of work in the teachers' college. A seminar for professors might be helpful.

I know an education professor who can teach only about the core curriculum; so back and forth he goes. He has one or two excellent lectures which even liberal arts professors would enjoy hearing, but his real contribution could be briefer and better. He could then have time to learn something new.

Once I visited a beginning class in philosophy at Vassar. The instructor was dealing with philosophy before Plato's time. At the rate of progress observed on the morning I visited, the instructor and class would do well to reach Plato six semester hours later. Both the educationist and the young professor of philosophy could do better.

A Professional Credo

Lest I be accused of ambivalence or something worse, I would like to state briefly my professional credo. I am by lifelong practice and belief an educationist. I believe in teacher education. No young man or woman should be certificated to teach in the high schools of the future without some period of definite professional preparation. I choose the side of the embattled professor of education and the teachers' college and mass education with a full knowledge of our limitations and weaknesses, with which I should be more conversant than the critics who devote only part time and little study to the business of mass education.

Having taken this position, I would be most flexible and reasonable about what should be taken by the teacher in training. I am glad a variety of methods are being tried. The experiment of taking liberal arts graduates and giving them a fifth year, under whatever particular circumstance, has been good. Of course it could not possibly "solve" the teacher shortage, because only a handful of the best students are going to be attracted into teaching by this particular procedure. Nevertheless it is all to the good.

Many of the high-school teachers of the future are going to come from the sources they have always come from, that is, from the small cities and towns and from rural areas. There are still thousands of young men and women of average and above-average mind and character who would like to teach, and not all of them have that opportunity. Teaching is still the open highway for many boys and girls who consider teaching an honor.

I regret the development of the sharp divergence of interests and attitudes between the liberal arts professors and the education professors. If I could, I would wave a magic wand and bring about a kind of integration, if that word can still be used without undue significance, of aims and efforts and understanding. The intransigence of the liberal arts professors brought about the teachers' colleges. Now more liberal arts colleges have, somewhat belatedly, evinced interest in their responsibility for preparing teachers for secondary schools. We should welcome their efforts if they are in earnest.

At George Peabody College I preside over a unique situation: our liberal arts professors in history, mathematics, and other areas rub shoulders daily with our education professors. The result seems, in the climate of American academic opinion, unbelievable. They actually like each other and show as much respect for each other as can be expected of a group of professors. There is a common interest in American public education. The education professors have their share of keys and other academic honors. Yes, we have our controversies, but rarely are they organized into warring camps of liberal arts versus professional education. The faculty has enough ingenious things to argue about without using up their polemic talents on each other. The reason? Well, we live close together in an institution long dedicated to the teaching profession on a campus with a laboratory school and many interesting efforts to improve schools and school buildings and school teaching.

Just as America of tomorrow has the most wonderful potential of any America we have ever had, so do you and I, liberal arts professors and professors of education and intelligent laymen and leaders, face the most wonderful opportunity of providing a finer education for more people than any which has ever been offered. As the former president of Harvard University, James B. Conant, well states it (and I paraphrase): "The mission of America has not been in the field of sculpture, painting, and the fine arts, or law-giving, but rather to extend to an increasing majority of people those privileges in other ages undreamed of except by the prophets and seers."[5]

An educational renaissance which includes the average is not to be dreaded but welcomed. A more imaginative teacher education of better quality is necessary if we do justice to the average or the bright. A more flexible program of general education is necessary. We can, if we will, share the best with more people in America and the world.

[5] James B. Conant, *Education in a Divided World* (Cambridge, Massachusetts: Harvard University Press, 1948), pp. 234–35.

V

*The Planning and Administration of the High
School Are Examined with Special
Attention to the Responsibilities
of Citizens*

Laymen Help Plan the High School
of the Future

Everyone now seems to agree with a statement made by Terry Fer-
rer, the new education editor of the *New York Herald Tribune:* "The
public is awakening to education as never before, and education is
at last awakening to the public's demands."[1]

If this is true (and I hope it is), the question seems to be: How
do we get the most mileage out of this great public interest? How
do we direct this general awareness to help shape more effective
educational programs? And how do we get for education the kind
of support that is still so sorely needed?

Conditions Requiring Educator-Layman Partnership

Those who have analyzed the emerging American scene have
made it unmistakably plain that the challenge of the new era is different in kind, as well as in degree, from anything we have known.
I am convinced that this unprecedented challenge means that both
laymen and educators must take a new, hard look at our partnership
roles, re-assess the size of the job, and try to tally the pluses and
minuses in our approach to it so far.

After trying to do so for myself, I am happy to say that I find
more pluses than minuses. We have learned a lot from each other.
Educators, on the one hand, have learned that they need more than
money from the public—that the layman's role in providing good
schools is, or should be, much more significant than just paying the
bill. William Carr, the National Education Association's executive
secretary, has emphasized this very point:

He who expects citizens' committees to concern themselves solely with
more money for schools expects the impossible. These committees are

[1] *New York Herald Tribune,* October 20, 1957, sec. 2, p. 3.

bound to inquire what changes would make our schools better. They cannot answer that question without considering what is wrong with the schools we now have.[2]

Just a few years ago this would have been a startling statement for a school man to make, and the occasional layman who had any questions about the schools was vague and incoherent in expressing them. Now, thousands of laymen have learned to ask questions intelligently, in a spirit of sincere co-operation with our new partners in education.

One of the postwar pioneers in this kind of questioning, Mr. Albert L. Furth, of Chappaqua, New York, started his fellow townsmen thinking about their local high school at about the time the National Citizens Commission for the Public Schools was launched. Speaking at a local parent-teachers' association forum, Mr. Furth said that, although their high school was generally considered one of the best in the metropolitan area, they were meeting "because, it appears, Chappaqua doesn't know where its high school is going."

The speaker went on to say that, in a month of intensive study and many personal interviews undertaken as homework for the forum, he had encountered "fully fifty definitions of education" which no one would be likely to disagree with. But he had also found that each citizen to whom he talked had some sort of doubt or misgiving about the high-school program.

He had concluded that the real split he had found in the community's thinking about how well the school was doing its job resulted from the lack of any real agreement on what the job was. There were those who argued that the high school was dominated by a college-preparatory influence, which neglected or misdirected the non-college-bound minority but at the same time failed to stir the highly gifted to their best efforts. Others argued in the familiar pattern that a "classical" education was best for all—that it was up to "inspired teachers" to awaken slow students rather than "shunting them off to shops."

As we all know, these disagreements still exist, in one form or another, in nearly every community in the land. It would appear that

2 William G. Carr, "New Forces in the Government of the Public Schools," in *Parents and the Schools* (Thirty-sixth Yearbook of the Department of Elementary School Principals, Bulletin of the Department of Elementary School Principals, Vol. XXXVII, No. 1 [Washington: Department of Elementary School Principals, 1957]), p. 9.

a basic trouble with secondary education is that people in general have not made up their minds what the high school should do. This is natural with any young institution whose size and functions have expanded so rapidly. The comprehensive high school, an American invention, is younger than many of my readers—a fact that is not realized by the public at large. But interested citizens are becoming increasingly aware that, if we do not establish a clear sense of goals and priorities, our high schools will do an excellent job of preparing students for the wrong things.

The birth of universal education has coincided not only with the birth of a new universe of knowledge but also with the greatest need for highly trained and broadly educated people in our history. And the American citizen is demanding that, in the face of ever increasing numbers of students, we must raise our standards higher than ever before, so that *all* our children, including those who will lead the nation in the decades ahead, will get educational opportunity equal to their capacities.

This dilemma, in Chappaqua, led to a two-year study of the basic questions: "Whom are *we* trying to educate, and for what?" and "What do *we* mean by education?" The study committee came up with two working hypotheses: that a community cannot generalize about its school from the experience of others but must define its own goals and that the *differentiation* among its students demands a program broad enough to develop the whole range of its students' capacities.

Now I submit that this was a fairly intelligent approach for a group of laymen to take toward the re-planning of their high-school program, and I have given this much attention to one citizens' study group to point up what I believe are some new attitudes, new approaches, new intelligence, and new understanding that our school administrators, as they try to help shape the high school of the future, can expect to find among parents and other citizens in many communities.

Parents Exhibit a New Understanding

In large part this new understanding stems from the success of our schools in the broadening of educational opportunity in our country during the past twenty-five or thirty years. For the first time in public school history, our administrators and teachers are now able to work with parents most of whom have had at least a high-school education. This fact, of course, creates problems as well as opportunities for the educator, but it is my hope and belief that the positive values will far outweigh the new problems it may bring.

We should remember that the present generation of school parents is providing the industrial managers and the skilled workers responsible for the tremendous industrial and technological advances made by the United States in the postwar years. If we can now turn their attention to our schools, this generation has the same great potential, it seems to me, for helping to achieve some of the advances that our educators would like to make in planning our high-school programs for today and the future. The often-mentioned "fifty-year lag" for the spread of new educational ideas has already been reduced, I have heard it said, to twenty or thirty years. But it is my impression that, if we make our educator-citizen partnership sound enough and broad enough, the intelligence and energy of this new generation can further telescope the age-old lag—perhaps wipe it out altogether.

American business is taking note of the important role that the educational level of today's families is playing in our rising standards of living. A nationwide *Study of Consumer Expenditures*[3] shows clearly the significance of education, even for marketers. Income level is no longer the sole reliable barometer of consumer taste or of upgraded demands. The study shows that the higher the level of education in a household, the greater the share of family income that is spent for home improvements or for things which make for the good life.

Some persons may say that many of these so-called improvements are merely material comforts. And I would agree that we still place too high a value on material things; what we spend for them compared to what we have been spending for education would certainly seem to prove the case. But there is another side to the picture. The return of the large family; the increasing number of protesters against materialism, mediocrity, and conformity; and the fact that some of our most heated arguments about the public schools concern moral and spiritual values convince me that the number and

---

[3] *"Life's" Study of Consumer Expenditures: A Background for Marketing Decisions* (conducted for *Life* by Alfred Politz Research, Inc. [New York: Time, Inc., 1957]).

influence of individualists among us is growing, rather than declining, and that the real heart of America is more dedicated to personal and social fulfilment than it has ever been.

I am sure of one thing about today's citizen: he wants the *best* high-school education for his children. And he insists that this education can be, and should be, provided in the public schools. He may not know what the "best" education for his children is, but he is trying to find out. He is rapidly acquiring a new awareness of the school's role and of his own role in supporting education, and, generally speaking, he has a new ability, and up to a point a willingness, to pay more for good schools.

In the past decade, twenty million of this new generation of educated Americans have migrated to the new Suburbia. Many of these now fast-growing centers were old, mostly well-to-do towns which attracted these newcomers as good places to live and bring up children. High on the list of their attractions were the schools, the churches, and other public services. What has happened in most of these cases is that, once the community has readjusted to the influx, there has been a general leveling *up*, not down, to maintain and advance the high standards that existed formerly.

The influence of this new type of parent is being felt, not only in the communities, but on the national scene. And a new point of view has been established by business and public leaders. One of its most effective proponents is the layman and parent who served as chairman of the White House Conference on Education and who is now our secretary of defense. On the eve of assuming his new duties, Neil McElroy said: "The greatness of our nation depends on the educational advancement of its people, on the constant outward push of the limits of learning." Mr. McElroy is but one of the many business and public leaders who hold this view.

The *will* for a general outward push is here. How to set it in motion?

Experimentation Needed in Educator-Layman Partnership

The experience of countless communities indicates that there is *no one way* to set the will in motion. There are many ways. Each of us—educator, businessman, politician, housewife, laborer—has his own contribution to make. And there are essential steps we must take to make such contributions possible.

It is my deep conviction that our revived partnership of citizens and educators must not, in the years ahead, be allowed to waver or dissolve. Instead, it must be strengthened and extended. When it is charged that we have failed, to date, in getting the needed financial support for our schools, can it also be said that we have sufficiently encouraged the involvement of lay citizens in planning and action in order to spread understanding of the schools' programs and problems?

Oldsters among our lay friends are fond of referring to the good old days of the little red schoolhouse, the rattan rod, and the three R's—much to our dismay. Among school people, also, are there not perhaps some "good-old-days" thinkers who are still fearful of "meddling parents" or fearful of making changes, even experimentally, because they might not be understood by the community?

Probably so. And the job is to make sure that the need for experimentation in education, as in everything else, *is* understood. Great progress has been made in many communities. But it is my impression that the process of change in the schools has, paradoxically, reversed itself in the past thirty years. In the 1920's the leadership for experimentation came from professional educators; it was the public that had to be convinced. Today some professional educators are among those who are apparently opposed to really sympathetic consideration of some of the experimentation that is under way in many communities. I am thinking, for example, of current experiments in school reorganization, early admission to college, open- and closed-circuit television in classrooms, teachers' aides, and merit-pay programs. Many lay citizens, quite understandably, want to test the potential of all these ideas.

We cannot be sure, of course, that any of these new things will bring better education. But there are two things we can be sure of. First, what we are now doing, broadly speaking, will not be good enough to meet the educational demands on our society in this last half of the century. Second, even if our current programs were good enough, all the facts seem to indicate that we simply cannot preserve them unchanged. Therefore, to the interested layman it seems that perhaps the least risk and the greatest hope for education lies in some courageous experimentation along new lines.

I believe it is time for bold, even venturesome, changes in the attitude of more educators toward the community—time to bring responsible, interested laymen wholeheartedly into administrative and policy planning, just as wholeheartedly as they would like their fellow citizens to respond to the inevitable need for higher taxes for school support.

The great need to involve laymen in planning for the schools is why I believe so strongly in the unique value of the National Citizens Council for Better Schools. The council was organized from the grass roots to expand the program started by the former National Citizens Commission for the Public Schools—the program of arousing citizen interest and increasing the broad public understanding necessary to proper support of our schools. To quote William G. Carr once more, "The complaint counter is going to be busy, but every merchant knows that a shortage of buyers is much worse than too many complaints."[4]

Citizens Ready To Support Improved Schools

Two successive Congresses have been unwilling or unable to respond to the call of the White House Conference on Education for federal support of an emergency program for building schools. Meanwhile, national publicity attesting to the growing citizen awareness of ever growing school financial needs has emboldened many state and local leaders to propose or to support considerably stepped-up taxes for school programs.

The great majority of these proposals have found wide local acceptance. Often, indeed, the political leaders have found that the people were far ahead of them. It is true that many needed proposals have been turned down or delayed by local taxpayer resistance. But in most such instances, our studies indicate, the public had not been brought in early enough on the planning which required the new tax proposals.

This hard-learned lesson apparently cannot be overemphasized. Too often, still, small groups of educators and citizens have worked out sound and essential plans only to have them rejected for lack of broad public understanding. Fortunately, however, most school communities which have experienced defeats of this kind now know that, once the people understand school needs and get involved in planning and action to meet them, money ceases to be a primary problem.

4 William G. Carr, *op. cit.*, p. 9.

That is not to say that the financial problem is on the way to being solved. It is becoming clearer every day that the cost of providing the educational programs we need is far beyond the sights so far set by citizen taxpayers across the nation. Today we are spending about thirteen billion dollars on our public elementary and secondary schools, or a per capita expenditure of a little more than seventy-five dollars—a total of less than 3 per cent of our current gross national product. We are getting our education cheap—much too cheap for our own good.

But here, it seems to me, we are up against a national mood with regard to the expansion of all our basic community services. In the face of an exploding population, it is distressing to note the general feeling that we have all the things we need and it is time to start cutting taxes. With regard to this delusion, dramatized in the closing speeches in Congress last summer, Columnist Walter Lippmann had this to say:

The country has been left with the impression, which will dominate almost every great problem, that if we could cut expenditures by a few more billion dollars, it would be possible to reduce the income tax. This is a dangerous untruth to propagate. . . .

There is no prospect now in sight of an agreement to slow down the race of armaments. There is, on the contrary, much evidence that the race is swifter. . . .

Nor can we escape the consequences of the fact that our population is increasing at a prodigious rate—and that almost every necessary public facility is overburdened. This is true of the public schools, the colleges and the universities, where as the school population rises, the quality of education is deteriorating. . . . What we should be hearing from Washington, and talking about ourselves, is not tax cuts . . . but how to meet our responsibilities and to do our duty.[5]

In my opinion, we have very little time to heed Mr. Lippmann's warning. We can no longer afford the lag in educational planning which inadequate support inevitably brings. Such a lag is likely to produce schools that can serve only yesterday's needs. In thinking of tomorrow's children, we must realize that they will live and work in a world as different from today's as today's is different from the world we grew up in. And to prepare them for the world of the future means that we not only must update and support, but must toughen up, our educational programs to a level of unprecedented challenge for both students and teachers alike.

[5] Walter Lippmann, "Today and Tomorrow," *New York Herald Tribune,* September 5, 1957, p. 18.

Students Ready To Work To Learn

Fortunately it appears that the atmosphere for lifting scholarship standards has never been more favorable. Not only do today's parents have a new seriousness and understanding of the value of education, but our students' attitudes have changed dramatically in the last few years. This began, apparently, with the G.I. Bill and the veterans' earnest approach to the privileges it gave them. Since then the word has gotten around to young people that education is important to them personally. Our college-bound high-school students are becoming more and more aware that they will not be able to get into the colleges of their choice, perhaps not into college at all, without records of high-school accomplishment which hard work alone can achieve.

Robert Marschner, the president of the school board in Homewood, Illinois, made a study of "outstanding high schools" in order to establish some guide lines for planning Homewood's new high school for 1,250 students.[6] He freely admitted that his investigations were limited; to begin with, he said, he could find no generally accepted criteria of a good high school. But one extremely interesting finding in this widely publicized one-man survey was the indication by most of the principals who were questioned by Mr. Marschner that the decisive factor in their students' scholarship achievement was plain hard work. As one of them put it, "We simply refuse to accept mediocrity." And another, "We started high and have raised our standards from year to year."

I would like to think that the report of Mr. Marschner's findings will prove to be an effective and significant document for any citizens' group helping to plan the high school of the future in its community. The basic ingredients of "hard work" and "high standards" must apply to the programs for all our high-school students to insure more solid groundwork for their continuing learning—whether in college, in the military forces, or on the job.

Raising the Status of the Teacher

An essential part of the citizen's job in helping to shape the high school of the future is to lift the role of the teacher until it is in proper proportion to his great importance to all phases of our na-

[6] *Time,* LXX (October 21, 1957), 52.

tional development. Simple logic places the primary resonsibility for this enormous and continuing problem squarely at the door of society. Therefore I submit that laymen must work at a much faster pace than they have been doing in recent years to end the shocking state of affairs in which our teachers have actually been penalized by inadequate status and rewards. Meanwhile, the layman asks, is it not possible through merit-pay programs, through other adaptations of some of industry's practices, to raise the pay ceilings for more of our outstanding teachers?

I am impressed by the special projects launched by many communities to enlist "resource people" for supplementary instruction and to fill the gap of an increasing teacher shortage. Many of our citizens from business, from science laboratories, and from law have much to give in such a program, and I would hope that there could be some broader formalization of opportunities for them to do so.

Assuming an increasing shortage of really competent teachers, I believe that we must depend more and more on the highly trained teacher to become the leader of a team of teachers (some trained and some not trained), who collectively would perform the various functions involved in effective teaching and learning. Would not the higher salaries paid these group leaders enable us to reward more adequately our most competent teachers and serve to attract more of our ablest youths into the profession?

A Concluding Word

These are questions the layman must leave with his educator-partner, in the mutual effort to meet the seemingly insoluble problem of maintaining quality goals in the face of ever increasing numbers of students. He does so with confidence and with the full knowledge that his partner represents the profession which has brought universal education in this country to the highest level the world has ever known.

In this lay-professional partnership, I think, we have what it takes to shape and support the high school of the future. But the future is very much with us; we are building tomorrow's schools today. God speed us all in our task!

WILLIAM HENRY SHAW

Responsibilities of Educators and Laymen in Developing the High School

The early schools of America were close to the people. In fact, they were created by the people. Every parent and lay citizen knew the school intimately and took part in shaping the community educational program. The teachers even lived in the homes of the children who attended school. Even today the board of education, in the small community at least, is about the most important group in the entire community. The selection of a high-school site, the construction of the new high-school building, and the employment of the high-school principal or coach still get the headlines in the local newspaper.

Today, especially in urban centers, community life has become more complex, and other agencies and institutions are competing for public interest and support. Many lay citizens feel that the school program is too complex to be understood easily. For a long time, people have taken the school for granted and have left policy-forming to the board of education and to the educators. However, if the schools are to reflect the interest and welfare of the community, citizens must interest themselves in the program of the high school and must participate in its future plans.

A half-century ago the American high school was primarily a college-preparatory institution, but this is no longer the case. Today the American high school enrols more than 80 per cent of the youth between fourteen and seventeen years of age. Of every one hundred youths seventeen years of age in 1953–54, sixty were graduated from high school.[1] Since 1890, with the exception of the years during World War II, the per cent of students of high-school age who

[1] United States Office of Education, *Statistical Summary of Education, 1953–54*, Table 15, p. 27, in *Biennial Survey of Education of the United States, 1952–54*, chap. i (Washington: Government Printing Office, 1957).

273

attended high school has increased steadily, rising from 7 to more than 80.

In the days when seven out of every one hundred youths of high-school age were graduated from high school, laymen were not greatly concerned about the high school. Today, with sixty out of every one hundred being graduated from high school, laymen have become intensely interested in the type of training our high-school students are receiving. This interest and concern are manifested in the remarkable growth and effectiveness of citizens' councils and committees throughout the nation.

If educators and laymen are to work effectively together in discharging their responsibilities for developing a high-school program to meet the challenge of the new era, they must first come to a common understanding of present-day goals and current trends in high-school education. Furthermore, there must be greater understanding of certain pressing and perplexing problems which face the schools today. This is not the place to attempt a thorough analysis of goals and trends, but it will serve our purposes in this discussion to draw attention briefly to some of them.

Goals and Trends of Secondary Education

For a long time, the American people have set certain goals for secondary education. Three of the major goals are rooted deep in the American democratic way of life. They may be stated as follows:

1. To make secondary education available to every boy and girl in the United States regardless of social and economic status, race, nationality, political affiliation, or religious belief.
2. To make the high school a tuition-free public school, supported by taxes and separated from religious organizations in administration and curriculum.
3. To provide curriculums which will be congruous with the needs, interests, and capacities of the boys and girls who attend the high school.

Among the trends reflected in the writings of educators and in current practices in the schools, the following may be cited:

1. To consider the nature and needs of the "whole child"—his intellectual, physical, social, and emotional development.
2. To relate the education of youth to their present needs as well as to life's future demands.
3. To make the school a part of the community and the community a part of the school—to use the school to improve the quality of living for all and to use the community to extend the learning experiences of youth.

4. To serve the needs of all youth in accordance with their talents and abilities—to educate the rapid learner, the slow learner, and other students in ways that are most useful to them and to society.
5. To consider the interests, educational needs, and goals of young people in planning the curriculum.

If the lay public understood these and other goals and trends in secondary education, we should hear less uninformed and reckless criticism of the schools. Informed criticism is wholesome and useful and should be welcomed by educators and laymen alike. It is the responsibility of educators, working with lay leaders, to interpret the goals of high-school education to the public and to indicate how certain trends are related to these goals. In the degree to which this is done, criticism is likely to be informed and constructive.

Let me illustrate with one example: the increased freedom of high-school students and their more active participation in a wide variety of extra-curriculum activities. Our students have a great deal of freedom in working together and in planning their work throughout the school day. They engage in a large number of activities which some critics consider foreign to the central purposes of the high school and which, these critics allege, interfere with academic achievement.

In this connection certain data about the entering Freshman class at Yale University in the fall of 1957 are interesting.[2] From 4,000 applicants, 1,010 Freshmen were admitted, who represented 476 public and private schools from 46 states. The study shows that these Freshmen, while in high school, had participated in many extra-curriculum activities:

> 554 had won varsity letters for at least one sport.
> 131 were varsity captains.
> 158 were presidents of their class or student council.
> 139 held class offices other than the presidency
> 118 were chief editors of school publications.
> 216 were on editorial boards.
> 312 sang in school glee clubs.
> 147 were presidents of extra-curriculum clubs.

These data give evidence that participation in high-school activities is not incompatible with academic achievement and college preparation.

[2] "Freshmen Are Culled from Many Applicants," *Lovejoy's College Guidance Digest,* X (September, 1957), 4.

The Problem of Organization

The organization of the American high school has undergone considerable change in the past half-century. First of all, the introduction of the concept of "secondary" education, as contrasted with high-school education, extended the period to include Grades VII through XIV. The traditional four-year high school embracing Grades IX through XII came to be only one of several patterns of organization. Today we have junior high schools, senior high schools, junior colleges, and a number of other combinations of Grades VII through XIV. In planning the high school of the future, educators and laymen together will have to examine the relative merits of these and other patterns of organization. The new era calls for bold experimentation with a variety of organizational patterns.

Another aspect of the high-school organization which calls for critical re-examination is the nature of the student body which should be grouped together for instruction. At present we have a variety of types of high schools: comprehensive, technical, commercial, trade, vocational, college-preparatory, and special schools for the gifted. Arguments can be advanced for and against each of these types. Indeed public discussion of this question is likely to grow more voluminous and intense as the demands for more science and mathematics and for a higher quality of high-school education increase. Here, too, educators and laymen must share responsibility for major policy decisions affecting the nature and quality of education offered in the high school. Perhaps school administrators have been too preoccupied with school buildings and school finance to give adequate attention to the quality of education that high-school students have been receiving. In any event, laymen today are taking a hard look at the product of the schools, and many are voicing dissatisfaction.

Economy in School Construction

Another area in which school men and laymen can work effectively together is in the planning of the building program. The sharp increase in school population in recent years has required the erection of new school buildings in virtually every community, and the rising tide in high-school enrolments will place unusually heavy burdens on many communities in the years just ahead. Coupled with this sudden demand for new schools is the sharp rise in building costs. The high costs have naturally caused many citizens to raise questions about our building programs. Have school men and boards of education become extravagant? Are our school buildings too luxurious?

No one will deny that new school buildings today, in both rural areas and urban centers, are commodious and attractive. But they are not extravagant. A recent release from the American Association of School Administrators, entitled "Stretching the School Building Dollar," presents evidence to support the assertion that communities today are getting "more mileage out of the school-building dollar than people in this country are getting out of the dollars they spend for nearly any other product or commodity."[3] Here are the facts:

> During the past twenty years the cost of—
> School buildings has increased 150 per cent
> All buildings has increased 210 per cent
> General construction has increased 275 per cent
> Medium-priced brick residences has increased 225 per cent
> Medium-priced frame residences has increased 228 per cent
> Highway construction has increased 200 per cent
> Automobiles has increased more than 200 per cent.[4]

It is not surprising that building costs have increased, for the stuff out of which buildings are made has risen sharply in this period.

> During the past twenty years the cost of—
> Structural steel has increased 215 per cent
> Face brick has increased 200 per cent
> Common labor has increased 330 per cent
> Skilled labor has increased 220 per cent
> Materials and components for construction, a widely used construction cost index, has increased 200 per cent.[5]

In communities all over this country, school administrators, architects, and laymen have teamed up to obtain maximum value for the school-tax dollar. School buildings have been carefully planned and designed to realize the best use of space and equipment. Their at-

---

[3] "Stretching the School Building Dollar" (Washington: American Association of School Administrators, September, 1957), p. 1.

[4] *Ibid.*, p. 2.   [5] *Ibid.*, p. 3.

tractiveness lies in their functional usefulness. As the report to which I have just referred points out, these savings have been achieved largely through functional planning:

> Gables, cupolas, parapets, decorative columns, and gingerbread in general have been eliminated. The long straight lines that characterize the new school plants in crossroad neighborhoods, towns and cities illustrate this streamlined simplified school-building design.
> Expensive decorative materials have been replaced by simpler functional materials. Colorful plastic tiles laid on concrete have replaced more expensive hardwood floors. Plaster on classroom walls is becoming less common. Finished roof decks have eliminated ceilings.
> Classroom heights have been dropped from the traditional twelve feet to nine or ten feet, or in some instances even lower. Corridor space, which seldom can be used for instructional purposes, has been reduced. Single-story buildings have eliminated the need for expensive stairways.
> Buildings have been made more useful by the use of movable partitions and large open spaces that can be used for a variety of purposes.
> Wherever possible, plans have provided for the use of stock materials. Expensive hand labor has been reduced by the use of heavy machinery in the construction process.[6]

Facts such as these should be made widely known to the public. If the taxpayers and patrons of the schools knew about the great strides which have been made in cutting school-building costs, they would respond more generously to the demands for new funds for buildings.

Co-operation between Industry and Education

For a long time, business and industrial leaders seem to have been too busy to look at the public schools and the program of education offered to the young people who go directly from high schools into the business world. General David Sarnoff, chairman of the Board of the Radio Corporation of America, has proposed that the industries release annually some of their engineers to teach mathematics and science in our high schools.[7] The proposal may have merit, but from a long-range viewpoint it would be better to provide adequate compensation to teachers and reduce the differential between teachers' and industrial workers' earnings so that a choice between teaching or a career in engineering will be made on the

[6] *Ibid.*, p. 4.

[7] "The Outline of Sarnoff's Plan for Educational Service," *New York Herald Tribune*, January 29, 1956.

basis of interest in the work rather than in the amount of pay. It is a well-known fact that business and industry, by offering attractive beginning salaries to new employees, have siphoned off potential teachers to staff the needs of industry.

Another layman, Joseph P. Sprang, Jr., has emphasized the need for business and industry to take a more realistic and unselfish view toward meeting the needs of the education profession, either by direct subsidy or by taking a more active part in finding new sources of funds for the public schools.[8] Mr. Sprang believes that an honest and sincere effort must be made to help high schools and colleges find the scientists needed on teaching staffs. Indeed some effort has already been made by business and industry to help colleges pay adequate professional salaries and to provide needed housing and equipment. The same thing should be done on the high-school level. But if we are to hold the outstanding teachers in the profession, we must find some way of rewarding teachers on a merit basis. Laymen have used this plan effectively in business, and I believe education could profit from the experience of the business world.

The United States Chamber of Commerce is showing an increasing interest in education. Recently the Chamber of Commerce has organized on the local level what is known as Business-Education Day, in which businessmen visit the public schools. This approach to the development of a better understanding of the schools started by having the teachers visit in the various businesses and industries in the community.

Laymen and School Men Co-operate

Many boards of education have found it necessary to go back to the community at close intervals for an increase in the tax rate and additional bond issues for school buildings. These boards have found it most important to give the laymen opportunities to assemble and interpret, at first hand, information concerning school needs, educational interests, and resources of the community. School officials must take the responsibility of assembling information and facts and placing them in the hands of lay citizens so that the citizens

[8] Joseph P. Sprang, Jr., chairman of the Board of Directors, Gillette Razor Company, in a speech given before the Poor Richard Club in Philadelphia, May, 1956.

will become better informed of the facilities and personnel needed.

When lay citizens get out and work for an increased tax rate in order to obtain better teachers, when they advocate a new bond issue in order to build additional classrooms and new schools, the average voter is more likely to support the measures than if the call comes simply from the superintendent of schools and the members of the board of education. Laymen have been active in learning about school programs in the community and in helping to finance better schools during the period following World War II. The interests of these groups lie largely in better school programs, planning new school housing, and securing the financial resources for the support and operation of schools. Other items have claimed the attention of citizen groups in recent years, but the important thing for any citizen group to do first is to study those problems that they feel need attention in their own school and community.

The extent to which laymen can help improve the high school of tomorrow will depend upon the extent to which boards of education and educators are ready and willing to receive help from lay groups. Laymen cannot render effective service to the American high school unless educators, board members, and teachers demonstrate ability and willingness to work with them. The following have proved most effective in bringing about such co-operation:

1. Having laymen attend and participate in board of education meetings.
2. Seeing that citizens from every segment of community life share in the work of the parent-teachers' association.
3. Holding parent-teacher conferences for giving assistance and direction to children's classroom work.
4. Arranging for laymen to visit the schools frequently and take an active part in the program.
5. Co-operating with the chamber of commerce in promoting Business-Industry-Education Days and Business-Education Days.
6. Asking lay persons to assist with teacher workshops.
7. Using the school plant extensively for adult-education programs.
8. Inviting selected laymen from the community to serve as resource people in the classrooms.
9. Keeping laymen informed of long-range plans for the schools.
10. Using excursions and field trips to important businesses and industries in the community as a means of instruction.
11. Providing students with real opportunities to participate in their own school government and relating this experience to the actual operation of government in the community.

I believe that laymen make their greatest contribution to the educational program in the community through participation in long-range planning. The experience of Muscogee County, Georgia, affords an example of effective co-operation between educators and laymen in long-term planning. When the citizens' groups in 1948 urged a merger of the city and county schools in Columbus and Muscogee County, they were looking to the day when it would no longer be necessary to extend the school district every time the city limits were extended.

The Muscogee County School District covers 220 square miles and serves 31,885 pupils. There are four high schools serving Grades IX through XII. Grades VII and VIII are located as parts of elementary schools and in three junior high schools serving Grades VII and VIII. The citizens of Muscogee County have had a major responsibility in participating with the fifteen board members in making the decision on the kind of school organization best suited for Muscogee County. In 1950, laymen contributed more than $100,000 for the purchase of 157 acres of land to serve as a new educational center for Muscogee County. This was done with the idea of building a new community high school, which would be operated as a comprehensive high school, and with the idea of having a community college. There has long been a definite feeling in the community that opportunity for education beyond the high school should be made possible for all youth desiring it. Without a university or college in the county, many youths are denied the privilege of education beyond Grade XII. It is felt that, for some, the junior college can be an extension of the high school and can provide general education; it can become a two-year terminal education for others; and, for a third group, it can offer two years of college-preparatory work that will enable the students to transfer to a senior college or university for further education.

To assist the school administration in obtaining the needed data and in appraising the situation, the services of the Division of Surveys and Field Services of George Peabody College for teachers were employed. Twelve professional educators completed a comprehensive educational survey of the county.[9] The survey staff rec-

[9] *Public Schools of Muscogee County, Georgia: A Survey Report* (Nashville, Tennessee: Division of Surveys and Field Services, George Peabody College for Teachers, 1957).

ommended that several junior high schools for Grades VII, VIII, and IX be built in Muscogee County in the near future. The over-all organization plan is K-6-3-3, eventually to be extended to K-6-3-3-2 when the community junior college is added. Following the survey, two hundred laymen spent a day visiting the schools, with the idea of formulating a plan for supporting a bond issue that would enable the Board of Education to carry out the plans recommended by the survey staff.

One of the crucial problems facing public education that can be met only through citizen action is district reorganization, particularly at the high-school level. In far too many places, pupils living in rural and suburban areas are denied adequate education because the districts in which their schools are located are financially unable to support schools of good quality. Laymen, largely, must assume responsibility for consolidating small school districts all over America. Unless this is done, many young people will be denied the kind of high-school education that the new era demands.

Summary

Many perplexing problems confront the high school as we face the challenge of the new era. Difficult as these problems may seem, I am confident that they can be met through co-operative action of laymen and school men. Indeed they are not likely to be solved at all unless laymen and educators work together to achieve their common goal of improving the high school of the future. As laymen and educators, let us join hands in providing for our youth the kind of education which they must have to meet the challenge of the new day and which our country needs if it is to remain strong and free.

ERNEST A. GRAY

Organizational Methods for
Effective Co-operation

The subject which I shall discuss is the layman's role in the high school of the future, with specific reference to organizational methods for effective co-operation. I shall consider exactly how laymen can best co-operate with boards of education and school administrators in building the kind of secondary education that will meet the challenge of the new era. I use the word "exactly" because I believe that the part laymen can constructively play in the schools of tomorrow has been clearly patterned by the experience of yesterday and today. The past ten years have seen a nationwide phenomenon that has given us great quantities of data on lay participation in education. That phenomenon is the birth and growth of citizens' committees, more than ten thousand of which are now in existence. Thousands of committees born over a decade ago are still very much alive today. Many hundreds more are being born each year. But unfortunately hundreds have been "dropouts," living brief, frustrated lives and vanishing into oblivion.

It is our great good fortune that this vast experience with successful and unsuccessful citizens' action for the schools has been recorded for us by the National Citizens Council for Better Schools and by state citizens' committees in Illinois, New York, and other states. The histories they have compiled and the conclusions they have drawn provide what seem to me some clear-cut answers to the question of the citizen's place in tomorrow's high-school education. They have given us basic principles of organization and operation that concretely define the difference between the committee that is here today and gone tomorrow and the committee that is here today and still here tomorrow.

Characteristics of Successful Citizens' Committees

It is true, of course, that each committee has a character all its own, a character shaped by its own community. But it is equally true that the analyses made by the National Citizens Council for Better Schools and by the committees of New York, Illinois, and other states have produced a well-defined composite picture of the successful committee—a basic committee personality. Definite personality traits and points of view are common to the successful committees. Let me depict for you what the typical successful committee is like and what it is not like.

The successful citizens' committee is *not* a vigilante group concerned solely with the protection of the lowest possible tax levy. It *is* a vigilant group, ever alert to the opportunities of education.

It is *not* a small, intrenched lobby of ingrown people, representing only their personal prejudices or self-interest and a backward-looking determination to stop the clock. It *is* a representative cross-section of open-minded people with an honest, objective interest in the facts and opportunities of education and a forward-looking determination to keep up with the times.

The successful citizens' committee is a great listener and learner. The unsuccessful citizen group hears nothing, fears everything.

Having drawn this contrast between the positive and the negative citizen committee personality, I should like now to report on the specific facets of the positive personality—of the well-balanced, well-adjusted lay group that has worked and will keep on working.

The successful lay group has, first of all, gained solid status. This is no easy task, for many boards of education view public participation with alarm, considering it a threat to board prerogatives. Many teachers dread the effects of amateur meddling in professional matters. In numerous communities, citizens' organizations have run the gamut of vilification, have been called everything from bumbling busybodies to camouflaged agents of Moscow.

How, then, have school groups been able to gain status and to maintain it? The experience of thousands of citizen groups provides some truths that will be as pertinent tomorrow as they are today. Status that results in lasting co-operation and effective action with school boards, school men, and the community at large is built on proved methods of organization, operation, and action.

How Citizens' Committees Should Be Organized

A citizen group can die the day it is born if it makes a basic mistake in the crucial area of membership—in short, if it fails to be truly representative of the entire community geographically, economically, philosophically. It must include parents and non-parents, home-owners and renters, progressives and conservatives. It should be composed of advocates and opponents in school controversies. I have seen almost unbelievable things happen to the chronic complainers when they are placed on a committee. As a board member in Elmwood Park, Illinois, says, "It's best to have dissidents where you can meet their arguments face to face."

There is something about sitting down with neighbors that makes a man more careful of the things he says and the things he does. It is easy for him to sit in the barber's chair and carp about "the foolish frills in the schools these days" or to blast away at "that crazy guidance program." But you can take the very person who makes the most disagreeable noise about school affairs, sit him down with a citizen group, and then watch Mr. Hyde become Dr. Jekyll.

Typical of the people I have seen go through this transformation is a fellow townsman. His favorite, and most effective, theme song to his friends and neighbors was this: "When I went to this school, they used to tell me it was one of the best schools around. Now all of a sudden, everything about it has to be changed. I don't get it."

This gentleman of the old school agreed to become a member of our citizen group. At the first meeting the steam he blew off filled the room. At the next meeting he let off some more steam but in staccato huffs and puffs. On the whole, he seemed to feel that he had had his say, and he was satisfied to sit back, relatively relaxed and relatively quiet. And that night, things began to happen to him. Some of the facts he heard began to soak in. Perhaps most important of all, he got a group feeling—the feeling of being part of a group whose only reason for meeting and working together was to help young people. He fought the feeling, but one night he said, "There's certainly no reason why our kids shouldn't have as much of a break in school as other kids." Before the first year's study was completed, he was not only on the team but was one of the team's toughest fighters. He took on any and all critics, always asserting his independence by declaring, "I'm not saying that the committee is always right or anything like that, but I do know this: they're always trying to do the right thing by the kids of this town."

Certainly not every story of the dissenter has such a happy ending, but, just as certainly, involvement has shown itself to be the best way to win over the complainer and quiet the complaints. As they say, a bird in the hand is worth two birds in ambush.

A few other observations about membership may be offered. Some committees have made the membership mistake of relying solely on what they think is the magic of big names. Too often, they find, big names are called upon by so many organizations that about all they can give are their names, but no time. And the magic of time is far more important to citizens' committees than the magic of big names.

What kinds of names make the best committee names? A few big ones do help in gaining prestige and acceptability. But a citizens' committee must have much more than that. It needs something deeper than high-level prestige; it needs everyday acceptance and confidence, the kind of confidence that comes only with inclusion of the real leaders around town. The banker, certainly, and the lawyer and the real-estate man; but also such recognized community contributors as the chief of the volunteer fire department and the lady who runs the Sunday school; and then some of the men and women other people listen to in the factory or in the office. The prestige of the members is far less important than the daily influence they exert on the groups in which they move.

One of the most exciting phenomena of the upsurge of citizen participation in education is what it has done to and for people. Many of you have seen what I have seen in community after community: the uncommon accomplishments of the so-called common man, the leadership of the "little man" that has surprised everyone, particularly the little man himself. I saw an electrician rise to such heights of leadership and accomplishment through a series of school-building crises that both the high school and the elementary school were named after him. I watched a normally reticent physical-education teacher snap a sleeping community out of a nightmare of school overcrowding and into the building of one of America's model junior high schools. I saw a middle-aged mother, who describes herself as "just another housewife," end the dominance of a do-nothing group over a school district of forty thousand people. She stimulated the majority to participate in school affairs for the first time in over forty years. She is credited with raising the school vote from 15 per cent to 55 per cent in only two years.

This leadership that citizen committees have created has done more than benefit the schools alone. Many of these good people, who have suddenly discovered their own capacities for constructive accomplishment, have gone on to show the way in other areas of civic service—improving parks, encouraging town planning, cleaning up corrupt local politics.

Teachers as Members

The relationship of teachers to the citizens' committee has been the subject of considerable discussion and experimentation. Based on many personal observations and on the reports I have heard and read, I would say that the relationship of teachers to the committee should be one of complete partnership. When a committee recognizes that the teacher is also a citizen and makes him a regular committee member, something fine is accomplished for the understanding between layman and professional. The teacher gets a new sense of belonging to the community—particularly if he works with other citizens on population studies or the character of the community or in some other field in which he and the layman have equal knowledge. Layman and school man can then come to know each other as people, instead of as expert and critic, or taxpayer and tax-paid.

Selection of Members

Let us consider now the ways in which committee members are most successfully selected.

With very few exceptions, committees work more efficiently and effectively if the cross-section is picked by the individual method rather than the organization method. Citizens who come to school meetings representing themselves are certain to say more and do more than they will if they are acting as delegates from organizations. It is challenge enough for any individual to face the facts of education and to come up with what he thinks or wants, without expecting him to second-guess the men back at the lodge or the women in the garden club.

Having determined the individuals who would make a committee function, how can you get them to accept membership on the committee and how can you keep them? The chief answers to both questions are the same. First of all, plan the use of their time carefully. Make it clear that undue demands will not be made on their time, and set up your organization so that such demands need not be made. Furthermore, make certain your committee is large enough so that it can be divided into good-sized subcommittees. Then parcel out the responsibilities during the committee year, so that no one committee and no one individual has an overload of work all through the year. Intense work for a brief period is permissible and, in order to insure involvement in the committee, highly desirable. But the committee that fails is one that loads the work on a few of the more willing or the more agreeable members.

Having organized the operation for proper work distribution, you are now in a position to recruit and retain the committee members you want. Tell them that their work period will be short. Tell them that, during the rest of the committee year, they will be contributing judgments on other subcommittee reports and on over-all committee action. Explain to them that the schools need their views. The members you want will respond.

Next, be sure you set sharply defined goals. What is the subcommittee aiming for? What is the entire committee aiming for? A report on merit rating? A survey of possible future school sites? A report on physical-education facilities? An analysis of other schools or of college-entrance problems?

Let each committee member see what he and his subcommittee and the whole committee are going to do and tell him when it is expected to be done. Show him specifically what his effort can accomplish. Give him a sense of purpose. Then watch him produce.

What Makes for Effective Leadership?

The productive group demands dedicated and skilful leadership. The leaders must not be working for "what's in it for me" or, as sometimes happens, for the purpose of exercising their egos. They must be entirely concerned with making the organization work, not at all concerned with proving anything about themselves. In fact, one of the first duties of a lay group leader is to train new leaders as replacements. For the lay group that renews and refreshes its public personality with new faces at the top avoids the danger of becoming a pressure group or the suspicion of being one, both of which are equally destructive. To insure changes in leadership, many committee constitutions write in specific provisions for regularly revolving leadership and membership.

Defining the Role of the Committee

Many committees also use their constitution or by-laws to make the role of the citizens' committee unmistakably clear. Such provisions can delineate, for all to understand, the relationship between the board of education and the citizens' committee. The successful citizens' committee is a fact-finding group. It is a liaison group. It reflects community attitudes to the board and the administration. It acquaints the community with the school problems and plans faced by the board and the administration. It provides information, and makes recommendations to board members and administrators. It does not make policy decisions or take over the duties of the board.

The lasting committee works with the board and the professional people from the first, making its reports and recommendations to these official groups. It can, of course, go to the community with its recommendations, but only after every possible means of working them out with the board have been exhausted.

The successful committee is an independent organization. All its studies and proposals must be dependent on just one thing—the sincere conviction that every report and recommendation represents what is best for education. But, in maintaining its independence, the group must always bear in mind the fact that co-operation does not mean domination.

Involving the Community

In working with the community, the successful committee recognizes there is no substitute for the open door. Its general meetings are open to the public. It makes certain, through publicity, that the public always knows what is going on and why it is going on.

Opening your doors and your doings to the public is an important step. Getting the public to come through those doors is equally important. Good attendance at meetings is never an accident. It must be planned. Simply inviting people to a meeting is not enough. They must be motivated to leave the comfort of their homes and their television and to come out and think.

In newspaper announcements, on invitation cards and letters, the meeting must be made to sound interesting and important. Tell the people what they will hear about, and stress the fact that it matters to them. Tell them they will learn something about "how our schools measure up to other schools in the area" or "what our town will be like tomorrow and its effect on our schools." Then make sure of a good attendance in the only way you can make sure: put a telephone-calling corps of citizens to work a day or two before the meeting.

Good public attendance at open meetings is one of the best ways to change public apathy to public appreciation—to involve the public and make them, like your members, part of what you are doing.

How Successful Citizens' Committees Operate

Now let us analyze what makes for successful operation of a citizens' committee. As has been said, the committee should deal only with facts. Personalities are not the business of citizen groups. They should assiduously avoid the politics of board elections. Their function here is to furnish the public with statements of standards of good board members. They can help the community choose wisely and judge well by providing a forum for board candidates to be seen and heard. These are the approaches to citizen committee operation that have been effective.

How Can Citizens' Committees Act Constructively?

Finally, I would like to discuss examples of the most constructive citizen effort in the areas of committee action. The areas of productive action by a lay group are limitless.

If a lay group is to keep its members enthusiastic and the public interested, it should maintain a happy balance of immediate-action projects and long-range planning. The most vigorous group is consistently getting things done—promoting building improvements or new buildings, helping to right teachers' salaries, advancing the curriculum.

Opportunities for Immediate Action

Operating in the area of needed immediate action, an Ohio citizens' committee overcame a 50 per cent teacher turnover by recommending, after study, the upgrading of the salary schedules. A Downers Grove (Illinois) committee spearheaded the passing of a school-bond issue that had once been badly beaten. And the Hobbs (New Mexico) committee executed a study of the tax structure that uncovered much taxable property not previously assessed. The result: tax income for the schools was doubled.

In New York's Northern Westchester County, a 168-member committee worked with the boards and administrators of seven school districts to bring about a centralization. This joining of districts made it possible for the area to finance the first curriculum program to meet the needs of *all* the children. It introduced a broad industrial-arts and commercial program for non-college students and, at the same time, brought new, advanced courses to the academically gifted children.

It is easy to see why, in each of these communities and in hundreds more like them, board members and administrators agree with the statement made by the Board of Education of Great Neck, Long Island: "The only thing we would like to see happen to citizens' committees would be to see their strength grow 100 per cent."

Opportunities for Long-Range Action

Important and dramatic as short-range or emergency action is, the continuing vitality of citizens' committees calls for more than meeting crises, more than building fires under a community or putting out fires. Long-range activity is every bit as vital to the survival of lay participation.

In the area of long-range action, perhaps one of the most helpful functions is providing periodic attitude reports to the board and the school administration—reports on citizen attitudes toward school courses, toward teachers and their salaries, toward the basic objectives of education. As an example, the Baldwin (Long Island) Citizens Committee, under the supervision of the executive director of the New York State Citizens Committee, worked out and distributed a questionnaire on teacher pay. The results of the questionnaire were presented at a town meeting for discussion and then for voting.

The results so impressed the school board that they voted substantial increases into the budget. The budget was overwhelmingly passed.

Other long-range studies under way around the country include investigation of district reorganization, studies of methods of housing teachers, population studies made to anticipate future building and site requirements.

Hundreds of long-range curriculum studies are under way, producing findings such as those made in Niagara Falls, New York. Niagara Falls citizens called for "more stress on academic subjects, increased guidance, more standardized courses with fewer electives." This, of course, raises that eternal question: Is curriculum any of the amateur's business? Henry Toy, Jr., president of the National Citizens Council for Better Schools, has said: "Traditionally, setting the general objectives for the schools is a job for the whole community. Citizens have proved that they can operate effectively in outlining school programs."

Challenge of the Future

Adding up all the experience and all the facts, the properly constituted lay group has been, and will continue to be, a powerful and, in fact, an indispensable force for the better and better education needed to meet the challenge of the high school of the future.

What will our citizens bring to that future? Will they be ready to do their part in meeting its challenges and grasping its opportunities? Yes, better prepared than they have ever been if they apply the lessons of the past:

If they are truly representative of all the community and all points of view.

If they focus on fact-finding.

If they rotate their leadership and their membership.

If they include teachers as citizen members as well as expert advisers.

If they apply every method of working with the school board and the administration.

If they hold to their independence, remembering that co-operation does not mean domination.

If they organize the responsibilities properly, by giving all members enough and avoiding putting too much of a work load on any one member.

If they maintain a proper balance between immediate-action projects and long-range planning.

If they provide for proper communication with the public at large.

If they make the most of the treasure house of knowledge and guidance available to them through the case-history libraries, the revealing studies, and the direct counsel of their state citizens' committees and the National Citizens Council for Better Schools.

Many challenges confront the schools. There is the challenge of striking a proper balance between science and the humanities, of investigating the values we can adopt from the European secondary schools, of preparing young people to meet the ever increasing demands on science and mathematics, of bringing out the best in low-ability and high-ability students, of introducing innovations in the high-school curriculum, of attracting outstanding young people to the teaching profession and of properly supporting good teachers and good teaching, of advancing the relationship between high schools and colleges, of correlating freedom and discipline among high-school students, of housing the high schools of the future.

Citizens now stand ready, in greater numbers than ever before, to take on these challenges of the future. They have developed the will and the skill to help make tomorrow a great day for education.

Administering the High School
of the Future

Common sense dictates the acceptance of the democratic concept of administration. Democratic administration, which seeks to elicit from the individual the maximum output of effort and creativity, would appear to be acceptable even in an entirely selfish approach to management devoid of a social conscience. For, after all, it works; it brings the best efforts out of most of us. Again the objectives of modern secondary education, with their concern for the worthwhileness of the individual, would make it seem logical that no philosophy of administration which did not have a similar concern could be considered acceptable. For if administration fails to deal creatively with the potentialities of educational personnel, this professional group, in turn, is not likely to deal creatively with the potentialities of children.

Stimulation involves the desirable elements of inspiration and of good example. Command involves the giving of orders backed by authority. In the latter connection, then, a person who has been given specific orders may be satisfied to do only as much and as well as his "commander" will accept as minimum satisfactory performance. On the other hand, a person who has been triggered to action through stimulation may unleash so much energy and creativity as to surpass by far the plan and the design of the leader who desired action to take place. A basic principle in the administration of the secondary school of the future, then, will subsume that administration is effective to the degree that it relies on stimulation rather than on command.

In projecting the problem of administering the high school of the future, it is necessary to make the following assumptions: (1) that the community will be willing to support not only the program which it will demand but also the program which it will need; (2) that the problem of teacher shortage will have abated to the point where the school will be able to attract, develop, and retain a faculty of continuing professional growth; and (3) that the administrative principles, procedures, and practices set forth in this paper are not essentially new when considered one at a time. These principles and practices exist now at either the theoretical or the practical level and, with time, will be adopted (if this has not been done already), modified, or cast aside as the wisdom of experience dictates.

Development of Administrative Policies and Practices

Administrative policies and practices will be developed in light of the local school situation. Under no circumstances will they be lifted lock, stock, and barrel from another context for specific local adoption. Such borrowing might tend to cause the valid practices of other schools to appear gauche, insensitive, and invalid as a result of the neglect of important variables and of the "psychological factors" in a second situation.

Consistent with the democratic philosophy of administration, there will be maximum involvement of the faculty in the development of administrative practices and policies. Where applicable, there will be similar involvement of the students and of lay advisory groups from the community. Through this means a valuable principle of operation is invoked: policies and plans tend to be more sensitively developed and more completely and enthusiastically carried out to the degree that those who are affected by their operation are involved beforehand in their development. It should be expected that innovations will be accompanied by the appropriate and concomitant education of personnel and that, in the process of being adopted, the innovations may themselves undergo change.

A logical outcome of the foregoing would be the development of an emerging administrative handbook. This handbook, to be developed as a co-operative staff activity, will be in a stage of continuous refinement. Thus it will tend at once to elicit creativity and to exercise control by fostering stability as well as change in light of the problems and the desired course of direction of the school.

Staffing the School

Age Distribution of Faculty

Careful effort will be made to effect an even distribution of the faculty within each age bracket. This practice should tend to prevent the faculty from suffering unduly from the inexperience of youth or from the diminution of energy and the loss of modifiability which tend to characterize the condition of a staff too heavily composed of persons of later maturity. Likewise this practice should lessen the danger of the faculty's being in a constant state of flux as youth experiments in a field unmarked by the guideposts of tradition, both hallowed and praiseworthy.

Versatility of Preparation

Teachers will be hired on the strength of both specialization and versatility as to subject-matter background and competency. It is well recognized that teen-agers develop the intellectual powers basic to learning the most difficult subject matter, skills, concepts, and understandings. Nevertheless our young people will be served best if their teachers are trained in breadth and in depth in order that correlation and integration of subject matter be realized, whether in core classes or in classes of the conventional type. Furthermore, every administrator knows how advantageous it is to have on the faculty a number of teachers who are qualified, able, and willing to teach a split program of classes. Doubtless the willingness stems in part from ability. Naturally the same principles of versatility will apply to teachers for co-curricular or special-service areas.

Importance of Strong, Interlocking Departments

Strong departments of instruction should exist in the school. At the same time the specter of over-departmentalization should influence our planning in order that all departments will work together with optimum concern for the integrated learning of the students. To effect the latter condition, the department chairmen should serve on the school's curriculum committee. In so serving, they may, under competent leadership, come to recognize the place of their departmental offerings in the broad education of the children as well as the gaps and overlaps which must be eliminated. Through interdepartmental and cross-departmental planning, they may learn how to, and attain a willingness to, co-operate in realizing the progress goals of the school.

Department chairmen will be selected on the basis of their competence in both their field of specialization and the field of human relations. Their positions will be functional rather than honorary; their duties will be both supervisory and administrative. Their supervisory and administrative roles must be implemented because the bifurcated nature of the principal's position is such that he requires assistance in the administration of the program and the supervision of instruction. And, finally, the department chairmen will be rewarded both in salary and in released time in proportion to the size of the departments supervised. Only in this way will it be possible to attract and retain persons well qualified for this important administrative post.

Effective Use of Administrative Time

The proper use of administrative time is a matter which will always be of concern to the professional administrator. How to do more things better and in less time is the specific problem. Since the most time-consuming task of the year is the development of the master program and the scheduling of children to classes within it, let us consider that task.

Committee on Programing

Since each department of instruction is vitally concerned with its own position in the curriculum and since it will continuously strive for more desirable and convenient organization and placement of classes in the school day, it is at once evident that all departments will never be fully satisfied with their lot at any one time. There are two basic causes of this condition. First, a sort of departmental partisanship appears to be both natural and desirable; and, second, it is a human failing to view our personal interests through a telescope, with the consequence that the resulting enlargement is out of focus proportionately to the surrounding field.

One means of bringing about proper focus is the use of a committee on programing. This committee, representing each department in the school, will meet regularly with the program chairman for the purpose of stating and hearing the special requests made by various departments. And since all requests will be heard in a sort of clearing-house situation, the persons involved will recognize that occasions arise when the requests of one department run counter to the wishes of another. Through discussion, a meeting of minds becomes possible; through reporting back to the various departments, understanding becomes probable. In any event, the help of a program committee will enable the program chairman to prepare a more sensitive and effective schedule. And this is no mean accomplishment.

Mechanical Assistance in Making a Class Program

The literature is rife with suggestions on how to develop a program with a mimimum of conflicts among single-section classes. We often decide, in retrospect, that, if we had had more time, we could have arranged our classes with fewer conflicts. It will be a great aid to the administrator to have the students' selections of classes for the next semester, or year, placed on business-machine cards by a key-punch system. With such an arrangement a clerk can run sorts on all the children in the school so that every potential conflict will be recorded. Armed with this information, the program-maker will be able to arrange classes to the best advantage.

Little elaboration is required to suggest the infinite possibilities which will be available to all high-school principals when they have at their disposal a facility whereby the most sensitive types of analyses and correlations can be made. Data can be obtained on the subjects being taken, trends in subject selection, correlation of subjects taken with grade-point averages, success on scholarship examinations, and the students' success in college and in various types of post-high-school experiences.

In-service Education of the Faculty

There must be a unifying factor in an in-service education program, and, since all things in education begin and end with the child, it is logical that the child should constitute the dominant idea in the program. No other center of interest will transcend the various foci of emphases and the subject-matter partisanship that may be found among people who are highly trained in special fields.

In-service Program as Part of the School's Daily Life

When the new teacher joins the faculty, he will be told that the program of in-service education will be part of his life as a member of the faculty. However, it will also be made clear to him that the program does not function because of any inherent weakness in himself or in his faculty colleagues. Rather it functions because providing optimum service to our students is a constantly evolving and developing task, which truly educated and professional persons must never be satisfied to regard as perfect. Logically, then, there will be time in the school day for teacher participation in in-service education programs. In the case of some teachers, arrangements will be made for non-teaching or reduced teaching programs in order to permit participation in especially significant programs at varying degrees of depth.

All too often administrators who consider themselves thoroughly democratic fail to see any inconsistency in setting down, by their own fiat, all the in-service topics and problems which are to be worked on by the faculty. Such a practice tends to result in superimposing a supposedly democratic relationship upon an unintentionally autocratic substructure. It is hoped that the faculty of the secondary school of the future will study their problems co-operatively with the principal and with other key persons, such as department heads, in order to identify and define the problems needing consideration and action. Such a practice will, of course, share all the advantages that result from involving in the planning stages of any activity those persons who will be concerned with, or touched by, the implementation of the resultant program.

University Courses in the In-service Program

Explicit in the teacher's contractual relationship with his school will be the agreement that courses taken for salary advancement are to have definite bearing on his specific and developing service to the school. This practice will mean that teachers will become more valuable to the instructional program, will be able to function effectively in more than one department and to render some needed noninstructional or co-curricular service. Nothing in this statement should rule out the possibility of rewarding a teacher for special growth leading to greater value in the school program when this growth has resulted from informal study. However, problems relating to accreditation remain to be worked out before certain aspects of such study may be recognized.

Program of Public Relations

Public relations, or social interpretation as it is sometimes called, will continue to be an important element in the administration of the high school. However, it is to be hoped that future public relations programs will be of the continuous type rather than the *ad hoc* type which is often initiated to cope with a crisis.

Increasingly, high schools will involve a lay advisory committee in the public relations program. The purpose of this committee will be not so much to tell the school what should be taught as it will be to understand the nature of the high-school objectives and the means by which the school seeks to achieve them. However, two-way communication between the committee of key citizens and the school administration will be so thorough that it will serve as a formidable leading edge of faith and understanding against even the perennial and compulsive critics of secondary education. It will also be so thorough as to serve as a basis for modification of school practices whenever convincing evidence is obtained from the facts of public experience.

It is hoped that we shall continue to gain knowledge of what our public desires to find out about the schools. Actually they wish to learn about their children and, specifically, how well the children are doing in their schoolwork—a true measure, in a sense, of how the schools themselves are doing. Accordingly it is hoped that the public relations emphasis will be more clearly directed, proportionately, to the academic life of the school and less to the extra-curriculum aspects of the program. In the final analysis, we shall continue to be judged on how well our graduates read, write, spell, communicate, compute, and think in problem-solving situations. We shall do well to continue to prepare for that judgment.

In Summary

The high school of the future will receive adequate financial support from its community. It will be administered in harmony with the democratic tradition. The faculty will be selected in terms of depth and versatility of preparation. Instructional departments will be led by carefully selected specialists, who will have status adequate to their function. Efforts will be made to simplify administrative routines through careful planning and mechanical assistance. The in-service education of the faculty will be built into the daily life of the teacher. Finally, the program of public relations will deal continuously with matters of true significance to parents and will evolve with the close co-operation of key citizens. If we do as well as we know, the future may be sooner than we think.

Clarifying the Role of the High School in the Face of Conflicting Demands

Three assumptions seem to underlie the topic "Clarifying the Role of the High School in the Face of Conflicting Demands." The first assumption is that some clarification is needed; the second is that the high school has a single role; and the third, that we can safely predict conflicting demands on the high school in the future. Before turning directly to my topic, it is appropriate to comment on these assumptions.

Validity of the Assumptions

First Assumption

Granted that some clarification may be needed (and I doubt if there is any enterprise of any sort in which clarification is not always needed), there remain the questions: Needed for whom? For the sake of the institution itself? For the sake of the public it serves? For the sake of the students enrolled? For the sake of the educators involved? I believe that clarification is needed for all parties.

Changing times have changed the institution. The public has been treated in recent years to a vast amount of advice from all sources, including admirals and historians, pedagogues and business leaders. Not all of this advice has been consistent. Teachers in the colleges have not seen the matter in the same light as have their colleagues in the high schools. And the amount of vandalism exercised on school buildings in recent years suggests that at least some of the students do not see the high school in the same role as do either the principal or the chief of police. Let us assume, therefore, that clarification would be helpful.

But, even with that assumption, one should understand clearly that clarification may not lead directly, or even inevitably, to the solution of the social problems or to the resolution of the differing attitudes concerned. It is not inconceivable that a sharpening of the definition of the role of the high school will tend to sharpen, rather than to resolve, some of these conflicting demands. I am myself enough of an optimist to think that, in the long run, clarification will help. But we must surely be realists enough to recognize that at times the opposite may seem to be the first result. When the only national school committee in the land (and I refer, of course, to the Supreme Court in Washington) clarified one educational policy, and that policy was applied in a city of Arkansas, the result was a situation which will long last in our memories. In that case, clarification did not lead at once to resolution of conflicting demands.

Second Assumption

The second assumption seems to be that there is a single role for the high school. Without attempting to use the word "role" in any strict sociological sense but rather in its more ordinary meaning, I still doubt whether this assumption is correct. The most obvious comment at the start would be that the role of the high school may well vary in communities with different economic and social compositions. But the matter goes deeper than the differences implied by the economic and social considerations alone. When we consider the role of the high school in the lives of the students, we recognize the school's responsibilities for general education and for specific training in particular fields. Probably this is the role most often considered in public discussions. Yet we must surely recognize at least two other roles of the high school.

One of these is its role in carrying out that part of the American dream which says that all men should have an equal chance and, to some, suggests that all men should be equal. Fulfilling this purpose might be described as the political role of the high school, and, as is often the case in political matters, the party platform is not always translated into action during the term of the executive. Yet if we strip away this notion of the role of the high school, we would have an institution which would not satisfy the deepest wishes of the American people.

To these grand considerations another must be added. In many parts of the United States, probably in the majority, the high school symbolizes the community it serves. As local ties are broken more and more by the nature of modern life, the high school more and more becomes the local institution which stands for man's pride in his home town. I submit that, were this not true, the nature of high-school athletics would be inexplicable. I doubt that high-school bands would have been made the showpieces they are were it not for community pride and a sense of competition with other communities. And I have often been struck by what seems to me the tendency of residents of a town either to overrate the accomplishments of their high school or sadly to underrate them. The reason probably is that they have an emotional attachment to the school, of which they may not even be aware. Without such emotional attachment, their judgment might well be more accurate. For example, the press reports on the visits made by Ambassador Conant to study the American high school reflect again and again a pride that he has chosen "our town." I sense in these reports, not alone pride in the high school or a concern for the state of secondary education, but rather a reflection of that localism which is deep in our society.

To summarize. Clarification is doubtless needed, but it will bring trouble as well as help. There is not one role of the high school; there are rather several roles. Consequently clarification is not a single, but a multiple, process, since the school serves several groups.

Third Assumption

Finally, in considering the assumptions underlying my topic, I turn to the nature of the conflicting demands. Should we assume that certain forces in society will reduce the conflict in the demands placed on the high school? Is there any likelihood that the schools will be allowed to develop independently of any larger social and political purpose and independently of community pride and symbolism? I doubt it. These conflicting demands are likely to grow more complex as the population shifts from town to town and state to state and as the interrelation of a single high school to the larger regional and national needs becomes more clear. It becomes important, therefore, to analyze some of the sources of these demands. If we deal with them in general terms only, we may not realize the underground currents of influence which will change the pattern of the future.

Sources of Demands on the High School

Let me suggest that there are six categories into which the demands on the high school may be placed. I have deliberately selected categories which now have, or are likely to have, ways of expressing the views of the groups assigned under them; for the word "demands" suggests a deliberate effort to influence and a way to express that influence. I do not for a moment suggest that these six categories include all the types of influence that will be exerted in the years to come. I suggest only that under them will be clustered those influences that are of the greatest importance for the topic at hand.

1. Children and Their Parents

The first category includes the demands of the children and their parents. The demands in the elementary school will more often be made by the parents on behalf of the children than by the children themselves, while in the high school the demands will frequently come from the students, often with the support of their parents. We may confidently predict an increasing pressure in the high school for programs which guarantee the prospect of further education. Most observers of the social scene would agree that this pressure is sure to be exerted if the United States continues to enjoy good times economically. I submit that it is likely to be felt even in a recession, because the American dream that education brings *both* opportunity and security is still deep in our nature. Of all the influences on the high school, I suppose this influence is the greatest. It is often based on a naïve faith in what formal education can do. It is both the hope and the despair of our schools. It is what makes American public education so radically different from educational systems abroad. To many of us, it is our strength. In it may lie our hope of being able to resolve the conflicting pressures from the sources named in the five categories that are mentioned below.

2. Community Influence

My earlier remarks have suggested one aspect of the influence of the community in which the high school is placed: the fact that the high school symbolizes the pride of the community in its own affairs. But the influence of the community is greater than that alone.

Obviously, with the American pattern of decentralization, the community influences the high school both by the nature of the school committee it elects and by the financial support it provides. The community, by its influence, can control the high school to a degree unmatched in any other land. I doubt that a high school, except in the large cities, can by itself remake the cultural life of the area it serves; for the influences on the high school are like alternating current. Even if some greater force were to dictate the curruculum in the American high school in great detail, the community could so change the quality of the enterprise as to make it unrecognizable to the authorities who conceived it in the first place.

3. Special-Interest Groups

The high schools are now influenced, and surely will be influenced for some time to come, by the views of enterprises and organizations of all sorts. These are sometimes located entirely within the community served but are more often parts of an interlocked group of associations of regional or national character. The local chamber of commerce or labor union, the local patriotic association, the association representing certain specialized technical interests, the group devoted to the care of children with mental or emotional deficiencies—all are examples. Many of these associations are powerful politically and can have a direct influence on the election of the lay boards that determine policy for the American schools. On no account should their influence be underestimated.

It is obvious that the demands of these groups are often in conflict with one another. The most recent example is the difference between the desires of certain patriotic groups with regard to the teaching of history and the desires of associations eager to forward international organization. Undoubtedly some members of these groups find that their associational efforts conflict with their personal desires for their children. For example, I have no doubt that some insurance company vice-president may deplore the diffuse nature of the high-school curriculum, since he wants his boy to get into some college, yet in his daily work is an ardent advocate of the National Safety Council, which is not without influence in the introduction of driver training in the high school. There may well be a man who is generously giving time to causes which attempt to reduce the incidence of juvenile delinquency, while at the same time he is persuaded that the high school should be an educational institution only, with no responsibilities for social welfare. On the horizon looms the possibility of profound conflict between religious groups with differing views on the high school's role in instruction in what have recently been called the "moral and spiritual values."

It is appropriate here to emphasize the point that the individual American will often find himself involved in a conflict because of demands placed upon him. The problem of clarification is not alone the resolution of differing group opinions; it is a problem that rests within the single citizen. Some aspects of the American high school's role remind one of that felicitous phrase used by Myrdal in naming the book which resulted from his study of the American racial problem, *The American Dilemma*. You will recall that Myrdal's central point was that the American dilemma in the area of race rested, above all, in the soul and the conscience of the individual American.

4. Interests of the Nation

Recent months have made it clear that, aside from the interest of the parents and children, of the community being served, and of special interests, there is a national interest in the role of the high school. This national interest currently expresses itself through three channels: the concern about our ability as a nation to compete successfully with our potential enemies in science and in mathematics; the national concern about broad social policies, such as that of integration as expressed through the rulings of the Supreme Court; and the economic concern that grows out of the increased population and the need for new school buildings. It is worth noting that this national concern is not expressed through any single agency, as would probably be the case abroad. The concern about science and mathematics tends to come from the scientific foundations of the government and from the Defense Department. As a matter of government policy, the views of Admiral Rickover are not related to congressional discussions on school buildings. The program of the National Science Foundation to aid in the training of teachers of science and mathematics was probably not worked out in relation to the policies of the attorney-general on integration. Nevertheless, these forces are national in their nature and in their intended influence.

It seems a safe guess that these influences will increase rather than decrease. The ever closer economic bonds between American communities will demand a leveling of the quality of high-school work. There is reason to believe that we are in a period of shortage of skilled manpower that will last for some time. While the national government may not soon organize itself into a single agency to express the national needs, the influence exerted will nevertheless increase (sometimes, as in the case of private associations, with the result that one agency of the national government is in conflict with another).

5. The School Subjects

The fifth category is difficult to define. The nearest that I can come is to use the words "the nature and influence of the subjects to be taught in the high school." This influence is expressed in several ways. Indeed in the description of an earlier category I have suggested one of them: the national need for scientists has caused scientific groups to attempt to influence the high-school work in mathematics and in the sciences. But the influence is felt in more than this indirect way.

There is an internal dynamic in the very subjects included in the curriculum. Research and scholarship in the arts, the social sciences, and the sciences change the disciplines themselves. The scholars are therefore in a position in which it is to their advantage to attempt to influence what is taught in the high schools, not only to see to it that the students who come to them for teaching are better prepared, but also to make sure that their particular scholarly interest may be properly weighed in the balance of American general education. This interest is expressed in several ways. The learned societies which draw together the specialists in the various areas by publications, conferences, and other means can, and actually attempt to, influence the high-school curriculum. It is to me a regrettable fact that the lines of communication between these societies and the teachers in the high schools have been sadly broken in the past half-century. The signs of increased contacts and relationships between college and high-school teachers, which I see on the horizon, are therefore welcomed.

In addition to scholarly associations, we must reckon with the influence of the publishing groups. I suppose the major channel of communication that still exists is the textbook. Indeed, when a foreign visitor asks me why the American high schools are as alike as they are, despite decentralization, I have found myself mentioning again and again the fact that the textbook, to be profitable, must be sold in more than one area and that the salesman plays a role not unlike that of the jongleur of old—the carrier of information and the distributor of ideas from town to town.

The breakdown in communication between the college and the school world has, unhappily, broken the personal relations between college teachers and high-school teachers. As a result the associational meetings of specialists in the several fields tend to be held separately, for example, separate meetings of the college teachers of science and the high-school teachers of science. I am well aware that there are exceptions to this statement, but, as a generalization, it will stand. The chances of a merging of the groups by subject fields in the years to come seem to me reasonably good. If this merging takes place, it will mean that the influence of the college and the world of scholarship on the high-school curriculum will increase substantially over the coming few decades. This influence will be exerted, not only because there will be more applicants for fewer college places (with the result that college-admission standards and requirements will have more influence in 1975 than they did in 1945), but also because the same influences which govern the admission policy of the college will be felt within the groups making the curriculums in the high school. These college and high-school groups will be reinforced by the learned societies and, in some areas, by the direct interests of the national government. School committees and school boards will, therefore, feel the pressure from all sides: from the high-school students seeking admission to the colleges, from the admissions directors of the colleges, from the teachers in the school system, and from national publicity and national fellowship and scholarship programs.

6. The Teaching Profession

The final category to which we might turn our attention is that of the teaching profession as a whole, as distinct from its specialized parts. Here again we must consider the influence of private associations. Here again, in answering the question of a visitor from abroad who marvels at the similarity of the American schools despite their decentralization, we must point to this network of personal and professional communication that spreads across the nation. What demands may we expect these associations to make? Can we assume that they will be in conflict with other demands made through other groups in categories?

To the latter question the answer is surely "Yes." The professional education associations will be less concerned with special interests and more concerned with teacher welfare as a whole. They will often find themselves in conflict with economic pressure groups. In the matter of standards for admission to the profession, it is probably inevitable that they will be in conflict with the demands of the scholarly fields, which will naturally insist upon training programs that specialize heavily in the area of their particular concern. It is probable that the professional teachers' associations will rank somewhat higher than do others the importance of the high school in American society. The teachers' associations will call for a higher allocation of national resources to their cause. And their influence will be considerable, for they are, after all, the group of adults with which the local school board is in closest touch. Their demands have already placed, and surely will increasingly place, the superintendent in a position of ever greater role conflict. Though their influence on legislation and on school policy is probably less than is estimated by some contemporary observers, it is nevertheless a significant factor and deserves a special category.

Balancing the Conflicting Demands

After this long analysis, the reader will doubtless be impatient for some effort to clarify what the role of the high school should be, or will be, or both. But if the analysis has shown anything, it has shown that no man is capable of giving a total answer to this question. He can perhaps give some idea of his special interests, and I think it is reasonable to ask him to assess the forces mentioned above and to indicate those forces whose influence, he thinks or hopes, may increase.

The analysis implies that American educational policy, and therefore a policy governing the roles of the high school, is the result of the fusion and the balancing of a variety of pressures. It implies that we are now proceeding, and probably should proceed, on a plan of deliberate checks and balances. There is an echo here of the pattern of government defended by Hamilton and Madison in the *Federalist Papers*. It means that those of us who have views and are willing to express them have to take into account the views and needs of others. Lacking anything like the Constitution in written form, the school board is faced often with the difficult task of being simultaneously the legislative, the judicial, and the executive branch of educational government. Under these circumstances, school boards across the nation are likely to find different definitions of the role of the high school, though we may hope for greater uniformity by the self-conscious analysis and balancing of the demands being made. Given the present American situation, I doubt that any formula is available for the proper balance and mixture of these demands. This result is inevitable in our system of decentralization.

Looking in this way at the problem of clarifying the role of the high school makes it a little easier to decide which demands are relevant and which are not—or, more accurately, which of the many entirely relevant demands are more important than others. Here the educator has a responsibility: to state his case as an individual who is devoting his life to the field. Here he may try to persuade all groups, or some groups, as he may think most expedient. For example, I am personally persuaded of the importance of a rapid raising of the high-school standards in mathematics and in English composition for all students, not alone for that much publicized group of the talented. I consider it quite fair for me to try to persuade the scholars in these fields that their influence should be cast on that side of the balance.

I also suspect that specific vocational training is unwise social policy and that it should be replaced by programs which, while giving full opportunity for actual participation in vocational work of various sorts, seek to generalize the training to a greater degree than is often done today. Here it seems quite appropriate for me to urge changes in the basic policies (as I understand them, although I probably do not), in federal aid to vocational education and in the policies of some of our commercial and vocational courses. It would seem perfectly fair that industrial and commercial groups particularly interested in the training of the young men and women who come to them as employees should exercise their influence.

It seems to me, an educator, that the high schools in many parts of the United States are not fulfilling the function suggested in the early part of this paper, namely, providing a place where children of all economic and social backgrounds have an even chance to start their lives and their careers. To me this failure suggests the need of increased federal support to even out the opportunities. It is surely appropriate in this connection to urge teachers' associations, and other private groups which entertain comparable social ideals, to take part in influencing both the national government and the local school boards to achieve such equality of opportunity.

The resolution of these conflicting pressures rests squarely on the elective body that governs the school system. Under our system, influence can be brought to bear on these bodies, but no instructions can effectively be given. One might therefore ask whether, under present circumstances, this system seems to be the best available to us. Should we take away from school boards substantial areas of their present responsibilities? Should the curriculum, for example, be set by state and/or national decision? Even if the making of such decisions were politically practicable, which I doubt, I would argue against it as a solution; for it seems to me that the removal of these decisions to a higher level of government would immediately reduce the influence of the first two categories of influences that I have mentioned: (1) the children and the parents and (2) the local community. As I read American history, it appears that we have made remarkable progress in good part because we have never wholly disassociated our policies from the attitudes and emotional ties of the localities. The result is a messy picture, which would not appeal to the aesthetic taste of most Frenchmen, but it appeals to me. Proceeding in the American way requires the self-conscious use of the idea of checks and balances. It requires patience. It requires educators to see themselves in context. It implies the need in school systems for administrative officers whose general education includes an understanding of American society and the courage to be willing to resist its multiple pressures. It implies that there will never be a total resolution of these conflicting pressures, and I, for one, am glad of it.

WALTER L. COOPER

Meeting Conflicting Demands on the High School

Any consideration of the vast area of pressures and demands, either conflicting or helpful, that serve to influence the scope, content, and performance of America's educational program should first be viewed in terms of the basic goals and desired outcomes of that program.

Our educational program stands unparalleled among all the programs of the world in the extent to which it serves all the children of all the people. Let us assume that this status is generally accepted as being right and essential. Let us also assume a general agreement on the concept that, without an enlightened citizenry, the principles of democratic living may be imperiled. Let us further assume that both lay and professional people agree that an educational program in a democracy must be a co-operative process, in which the most mature thought of one group serves to complement and supplement the other. Let us assume, moreover, that there is reasonably universal acceptance of the broad general objective that the product of our secondary school should be people who possess a basic understanding of the rights, privileges, and responsibilities of democratic citizenship and who, to the extent of their individual capacities, possess social and economic competencies.

During the past quarter-century there has been an increasing interest in, and concern about, the program of the schools. This interest is a logical sequel to the great increase in the number of school patrons, to an ever expanding membership in the parent-teachers' association, and to an ever increasing membership in professional organizations of all kinds. Most of the concern has been with the end product of the schools, as well as with what is taught in the classrooms. Another source of the interest has been the increasing competition for the tax dollar.

These influences have not been strictly local in nature but have extended even to the national scene. Few have forgotten the period during World War II when it was found necessary to ration gasoline and certain food products. How to carry out this program effectively was a problem. Because of the community nature of the schools, they became the logical avenue for carrying out the project. Since we were in a period of national emergency, the schools accepted the challenge and did an excellent job of reaching all the people. Not a high percentage of school and lay people would maintain that a significant learning experience resulted from this effort, but it made the public aware that, when called upon to do a job, the schools could do it and do it well.

It must be said that the ultimate results from some of the external demands upon the schools have been desirable. School people have not always shown a pioneering, aggressive spirit in attempting to meet the needs of boys and girls in a changing society. Often the preservation of the status quo has been more nearly the aim. Particularly is this true at the secondary level. Some of the changes that have come about have been the result of pressures exerted from the outside by persons or groups who recognized the needs. Each successful venture opened the door to others and has made their accomplishment easier.

It is difficult to determine how much influence these demands and pressures exert upon the school curriculum or upon the effective administration of a school program. Let us examine some of these demands and pressures and attempt to assess their influence on the high school.

Local Influences

In most communities there are various professional organizations which originated in collegiate educational institutions and the membership of which is composed of persons whose educational careers were marked by superior achievement. It is only natural that such organizations should have a vital interest in the school program, particularly in the quality of the offering. Quite frequently these people are interested in course content and have definite ideas about what should be taught. There is a danger that the rather high selectivity of the membership of these organizations limits their understanding and acceptance of the broad scope and objectives of the modern school. The activities of these organizations are frequently identified with public forums and discussion programs concerning some phase of education.

In less than twenty years the number of American citizens eligible for membership in patriotic organizations has reached a staggering figure. Few communities are without local chapters of these organizations, and the opportunity for exercising significant influence is almost universal. For the most part their purposes are worthwhile, and their activities may contribute to the establishment of real values in the minds of students. These organizations are essentially concerned with keeping a close watch upon the offering and content of the school program to see that no instruction inconsistent with their established policies and beliefs is offered. These organizations have assumed the responsibility of maintaining and perpetuating ideals of patriotism, and they interpret school activities in light of these ideals. A very significant percentage of the American public can be influenced if activities that involve school children can be arranged. Perhaps that is one reason why the activities of patriotic organizations are largely associated with essay, oratorical, and good-citizenship contests. Even though the activities may be of questionable value as learning experiences, they are certain to be supported with sincerity and enthusiasm.

Increasing competition for the tax dollar and growing awareness of the mounting tax bill have caused many groups and individuals to look for ways to obtain education for less. In most communities the largest single tax is laid for schools. Little wonder, then, that the school becomes the target of attention. Local tax groups demand justification of any program in the schools that may deviate from the traditional. Most of these groups or individuals have solutions that would "improve" the schools. No other group attracts so many experts or so many who will discuss the "ills" and the "treatment" at any time and any place before any audience. Such persons usually draw broad generalizations from specifics which may have little basis in fact.

Consciousness of the tax burden, coupled with a strong motivation in the area of personal interests, brings other individuals and groups into the scene for recognition. Business interests that find an insufficient number of young people entering their occupational fields sincerely believe that the schools could, and should, offer specialized courses designed to further interest in these occupations. Two obvious examples may be found in the present high interest in economic education and the pressure for developing physicists, chemists, and engineers.

In many communities there are a few vocal individuals who "carry the torch" for a cause. These persons may not gain too much public support, but they can become a constant source of annoyance to those responsible for planning and executing the school program and may even become a deterrent to normal progress.

National Influences

For the most part the organizations identified above are local in nature. Some of them, however, are affiliated with parent organizations operating at state and national levels. Such organizations not only conduct their activities as local initiative dictates but are required to conform with general policies of the so-called parent groups. Still other organizations, somewhat detached from the local community, exercise varying degrees of influence upon the schools. For the purpose of bringing about a better understanding of the interests they serve, business and industrial interests, for example, spend large sums of money in the development of pamphlet materials designed to be used as supplementary text materials.

A careful study of course offerings in the typical American high school indicates the strong influence of colleges and universities in shaping curriculum practices. The number and the per cent of high-school graduates who go on to college is rapidly increasing, and predictions indicate that this trend will continue if not increase. In anticipation of this expanding enrolment, even beyond existing facilities, more and more colleges and universities are requiring that prospective students pass the tests of the College Entrance Examination Board before they can be admitted to the higher institutions. It is entirely possible that curriculum planners in the high school will step up consideration of the program for college-bound students, with a resulting loss to students who will terminate their formal education with the high school. Recently Robert Marschner, president of the Homewood (Illinois) Board of Education, released, through a national magazine with a large circulation,[1] the names of the thirty-eight top-ranking high schools in the United States based solely upon the number of finalists in the National Merit Scholarship testing program. It is easy to imagine the amount and character of discussion from all quarters that such a pronouncement would provoke. At least one newspaper editorially assailed the school serving its district because of the school's absence from the list.

Closely related to testing programs is the whole area of scholarships, which is currently receiving much attention. More and more business and industrial interests are arranging for substantial scholarships and grants to individual students on various competitive bases. Also closely related is the current emphasis, both at local and national levels, upon appropriate ways of meeting the needs of the gifted or talented child.

Other Influences

The foregoing descriptions do not comprise an exhaustive list of the influences that create either direct or indirect demands upon the school, nor is it implied that all exert conflicting pressures. Two other situations by which serious influences are exerted upon the schools should be presented. These are less direct, perhaps, in application, but they may produce more serious and lasting effects upon the curriculum and the administration of the school's program than those that have been previously identified.

The first deals with the familiar concept of academic freedom both for the student and for the teacher. Since any inhibitions upon the academic freedom of the students is likely to be teacher-induced, the principal emphasis here should be on the effects that some situations exert upon the teacher. Academic freedom, or the lack of it, may result from pressures externally imposed which create inhibitions in the teacher. Frequently these inhibitions are associated with the teaching of controversial subjects. Whatever the source of the influence, the result is that the student is denied his natural right to explore all facts relating to a subject and thereby to form independent judgments and conclusions. There is some evidence that the teacher in general enjoys more freedom today than in former years, but the situation drew this statement from Mrs. Newton P. Leonard.

[1] *Time*, LXX (October 21, 1957), 52.

president of the National Congress of Parents and Teachers, in speaking before the 1953 meeting of the National Education Association:

> Teachers want freedom—the personal freedom that is the right and privilege of all citizens. But to attain and hold that freedom they must have the courage to speak up and act in their own behalf.
> It is true that our fears make us cautious, wary of speaking up. But fear only invites deeper and deeper inroads on personal freedom. If each new attack awakens only a more intense fear, we become in the end victims not of outer threat or assault but of our own inner terror.[2]

Other authorities have similarly spoken and written, emphasizing the need for schools to be operated with the needs and interests of the young people and the entire community in mind.

The second influence deals with an area that in the past decade has seldom been absent from the programs of professional school groups, whether local, regional, or national. It may be described as "attacks" upon education, or perhaps a better term is "criticisms." Critics of the schools have generally been divided into two classes: those who are sincere in wanting to improve education and those whose apparent motive is to undermine confidence in it. The latter group has made various and sundry charges, which, for the most part, have been made to look ridiculous but which cannot be ignored. The persons who would destroy the schools dare not reveal their true purpose. The opponents of free public education are so few in number that they resort to subversive methods. They organize or join groups in which there are likely to be honest critics who are sincerely working for the betterment of the schools. When they are intrenched in these groups, they arouse emotionalism and suppress reason. They hope, in the midst of bitter discord and confusion, to divide the friends of the schools. Thus the enemies of free public education strive to gain their ends. During the past decade more than a hundred communities have been subjected to pressures of this type.

Today the situation is somewhat changed because several of the organizations through which the extremists propagandized are out

[2] Mrs. Newton P. Leonard, "Greetings from the National Congress of Parents and Teachers," in National Education Association, *Proceedings of the Ninety-first Annual Meeting Held at Miami Beach, Florida, June 28–July 3, 1953* (Washington: National Education Association, 1953), XCI, 55–56.

of existence or are ineffective. There is some evidence that grounds for undue alarm about "attacks" are diminishing. The more moderate and logical critics now have the upper hand, and the climate of opinion is more favorable to constructive criticism. Although the views of the extremists have died down, the seeds already planted have been sufficient to arouse other critics. The latter, for the most part sincere, are not in sympathy with the aims and objectives of modern education, and they resent what is often termed "intrusion by educationists" into areas that should be controlled by the scholarly disciplines.

Ways To Meet Demands

In pointing out methods by which conflicting demands have been, and may continue to be, met, it would be appropriate to adopt the premise that "the schools belong to the people." The people provide the facilities and the money to operate the program whether public or non-public. The people also provide the children who make up the membership of the schools. The premise carries with it three major implications: first, the people have a right, and an obligation, to determine the kinds of schools they want; second, the people have a right to know what is going on in the schools; and, third, the people must reserve the right to evaluate the results. The last prerogative is likely to be exercised whether or not the others are, and the results may sometimes be disturbing to school people. The lesson is that, as the school program evolves and is developed, people of the community should be involved, the talents of special groups should be employed, channels of communication should be kept open, and the confidence of the community should be gained. Some promising approaches to meeting the problem are suggested below.

1. If the secondary school is to develop and carry out an effective educational program, the program must be given direction by a definite, well-formulated educational philosophy. It is not sufficient that the guiding objectives for the school be formulated in a broad general statement of the function of secondary education in society. Rather a very intimate statement should be developed by, and for, the local community, embracing the goals which the community desires for its schools.

An understanding of the goals of the school will give direction to curriculum planners in making decisions about what shall be taught, about methods of teaching, and about the evaluative process. If the patrons of the school have the right to help determine the what and the why of education, intelligent use of lay people on a representative basis is important when developing the school's goals.

To develop a carefully formulated philosophy with specific aims and objectives is a forward move, but it is not complete. The goals should be accepted by all teachers and so well understood by them that their teaching activities are continuously directed toward the accomplishment of the goals. It is equally important that the community understand and acccept the goals. In order that the aims and objectives will always reflect the changing needs of the community, a process of continuous re-evaluation needs to be instituted.

2. A well-functioning curriculum committee, certainly representative of the professional staff and preferably containing lay representation, can become a vital force in shaping the curriculum to accomplish the desired goals. Such a committee, with diverse interests and relationships, can serve to bring a necessary balance to the school's program. Many schools today have such committees or councils, through which all problems related to the curriculum are channeled. For example, such a committee can screen the vast amount of supplementary text materials provided by special-interest groups and can recommend for use those appropriate to the instructional needs of the school. The channels of communication should be kept open to and from this committee so that the professional staff and the community are aware of, and understand, developments that are taking place.

3. Professional and patriotic organizations and other groups interested in the welfare and improvement of the educational program can be profitably utilized by (a) furnishing them with leaders who will assist in organizing and conducting public forums where problems of local interest to the schools can be discussed freely but with dignity and understanding; (b) securing their participation in school-sponsored projects (this is very commonly done when referendums and bond issuse are being voted on, but there are a great many other projects with which such groups could well be identified); (c)using them in the collection and the preparation of pertinent data necessary to answer specific questions about the achievements of the school program.

4. Educational leadership would do well to recognize that the schools' most severe critics should be the school people themselves. Consequently a carefully planned program of self-evaluation should be carried on. Strengths should be detected and capitalized upon, and weaknesses discovered and efforts made to overcome them. When community help is needed, the school faces the facts. Frankness is as important in weakness as in strength.

5. If the community has enthusiasts for a cause, such persons should be heard. Perhaps an audience with the superintendent or even the board of education would be proper. In many instances just the chance to be heard satisfies these persons and stills their criticisms.

6. Most schools could profitably expand the use of community resources by inviting persons with special knowledge to appear before class groups and enrich the teaching situation. The organization of the school program to provide for excursions and field trips to points of interest in the community will help provide valuable learning situations for the students. Such procedures will also assist in identifying the school with the community, thus providing a "we-ness" in the program.

7. A number of schools have developed instruments for reporting to the parents and to the community on a periodic basis the salient facts and features of the school program. These instruments take the form of newsletters, newspapers, annual reports, and others. In many instances the services of parent-teachers' association members are used in preparing and distributing these instruments of information.

8. Open houses, parent nights, and school programs which bring the parents into the school offer opportunity for the public to learn at first hand what is being taught in the schools.

9. On a national and regional basis, organizations are diligently at work in the articulation of high school and college, attempting to bring high-school and college people together to identify and better understand the mutual problems of both institutions. The high schools must come to understand that the colleges have a particular function to perform in society and that appropriate and adequate preparation at the high-school level can materially assist the college in performing that function. By the same token, the colleges and their staff members must realize that the function of

the high school is much broader than mere preparation for college and that the high school's influence reaches a major percentage of the youth of this country who will never be identified with the college.

10. The increasing pressure to secure participation of school children in contests of many types has been partially alleviated through the activities of the National Association of Secondary-School Principals. There is now available to the schools a list of approved contests, and many state organizations have adopted this list for use in their particular states. Some schools have gone beyond this point and have adopted policies which prohibit highly organized participation in contests but still do not deny individual students from participating on a voluntary basis.

11. Throughout the years the schools have assumed an increasing role in the total education of the child until today the school is fast approaching the point of being "all things to all children." It may be time now for the schools, in co-operation with the home, the church, and other educative agencies of society, to redefine the role of the schools and recognize that it is not appropriate or even possible for schools to perform every educative function in society.

12. Most of the suggestions listed here have emphasized the need for involving people of the community in the development of the school program. The reason for this emphasis is the fact that individuals are slow to attack or criticize themselves. Likewise, people who feel themselves a part of the educational program will offer constructive criticism rather than exert damaging pressures or make highly conflicting demands.

13. Finally, the effectiveness of any of the suggestions made here for meeting conflicting demands is proportionate to the sincerity and courage of the educational leadership in the community. Education needs leadership that is willing to utilize all the community resources available in determining the goals of the high school and in developing programs designed to achieve those goals. If maximal effectiveness is to be achieved in the learning process for boys and girls, the same degree of professional courage is essential in all teachers. With teachers and administrators of such professional stature at work on the educational scene, the ill effects of conflicting demands will be minimized.

VI

Consideration Is Given to Guidance, School-College Relationships, the Needs of Fast and Slow Learners, and Achievement Standards

Student Personnel Services in the High School

The development of the secondary school as an institution for all children has presented new problems. It is now necessary for us to think in terms of the gamut of individual differences and the total range of abilities found in the large unselected student body making up the high-school enrolment.

Although our schools serve the many, education is, in a real sense, an individual affair. The effectiveness of our program must still be measured in terms of the learning level of each student and of the success attained by each young person in his progress toward mature, effective adulthood. A modern program of student personnel services in the high school is geared to recognition of the individuality of the student. It includes accounting for attendance, maintenance of appropriate student personnel records, arranging appropriate student placement, and reporting to parents, as well as educational, vocational, and personal counseling for facilitating effective adjustment. Thus we may say that student personnel services translate the broad concepts of the educational program into its impact on the individual.

Guidance and Administrative Planning

The guidance point of view should have a primary place in the strategy of administration and curriculum planning. Student personnel services and the intellectual understandings on which they are founded must undergird all our educational thinking. Some authorities have said that the challenge to student personnel services is to take curricular plans and administrative policies and translate them into programs of education. I suggest that this is introducing the student personnel concept too late, and perhaps at a time when an effective translation is impossible. In my view, the guidance point of view must be represented in the original deliberations in which curricular plans and administrative policies are formulated. Only in this manner can we guarantee that full consideration will be given to the implications of the wide range of individual differences, to the students' needs and the relation of needs to the learning potential, and to the necessity for appropriate evaluative techniques. Only in this manner can we guarantee that the important information from the world of work and from the social and family setting will be translated into appropriate curricular developments.

It is through the guidance service that the school reaches into the home and integrates the influences of home and school into a unified, effective program for the student. Guidance takes cognizance of the fact that the teacher of each class faces students with a wide range of individual abilities; it provides the teacher with basic materials for effective grouping for instruction. The guidance service high-lights the fact that educational programs are effective only when they make possible an optimum growth for each student and when the instructors are provided with the basic information about each student necessary for planning an instructional program to attain these goals. Through guidance services, students get the assistance which helps them develop problem-solving abilities adequate to meet their current challenges and the problems ahead of them. Guidance is the process whereby all the educational staff is continually reminded that young people have needs other than academic needs. Guidance emphasizes that an effective organization of a secondary school must provide for each person in terms of his needs for acceptance, affection, a feeling of belongingness, and his strong need to taste success and to accomplish adequately.

It may seem that, in defining the total nature of guidance, I have labored the necessity of providing for each person. If so, it is because, in my experience, this concept is accorded much lip service but little practical application in many secondary schools today. In some schools, guidance is still the program provided for those who are retarded or emotionally disturbed. In some, the guidance department seems to occupy the role occupied by the fire department in our modern cities—taking care of emergencies. To be sure, the guidance worker must always take a leading role when corrective or therapeutic work is essential and when the trauma of daily living makes it necessary to provide special attention for the individual.

However, it is essential to recognize that the guidance worker can make his most effective professional contribution by diffusing his understandings and principles throughout the school organization. This will be done to the extent that student personnel workers play an active role in administrative strategy, planning, and decision for the total educational program.

The Emerging Guidance Profession

The past quarter-century has seen the emergence of guidance as a profession that reflects many factors present in society and incorporates the basic core of psychological knowledge as a theoretical foundation. Perhaps there are some who wonder if this new profession, with its additional budget demands, has come into being to serve the needs of the personnel workers themselves or the needs of students that would otherwise be unmet.

It can easily be shown that the great changes in our society in the past quarter-century have made a guidance program essential in any secondary school. In a world of work with an overabundance of opportunity, our students face much pressure in making the correct occupational choices. More than thirty-nine thousand ways of earning a living in our society have already been classified. There are more than a hundred families of occupations requiring different academic preparation and utilizing different interests, aptitudes, and abilities. The lengthening of preparatory programs for each of these fields has likewise emphasized the necessity of correct choices. It is no longer possible for a person to try one professional field and switch to another without losing much time and money and without experiencing frustration. In addition, both the diversification of work and the evolving pattern of universal education have caused young people to depart from the tradition of following in their fathers' footsteps vocationally. In the fullest sense today, young people are free to strive, free to experiment, and free to succeed or to fail. We defend the preservation of these opportunities for young people, but we must also assume the corresponding responsibility to provide them with the needed counseling assistance, the basic information, and the necessary psychological support during their time of exploration, choice, and preparation.

Apart from all this, a guidance profession could not have emerged unless there had been a basic field of knowledge to support the services offered. Only during the last twenty-five years have we learned much about how the individual matures and develops. Much of this knowledge comes from studies in the fields of medicine, psychology, sociology, and cultural anthropology, as well as from interdisciplinary studies. Through guidance, the findings from all these fields are now being assimilated into the educational services and are having an impact upon the guidance worker and his methods of working with young people.

All signs indicate that our society will continue to grow in complexity and diversified opportunities for our young people, requiring comparable diversification of opportunity for them in high school. In addition, the professions providing the basic information from which the guidance worker draws his techniques will continue to grow. As a result we can look forward to better methods and understandings in the years ahead. Thus in terms of need for the service and of promise for better service through professional improvements, we can predict that the guidance profession will grow in stature and importance and will become an increasingly valuable arm of the educational administrative planning team.

The Role of the Teacher in Guidance

In the early stages of guidance the professional worker seems to have envisioned that all good guidance work would be done by specialists and that the teacher would have little responsibility in this field. For some workers, this was a sincere point of view, reflecting their recognition of the complex factors in the guidance process and the importance of developing professional techniques to handle the complex problems. However, on the part of some, it may well have been a symptom of insecurity and of their need to establish a profession of stature and recognition. Commenting upon this point, T. R. McConnell, while he was chancellor of the University of Buffalo, said:

> I think I have detected a desire on the part of some professional counselors to establish a priesthood. As members of the order, they speak with authority, and like the medical profession, they do not want their authority questioned, either as to substance, or as to the methods by which they arrived at their conclusions. Furthermore, they act as if their knowledge were esoteric. . . . I know how intensely counselors want to acquire status, if not

as much for themselves individually, as for their profession. But it actually might be better strategy in educational institutions for them to share their special knowledge as fully as their academic colleagues are able to understand or appreciate.[1]

In the main, this concern is now behind us in the field of guidance. Almost all guidance workers are now agreed that an effective program depends directly upon involving teachers to the fullest extent and that the guidance worker is a team member, working with and through parents, teachers, and administrators in planning a total student personnel program. Guidance workers recognize the fact that, because the teacher is in contact with the student for the major portion of the day, the teacher is, in the fullest sense, a key person in the total guidance program.

From one point of view the teacher is a manager of a social system; he controls the group processes in which young people function for many hours a day. Within his power of manipulation are the interpersonal relationships of young people. Through the selection of classmates and partners for various group activities and through the demonstration of courtesy, appreciation, and respect, the teacher controls the emotional climate for the student. As we have increasingly recognized the school as a laboratory for teaching the democratic processes, the teacher has accepted the responsibility for creating an appropriate climate and for basing his social decisions upon respect for the rights of individuals.

Sometimes, it has been said, the guidance worker expects the teacher to be a mental-health expert as well as a subject-matter specialist. This charge usually reflects misunderstanding of the guidance worker's intention. The guidance worker recognizes that the teacher is always responsible for determining the atmosphere in the classroom. It is apparent every day in the teacher's every contact with students that he is guiding and directing a program with a mental-health impact. In assessing the teacher's effectiveness in this area, the basic question is whether through the teacher's efforts the atmosphere of the classroom is conducive to good learning, whether it stimulates students to effective performance and affords constructive, wholesome experiences. The teacher who achieves this goal

[1] T. R. McConnell, "A University President Looks at Student Personnel Work" (Paper read at Conference of American Personnel and Guidance Association, Buffalo, New York, April, 1954).

may do so naturally, because of his type of personality, even though he is not professionally trained in mental-health matters. However, in many instances the teacher needs assistance in this facet of his professional development as much as he does in other facets.

The teacher has the natural opportunity to make a constructive guidance contribution in day-to-day contacts with youth. To separate the teaching and guidance functions would be an artificial administrative device. However, it would be equally unrealistic to presume that the teacher can handle all problems no matter how complex they may be. It can be anticipated that handling the majority of daily contacts with students is within the scope and the capabilities of the classroom teacher. Nevertheless, to handle them adequately, the teacher should have constant access to advice and information from the professional guidance workers. In addition, the teacher should have the full confidence of these professional workers and should be free to refer special problems to the guidance department with no feeling of personal threat or incompetence.

The Role of the Professional Guidance Worker

The professional guidance worker influences all the participants in a school system. He provides the basic information that teachers need to make effective instructional plans for their groups and for the individuals comprising the groups. The guidance worker cooperates with parents in developing an understanding of their children and the problems facing them at various stages of development. He assists the school administrator in planning an appropriate instructional program and in evaluating the effectiveness of the program.

Part of the work of the professional is done in face-to-face contacts with students with specialized problems. Often these problems relate to emotional issues and to personal tensions between the student and members of his peer group or between the student and adults. The professional uses the full gamut of counseling skills and insights from his broad background in psychology, sociology and personality dynamics. This broad preparation helps him to recognize the early symptoms of serious maladjustments and to understand the need of referring individuals to clinical resources, in time and under conditions that will make effective treatment by the clinic possible. Often the professional must secure parental under-standing of a problem and parental co-operation in supporting the student during the arduous experience of referral to the clinic and during the lengthy period of psychotherapy.

In addition to his skills in working with individuals in a coun-seling situation, the professional worker must be a team member par excellence, adroitly assisting the other members of the team to identify problems and to suggest solutions. He seldom fulfils his role when he superimposes his insight and his superior knowledge. Rather he will be most effective when he asks searching questions and suggests broad viewpoints likely to lead to solutions of instruc-tional and administrative problems. In other words, his qualifica-tions must include great adeptness in working with his professional peers and other adults, as well as skill in developing warm, close relationships with students. Unquestionably our secondary schools of the future will need to attract and encourage superior counselors with broad professional preparation and with exceptional personal qualities of leadership.

Guidance as a Form of Teaching

An additional trend may be noted in the field of guidance: mod-ern guidance techniques and modern teaching techniques have moved closer and closer together. Much of our modern clinical psy-chology, as well as our educational theory, relies on principles de-rived from research in the psychology of learning and on the recog-nition of the importance of habits, attitudes, and past experiences. Both the teacher and the professional guidance worker have become increasingly aware of the importance of emotions and of the varying motivation levels of students. Techniques in both teaching and counseling rely heavily on stimulating students to act and think for themselves and to learn, through experience, appropriate modes of response and habit patterns.

This has not always been so. Formerly teaching was much more likely to be conducted in an autocratic setting with emphasis on rote learning and on the reciting of lessons. The dominant theories in psychology formerly stressed the mysterious labyrinths of the unconscious in accordance with Freudian teachings, and the coun-selor dispensed advice instead of listening and eliciting self-direction. It is interesting that current trends both in education and in psychology seem to be moving toward the acceptance of individual responsibility and the importance of self-realization by the adolescent. Perhaps this trend, as much as anything, has helped the guidance worker and the teacher to join forces on the academic team and has assisted guidance workers to function harmoniously with teachers, parents, and administrators in the academic setting.

The Use of Psychological Tests

Perhaps the major contribution made by the guidance worker and allied professions is the development and interpretation of instruments for effective appraisal of the psychological attributes of individuals. Nearly all secondary schools today have regular programs for testing entering students, and they make periodic reappraisals of student achievement in various fields. In addition, the increasing attention given to college preparation and to competition for college entrance has increased the emphasis on broad areas of learning and on preparation for competitive examinations. Tests thus provide, for the student and for the administration, some insight into the effectiveness of the academic work done by the students.

Psychological testing was the cornerstone of the early guidance movement. Unquestionably, testing had great "sales" value for the movement, for it was something tangible that the guidance worker could offer to the teacher and the administrator to help them understand students. It was of obvious advantage in interpreting the work of the school to the parents. In the early days much testing was done primarily for this public relations goal.

In recent years, however, emphasis has been placed on the importance of using test results to help students personally and individually. A maxim now is that tests should not be given to collect data for the file or merely to contribute to research studies. Taking a student's time for testing implies an obligation for the counselor to interpret the results to the student and to counsel with the student concerning the implications of the findings. However, there is a difference of opinion on how far we should go in sharing test information with parents and students. Most of the psychological testing at the elementary-school level is done for the information of the teacher and the administrator. In general, as little information as possible is given out, whether performance is favorable or not. The situation is different in secondary schools.

Secondary-school organization, in the main, is predicated upon the student's acceptance of responsibility for his own actions, for the selection of his program, and for the effectiveness of his performance. Counselors working in this setting have usually been oriented toward a fuller sharing of information with students and parents. Some counselors with a great sensitivity to the components of mental health fear that realistic information may have an adverse effect on the morale of students. My own conviction is that the secondary-school guidance program should be based on the concept of full partnership of student, parent, and counselor; such a program will enable student and parent to accept information and responsibility on a realistic basis. When a counselor has established effective rapport with students, parents, and teachers, it is possible for him to discuss, in an objective manner, personal information from test results and class marks. When this discussion is pointed toward sound planning for the student, it is doubtful that harm will be done to the motivation level of the individual. The basic psychological principle that "knowledge of results improves performance" seems to apply here.

One additional comment should be made concerning the quality of psychological tests. In discussions of the use of psychological tests for ability grouping, for evaluating progress of pupils, and for special class placements, educators too often apologize by saying something like this: "We all know the weaknesses of tests, but they are the best instruments we have." If this comment once had a place in our conversations with teachers and parents, it is no longer accurate and has long outlived its usefulness. As the result of extensive research programs conducted by colleges, universities, the military services, and professional publishers, psychological tests today give comparatively accurate anwers to the basic questions that they purport to answer. In light of the accomplishments in test construction, the educational profession does itself a disservice by offering evidence from psychological tests with an apologetic attitude. The potential for more effective use of psychological tests is there if we but have the courage, understanding, and wit to use it appropriately.

Group Processes in Guidance

To many an administrator and parent, the word "guidance" calls forth a picture of a counselor and a student sitting in a private office discussing the student's personal problems. Perhaps some members of the guidance profession have fostered this concept and have perpetuated it in spite of recent trends and developments in the field. As a result of our increased understanding of group dynamics and our recognition of the close kinship between personal adjustment and the learning process, the secondary schools during the past decade have been turning more and more to group techniques to provide for the guidance of the students. Our students need basic information concerning the world of work, assistance in planning their secondary-school work and their programs for college preparation, and the opportunity to discuss their problems with peer groups under the sympathetic supervision of a trained guidance worker adept in group-conference techniques.

Recent years have seen a dramatic growth in group-guidance programs for all students. During the adolescent period, when young people are searching for a sense of identity, they draw closer to others in their age group who are experiencing many of the same tensions and frustrations. Because adolescents often feel that parents and teachers are too remote from their problems, young people find themselves unable to discuss their feelings meaningfully with adults. They can, however, accept assistance and advice from fellow students.

At present several youth-opinion surveys offer us insight for planning group programs with youth. The Purdue program, for example, has shown that adolescents have questions concerning health, vocational adjustment, family relationships, relationships with the opposite sex, and spiritual meanings. It is doubtful that any counselor in a modern secondary school can find time to discuss all these issues with individual students or that he can do so effectively even if he has the time. Evidence from the counseling field indicates that problems of this type are better explored in a group setting, with the students taking major responsibility for the discussion and the counselor functioning more as a catalyst than as a participant. To be sure, he must be ready to enter the discussion as a full-fledged participant whenever he judges it is necessary for him to do so. But, with skill, he can often limit his own contributions and give major emphasis to student participation and student growth.

Additional Crucial Areas

Space does not permit full discussion of other crucial areas in which the student personnel program functions in the modern secondary school. Some of the issues in these areas are exceedingly complex. Much could be said, for example, about the discipline problems in a secondary school and about the assignment of this function to the counseling department.

The extent to which the school should provide adequate counseling services and family casework could likewise be explored with profit. One critic has protested that the guidance profession should remember that an educational institution is neither a hospital nor an intellectual hothouse. This critic contends that guidance workers have acted in the apparent belief that the only purpose of secondary schools is the treatment of maladjusted adolescents. Exaggerated as this criticism is, it emphasizes the need to think through the extent of the school's responsibility in problems essentially socioeconomic and the resources that the school must be prepared to muster. In the matter of health the school has accepted the responsibility for identifying health problems and for referring them to parents and to community health agencies, leaving therapy to other community agencies. However, this definition of responsibility has not been so clearly possible in the field of personal adjustment, for adjustment occurs in the setting in which the student lives. This area could also stand full discussion.

One of the most complex areas in which the guidance worker functions is that of value choices in our society. The guidance worker confers with young people in their developmental stages, when they are groping for a personal value system. Often these young people experience much difficulty in choosing between a life of service and a life devoted to acquisitiveness. This conflict is a conflict of values, as are the conflicts between co-operation and competition in our times. On occasion there is confusion for young people in interpreting the "public will," since the "public will" is not always clearly defined even in the minds of adults. Passing through the turbulent years of adolescence, young people experience many conflicts concerning their relationships with the opposite sex and with parents. Such matters abound in counseling interviews. As these are basic questions with long-term significance for students, they pose for schools a great challenge in organizing and staffing guidance departments which are adequate to cope with issues of such major significance.

Sometimes the frank discussions that take place between counselor and student pose difficult decisions. Sometimes, for example, illegal or immoral acts which are discussed with the counselor have import for the administration, for parents, and for the enforcement authorities and correctional services in our society. In such cases what about the counselor-student relationship? Does the counselor owe his greatest responsibility to the student, or to the administration, or to the parent? These are not easy questions to answer.

This paper has been a sketchy portrayal of a major department of our secondary schools at work. As long as we are concerned with the individual and his special needs, we shall want strong pupil personnel programs in our secondary schools. The test of the effectiveness of our efforts will always be measured in terms of the progress made by the individuals comprising the student body. Though our plans encompass the many, our goal is to provide for the individual, to afford an appropriate experience and challenge for each student. Our student personnel program is organized to implement this concept.

A High-School View of Relationships with the College

How should one attempt to express the viewpoint of the American high school? It is parochial, private, and public. It is academic, comprehensive, and specialized. It is rural, town, and urban. It is small, and it is large.

The typical American high school is public. It is essentially a creation of the state. In the American tradition, it is supported and administered by the local community; its basic allegiance and obligation is to the local community. In brief, there are thousands of American high schools which are diverse as to size, as to means of support, and as to basic community obligation.

The image of a so-called typical American high school in the current era is further blurred by the pressure of ever increasing numbers and by the mobility of our population. Many schools of today have lost sight of their proposed goals and functions because of overcrowded plants and inadequate staffs. Others, because of hurried expansion, have staffs dominated in numbers by beginning and substandard personnel.

Under these circumstances it would be presumptuous to attempt to present a completely representative viewpoint. This paper will, however, describe what seem to be trends in current writing and research concerning the problem of high-school and college relationships as viewed by the high school.

New Look at High School–College Relations

It is not the tidal wave of numbers that is the most significant and sobering challenge to high-school and college relations in the decade ahead. Nor are these the questions of this era: Whom shall we educate? How long shall we educate them? Rather, the question is:

How and where shall we effectively train and educate *all* our human talent to live and share this complex life?

Education must no longer be considered terminal; it must be continuous for life. The young person must make a smoother, more effective transition from his non-productive, formal school period to the productive. The man whose job has been displaced by occupational change must prepare to move to another productive opportunity, and the man who must retire from his regular job must prepare to move to a less active productiveness but one which permits him to contribute in terms of his vitality and experience.

It should be added that the necessity for training all in no way denies the need for quality in the training of all. Perhaps the challenge of the day, then, is not merely to provide for the tidal wave of numbers. It is to provide a higher quality of formal education at all levels.

If these new demands are imperative, they imply a re-examination of the unique function of each level of education and a faithful adherence to its expressed obligation. Each level must do careful research to identify more effective practices and processes for fulfilling its own function. Each level must co-operate with the one above and below in study and research which are of mutual concern. Each level must point out those responsibilities and services which have been thrust upon it, those which cannot be definitely related to its unique function but which might be equally well or better served by other agencies. Each must delimit its program and services to its unique function and, at any given time, to the limitations of its existing staff and plant. Each must make a sincere, honest, and patriotic effort to extend its resources for serving more people more effectively.

What is the obligation of the high school and the college to youth in this atomic-electronic-technical age? What is our obligation to our nation, to the free world, as two major ideologies compete for the allegiance of the peoples of the world? How shall we prepare youth to survive as free men? How shall we prepare youth to adjust to the ever increasing tempo of change? These obligations are a sobering challenge to our creative leadership.

The obligation of high-school–college co-operation is aptly expressed by Traxler and Townsend:

Entrance requirements and the improvement of transition from school to college cannot be considered apart from a broad educational philosophy covering the entire range of school and college. . . .

The education of a boy or girl—the making of a man or woman—is all of one piece, and, logically, the same pattern ought to run throughout the making of the whole cloth, if symmetry and harmony are to characterize the end product. . . .

The point is that college ought to be a continuation of a broad, liberal, individual-centered and community-oriented education begun in school. Ideally, the curriculums of both institutions and the point of transfer from one to the other should always be flexible enough to take account of individual needs and drives and to provide that kind of continuity in progress toward distant but well-defined goals which helps to create intellectual maturity.[1]

In this obligation to youth, what are the problems as viewed from the high school? My presentation is concerned largely with college-bound youth, an ever increasing number and, in many respects, an increasingly heterogeneous group. This growth in numbers and in heterogeneity may call for better selection; if so, selection must be the result of earlier and more effective guidance. It must be a result of efforts to recruit all students who are able and talented.

Early Identification of Able Youth

As we consider the responsibilities of the high school toward young people who should be college bound, a most timely need is seen to be early identification of the able youth. Gardner, in the *Annual Report* of the Carnegie Corporation for 1956, expresses the crucial need in these pertinent words:

It is not just technologists and scientists that we need, though they rank high in priority. We desperately need our gifted teachers, our professional men, our scholars, our critics, and our seers.

The immensely increased demand for educated talent has placed a wholly new emphasis upon the role of colleges and universities in our national life. Virtually the total future leadership of our society—political, cultural, industrial, technical, professional, educational, and agricultural— is today being channeled through the colleges and universities and, increasingly, through our graduate and professional schools. It follows that these institutions will play a far more weighty and powerful role on the American scene than anyone had anticipated. As the cradle of our national leader-

---

[1] Arthur E. Traxler and Agatha Townsend (eds.), *Improving Transition from School to College* (A Study of College Admission by the Committee on School and College Relations of the Educational Records Bureau [New York: Harper & Bros., 1953]), pp. 115–17.

ship, their vitality and excellence become a matter of critical importance.
...

Concern for the full use of human capacities will produce intensive efforts
to salvage the able youngsters who are now lost to higher education.[2]

A joint committee of secondary-school principals and college officials proposes to begin this search by at least the ninth grade and
recommends that:

Further study be made of the ways and means by which talent, competencies, and special abilities can be *discovered* and developed early
enough so that proper and continuous guidance may be effective. This may
involve the use of a national test administered at the national, state, or local
level.[3]

In the comprehensive high school with multiple sections of English, language, mathematics, science, and social studies, should we
group to serve aptitudes, interests, and goals? For instance, grouping in English might place together the students who have advanced English mechanics skills; in elementary algebra and geometry, those who have an engineering or scientific goal might be
separated from those who are largely concerned with college-entrance credit. This practice would apply also to the languages.
Perhaps it should be said that grouping of the college-bound
through the daily schedule should not extend beyond the point at
which it can be justified as an effective motivational and educational device. Further it is agreed that there would be less justification for grouping in classes with a small pupil-teacher ratio.

A. Harry Passow, who has been closely associated with much of
the recent study and research on the gifted, states our responsibility
in these terms:

Gifted children need to cultivate their abilities to think searchingly and
critically, to build meanings and concepts, to see relationships between
past, present, and future learnings. They need training in how to learn and
how to discipline their intelligence in the interest of scholarship. The dis-

[2] John W. Gardner, "The Great Talent Hunt," in *Annual Report for the Fiscal
Year Ended September 30, 1956* (New York: Carnegie Corporation of New
York, 1956), pp. 12, 20.

[3] Joint Committee of the School-College Relations Committees of the American Association of Collegiate Registrars and Admissions Officers and the National
Association of Secondary-School Principals, "1957 Report: A Summary of Conclusions and Recommendations Resulting from the Joint Meeting Held in Chicago, January 11–12, 1957" (Washington: Paul E. Elicker, Secretary, National
Association of Secondary-School Principals), p. 6.

tinctive characteristic of the intellectually gifted youth is his fertile, creative mind; the optimum development of this creative intellect is another specific objective.[4]

One might ask if these are not worthy aims for all learners, especially the college-bound. That is agreed, but in typical practice today, are we not permitting the gifted to squander his fine intellectual, creative resources? Passow further challenges the high-school leaders in these words:

With imaginative planning, comprehensive schools, more than any other agency in the land, can develop socially precious gifts with certainty of a good yield—but they must use more creative approaches than they have to date.[5]

One channel for serving the very able and highly motivated youth is the Advanced Placement Program of the College Entrance Examination Board. A College Board brochure describes the program:

The College Entrance Examination Board offers the Advanced Placement Program in the interest of able students, secondary schools which enable these students to undertake work commensurate with their abilities, and colleges which welcome Freshmen who are ready for advanced courses.

The Advanced Placement Program provides descriptions of *college-level* courses to be given in schools and prepares examinations based on these courses. Colleges, in turn, consider for credit and advanced placement students who have taken the courses and examinations. The program is thus an instrument of co-operation which extends the educational opportunities available to able and ambitious students by co-ordinating effectively their work in school and college.[6]

The College Entrance Examination Board gives advanced-placement examinations in twelve subjects: English composition, English literature, French, German, Latin, Spanish, American history, European history, mathematics, biology, chemistry, and physics.

A paraphrase of a terse summary of the advantages of advanced placement may be stated as follows:

1. It pays attention to superior ability and stimulates the able.
2. It starts students on independent study, which can lead to college honors program.

[4] A. Harry Passow, "The Comprehensive High School and Gifted Youth," *Teachers College Record*, LVIII (December, 1956), 150–51.

[5] *Ibid.*, p. 152.

[6] College Entrance Examination Board, *Advanced Placement Program* (New York: College Entrance Examination Board, 1956), p. 7.

3. It breaks down artificial lines between high school and college, thus helping to eliminate duplication of work covered.
4. It encourages outstanding high-school teachers to keep abreast of college requirements and to keep after the abler students who can meet them.[7]

As we close this phase of the discussion on identifying able youth, we should be reminded that it is the high school which is responsible for discovering the college-bound boy or girl. Not many young people decide, after leaving high school, to go to college. Not many can retrieve their loss of preparation and background if they have not planned on college before graduation.

Earlier and More Effective Guidance for All

Along with the early identification of the able, there should be the early discovery of *all* students who are capable of doing post-high-school study. Since parental interest and consent figure heavily in a youth's post-high-school plans, the pupil and his parents should be encouraged, early and continuously during the secondary-school years, to explore areas of occupational interest. Parents and pupils should be helped to measure the youth's abilities, aptitudes, and limitations. If his tentative goals presume college training, a pattern of high-school work which will reveal evidence of competence to do college work should then be recommended. The student and his parents should be progressively informed of his successes, his limitations, and any deficiencies that will hinder his college work.

Once the student's tentative goal and his high-school performance point to college work, he and his parents should be invited to learn about the types of colleges which might serve his interest, fit his budget, and meet other requirements which the family may have. A search for the right type of college should start as early as practicable, perhaps by the tenth grade.

As he moves closer to graduation, the student should be helped to identify particular colleges which fit his ability to compete, which fit his maturity in self-direction, and which he can afford. At this phase he and his parents should be informed of available scholarships and financial-aid plans. He and his parents should be made

[7] "Will Your Child Be Going On to College?" *Better Schools*, III (February, 1957), 7.

aware of the various military-service programs that will most satisfactorily fit into his post-high-school plans.

Throughout the precollege counseling the student, his parents, and his counselor should check frequently with the admissions officers of the colleges in which he has a particular interest. This is especially important for the student in a high school which cannot offer some of the prerequisites which the college recommends. In this instance the student should ask the college's recommendation for acceptable substitutes which are offered by the high school. The student and his parents should be prepared on how to take advantage of the visits of college representatives, college-day programs, interviews with graduates in college, visits to college campuses, and similar channels for learning about college life and particular colleges.

At this point many high-school principals would express a note of caution concerning the need of mutually agreeable plans for the visit of college representatives, the invitations to visit college campuses during the school week, and similar contacts which can interrupt class work. Many large high schools which send half or more of their Seniors to college have a surprising number of requests for interviews with students on school time. In urban schools it is often awkward to say "No" to the request of college alumni for an assembly of the Senior class to hear a prominent dean or president, and it is not uncommon to have several deans make a given metropolitan area in one season.

This discussion of guidance has been concerned largely with the high school's responsibility in terms of transition to college. Guidance for the individual begins much earlier and continues through college. The report of the Committee on School and College Relations of the Educational Records Bureau relates guidance to college placement in these terms:

Guidance includes the collection of information about the individual pupil through measurement and other means, the maintenance of comprehensive cumulative records of development, the use of cumulative information in counseling the individual, and the building of attitudes and understandings that will enable the individual eventually to reach valid and mature decisions of his own accord. Thus, placement of students in college is to be viewed not as an end in itself but rather as an integral part of the whole guidance process.[8]

[8] Arthur E. Traxler and Agatha Townsend, *op. cit.*, p. xvi.

Burton P. Fowler, in the Foreword to the committee's report, makes this observation:

> How can we best identify the characteristics of a promising candidate for college? Such intangibles as maturity, intellectual curiosity, a sense of social responsibility, and capacity for painstaking, sustained effort are still only inferences which must be drawn from insufficient data. Studies need to be made of the factor of emotional maturity in the successful adjustment of students to college life. At present we know much more about preparing students' minds than their emotions. In dealing with the latter we have neither curriculum nor dependable tests.[9]

In other words, we have much to learn about effective guidance in terms of college entrance. The transition from the teen-age high-school pattern to that of the young-adult college pattern is no less complex than that from the elementary school to the junior high school. Again, the high school and the college must find new means for co-operating in making guidance continuous, evolving from a sheltered, closely guided high-school pattern to one largely of independence and self-direction in the college.

Preparation for College

Gaining proficiency in certain skills, such as English mechanics, reading, writing, listening, speaking, and study habits, is essential preparation for college. Deficiencies in these skills are a real handicap to college success. Much remains to be done at the high-school level to reduce these deficiencies.

There are other causes of college failure or of mediocre performance, which Fowler described as "intangibles." How can we reduce such hazards as immaturity and lack of motivation? Basic self-discipline and self-direction are difficult to develop in the typical high-school classroom. If we are strictly honest, we will admit that these valuable qualities of self-direction and motivation have been largely learned through participation in drama, student government, publications, sports, and like activities.

As we upgrade education, we shall undoubtedly be inclined to de-emphasize activities and stress the academic. How shall the high school then meet its obligation for more effective preparation in self-direction? How shall it build a stronger motivation for a college education? Where in the educational process are we losing natural

[9] *Ibid.*, p. xii.

curiosity, personal drive to want to know, and a sense of wanting to share and contribute in the ongoing life processes in this awesome technical age? In the steady prolongation of childhood characteristic of our American culture, are we leaving youth stranded on a static plateau where he learns to do wishful thinking, to twaddle, to squander his talents? If more students are to go to college with a purpose and if all levels of formal education are to have greater meaning, we must find new ways of relating education to our complex, technical life. The high-school age is the crucial period for initiating self-discovery, self-direction, and basic personal motivation.

Until we discover more effective means of developing the important intangibles, we must make a wiser and more stringent use of the methods now known. If success in college depends heavily upon adequate motivation and upon emotional and social maturity, the home and the school should use every co-operative means to instil these qualities. For instance, do parents too frequently refer to college in terms of its social life and prestige? Does the high school too often permit the Senior to carry a reduced load so that he may have a good time in his last year? By studies and reports, colleges can provide much valid information to impress on high-school students the importance of such qualities as maturity and motivation to succeed in college. High schools should provide as many special incentives as possible, in and out of class, to open new vistas of interest in the scientific, economic, and political world. These could include such devices and opportunities as model United Nations assemblies, science fairs, the use of community and professional leaders as consultant-resource people, and community surveys based upon a current need.

Mechanics of College Admission

The mechanics of college admission are also important. There are numerous unresolved problems, but they have received more attention and careful joint study than any other aspect of school-college relations. Such familiar questions as these are met:

What are the comparative merits of a transcript of high-school marks, of rank in class, of the record of test scores, of personality descriptions, and of the principal's recommendations as standards of college admission?

How inclusive shall be the transcript of record and the references? Shall they be reported on a uniform type of blank?

How important is the testing program—the college aptitude, achievement, proficiency, and placement tests? How much duplication is there between school and college testing?

What about applications to several colleges? How soon should the college advise the student of admission? what is the student's responsibility when he has made several applications?

How important is the Carnegie Unit as a determiner of admission?

What should be the basis of awarding scholarships?

What are the merits of "college days" and "campus days" in informing students and parents about college?

Several studies of school-college relations provide answers to some of these questions. For example, Traxler and Townsend summarize the guiding principles of college admission in about these words:

1. The purposes of admission will be best served if the welfare of the individual student is made focal.
2. Admission is, or should be, one step in a continuous guidance process from the pupil's early school contact through college.
3. Selections should be based both on what the college has to offer the applicant and on the abilities, preparation, and interests of the applicant that may enable him to profit from the college's offerings.
4. Requirements for admission should allow for the evaluation of the candidate's record as a whole.
5. If the qualifications and potentialities of the applicant are to be adequately studied, a thorough assessment of ablilities, achievements, interests, and personal qualities must be made.
6. The individual's fundamental habits, skills, and qualities are frequently the prime determiners of college success rather than courses studied or specific learnings mastered.
7. The curriculum of the college-bound student is a matter of major interest to both the high school preparing him and the college to which he applies.
8. An experimental or research attitude should be maintained in the program of admissions.[10]

Critical Areas for School–College Co-operation

Several aspects of the problem of school-college relationships need further co-operative effort. One of these is guidance. Criticisms expressed by college Freshmen and Sophomores indicate that counseling at the college level, especially in large schools, is far from adequate. Some complain of having as many as three or four differ-

[10] *Ibid.*, pp. 9–15.

ent advisers within the first two years. The larger the school and the more extensive its offerings, the greater is the need for effective individual counseling.

Co-operation in curriculum planning scarcely has been touched. We are aware of the monotonous duplication and repetition and of the frustrating gaps about which beginning college students complain. Indeed these may be one of the initial and crucial deterrents to motivation in college.

The Minnesota study of high school-college curriculum articulation in 1946–49 was perhaps one of the first state-wide efforts to reveal the need and status of co-operation. Since the typical high school of Minnesota was, in terms of numbers of students, concerned primarily with the education of youth who were not college-bound, the study was slanted toward the colleges' obligation in articulation. The study asked these four questions:

1. What provisions for curriculum articulation and student adjustment are made by the colleges in their guidance of entering Freshmen?
2. What provisions have the colleges made for developing courses appropriate to the different levels of ability and achievement among Freshmen?
3. What are the means by which colleges now attempt to articulate the content and instruction in Freshman courses with those in the high school?
4. What are the colleges doing to improve the present articulation of Freshman courses with those in the high school?[11]

A promising program in school-college co-operation in curriculum articulation is that of the school-college conferences held each summer by the Advanced Placement Program of the College Entrance Examination Board. At least ten such conferences were held during the summer of 1957. The aim is to develop communication between school and college teachers and administrators and to improve articulation of the work done in school and college. Participants include members of the examination committee, readers, and the school and college people interested in the Advanced Placement Program. The conferences of last summer included two sections on English, one at Haverford College and one at Ann Arbor High School in Ann Arbor, Michigan. The conference on foreign lan-

[11] University of Minnesota, *High-School-College Curriculum Articulation in Minnesota* (Minneapolis: Bureau of Educational Research, College of Education, University of Minnesota, September, 1950), pp. 2–3.

guages considered French, German, Latin, and Spanish. There was a conference on each of these subjects: history, mathematics, biology, chemistry, and physics. High-school and college administrators met to discuss the problems of administering the program and ways of improving articulation.

In Conclusion

This paper is easily open to criticism for being idealistic and unrealistic. There are undoubtedly many frustrating hazards to school-college co-operation. The more pertinent may be enumerated as (1) the many institutions of diverse size and goals, (2) the ever increasing and overwhelming numbers of students, (3) the lack of finances, and (4) the tremendously overloaded work schedules for the staff. These must be admitted. Surely ways and means can be found for representative groups of persons who guide and teach at both levels to extend and improve co-operative efforts in the interests of the college-bound student. This critical need for improved communication and co-operation is a challenge to educational leadership.

This realistic concern for the college-bound should in no way hinder the effectiveness and the quality of the training of the non-college youth. The high school of the future must provide improved programs for both groups.

CLYDE VROMAN

A College View of Relationships with the High School

The relationship of high schools and colleges has been important for many decades. It began to receive major attention about the end of the nineteenth century and has continued to receive consideration in varying degrees ever since that time. In the early decades the colleges dominated the thinking. In the thirties and the forties, college restrictions on the high schools were reduced, and the high schools have struggled valiantly to find how they might best use their new-found freedoms. The present decade has seen many cooperative efforts to establish the relationship of high schools and colleges on a sound and functional basis.

For example, in 1951, the American Association of Collegiate Registrars and Admissions Officers established a Committee on High School–College Relations, which I served as chairman. In 1955 this committee published a comprehensive report of its findings.[1] Two-day meetings of this committee are held each January with a similar committee from the National Association of Secondary-School Principals. The recommendations of this joint committee are then implemented by the two national associations.

At its annual meeting in Washington on October 10–11, 1957, the American Council on Education addressed itself to the topic "Articulation—A Consideration of Desirable Relationships among Levels and Types of Education to Insure Better Education for the Individual Student, Now and in the Coming Years." A resolution passed by the Council was related to this topic. It reads:

[1] Clyde Vroman (chairman), *Secondary School—College Co-operation: An Obligation to Youth* (A Study of Secondary School—College Relations, Committee on High School—College Relations of the Special Projects Committee, American Association of Collegiate Registrars and Admissions Officers [Lawrence, Kansas: James K. Hitt, Secretary, American Association of Collegiate Registrars and Admissions Officers, % University of Kansas, 1955]).

WHEREAS, The representatives of members of the American Council on Education here assembled agree that the growing numbers of our population who are seeking college opportunities make improved articulation among the various levels of education highly essential; therefore, be it

Resolved, That the members of the Council be urged to make needed studies and to seek other ways to further communication and co-operation among the various levels and types of educational institutions, for the purpose of meeting more effectively student needs.[2]

In this paper I shall try to analyze our problem as I have found it in my many-related activities of the last several years and particularly as I see it at the present time. I shall try to summarize the basic points of view, problems, and trends.

Colleges and Universities in the United States

The points of view held by college representatives on the high-school and college relationship usually depend on the kinds of institutions in which they serve. Therefore, as a basis for discussing this topic, we first must recognize the many differences in size, nature, and purpose of post-high-school educational institutions. The *Biennial Survey of Education in the United States, 1952–54* reports 1,863 institutions of higher education in the continental United States.[3]

The first major difference in colleges is their control and support. Of these 1,863 institutions of higher education, 662 were publicly controlled and 1,201 were privately controlled. These institutions can be differentiated further into at least seven major types. Table 1 shows the enrolment in 1953–54 for seven types of institutions.

Certain facts stand out in these data. Although about two-thirds (1,201) of the institutions of higher education are privately controlled, slightly more than half (53.9 per cent) of the students attend publicly controlled institutions. Furthermore, there are some striking differences in the enrolment of students in types of institutions. Seventy-one per cent of the liberal arts students are enrolled in privately controlled institutions, while only 4.7 per cent of the students in teachers' colleges are enrolled in privately controlled institutions. Only 21.1 per cent of the students enrolled in other pro-

[2] "Minutes of the Fortieth Annual Meeting: Report of the Resolutions Committee," *Educational Record,* XXXIX (January, 1958), 80.

[3] United States Office of Education, *Statistical Summary of Education, 1953–54,* Table 34, p. 52, in *Biennial Survey of Education in the United States, 1952–54,* chap. i (Washington: Government Printing Office, 1957).

fessional schools are in publicly controlled institutions, but 83.5 per cent of the students in junior colleges are in publicly controlled institutions. It is understandable, therefore, that the attitudes and actions of college representatives toward the relationship with high schools vary according to the type of college in which these persons are serving.

Of course, at least four years have elapsed since these data were collected. Meanwhile enrolments in institutions of higher education not only are growing rapidly but also are shifting among the types

TABLE 1

ENROLMENT IN INSTITUTIONS OF HIGHER EDUCATION, BY CONTROL OF INSTITUTION: CONTINENTAL UNITED STATES, 1953–54*

ITEM	TOTAL	PUBLICLY CONTROLLED		PRIVATELY CONTROLLED	
		Number	Per Cent	Number	Per Cent
Resident, College Grade:					
Universities..............	1,138,046	632,006	55.5	506,040	44.5
Liberal arts colleges.......	635,021	184,091	29.0	450,930	71.0
Teachers' colleges.........	208,573	198,721	95.3	9,852	4.7
Technological schools......	114,077	56,559	49.6	57,518	50.4
Theological schools........	31,205	....	......	31,205	100.0
Other professional schools..	61,986	13,068	21.1	48,918	78.9
Junior colleges............	325,804	272,036	83.5	53,768	16.5
Total					
....	2,514,712	1,356,481	53.9	1,158,231	46.1

* Adapted from United States Office of Education, *Statistical Summary of Education, 1953–54*, Table 35, p. 53.

of colleges. To illustrate, in Michigan in the autumn of 1957 we had an increase in college enrolments of about 6 per cent, but our community junior colleges reported an increase of 24 per cent. Senior colleges increasingly will have to plan for students who will want to transfer from junior colleges.

These few facts on the nature, scope, control, and enrolment trends in institutions of higher education have been presented to support my conviction that colleges cannot, and should not, have a single, unified philosophy or program of action on the high-school and college relationship. There are, of course, some basic attitudes, understandings, and principles which should be used by all colleges, but the functional relationships and action programs can vary considerably according to the type of college and its purposes. The major implication of all this is that each college, in addition to observing the basic principles of school and college relations, will have to develop and implement its own concepts and programs of appropriate relations with high schools.

Common Problems of the High School and College

It is important for colleges to recognize that they have many problems in common with high schools, for through these problems, both levels learn to understand each other and to work together for the solution of their mutual difficulties. If they do not achieve this relationship, the student suffers. These common problems can be divided into two groups—general problems and specific problems—and I shall now discuss a few typical ones under each category.

General Problems

There are many general problems[4] in the area of educational philosophy and objectives which must be considered jointly by high-school and college leaders.

1. *How can we most effectively educate the youth of America?* What patterns of secondary education and of higher education shall we use to meet the growing needs of an expanding population and economy? What shall be the scope and sequence of our educational offerings?

2. *How can we better understand the youth we educate?* We need to know a great deal more about how young people grow, how they learn, what is important to them, how to understand and evaluate them as individuals, and how to help them. We are accumulating a great deal of knowledge and experience both on the high-school level and on the college level, but we have all too little exchange of such information.

3. *How can we place primary emphasis on the student as an individual?* Enrolments in high schools and colleges are already at record levels, although the major tidal wave of students has not yet hit the colleges. We must find ways to treat and serve every student as an individual. He must not become a mere number, either in the high schools or in the colleges.

[4] The problems discussed below are taken from Clyde Vroman, *op. cit.*, pp. 1–4.

4. *How can the high schools and colleges adequately understand each other?* Probably no single factor is more important in understanding students than a thorough understanding of both secondary education and higher education. We must strive to know each other better and to use this knowledge for the benefit of students.

5. *How can we adjust to major changes and pressures occurring in American education?* In addition to the much-publicized increase in population, various other changes are having great influence on our schools and colleges. More students are staying in schools and colleges for a longer time. More adults are pursuing formal education. Scholarship money is being provided for the education of talented youth. In the fall of 1957 some three hundred thousand high-school Seniors hopefully wrote the Scholarship Qualifying Test. They and their schools were certain to be involved in the scholarship race throughout most of the school year. There is strong pressure to increase the emphasis on mathematics and sciences in the curriculum. Surely these changes and problems demand mutual understanding and co-operation between high schools and colleges.

6. *What are the common and individual roles of high schools and colleges?* There is a growing lack of understanding on this important question. Public secondary education is intended to meet the needs of all young people. The major objectives of secondary education include both general education and specialized education. College education, likewise, has an obligation for general and special education, but it also has additional purposes and characteristics. Most college students are preparing for special occupational fields and therefore have very definite goals and needs. We must strive to clarify and understand the similarities and differences in the roles of high schools and colleges and to establish these facts and understandings clearly in the minds of our citizens.

Specific Problems

Although we must first establish a common ground of philosophical principles on which to conduct American education, we can implement our purposes and solve our mutual problems only by identifying and attacking specific problems,[5] such as the following:

1. *Who should go to college?* Some authorities have believed that

[5] Clyde Vroman, *op. cit.*, pp. 4–9.

only students with above-average ability and preparation should be given college education at public expense. Many colleges which formerly had no selective admissions are considering a change of policy.

The tensions of the world situation make it imperative that we educate all our youth to the full limits of their capacities and motivation. And this is happening at a time when colleges are facing their greatest shortages of facilities, faculties, and financial support. There is real danger that the effect of these conditions may be to restrict the proportion of our youth who will receive a college education. Thus the problems now are: What kind and amount of education should the individual student have? Where should he procure his college education? How can he finance that education? What are the respective obligations of the high schools and colleges in giving him his total education? Unless we voluntarily find ways to work out our problems, we may have unacceptable answers forced upon us, such as quotas for admission.

2. *What curricular offerings in secondary schools best prepare students for college?* Fifty years ago this was no problem; the colleges prescribed the entire curriculum of the high schools, which accepted as their basic purpose the preparation of students for college. In the last twenty-five years the high schools have become comprehensive schools, attempting to serve all the children of all the people. The majority of high-school students end their formal education with high-school graduation. High schools now feel seriously restricted by the structure of American education, the foundation of which was established a half-century or more ago. Strenuous efforts are being made to remove what is thought to be serious blocks to the most effective operation of the secondary-school program. Colleges are paying less attention to the specific courses which the student has in high school and are more interested in standardized measures of aptitude and achievement regardless of the pattern of his high-school courses.

Schools now are in a dilemma. How can they get the freedom they want to organize their instructional programs without bringing in such Trojan horses as institutional, state, and national testing programs? The subject of testing is causing considerable concern and is receiving increased attention from various state and national associations.

The colleges are caught in a similar predicament. They, too, need to prepare their graduates for life, and this life obviously will be a complex one, requiring advanced knowledge and skills in all branches of learning. As education moves away from the use of the Carnegie unit and specific course requirements, the colleges are forced to seek other measures of the nature, ability, and achievement of students who apply for admission. What shall these be?

3. *How can college-admission requirements, policies, and practices be made more clear and helpful to high schools?* This has always been a major problem both to high schools and to colleges. Now the problem has become acute, mainly because of the "scare" articles which have appeared in the press recently. Rumors are flying in a most disturbing manner. I have talked with many parents of good students, who are extremely alarmed about the problem of gaining college admission for their children. Colleges can no longer be content with general, meaningless statements about their admission requirements, standards, and practices. They have a serious obligation to issue clear and definite statements which give the whole story to students, parents, and schools. At the University of Michigan we annually issue a leaflet, *Admission of Freshmen,* which we think serves this purpose. Such pronouncements will be better if the advice and counsel of school people is used in their preparation.

4. *How can students' high-school records be transmitted to colleges most easily and efficiently?* This perennial problem never has been solved satisfactorily. And now in this period when students are applying to several colleges and when the colleges need supplementary information about students in addition to their academic records, the problem is increasing. High schools are using reproducing equipment to prepare information for the colleges, but the permanent records of students often are not suitable for use as transcripts.

However, important progress has been made on the problem of adequate and uniform forms for reporting students' scholastic and personal records to the colleges. Through the efforts of their Joint Committee on High School–College Relations, the National Association of Secondary-School Principals and the American Association of Collegiate Registrars and Admissions Officers have agreed upon a uniform "Secondary-Record" form and a uniform "Personality Record" form. The revised forms are based on the standardized forms in use for many years by the National Association of Secondary-School Principals. These standardized forms are the most widely used of all forms of this kind, and they should be considered for possible use by all high schools and colleges.

5. *How can we gain a common understanding of the instructional programs and methods of high schools and colleges?* When a student enters college, he moves abruptly from the instructional program and methods of his high school to those of his college. Both high schools and colleges have a major obligation to help students make this change one of gradual transition. It can be done by the exchange of information between high schools and colleges and by serious efforts to articulate both subject matter and methods of instruction.

6. *How can the transition of the student from high school to college be made most effective?* Both high schools and colleges want to do this job well. Colleges in general are doing a great deal to meet this problem. Sometimes their efforts are viewed by the public as high-pressure recruiting. Nevertheless the transition of students is a major problem which must be met co-operatively by the high schools and colleges.

7. *How can colleges best report student progress and adjustment in college?* A fundamental corollary of guiding students toward college is that reports of their progress in college shall go back to the schools which educated and guided the students. This is largely an undeveloped frontier of service among colleges. Some colleges, of course, send grade reports to the high schools, but it is difficult to find a college that sends back much information about students other than grades. We need to attack this problem through joint action on both levels of education.

The Problems of the Colleges

Naturally, colleges first view their relationships with high schools from the standpoint of their own major problems. Most college programs set up definite goals to be achieved in a given time. Engineers currently are prepared in four years, dentists are graduated in six years, and medical doctors are graduated in seven years. In this age of increasing knowledge and technology and of higher levels of performance throughout our society, colleges are feeling increasing pressures to improve the quality of their graduates. The colleges can do only so much in the time they have their students. It is only natural that colleges are urging high schools to assume a larger share in the basic preparation of college-bound students. The alternative for the colleges is to admit only students who have the ability and the preparation to complete the college program successfully in the allotted time. Many colleges are content to follow this alternative.

One philosophical concept is held by many colleges on which it is hard to get high schools and colleges to agree. This concept holds that, when a student is graduated from high school, he has completed his custodial period of legally required education and of adolescent growth and that, when he enrols in college, he enters an adult world and should be treated as an adult. Of course this change must be gradual and must be accomplished without undue disturbance. Here the relations of the high school and the college must be so structured that the student receives all possible assistance in making the change. Here the objectives are tangible and specific, and the effectiveness of the co-operative relationship between high school and college stands its first test. Once the student is in college, the process of achieving independent adulthood should move as rapidly as possible.

Probably the most complex aspect of the problem of the high school and college relationship lies in the great differences in size, nature, purpose, and control among both the high schools and the colleges of this country. The high schools range all the way from the very small schools with as few as four teachers to the large high schools which are able to give college-level work to superior students. High schools also range from those with a single curriculum for all students to those which can offer several-track programs to homogeneously grouped students. Add to this great diversity of secondary education the fact that colleges likewise vary in almost every possible aspect, and we can only wonder that we do not have more trouble. Meanwhile, great numbers of our citizens hold the simple concept that any student should be able to move from any high school to any college as easily as he moves from one grade to another in high school.

Insofar as a college has special purposes and objectives not attainable by all high-school graduates of this country, it should select and admit only those students for whom it has appropriate instructional programs and only those who have reasonable probability of success in these programs. In effect, it is a matter of matching the student and the college in a manner most appropriate for the student. Herein lies our most challenging problem: How can the colleges effectively carry out their purposes and obligations with a minimum of influence and hardship on the high schools, most of which send their graduates to all kinds of colleges? Conversely, how can the high schools help the colleges in the education of the youth they both serve?

What Colleges Would Like from High Schools

I believe that there are some things which most colleges want from high schools and that these things can be provided or accomplished.

1. High schools should become acquainted with the colleges to which they send students. This can be done through college publications, visits to campuses, conferences on campuses, invitations to college personnel to visit the high schools, and interviews with former students. Such devices as conferences between the high-school principal and college Freshmen and invitational conferences for counselors are current successful techniques.

2. High schools should develop a sympathetic understanding of the roles and problems of colleges. I recognize how difficult it is to become acquainted with, and understand the details of, another level of education. However, the key that unlocks constructive action is attitude, and good attitudes are fostered when we sincerely try to know about, and to understand, each other.

3. Colleges would like the high school to help students under· stand the colleges. It is normal for most students to consider more than one college for their education. We in the colleges hope the high schools will have an effective program to provide students with adequate knowledge and understanding of the colleges in which they may be interested.

4. Colleges would like high schools to give students good guidance about attending college. We hope the high schools will help the student make a wise choice of college and a field of study. We also hope the high school will help the college to make a similarly wise decision concerning the admission of the student and the studies of his Freshman year. All this requires much extra effort, but it is the crucial time in the student's career when all possible assistance should be given him.

5. Colleges would like high schools to prepare students as well as possible. What constitutes the best preparation for college is, of course, one of the major issues in education about which there is much heat and little light. The problem cannot be, and should not be, resolved unilaterally by either the high schools or the colleges. For the foreseeable future it is likely to remain the responsibility of the high schools, perhaps with increasing influence from the colleges. Meanwhile the colleges hope that the high schools will give serious thought to the preparation of their college-bound students.

6. Colleges would like high schools to provide a clear analysis and evaluation of each student who enters college. The revolt against the Carnegie unit is known to all of us, as is the concern of high-school leaders that colleges may make inappropriate use of test scores. I believe a possible answer to this dilemma lies in some improved system of analyzing and evaluating the growth and outcomes of the high-school education of students. Such a system might include such factors and student characteristics as follow:

a) General aptitudes for college interpreted in terms of the college in which the student wishes to enrol.
b) The student's special aptitudes, abilities, competencies, and interests as related to his chosen or probable field of studies.
c) Vocabulary and reading levels.
d) Mathematical aptitudes and competencies.
e) Achievements and interests, both inside and outside the formal classrooms.
f) Clarity of purposes and goals.
g) Seriousness of purpose and motivation.
h) Interest in college education.

7. Colleges would like information about the high schools. Just as it is important for the college to know a lot about each student, it is equally important for the college to know the high school from

which the student comes. We would like information about the high school—its curriculum, its student body, and what becomes of its graduates. What proportion of the graduates go to college? Which colleges do they enter? How well do they do in those colleges?

The Process of Co-operation

As I near the end of my paper, I wish to emphasize the importance of method in achieving desired goals in the high-school and college relationship, and I find no better way to do this than to quote the following statement from the publication *Secondary School—College Co-operation:*

> Both secondary schools and colleges are becoming increasingly aware that many of the objectives they hope to achieve and the solutions to many of their problems require co-operative action between the two levels of education. However, many of the most sincere and energetic leaders in both schools and colleges are not familiar with trends and problems on the other level of education. Thus the first step is to create situations in which people from secondary schools and colleges can become adequately acquainted with each other and familiar with both their common and individual problems. In some areas of our country this mutual understanding has already been accomplished to a gratifying degree; in many places it unfortunately is conspicuously absent.
>
> Once it is resolved to work co-operatively on mutual problems, the important factor becomes *process.* How can we create friendly and sincere working relationships among us? How can we insure a feeling of equality of status and a mutual respect for each other's problems and opinions? How can we identify problems and take constructive action toward their solution?
>
> These and many other fundamental questions confront those who initiate co-operative action between secondary schools and colleges. In new situations it will be profitable to choose minor problems and use them to develop experimentally the process and structure of co-operation. With these successful experiences as a background, we will be organized for and capable of constructive action on the major problems we now have and are likely to have to an increasing extent in the future.[6]

I also wish to emphasize the great challenge each of us should feel as we consider the obligation we have to the young people who pass through our hands. The many differences among institutions, our tendency to operate along the lines of our own special interests or in geographical groups, and the freedom of each college to act as it desires have led to many approaches to this problem. The chal-

[6] Clyde Vroman, *op. cit.,* pp. 9–10.

lenge to each of us is to be well informed on these matters and to develop a program of co-operative relationships which will enable each of our institutions to serve its students most effectively. I can think of no more fitting close for my paper than this paragraph from the publication on which I have just drawn at some length.

Leaders in secondary education and higher education thus have an obligation to understand the similarities, differences, and interdependence of these two levels of American education. As new problems emerge and new solutions are found, there must be adequate awareness of, and consideration for, the total educational program in schools and colleges. Some roles will be common; some will be individual. Clarity and co-ordination can be achieved by adequate co-operation.[7]

[7] *Ibid.*, p. 4.

Educating the Gifted in
Our High Schools

Even a casual examination of the topics discussed at educational conventions, in educational literature, and in the lay press reveals a sharp increase in recent years in the nation's concern about the education of the gifted. This marked interest in the educational welfare of the more gifted child at once raises the question: Why? Why, in a period of a few years, has the gifted child become the center of attention? Why this new urgency in regard to the gifted? A number of factors account for the urgency. I have time to discuss only three of them, and those only briefly.

Reasons for Concern about the Gifted

Certainly one of the major factors is the troubled times in which we live. The rapid acceleration of the training of scientists in Russia and the Soviets' apparent bid for technological supremacy, dramatized by the launching of sputniks in the sky, have served to shock the American people into a fuller realization of the need for maximum development of our creative manpower. For many years our people have been alerted to the need for conserving our natural resources. Now, all of a sudden, we have begun to be concerned about our human resources, especially scarce human resources. Much of the current thinking about the education of the gifted is, in fact, couched in terms of manpower.

This emphasis upon the education of the gifted for furnishing the creative manpower needed to cope with the dangers to our national security and that of the whole free world is understandable. The danger is real, and the need for highly trained minds is genuine. Yet many people are disturbed by the notion of stockpiling gifted men like war materiel. Equally disturbing to some is the prospect that

362

the present crisis might siphon off, through attractive scholarships and other inducements, the most creative talent into science and technology, leaving to the humanities and the social sciences the less able. These people would argue, and rightly so, that, if there ever was a time when talent was sorely needed in the social sciences and in the humanities, it is now. Winning the peace, which is our only hope for survival, calls for creative talent in the arts of communication and for wisdom in contriving ways for men to live together amicably.

A second compelling reason for the current interest in the education of the gifted is the growing complexity of modern life. The amazing unlocking of the secrets of nature; the astonishing development of technology; the extension of the frontiers of knowledge on every side; and the interpersonal, intergroup, and international tensions of our day—all call for talent of the highest order. Scientists today who hope to break through new frontiers must have a command of knowledge undreamed of a few generations ago. This demand for new knowledge is characteristic of virtually every aspect of modern life, whether it be engineering, medicine, communications, or the field of human relations. We are living in troubled times, to be sure, and the need for talent in the sphere of national security is great; but we are also living in times which call for maximum development of talent for purely peaceful pursuits. The talents that the gifted have to offer are needed in law, medicine, the ministry, education, communications, government, technology, business and industry, social service, aviation, to mention only some of the aspects of modern life. There is likely to be no oversupply, even though we husband all of our most talented human resources.

A third factor which may account for the present interest in our brightest youth is the growing realization that our concept of democratic education may be somewhat warped. In the last half-century our nation has made remarkable progress in extending educational opportunities to all the people. Elementary education is virtually universal, and more than 80 per cent of our young people of high-school age are in high school. We can be justly proud of the educational opportunities afforded the handicapped of all descriptions. The slow learner receives special attention in clinics and remedial classes. All this we have been doing, and justly so, in the belief that in a democracy all children are entitled to equal educational opportunities.

However, many educators and laymen have recently expressed the view that, in our efforts to provide equal educational opportunities for all, we have inadvertently neglected the gifted. It is probably true that, in altogether too many classrooms, curriculum materials and instructional procedures are geared to the average, if not the below-average, students. As a consequence the abler students have been left unchallenged, and their needs unserved. There is nothing democratic about neglecting the gifted children. There is nothing undemocratic about meeting their needs. We have begun to see more clearly that equality of opportunity does not mean identical opportunity. Hughes and Lancelot put the matter this way:

> We have long held a confused idea of "democracy." It does *not* mean that all men are equal in ability. It does not mean that identical schooling must be open to all. It does mean that *opportunity* to reach the highest posts should be provided for all, regardless of wealth or poverty, or of high or humble birth. It means that *every* promise of ability is entitled to recognition and encouragement. It means that each youth should have the education that is best fitted to his needs and capacity.[1]

A sound school program for the gifted, then, is one which provides special arrangements for the abler students because they, too, are entitled to educational opportunities which meet their special needs. The concept of equal educational opportunities implies opportunities equal to the needs and aptitudes of all students, the gifted as well as the less gifted.

Identifying the Gifted Child

Who is this gifted person? What is he like? How does he differ from the less gifted? These are questions which must be answered if we are to provide programs for the education of the gifted. The answers are not easy to supply.

First of all, there is little agreement on the definition of the gifted. Some apparently think in terms of genius, of those very few persons of extraordinary intellectual power. A more common view is to include the top 10 per cent of children in measures of intelligence.

---

[1] Raymond M. Hughes and William H. Lancelot, *Education—America's Magic* (Ames, Iowa: Iowa State College Press, 1946), p. 133.

Obviously the number of children to be included in the category of the gifted will always be arbitrary. Giftedness is not absolute; it is a relative matter. It seems to me that it does not matter much whether the cut-off point is 5 per cent or 10 per cent or 25 per cent. The important thing is the provision we make for the abler students, whatever the portion we may choose to place in that category. Indeed the important consideration is to provide the right kind of educational opportunity for every boy and girl who has some special talent.

Another area in which there is disagreement is the nature of giftedness. Far too many people limit the concept of giftedness to intellectual giftedness. The gifted are defined in terms of performance on intelligence tests. Even if we grant the validity of these measures, such a definition is restricted to one kind of giftedness— the ability to perform the tasks set in these particular tests.

It has been encouraging to note in more recent educational literature the extension of the concept of giftedness to include the artistically gifted, the athletically gifted, the socially gifted, the morally gifted, to mention some of the categories. This concept of giftedness recognizes that society values inventiveness, leadership, physical prowess and dexterity, artistry, managerial skill, and forensic skill, to mention only enough to suggest this wider view. Some educators are proposing that the schools identify the top 10 per cent of the children who are gifted in these several areas and then provide educational programs designed to develop these talents. If this concept were adopted, our approach to the problem of the education of the gifted would be quite different from what it is in most schools today. With this concept of the gifted, we should probably find gifted children in unsuspected places.

At this juncture I should like to comment briefly on the notion held by too many that gifted children are "queer." Some are, to be sure. But so are some of the less gifted children. Most studies show that bright children are, on the whole, quite normal in physical fitness and social relations, the two areas of usual concern. I should like to share with you a sound observation made by a school principal, Miss Edith Peters, formerly of Hazeldell School in Cleveland, when speaking to a parent-teachers' association meeting:

The boy or girl with a high intelligence quotient is just an ordinary child with the power to think a little faster than the average. He is not, as we have thought of him for too many years, a small, bespectacled child with an armful of books. He is not uncommon. You have him in *your* families, and you meet him in the homes of *your* friends. The typical gifted child is neither a genius nor a freak, an angel nor an imp, a paragon of all virtues nor a conceited prig.

Before a school can undertake a program for the education of the gifted, it must, of course, identify the gifted. Before it can identify its gifted, it must define what it means by giftedness. We have a long way to go before agreement will be reached on the concept of giftedness and before we can identify these pupils with certainty. In Cleveland we have been working with groups of gifted children for a number of years. We have found that the typical gifted child can be described about as follows:

He is well-developed physically.

He has a high degree of general intelligence.

He knows much about, and is interested in, many things.

He has unusual powers of analysis.

He has a long attention span.

He has a high degree of reasoning ability.

He has a high degree of originality and initiative.

He is energetic, active, curious.

He responds quickly to the reactions of others and is quick to sense appreciation, sarcasm, and criticism.

He adjusts quickly to new situations.

He is socially adaptable.

He usually has a desire to challenge, to prove, to find out for himself.

Teachers in the classroom soon learn to spot these children, and teachers' judgments have been found to be a fairly reliable means of identifying the gifted. This is especially true when teachers have a clear notion of what is meant by giftedness and what traits to look for.

A second useful means of identification is supplied by the scores on standardized tests of intelligence and achievement. It should be pointed out in this connection, however, that at the present time we do not have available tests which measure a number of achievement or aptitude areas. Tests are needed to measure creative ability in art, music, and writing and in such areas as social leadership and moral judgment.

In the Cleveland public schools we have established 125 as the intelligence-quotient level required for entrance to our special classes for gifted children. We also screen the children in terms of emotional stability, social adjustment, and physical fitness.

Programs for the Gifted

After the gifted children have been identified, they should be placed in school situations that will provide the best opportunities to develop their talents. The best placement may be in regular classrooms, in segregated classes, in special schools, or in accelerated programs. The primary requisite is a classroom atmosphere that will stimulate optimum development and growth. Observation has shown that optimum growth is best assured for gifted students when:

They are surrounded by other students of like mental ability.

They feel free to carry out their own ideas.

They feel free to change their minds and make mistakes without embarrassment.

They have the opportunity to select their own materials and working partners.

They can select their own programs in accordance with their own interests.

They work in well-equipped classrooms, furnished with tables, chairs, pictures, maps, globes, encyclopedias, and reference books.

The atmosphere of the classroom is permissive.

They have the opportunity of give-and-take relationships among the members of the group.

They have teachers who believe in them and understand their problems.

Program Enrichment

In Cleveland we have relied heavily on program enrichment for meeting the needs of the gifted. We have formulated a concise definition of "enrichment." It means simply an effort to develop curriculum materials and teaching methods designed to meet the individual needs of children. Using the regular course of study as a springboard, we broaden it, widen it, and deepen it. The curriculum is broadened through extensive use of art, music, a foreign language, field trips, and community contacts. We emphasize class discussion, independent research, making judgments, formulating ideas, drawing conclusions.

Through these means of enrichment, the students develop self-reliance and purposefulness. They appear not to be overstimulated and tense. The day's work offers as much training in emotional vigor and stability as it does in intellectual growth. As one visits these classes, one observes that know-how rather than a knowledge of facts is important; that there is much studying and little recitation; that much attention is given to building habits of independent study and to supplying the tools with which to work; that there is little instruction of the type in which the teacher asks questions and students answer but there is much instruction in which students report on their own projects and in which the class engages in lively discussion.

Special Classes

Another common approach is the provision of special classes for the gifted. Sometimes these special classes are composed of able students who can pursue a given subject more rapidly or more thoroughly than can their age mates. In other forms of special classes the children are enrolled in honors classes, pursue college-level courses while in high school, and study courses in special subjects designed especially for the gifted. In Cleveland three junior and senior high schools have been designated as schools in which special classes are available for all the "major work class" students who graduate from "major work classes" in the elementary schools.

Elective Courses

A large percentage of the gifted students in the Cleveland schools go to college. To meet their needs, opportunities are provided for electing subjects which prepare these students for virtually any field of specialization they may choose. We have found that students want, and need, substantial groundwork in the biological, physical, and social sciences. They also profit from rigorous training in the communication arts and in quantitative measurement.

Acceleration

Another fairly common provision for the gifted is acceleration. This takes several forms: skipping grades, carrying more than the regular number of subjects and hence graduating earlier, entering college early through demonstration of ability on performance and aptitude tests, taking college-credit courses in high school. In Cleveland we have followed what might be described as a *moderate* program of acceleration, limiting acceleration usually to not more than two years. Since many of the gifted enter the learned professions, it is important for them to enter their chosen profession early. Thus they can make greater contributions to society, to say nothing of contributing to their earning capacity. So far we have found little evidence of social and emotional maladjustment as a result of acceleration.

Teachers for the Gifted

The success of any program for the gifted depends, as does any education program, on the qualifications of the teacher. The qualifications for teaching gifted boys and girls are those which are necessary for good teaching anywhere, together with a few additional requirements which are needed to meet the exceptional situations inherent in any special class. The well-qualified teacher of the gifted child may be described as follows: intellectually gifted, well informed, modest but confident, sympathetic and patient, interested in the creativity of children, free from jealousy, possessing positive personality traits, possessed of good mental and physical health, ingenious and resourceful, open-minded, having a high degree of understanding of the learning and teaching processes, and experienced in teaching and counseling.

Follow-up Studies

Every student who has been a member of the special classes for the gifted in the Cleveland schools is interviewed just before he is graduated from high school. He is asked to co-operate in a very simple follow-up plan: a double postcard is sent to him twice a year for as long as he sees fit to return the required information. Each time these cards are returned, twelve or fifteen graduates are selected at random for special study. Personal letters are sent to these former students, asking them more about their schooling or their work. The last sentence in this letter usually asks them to comment on their experience in the special classes.

I am pleased to report that the overwhelming majority of these graduates have indicated their approval of the special classes made available to them while in school. I wish I could share with you a whole sheaf of letters received from our graduates who have been members of our special classes for the gifted. For us, these letters have been sufficient evidence to support our belief that we have helped these students develop their potential talents.

Someone has said that the greatest resource of a nation is its gifted citizens but that latent intelligence is no more valuable than unmined gold. I wonder how much "gold" this great country of ours is leaving unmined!

Improving Provisions for
Low-Ability Students

The democratic ideal of equality of opportunity for all citizens of our nation is of cardinal importance is our great American culture. All individuals in our society have an inalienable right to develop and utilize their talents. American schools are charged with the responsibility of aiding the younger members of our society in the nurture of these potentialities regardless of any inequalities in endowment.

For some time our states have had strong laws to compel school attendance. We have found effective ways of forcing the disinterested adolescent to attend high school. Legal provisions have set the machinery in motion, but our American high schools have not geared the curricular machinery to the mandatory enactments. Today a serious gap exists between the compulsory-education statutes and the specially designed, specially executed programs of training for teen-agers who have found school boring and unrelated to their practical existence.

In considering the challenge of the new era, thought should be given to means of aiding this group of lesser-endowed citizens in the American high school. Our less capable young citizens need an education designed to make them contributing members of our working community. This paper describes one approach to providing for the retarded students in our high schools. In looking at a few of the many facets of this perplexing problem, I shall use the technique of raising basic questions and suggesting possible answers.

Which students can be rightfully designated as mentally retarded adolescents and how shall we select students for a special-education program?

Generally speaking, this special group is identified by marked intellectual retardation and limited social competence. It is made up of individuals with little ability to comprehend difficult, complex, and abstract concepts. Each student enrolled in a special program should have the benefit of an individualized diagnosis. Specific criteria that might be used to select students for the secondary-school program for the retarded are as follows:

1. These special-program students should have intelligence quotients in excess of 60 or 65. More seriously retarded youth will not be able to live comfortably in the complex organization of the average high school. Probably the upper limit for a special group should be in the intelligence-quotient range of 80–85.

2. Social-competence evaluations should indicate that the special-class student has a social age of at least ten years. The Vineland Social Maturity Scale might be used as a tool in determining social age.

3. Academic attainments in the three R's should be at the fourth-grade level or higher in order that the special curriculum can utilize the printed word and simple arithmetic concepts.

4. The special-class student should be free of major personality disorders so that the program can be based on an educational, rather than a psycho-therapeutic, foundation.

5. The student and his family should recognize the need for this place-ment. They should actually be more interested in this program than in immediate employment or continued special education at the elementary-school level.

6. Chronological ages should range from approximately fourteen years to nineteen years in order that the retarded students may resemble their normal peers.

Why is the American high school the proper setting for the training and education of the slow adolescent?

For a number of reasons the secondary school is best equipped to meet the needs of the teen-age retarded. In the first place, the psychological, biological, and sociological needs of the retarded adolescent cannot be met in the elementary school. Second, high schools have the diversified non-academic offerings that can develop the practical potential in the retarded. Third, the retarded adoles-cent is psychologically and physically identified with his chrono-logical peer group. He can simulate the more sophisticated actions of the secondary-school students if he is given the opportunity to attend high school. Fourth, the slow learner and his family have a sense of success and of recognition because of the student's physi-cal presence in the high school.

What are the goals of a secondary-school program for the slow learners?

In general, this program should give the retardate a feeling of belonging, a sense of achievement and self-sufficiency, and an opportunity to contribute to the "common good." Specifically, the following goals should be sought and achieved as far as possible:

1. Appreciation of social and civic values and an understanding of the need for participation in social and civic activities.
2. Sufficient knowledge to enable the student to keep physically and mentally healthy.
3. Ability to plan, to choose, and to participate in worthwhile leisure activities.
4. Sufficient skill in reading, writing, language, arithmetic, and related areas to give him minimal literacy and a means of communication with his fellow citizens.
5. Ability to earn enough to cover his cost of living and to allow some savings for future use.
6. Art of being a good co-operator and a good follower.

How many students need these services? Will a high school of four hundred students have enough slow learners to warrant a special program?

Statistical references to the incidence within levels of intelligence are expressed in distances from the mean in multiples of the probable error. The retarded group herein discussed includes those children whose intelligence quotients fall between a deviation of -3 P.E. and -2 P.E. Wechsler,[1] in his development of the Wechsler-Bellevue Intelligence Scales, found that 6.7 per cent of his sample population (with chronological ages of 10–60) had intelligence quotients between 66 and 79. Wechsler placed this borderline group completely within the limits of -3 P.E. to -2 P.E. Observations in Wisconsin high schools indicate a smaller percentage of students with this degree of retardation. Approximately 4–5 per cent of our Wisconsin boys and girls of high-school age manifest the abilities and disabilities previously outlined. This estimate implies that every high school with 350–400 students might feasibly establish a special class to meet the needs of these teen-agers, since each special unit can enrol from fifteen to eighteen slow learners.

[1] David Wechsler, *The Measurement of Adult Intelligence* (Baltimore: Williams & Wilkins Co., 1944), p. 40.

Should these students be integrated with regular students at any time?

Many students with intellectual potential in the low dull-normal and borderline ranges can benefit by enrolment in a regular class activity. If a slow learner can achieve at the level asked of the lower quarter of a given school population, he should have the opportunity to learn with his more competent peers. Usually it is not possible to place retardates in academic sections such as literature, biology, algebra, chemistry, French, or Latin, but many secondary schools schedule the retardates for regular courses in art, general metal work, general woodwork, physical education, foods, homemaking, music, and typewriting.

Whenever special-class students are enrolled in regular activities, the administrator and/or the psychologist should confer with the instructor and outline what may be expected of the retardates. Such a pre-placement conference will help the special sudents and the teacher to become productive and satisfied. Inclusion of special students in non-academic activities of the secondary school, such as drama, music, athletics, and social groups, aids in making them feel that they are part of the school. The movement from the special classroom to another classroom develops a feeling of "regularness" for the retardates and gives them greater poise in social situations. But the faculty supervisor of the activity must be adaptive if these experiences are to be profitable.

In what manner can retardates be recognized for their attainments and attendance?

In the development of a special-class program in the high school, an objection, often unmentioned, is the full accreditation of the class work taken by the students. Many administrators hesitate to institute and develop a program for the retarded adolescents because of this threat to the academic standards of the secondary school. The objection may be removed by granting special certificates of attendance, certificates of graduation from special courses of study, or certificates of merit. At the present time, only a few schools grant to special-class students the diploma traditionally given on completion of the normal high-school requirements.

In most schools the special-program graduates walk across the platform as do the students with regular diplomas. They receive a document similar in appearance to the diploma of their more competent friends. This formalized recognition of tenaciousness is often a strong incentive for a slow student and is a goal that is obtainable and cherished. It also indicates to the potential employer the student's ability to master a specially designed sequence of training and experience.

What special abilities and attitudes must the special-program teacher possess?

A teacher with special training and strength of personality is needed to help the retarded adolescent accomplish his goals. The teacher of secondary-school retardates should be well accepted within the faculty and by the student population of the specific high school. He should be capable of transmitting a positive attitude to the program and to the slower students. He must recognize that he has an integral place within the school structure, must avoid being a "special" faculty member. He must know the school's entire program so that he can integrate the work of his students with that of the more competent students.

The special-program teacher must know how to convey adolescent and pre-adult concepts of work, family life, and community participation to his students and how to accomplish this by using language that can be assimilated by a person with a mental age of ten or eleven years. The teacher needs the ability and the desire to work with community groups, such as potential employers of the retarded and labor unions that will be considering membership of the retarded worker to be.

The special-program teacher must know the assets and liabilities of his students. He must be thoroughly convinced of the retarded adolescents' ability to adjust to our increasingly complex workaday world. He must know realistic subject-matter resources for his slow group. He must be able to create in his charges a feeling of worthwhile accomplishment.

At the present time most teachers of the adolescent retarded have had only minimal specialized training in such areas as secondary-school organization, leisure activities for the retarded, special guidance and counseling techniques for use with slow students, and techniques of adapting curricular content for the specialized needs of the less endowed. It will be necessary for colleges preparing special teachers to enlarge their staffs and the course offerings to supply the additional number of well-screened and well-trained teachers that are needed for the high-school-age slow learner.

Is work experience of value in working with the high-school retarded group?

A work-experience program is often the adhesive that keeps the slow learner in school. It gives him a positive sample of what adult life has to offer and yet impresses him with his need for more education. It affords the special-class teacher the opportunity to relate work in the academic areas to the job experiences of his special pupils.

A special-class teacher in high school should have a schedule that allows him to work with co-operating employers and labor unions. Thus he can relate the content of his teaching in the classroom to the actual working conditions of his adolescent students. This type of programing stresses the direct needs for language and communication and gives the instructor a direct avenue for person-to-person guidance conferences.

The work-experience program of the special department is the key transitional step between the classroom and "open" employment in the community. It should be a time for "tuning up" the slow learner for his role as a self-sufficient citizen. The per capita cost of this work-experience program is often large, but we recognize that the money is truly well spent when we see a marginal citizen become an independent member of society.

Specifically, what content can be included in the special class program?

The curricular emphasis in a secondary-school program revolves about the retardate as a contributing citizen, worker, homemaker, and social being. All the previous training and learning is crystallized and augmented.

A brief overview of the content of subject matter in each of the major academic fields indicates the direction that curriculum planning might take in this area.

MATHEMATICS

1. There should be provisions for review and improvement in fundamental arithmetic operations.

2. The student should engage in simple, practical, problem-solving activities built around daily purchases in stores. This type of activity should emphasize the relation of money to social and business practices. For example, a student in a slow group should develop a concept of the usual price of objects and special prices obtainable through discounts and sales.

3. Simple budgeting procedures should be outlined and practiced. Saving of money should be stressed.

4. Experience should be provided in the mathematics of instalment buying; various types of liability, health, and life insurance; union dues; social security; income tax; church contributions; and utility payments.

5. Minimal information should be supplied about simple banking and contracting. The retarded adolescent should know about such things as checks, savings accounts, receipts, and money orders.

6. The students should have practice in all types of practical measurements. Finding mileage on maps; using liquid measures; noting contents of food containers; apprehending the dimensions of a piece of property; using the home measuring devices of ruler, teaspoon, cup, and tape measure should be mastered by the adolescent retardate. Simple fractional parts of small and large portions of a given measurement should also be studied.

ENGLISH

1. Reading for information and pleasure would include the use of adapted books, of special teacher-prepared materials, daily newspapers, magazines, and simple publications related to everyday living in a work situation.

2. Remedial reading should be provided students who are attaining at a level below the educational optimum indicated by their mental ages.

3. The students should learn to read and write simple letters and notes that can give a retarded citizen a means of communication beyond the range of his voice.

4. Completion of printed forms related to work, play, and community participation should be stressed.

5. Oral expression should be stressed. The slow learner will need to express his wants and opinions to other citizens. Proper training in oral communication can be developed through dramatization of typical social situations, such as answering the telephone, greeting a guest, introducing people, and meeting employers and superiors. The art of inhibiting speech is also highly recommended for slow learners.

SOCIAL STUDIES

1. Elements of citizenship should be stressed. The role of every citizen as a taxpayer, a voter, and a contributor to the sociability of the neighborhood makes good subject matter for the special class group.

2. Simple concepts of local, state, national, and world geography should be developed so that the retardate can find his way about his home com-

munity and can speak with minimal competence on such matters as our national capital and important cities in the United States and the world.

3. Current events will play a big role in the special program since the retardate must know about, and desires to know about, everyday happenings so that he can derive the pleasures of conversation with his friends and neighbors.

4. Elementary United States history should play a big part in the silent-reading activities of the academic classroom for the high-school slow learner. A few well-chosen bits of information about our early development and the people involved appeals to the retarded and gives them hero images that they respect. Many adapted reading materials can be found in this area.

5. Occupational information should also be included in the social-studies area. Students in the special class will enjoy studying about the job areas that will be available to them. Many visits to local industries that employ retarded adults should be planned.

6. Recreational facilities of the community should be explored.

7. The students should be prepared for family participation and for assuming the responsibilities of the male or the female role in our society.

8. Work in the area of human relations will aid the slow learner in understanding himself and his fellow man.

9. Attitudes of safety and good habits in health and accident prevention should be instilled.

Rough surveys such as these can also be made in the fields of home arts (cooking, sewing, child care, home management, and simple housekeeping) for the girls and in household mechanics and woodworking for the boys. Physical education for all students is a big need, and a course in corrective gymnastics will benefit many retarded adolescents. Arts and crafts should also be stressed in a special program. These non-academic activities give the low-ability student a chance to succeed and also give him a vent for any frustration that his retardation may have produced.

The benefits of dramatizations, audio-visual aids, concrete teaching devices, and field trips should be emphasized. The relatively small size of the group and the possibilities of using block-time units give the special-program teacher more time for visits to local industries, stores, recreation sites, and other real laboratories. In general, the curriculum for high-school retardates should be realistic and flexible, with ample opportunity for the slow to learn by seeing and to learn to do by doing.

What special consideration should be made in the administrator's planning of this unit?

In planning a special unit in a secondary school, the following suggestions may help to avoid conflict with the ongoing regular programs. The special-education program must be acceptable to the building administrator, must be understood by the school's faculty, and must be "sold" to the student body so that each can be proud of the service rather than considering it a scholastic scrap-heap. State support should be made available for the excess cost of this special service. In Wisconsin, approximately 75 per cent of the cost of special instruction at the high-school level is paid by the state. Thus special education costs the local government no more than does regular education of average pupils. Special-program pupils should be assigned to a regular class only when the receiving teacher approves and when the chances for success are not below the norm for the slowest of the average group. The special-education department and the child-study department must work closely with the school staff conducting the special program so that problems may be attacked and solved before they affect adversely the total usefulness of the special service.

In this paper I have raised a few questions and suggested a few answers on the improvement of curriculum services to the high-school student with low mental ability. I am sure there are other ways of approaching these problems. We in special education hope to join secondary-school planners in developing a dynamic new program of instruction for retarded youth. The American high school can and will meet the challenge of the new era. It will provide a tailored education to fit all retarded students and thus help them become happy, poised, self-sufficient citizens of our society. Our democratic ideal of equality of opportunity for all citizens of our nation will then approach a reality.

Maintaining Achievement Standards
in the High School

The first public high school was established in Boston in 1821, but high schools developed slowly until after the Civil War. Even as late as 1900, the high school was still a highly selective and exclusive institution. At that time, in fact, its student body was much more selective than the college is today. Then only 11 per cent of youth of high-school age were in school, and about 6 per cent graduated.

A basic change in the conception of the role of the American high school occurred between 1890 and 1920. As the Educational Policies Commission has pointed out:

At the beginning of the period a committee of American leaders—the "Committee of Ten"—issued a report (1893) on the kind of secondary education needed for American life; at its conclusion, another committee formulated the "cardinal principles" of American secondary education (1918). The first report viewed the secondary school as a highly selective agency which would train a small percentage of American youth in certain approved bodies of subject matter. The second report set forth an infinitely broader view of education, holding it the duty of the high schools to prepare all American youth for citizenship, health, vocation, family life, and a variety of other functions.[1]

After 1900 the high school grew rapidly. By 1930, 51 per cent of the youth of high-school age were in school and, partly as a result of the depression, the figure had increased to 73 per cent by 1940. Today over 80 per cent of the youth of high-school age are in high school, and about 60 per cent are graduating. Thus, during the twentieth century, the high school has become a school for most American youth, a common school rather than a highly selective one.

[1] Educational Policies Commission, *Public Education and the Future of America* (Washington: Educational Policies Commission of the National Education Association and the American Association of School Administrators, 1955), p. 81.

Not everyone is pleased with the change in the American high school. Some people believe that the increase in numbers and the broadening of the school's functions have resulted in a disastrous lowering of standards, that the education of the masses has produced a neglect of the gifted, and that the essential intellectual function of the school has been weakened seriously by the addition of fads and frills. It has been said that the marking and promotion policies of the public high schools lead to laziness, incompetence, and the expectation of receiving something for nothing in adult life.

Evidence of Rising Standards

The degree to which the high school is succeeding in attaining desirable standards of achievement is difficult to determine because of the lack of a clear definition of what standards are to be expected from high-school graduates, the meagerness of objective research, and the wide variations in the quality of high schools. The extensive decentralization of the control of the high school makes a uniformity of standards practically impossible. However, there is some evidence of achievement trends in the high school on a nationwide basis. The periodical *Changing Times* reported in 1954 that the College Entrance Examination Board found "no decline in the quality of the entering college Freshman today when he is compared with the college Freshman of a quarter of a century ago."[2]

In 1943 the Armed Forces Institute administered its Tests of General Educational Development to a sampling of students in the last two months of their Senior year in regular public high schools throughout the United States. This battery of tests includes comprehensive examinations in English composition, the social studies, the natural sciences, literature, and mathematics. In 1955 the University of Chicago administered the test to a comparable sampling of high-school Seniors under like conditions. In reporting the results, Bloom states:

In each of the GED tests the performance of the 1955 sample of Seniors is higher than the performance of the 1943 sample. These consistent results give evidence that today's students are achieving to a greater extent the objectives measured by this battery of achievement tests than were the students of 1943. The greatest change is in mathematics, while the least change appears in the social studies. One way of expressing the change

2 "The Truth about Our Public Schools," *Changing Times* (June, 1954), p. 10.

is to note that in mathematics the average Senior tested in 1955 exceeds 58 per cent of the students tested in 1943. In the natural sciences, literary materials, and English, the median Senior tested in 1955 exceeds approximately 54 per cent of the 1943 students, while in the social studies, the median 1955 Senior exceeds approximately 52 per cent of the Seniors tested in 1943. These differences are not attributable to chance variation in test results.

In general, the differences are such that the entire distribution of scores has shifted up by about 5 percentile points. Assuming comparability of tests, test conditions, and samples of students, these test results indicate that the high schools are doing a significantly better job of education in 1955 than they were doing in 1943.[3]

Bloom reports further that there were wide variations in test results from the various states. In the test of Correctness and Effectiveness of Expression [in English], for example:

Seventy-eight per cent of the students in the top state receive higher scores than the average student in the bottom state. For the top state, the median student scores above 66 per cent of all high-school Seniors in the nation, in contrast with the lowest state, whose median student has a score above 34 per cent of all high-school Seniors. Another way of looking at the comparison is to note that, if students were admitted to a college because they were in the upper half of the national distribution of high-school Seniors in competence in English, as measured by a test like this, 65 per cent of the high-school Seniors in the top state would be admitted, while only 33 per cent of the Seniors in the bottom state would meet such an entrance requirement.[4]

In order to discover some of the possible causes of differences in test scores on the achievement tests between states, the study analyzed "some of the relationships between what is 'put into' the educational system and the 'outcomes' of the educational system." On the basis of this analysis, Bloom concludes:

The differences in the median level of performance on the GED tests of Seniors from the different states are related to the extent to which financial support is given to education, the level of education of the adult population, and the extent to which young people make use of existing educational facilities.[5]

There is also some evidence that the intellectual atmosphere of both high school and college is changing as a result of the emphasis on competition for college entrance and scholarships and a recognition that entrance to graduate school to pursue advanced study

---

[3] B. S. Bloom, "The 1955 Normative Study of the Tests of General Educational Development," *School Review*, LXIV (March, 1956), 113.

[4] *Ibid.*, p. 115.   [5] *Ibid.*, p. 124.

in science and the professions depends heavily on undergraduate grades. Eugene Gilbert, president of the Gilbert Youth Research Company, reported in the *Palo Alto Times* on May 23, 1957:

> Grades, not girl-boy problems worry today's teen-agers most. . . . Our survey of youngsters across the country shows that 42 per cent worry "a good deal" about getting good grades. More than 25 per cent say it is their chief concern. [One youth] has done a bit of soul-searching. He says, "I believe I have become too caught up in the competitive spirit of modern education."

The Demand for Quality

There will probably continue to be wide differences of opinion concerning achievement standards in the high school, but there is no doubt that the high schools need to raise their standards in the light of current cultural demands. The rapidity of change; the vast accumulation of knowledge; the increasing technological and cultural complexity; the intensity of contemporary problems; and the need for mathematicians, scientists, engineers, and highly trained professional workers—all mean that an upgrading of education is essential to our survival as a free society.

A free society depends for its existence on the making of effective choices by its citizens. Effective choices are informed choices. As knowledge accumulates with greater and greater rapidity and life becomes more complex, the educational task of developing citizens who can make informed choices becomes staggering, and the pressures on the schools to produce higher and higher levels of achievement becomes intense. As Fred Hechinger expressed it in the *Saturday Review:* "The first phase of the American public school epic is coming to an end. In the second phase it would have to be demonstrated that quality need not be plowed under by quantity."[6]

Thus current cultural changes are demanding ever higher levels of quality in the high school while we are struggling with the problem of rapidly increasing numbers and the accompanying shortages of teachers, materials, and classrooms. All these things cost money, and the problem of adequate school support is becoming ever more insistent. As Hartung has pointed out:

> Nationwide testing programs support the really obvious conclusion that good achievement by students as a group (but not necessarily as individ-

[6] Fred M. Hechinger, "Wanted: Quality as Well as Quantity," *Saturday Review*, XXXIX (September 8, 1956), 19.

uals) depends upon the quality of the educational services provided. In general, these are related to expenditures for education. With education, like everything else, you get what you pay for.[7]

In light of this situation, it seems unwise to engage in recrimination about the past. Instead, we should work together in mutual respect to improve high-school achievement standards in every way possible, now and in the future. Differences in point of view are to be expected and welcomed in a free society. Out of the ferment of conflicting ideas may come solutions to some of our problems in secondary education.

Dual Function of the High School

The high school serves both societal and personal functions. The societal functions include (1) cultural transmission, maintenance, and improvement and (2) participating in the selection and the training of individuals for various societal roles. The selection process involves the identifying of potential leaders and motivating and preparing them for higher education. The personal functions of the high school include (1) providing individuals with equality of opportunity to develop their potentialities to the fullest; (2) helping to prepare them for practical life affairs; and (3) developing their personality and character in co-operation with the family, church, and other agencies. Our ethic requires further that the infinite value of every individual be recognized and that he be treated with consideration and respect.

The standards of achivement in the high school should be in harmony with both its societal and personal functions. They should provide for the identification and fullest possible development of the talents of the intellectually gifted but, at the same time, discover and develop the talents of all in a way that will result in self-confidence and self-respect for those who work to the highest level of their abilities.

Factors in High Achievement

In a highly complex and rapidly changing society, education is a lifetime process. Hence the high school has the responsibility to develop deep and abiding interests in the important areas of living

[7] Maurice L. Hartung, "Are We Getting Our Money's Worth?" *School Review,* LXIV (April, 1956), 169.

and to develop self-discipline and self-direction in learning. It is possible to set standards and enforce them in such a way as to develop a dislike for the areas of knowledge in which the student ought to be developing a strong continuing interest.

Motivation is needed to stimulate students to work up to the highest level of their ability. Students should understand what they are expected to learn and why it is important. They need to be given more responsibility for their own achievement and held to high standards of performance. There should be more individual conferences with students to discuss their achievements and more class discussions to evaluate what the group as a whole has achieved. Each individual should learn to accept responsibility for his own success or failure, but the classroom situation should be such that every student has the opportunity to achieve some measure of success.

The achievement standards of the high school are related to attitudes in the home, the community, and in our culture generally. Parents are of supreme importance in the nourishing of intellectual excellence and in helping children to develop good work habits, self-discipline, drive, and a willingness to "stick their necks out." Many parents do not have a high regard for education, and some who regard learning highly do not take the trouble to encourage their children to work to the highest level of their ability. Pressures toward conformity and anti-intellectual attitudes are far too prevalent in many areas today. Performance standards in contemporary culture often are not what they should be. The get-something-for-nothing attitude is not confined to the school.

The holding power of the high school has increased, but, in the light of our ideal of equality of opportunity and our need for talent, the dropout rate of able youth from high school is still too high. The United States Department of Labor and the Department of Health, Education, and Welfare, in co-operation with the Department of Defense, are now conducting a national stay-in-school campaign. A stimulating atmosphere and the maintenance of high achievement standards in relation to the abilities of youth will, in all likelihood, contribute to the holding power of a school. The professions have learned that the high-standards approach is the best method of attracting and holding able individuals.

The greatest loss of talent, at present, is the result of school drop-outs and the fact that many individuals of high ability and talent do not go on to college. Many of these able persons come from families of low socioeconomic status and from minority groups, particularly Negro, Mexican-American, and Puerto Rican groups. Youth of talent in all groups should be identified early; motivated to stay in high school and to enter college; and be assured, through scholarships and other means, of the financial assistance they need. Early identification and motivation to high achievement are particularly important. It has been pointed out that today most scholarships are granted to youth who would go to college anyway.

The evidence concerning high-school promotion policies does not present a clear picture. There is a widespread belief that high-school promotion and graduation are automatic. This is certainly not generally true, even though promotion and graduation policies are, without doubt, much less stringent than they were when the high school was a more selective and exclusive institution. A study from the Office of Education on *Retention in High Schools in Large Cities* states: "The problem of retention is a problem only in the fact that pupils *do not finish high school*. It is not a particular problem that youth do not attend school long enough. Actually, dropouts stay in school, in number of years, almost as long as high-school graduates."[8]

Regardless of the marking and promotion practices, an effective guidance program is important in the maintenance of achievement standards. Guidance procedures are needed to measure individual differences in ability and to discover and help keep youth in school. Every high-school youth should know what he has achieved and how his achievement is related to requirements for college entrance, vocational opportunities, and the like. No youth should ever be led to believe that he has reached a standard of achievement he has not, in fact, attained. Accurate records of his level of achievement should be available to parents, college-admission officials, and prospective employers. Pupils and their parents should have a realistic appraisal of what the pupils have achieved and its meaning and significance for them and their future. No youth should have a sense of high

---

[8] David Segel and Oscar J. Schwarm, *Retention in High Schools in Large Cities* (United States Office of Education Bulletin 1957, No. 15 [Washington: Government Printing Office, 1957]), p. 16.

achievement if he has not worked up to the level of his ability, and no youth should have a sense of continual failure if he does his best. Both teachers and guidance specialists have the responsibility to help youth understand the demands of society and their own potentialities and how fully they are developing them. Self-discipline, ·elf-direction, and good work habits should be stressed within an atmosphere that stimulates interest and thought about that which is truly important.

There is need in many high-school classrooms for higher levels of expectation of achievement for able students. More courses of college difficulty should be available in high school, and students should be given college credit for such courses if they reach a certain level of achievement. This already is being done in a limited way, but the practice needs to be extended greatly. There should be a careful study of the articulation between the high school and college. Too many college Freshmen find they are repeating material that they already have studied in high school. In my judgment, as a result of advances in the mass media and other factors, high-school youth generally are more sophisticated today than they were before the war, and they are capable of handling much more solid intellectual fare than they are offered in some high-school classes.

There needs to be much less rigidity and much greater flexibility in the high-school program. There should be experimentation with a variety of kinds of grouping, and graduation from high school at varying ages should be accepted as normal. Woodring's proposal for a more flexible school program should be given serious consideration. As Woodring points out, many people "find themselves torn between two points of view" about education:

> We would educate for excellence and hold to high standards—and yet we know that many children cannot meet such standards and we are reluctant to let the slow learner suffer the consequences of repeated failure. We would stress knowledge and clear thinking—yet we are not at all sure that we want the school to neglect the child's health, his social and emotional adjustment, or even his recreation. We want each child to move through the school at his own best rate—yet we are reluctant to remove him from his social group.[9]

[9] Paul Woodring, "Reform Plan for Schools," *Life*, XLIII (September 2, 1957), 127.

To meet this dilemma, a reorganization of the present elementary and high school may be necessary.

At the heart of the problem of achievement standards is the teacher. Improvements in high-school standards, in the long run, must come through improved teachers. There are many excellent teachers in high schools now, but we need more of them. The recruitment, selection, and education of teachers will become increasingly important as the high-school population increases in size and the competition of colleges and universities for teachers becomes more intense.

There needs to be a clearer definition of what achievement standards are desirable for the high school. There ought to be a clearer conception of what the high-school student should know and be able to do—a more precise definition of standards in terms of knowledge and understanding, values and ideals, skills and abilities. Then there should be more careful studies of the standards that high schools are actually achieving today. At present there is too much controversy based on too few facts.

I have tried to stress that, while there is evidence of improvement in the achievement of high-school standards, there is need for still greater improvement if the survival of our free society is to be assured. However, in raising achievement standards, we should take into consideration both the demands of society and the uniqueness of the individual. The kind of high school we are trying to build is one where every pupil is challenged to work to the highest level of his abilities, where he develops his potentialities to the fullest, where he becomes deeply interested in the truly important, and where he is given sufficient responsibility eventually to become self-disciplined and self-directing in learning.

The ideal of America is that the good society is one in which every individual has an equal opportunity to develop and use his potentialities to the fullest. The high school is a key agency in achieving this ideal. It already has made a considerable contribution. Let us appreciate what it has already accomplished, but let us continue to improve it until it more nearly meets our heart's desire.

VII

*Specific Suggestions Are Offered for Mathematics,
Science, and Vocational Education*

School Mathematics for Tomorrow

The school mathematics of tomorrow will be very different from the school mathematics of today. I believe that all the thought and all the money being expended now in the effort to change the mathematics instruction in our schools will bring this about very rapidly indeed. The teaching of mathematics is going to be better adjusted to the needs and the capabilities of the different kinds of young people brought together in our schools. It is going to deal with many more aspects of mathematics, and it is going to treat both old subjects and new in a modern spirit which will reflect in some measure the vigor and power of the best mathematical thought of our times. In the elementary schools much more will be done to prepare children for the more demanding mathematical subjects they must master in the high schools. Teachers will be better grounded in the fundamentals of the mathematics they are to teach, and, in order to increase their effectiveness, they will make use of all sorts of new-fangled gadgets—films, filmstrips, television, Professor Skinner's didactic machines[1]—and various kinds of special apparatus.

If anyone thinks that these prophecies are over-optimistic or utopian, he should take note of the things which are being done now to lay new foundations for the school mathematics of tomorrow. He should look at the experiments under way in modernizing and diversifying high-school mathematics in the light of modern progress in mathematical research, or at the numerous special institutes organized to give teachers a better knowledge of this progress and its significance for them, or at the beginnings of the systematic exploration of what can be done with mechanical aids to improve teaching and to alleviate the impending shortage of teachers in our schools. Perhaps the mathematicians of the country are lagging behind the

[1] B. F. Skinner, "The Science of Learning and the Art of Teaching," *Harvard Educational Review*, XXIV (Spring, 1954), 86–97.

physicists, who have already succeeded in launching at least one ambitious and generously supported program for a co-ordinated attack on the problem of what the school physics of tomorrow shall be. If so, they are lagging only a little, because there is hardly any professional mathematical organization in America which has not begun or planned some major effort to help solve our teaching problems, while many of our colleges and universities have initiated new teaching and new research directed toward the same end.

The time is not far off when the mathematicians, like the physicists, should be able to draw some of these separate activities together into one or more integrated programs capable of producing the intellectual and material bases for the school mathematics of tomorrow. This is not to say that what the physicists have done should be imitated exactly by the mathematicians. On the contrary, essential differences between the problems confronting these two groups suggest that the mathematicians should be encouraged to develop their own organizational approach to the work which has to be done. To my mind, the public and private foundations interested in education would perform a highly constructive service by offering the necessary encouragement and fostering some of the more promising programs which might result from the impulse thus given.

Reasons for Aroused Interest in Mathematics

How has it come about that I can speak with such glowing but, I hope, justified confidence of what will take place in our schools? If anyone had told me five years ago that a professor of mathematics who had taught none but research-oriented graduate students for many years would today be asked to address an audience critically concerned with the shortcomings of our high schools, I would have been incredulous. Like many another teacher of mathematics, I have raised my voice in the wilderness for no less than twenty years and have been accustomed, until very recently, to have my pleas fall on deaf ears. If we mathematicians were not heeded, neither was so authoritative a critic as Admiral Nimitz when he took up his pen to report some sobering truths about the teaching of high-school mathematics in America.[2] We may indeed be thankful that the climate of

[2] "The Letter of Admiral Nimitz," *American Mathematical Monthly*, XLIX (March, 1942), 212–14.

opinion has recently changed in a way which is little short of miraculous.

It has suddenly become fashionable to do something about the teaching of mathematics in our schools. Why? The obvious answer, which might seem to be justified by a superficial view of recent events, is that, for the sake of keeping ahead in the military race with Russia, we need to train more engineers and more scientists. Certainly we must do whatever is necessary to lead in that race, and certainly this means that we must also do whatever is necessary to procure the engineers and the scientists upon whom we must count for superiority in the technological phases of military preparedness. In particular, we must improve the teaching of mathematics with this end in mind. Nevertheless most thoughtful pronouncements on the challenge confronting American education agree that it cannot be met by concentrating our attention on training more and better technologists. It is quite plain that the discussions among physicists and mathematicians about the future of high-school instruction in their fields envisage much broader and much more fundamental problems than this. In short, a closer look at the effect of the military competition with Russia shows that it has in reality been catalytic, putting into action powerful forces which have been accumulating gradually over a long interval of apparent stability and will now play a major part in shaping the education of tomorrow.

These forces have been created by the expansion of scientific knowledge and its applications to human affairs. It is almost self-evident, I think, that such forces must be generated in any progressive society and must exert an important modifying influence upon education, along with other social activities. If knowledge expands, then the content of education must be altered accordingly; and, if knowledge is to be applied at all extensively, then education must include training those who are to make the applications. What requires explanation in a progressive country like the United States is the faith—shared, to all appearances, by so many American educators—that in an age of luxuriantly flourishing science our schools could proceed on the principle of teaching less and less science and less and less mathematics to fewer and fewer young people. I am not talking now about the doctrine that it was expedient to sacrifice some standards in the teaching of science and mathematics in order to bring all young people into our schools. This doctrine is one which could be defended, and all I need to say about it here is that its application was so ruthless as to make inevitable the corrective movement which is now gathering strength. I am talking rather about a kind of philosophical conviction that, in the secondary-school curriculum, science and mathematics are purely technical subjects of interest only to a limited number of future specialists and in no sense essential components either of a general education or of a general practical training. While for mathematics this view decreed dislodgment from a traditional place of honor at the very heart of the curriculum, for science it meant relegation to a humble spot on the periphery. This view thus provided respectable intellectual grounds for those who thought it expedient to teach but the barest minimum of science and mathematics in our schools, but it certainly appealed to many more who were not directly concerned with the problems of secondary education. It is easy to say that such a belief as this must have sprung from ignorance of science and mathematics. While this is certainly true in part, I think that an explanation of its appeal must also be sought in the nature of the scientific legacy of the nineteenth century.

As one looks back upon the state of science and of mathematics around 1900, one has the impression that there must then have prevailed a general sense of pride and satisfaction in the achievement of a broad rational comprehension of the universe, which would very soon be brought to perfection by a little systematic tidying-up here and there. Many scientists had certainly been inspired by the goal of elaborating such a complete scientific theory of nature, and their efforts might well have appeared, by the end of the nineteenth century, to have brought them within easy striking distance of that goal. In physics, for example, it was thought that a closed deterministic theory could be founded on the dynamics of Newton and the electromagnetic theory of Maxwell. It was easy to extrapolate to the likelihood that chemistry, biology, and eventually even psychology would be embraced in a single system built on the same foundations. In the formulation and elaboration of this system, the role of mathematics was recognized to be indispensable; and mathematics, in its turn, was seen to rest squarely on the principles of logic. Furthermore, in his famous Paris address of 1900 the mathematician

David Hilbert boldly envisioned demonstrating the consistency of logic itself. Eventually he was to propose the search for systematic means of deciding whether any given mathematical proposition, correctly stated in logical terms, is true or false.

In such a climate it must have been easy and natural for many people, even the cleverest and most intelligent of the day, to reach the conclusion that nothing much of intellectual significance need be added to science or mathematics and that nearly everything of interest to be derived from those disciplines in the future could safely be left to a small number of technicians, trained for their specialized tasks in colleges, universities, and engineering schools. That something of the kind did indeed occur and on a very large scale, with grave and long-lasting consequences, was pointed out some thirty years ago in a devastating analysis of our times by a remarkably astute observer of the contemporary scene, the Spanish philosopher José Ortega y Gasset. I shall summon him as a witness, quoting from one of his most famous works, *The Revolt of the Masses*, which deserves to be reread from time to time as events unfold.[3] He wrote:

There have been various periods in history which have considered themselves as having arrived at a lofty and definitive height; various times in which people believed that they had reached the end of a journey, in which some ancient task seemed to have been brought to completion and a hope fulfilled. . . . Thirty years ago, indeed, the European believed that human life had come to be what it ought to be, what many generations had yearned for it to be, what it would indeed have to be forever.

He touched more directly on our present theme in another passage:

Thus it happens . . . that the world of the nineteenth century and the beginning of the twentieth not only has the perfection and amplitude which it actually possesses, but also imparts to its inhabitants a deep confidence that tomorrow will be still richer, more perfect, more ample, thriving, as it were, on some spontaneous and inexhaustible source. . . . In fact, the common man, finding himself in a world so perfect both technically and socially, believes that all this has been produced by Nature and never gives a thought to the efforts of individual genius which its creation presupposes. Still less will he admit the idea that all these conveniences continue to rest on certain rare virtues of man, the slightest failure of which would cause the whole magnificent structure to vanish with the utmost rapidity.

[3] My free translations are based on José Ortega y Gasset, *La Rebelión de las masas* (Buenos Aires: Colección Austral, 1941), pp. 54, 75–76, 93–94.

Ortega put his finger on one of the inevitable consequences of these attitudes when he wrote:

Since the beginnings of the physical sciences—that is to say, since the Renaissance—the enthusiasm for them has grown without halt as time has passed. More precisely, the number of people dedicated to pure research was proportionately greater in each successive generation. The first instance of a decline—I repeat, proportionately considered—has been produced in the generation which is now between twenty and thirty. It is beginning to be difficult to attract disciples into the laboratories of pure science. And this is happening when industry is attaining its greatest development and when the people show the greatest appetite for the machines and the medicines created by science.

This may sound very much like a current analysis of the status of the sciences in our schools, but it was written several decades ago.

The destiny of the twentieth century was to sweep away, one by one, the foundation stones on which the nineteenth century had built the house of science. Newtonian dynamics was rejected in favor of relativity; the deterministic corpuscular view of matter was abandoned in favor of the statistical wave conceptions fundamental in quantum theory. Mathematics was not spared the effects of the revolutionary trend. Indeed Gödel's discovery of undecidable propositions in arithmetic was more profoundly disturbing than anything which occurred in physics, because it disclosed an irremediable and unwelcome complication in logic to which we can only resign ourselves. While the foundations were thus being overhauled and replaced, the architects were busy also on the superstructure, adding new rooms and new stories to the mansion of science. Only half-way through the present century we cannot survey the extent of this expansion without a sense of wonderment and awe, which is greatly increased when we turn our eyes toward its tremendous implications for the conditions of man's life and the conduct of his affairs.

We have been taught by bitter experience that the dream of a closed and perfect rational system for comprehending the universe is an illusion. Instead of representing the mere patient accumulation of mechanical inferences from all-embracing principles, science and mathematics are once again seen as the fruits of high adventure in the realm of ideas and of exploration, where unimaginable surprises and formidable traps still lie in wait for us. This sense of the adventure and the power of science, in particular of mathematics, is the ultimate guaranty that the educational reforms of which I have been speaking will be achieved. If this sense is not yet shared by the majority of thinking men and women, it soon will be; and then nothing can prevent the restoration of science and mathematics to that place in our schools which intellectual and cultural, as well as practical, reasons compel us to accord them.

Adjustments to Supply and Demand

It is supremely ironical that, at the very time when we have begun to recognize these reforms as necessary and urgent, we find ourselves faced with a shortage of teachers which nothing we can do will keep from becoming progressively worse for a good many years to come. Needless to say, this shortage will be especially acute in science and mathematics. Much closer students of the problem than I have come to the conclusion that we shall not be able to solve it simply by increasing our efforts to recruit and train teachers in these fields. In circumstances such as these, where it is idle to imagine that we shall succeed in closing, or even narrowing, the gap between supply and demand, we must inevitably seek some way of transforming the problem by the introduction of new factors designed to alter the relation between the teacher and the taught. This is why there is such a lively and growing interest in exploring the potentialities of all kinds of mechanical aids for increasing the effectiveness of our teachers. It is hard for us to imagine what it must have been like to teach before the introduction of the printed book. It will be even harder, I suspect, for our descendants to imagine what it must have been like to teach without the use of films and television. Right now we are woefully ignorant of how best to employ these and other mechanical aids. An enormous amount of hard and closely reasoned study will be necessary before we can master these new means in the art of teaching. The results will certainly repay the effort required because the good teacher will be enabled to reach a far greater number of pupils and to concentrate his classroom work upon those particular activities in which the advantages of personal contact are most marked.

I must point out that mathematics is probably the subject in which it will be hardest to make proper use of mechanical aids. In mathematics we aim to teach, in essence, two kinds of skills: skill in carrying out the calculations and demonstrations needed in treating a given mathematical problem, and skill in making and understanding mathematical abstractions. It is not enough for us to tell our students how calculations and reasoning are done by someone else; we have to initiate and drill them in doing such things themselves. It is not enough for us to give our students an intuitive grasp of mathematical situations by using concrete analogues and illustrations; we have to lead them on from this level of understanding to the higher one of abstraction and logical analysis. Furthermore, we aim at developing in our students the ability both to handle the specific situations which we have examined with them in the classroom and, even more important, to master new situations which are not merely simple variants of the ones they have studied in school. Anyone who has ever taught a mathematics class knows how incredibly fertile students can be in discovering new pitfalls in the form of blunders, fallacies, and misconceptions. Do what we may to mechanize as much of mathematics-teaching as possible, it thus seems that there must forever remain a large central portion in which direct personal contact betwen teacher and pupil is absolutely indispensable.

While it is necessary and intrinsically very interesting for us to devise ways of using every conceivable mechanical aid, we must constantly remind ourselves of a fundamental fact, which I can best express in the language of physics: the only didactic system in which true resonance can occur is the system comprising teacher and pupil. In any system comprising only a pupil and some mechanical device, there is no true resonance: the pupil may respond to the book, but not the book to the pupil; the pupil may respond to the film, but not the film to the pupil; and so on, as far as one may please. And, as I have said, this fact seems to me to be particularly important for mathematics.

What we have just been discussing are the means by which a helpful adjustment can be made on the side of supply. We should also consider whether other adjustments cannot be made on the side of demand. The encouragement of home study and of self-instruction would be ways, for example, of reducing somewhat the pressure exerted by rising demand. Since the possibilities in this direction are severely limited and since it is of primary importance to welcome and encourage any demand whatever for increased instruction in science and mathematics, we are forced to examine the problem as a whole, considering not merely the demand in special subjects but also the total demand for expanded school facilities. As soon as we do this, we shall certainly be faced with some deep and fundamental educational questions. The answers given to these questions will affect very importantly the climate in which we must proceed to increase and improve the teaching of science and mathematics. For this reason I propose to discuss these questions and their bearing on the school mathematics of tomorrow. The essence of the matter is that there are insurmountable limitations placed upon our educational means and few corresponding limitations on the kind of educational services which are contemplated for the future. We are coming to the point where we shall have to decide which of the proposed services are sufficiently valuable that we should devote the appropriate portion of our limited means to their support. We shall have to muster the courage required to make this agonizing reappraisal.

The educational philosophy and practice of our schools appear to have revolved around two key phrases, "democracy" and "education for life." The test for any educational proposal has not been to measure its worth in any general system of intellectual or cultural values but to ask, "Is it democratic?" "Is it related to a life situation?" In the main these key words have been perverted into the slogans of covert anti-intellectualism in the United States and have been used as the dialectic tools for reducing American education to the lowest common denominator. This has been possible because the words themselves are ambiguous. No one wants our schools to be undemocratic or divorced from life. It is time that we redefine "democracy" to mean something closer to the ideals of Jefferson and Lincoln than the sentimental egalitarianism practiced in educational circles. It is time for us to take a long look at "education for life" to see whether it may not have to be something different from what educators, lost in some half-utopian view of what America and the world are like, have been telling us these many years. In fact, we should go one step further and try to redefine the goals of American education in positive terms bearing some sensible relation to the kind of world in which our children will be living.

I suggest that our aim should be to see that each child is educated up to a level determined by his intellectual capacities and his manual dexterity, but only on the condition that he maintain a genuine interest in his studies and strive for progress in them. If we hold to such an aim, we shall no longer close the door of opportunity to many of our young people, as the public schools have been guilty of doing in the name of democracy and education for life. We shall not have to argue the merits of giving our gifted children the chance to grow intellectually while still in high school. We shall not any longer be shamed by the existence of high schools in which no geometry is taught. We shall not continue to be smug about sending into the world of modern industry and commerce a flood of high-school graduates who are, at the most elementary level, mathematically illiterate. Furthermore, we shall be able to review the work done in our schools—and, I might add, that done in our colleges—with the purpose of eliminating those activities which serve no clear and necessary intellectual, practical, or moral end and concentrating our limited educational resources on the cultivation of those that remain. Finally, we shall be able—in sorrow, perhaps, but with no sense of guilt—to send away from our overcrowded schools and colleges the incompetent, the wasters, the idlers, and the escapists, on whom we are still squandering efforts which would much better be turned to the benefit of those who are both competent and eager for learning.

So far as science and mathematics are concerned, the pressure has become so great that our schools will find it expedient to do many of the things which they have refused to do for at least thirty years. However, these changes will be easier to accomplish if they are in harmony with our general goals; and the fact that they have to be made now in haste and with all the fanfare of reform is the surest sign that there was something fundamentally and radically wrong with the old goals. That is why I would like to see them replaced as we prepare ourselves to enter the new era which lies ahead.

Reshaping the Mathematics Curriculum

After these general considerations, which I think we cannot afford to leave out of account, it is time to pay some attention to more concrete and specific questions. In the field of high-school mathematics, the subject under the liveliest discussion is without doubt the reshaping of the curriculum. What the school mathematics of tomorrow will be is a question which will be determined largely by this discussion. It is now clearly recognized by teachers of mathematics that, in order to give our high-school graduates the kind of mathematical knowledge and mastery they will need in the more scientific and more technological world of tomorrow, we shall have to make many changes in the arrangement and content of our high-school courses in mathematics.

First of all, we have to make the curriculum reflect, in greater measure, the progress of mathematical science and the current trends in its growth. This means examining closely the subjects to be taught, with a view to eliminating elements which are obsolescent or outmoded and incorporating new ones which are more important or more useful in accordance with modern conceptions of what mathematics is. This difficult task will not be completed until a comprehensive series of textbooks and other teaching materials has been prepared, in conformity with the highest standards of mathematical accuracy and pedagogical effectiveness.

The details of this program are so prominent in current discussions that I do not intend to dwell upon them here. In summary, what is involved is not only the recasting of the traditional high-school subjects (algebra, geometry, and trigonometry) but the introduction of entirely new subjects (such as symbolic logic, probability and statistics, and mechanical computation) and the incorporation of traditional college subjects (such as analytic geometry and elementary calculus). I think it may be useful to suggest that no general agreement is likely to emerge from current discussions of the many different proposals of this kind which have been put forward. I am told that, when a large group of physicists met at the Massachusets Institute of Technology to launch a pedagogical program, they very quickly agreed on the contents of the high-school physics course which they proposed to plan and elaborate. In contrast, we mathematicians shall probably agree only to disagree. In consequence, we must expect tomorrow's high-school curriculum in mathematics to emerge in a variety of different forms, none demonstrably superior to the rest and all well established in different schools.

In the current discussions, not enough attention is being paid, I feel, to the reform of courses in general mathematics or to the revision of the mathematics curriculum in the elementary schools. I am convinced that we shall have to give very careful thought to both these matters if we are to meet adequately the challenge of the future. It is not enough for us to bring our teaching of high-school mathematics up to the level necessary for the young people who expect to continue their education in college or to go on into scientific or technological pursuits. We must keep in mind also the needs of those who will not, or should not, go on to further study. I believe that we should begin by making a new study of the needs of the latter group. It seems to me that we have made assumptions about them which, if ever true, have been rendered false by the changes that have taken place in our society. The number of activities demanding simple mathematical skills and simple mathematical understanding has been tremendously increased by the expansion of technology and the extension of government into more aspects of our lives. Concrete evidence of this exists in the massive educational activities of industry and the armed forces and in the political discussions of such problems as taxes, social security, and farm price supports. I think our educators have failed to recognize how often in his life the average citizen and worker in our complicated modern society must make contacts with the world of mathematics. When the need is better understood, I am sure that educators will take the lead in improving instruction in general mathematics and bringing it closer to the realities of modern life.

It seems obvious that the discussion of high-school mathematics, whether general or special, cannot be separated from a consideration of what is done with mathematics in the elementary school. My own educational interests are directed especially to the problems of elementary instruction because I am convinced that they are the most difficult and the most important educational problems of all and that they will eventually lead us into the most profound and challenging aspects of pedagogy and educational psychology. It is clear that, until we can achieve much greater success in teaching mathematics in the elementary schools, we shall be seriously hampered in our effort to make high-school mathematics what we believe it should be. For this reason, if for no other, I urge that these problems from another sphere of interest should not be overlooked in our concentration upon the high school.

In the teaching of mathematics, we have to measure our success by the degree of mastery we are able to impart to our students. As I suggested earlier, mastery is measured by skill in carrying out the calculations and demonstrations needed in treating a given mathematical problem and by skill in making and understanding mathematical abstractions. To acquire these skills, our students need drill, practice, and the experience of struggling with hard problems and difficult concepts. In short, they need discipline—first, the discipline imposed by a good teacher; ultimately, the self-discipline learned under his guidance. It is still true that there is no royal road to the mastery of mathematics. If we judge our high schools by their fruits (and that, after all, is how they will be, and should be, judged), we are justified in condemning them for their long neglect of discipline, in the good sense of the term. In my own teaching I have observed the weaknesses and deficiences of a long line of students, both undergraduates and graduates. These students included some of the best in the country; many of them are already professors in some of our leading universities and important contributors to the progress of science and mathematics. As the years have gone by, I believe I have seen a steady deterioration in the preparation given students in school, if not in college. It is heartbreaking to see young men of real ability flounder and waste unconscionable amounts of time and energy in their first years of graduate school simply because they have never learned anywhere to think or to speak with precision, to write clearly and in good order, to finish a task down to the last detail, or to persist in the face of real intellectual difficulties. My colleagues and I have to teach them all these things by indirection and example because they are too old to be treated as the intellectual children which they still are.

When American sicentists and scholars are compared with their European colleagues, as they so often are, to the advantage of the latter, the only difference which can clearly be attributed to a difference in education is that as a youth the European has generally received the benefits of a thorough intellectual discipline such as the American has never experienced. From my own personal and scientific knowledge of foreign mathematicians, I am convinced that this is the essential and decisive difference which explains the continuing superior quality of the best European achievements in the field of mathematics. Approximately one-third of the world's mathematicians who are just more than slightly active in the publication of mathematical research live and work in the United States, but a considerably less than a third of the important research currently produced comes from this country. In addition, it must be pointed out that many of the most active and prominent mathematicians in America were trained abroad and came to this country after they had started their university careers.

If American mathematics is to meet the challenge of the new era, it is absolutely essential that our high schools should restore intellectual discipline to the teaching of mathematics. I recognize that this may be difficult to do because so many of our educators no longer see any virtue in discipline, and the mathematics teacher who understands that, without discipline, there can be no mastery or true understanding of mathematics finds himself isolated and his efforts paralyzed. Nevertheless the effort must be made. Actually it is only too evident that the problem of discipline is one which is forcing itself on our attention in numerous pressing and alarming forms. I expect a reversal of the attitudes which have made our homes and our schools the nurseries of intellectual sloth, of self-indulgence, and of irresponsibility. In that case the return to old standards of discipline and achievement will seem a perfectly natural feature of the school mathematics of tomorrow.

In treating at such length and in such detail the various changes which seem to be in the making, we have risked overlooking the most essential things of all. There are so many concrete problems to be described and solved, and in some ways it seems so much easier to master the concrete difficulties which they offer, that there is always a temptation to let ourselves be fascinated and submerged by these innumerable details. In bringing these remarks to a close, I therefore want to return, if only briefly, to the most important element of all in our thinking about the school mathematics of tomorrow—our concern for the stimulation and fostering of intellectual curiosity. Let us elaborate new curriculums, invent new methods of pedagogy, revive the virtues of intellectual discipline, with all the zeal and wisdom of which we are capable; we shall still fail if we have not left a large place to intellectual curiosity. For the student it is his own curiosity which brings the curriculum to life, which guarantees his responsiveness to the teacher's knowledge and skill, which gives a compelling motive to experience the virtues of discipline. Our great task is, and will continue to be, the task of kindling that kind of curiosity in our students.

The Mathematics Curriculum for the High School of the Future

The present high-school curriculum in mathematics is a traditional one. It is outmoded, is oriented to nineteenth-century mathematics and physics, and no longer provides for present or anticipated needs of high-school students. The mathematics curriculum of the future must meet the needs of mathematics, physical sciences, social sciences, engineering, technology, industrial management, and other areas of human endeavor as they are carried on in the second half of the twentieth century. If we are to proceed wisely in constructing a curriculum for the future, we must examine some defects of the present curriculum, the present mathematical needs of our society, and the changing concepts and new developments in mathematics. Then we must temper this mathematical knowledge with our knowledge of the maturity and learning ability of the high-school population.

The Traditional Program

Today the ninth-year mathematics program is commonly given to a study of elementary algebra. What is this study? The manipulation of symbols according to rules in a structureless system.

There are no proofs, no system of axioms, no undefined terms. The instruction is mostly "how to do." Such terms as "literal numbers," "general number," "unknown," and "algebraic numbers" are for the most part meaningless and, worse, confusing. A student learns how to solve equations, but not what an equation is, or what operations are allowable and why, or what the solution indicates. If he is asked to apply his knowledge of solution of equations to problems, the latter must be explained in great detail. Again and again it has been shown that a student learned a set of operations,

406

mostly meaningless to him, and that he can do little with them in any original setting.

In the tenth or eleventh year the study of this algebra is continued as intermediate algebra. How? By first reviewing the skill algebra of the ninth year in exactly the same way but with more complex situations. Then the students learn *how to handle* exponents, logarithms, systems of equations, progressions, and the binomial expansion without being given any hint that proof in an axiomatic system is as essential in algebra as it is in dealing with geometric elements. If he is introduced to any other topics, they are usually permutations, combinations, and probability. But these are taught in an antiquated manner, ill-adapted for application to modern problems in statistical processes. The function concept present in most textbooks is one no longer generally accepted by mathematicians, and, even when presented, it contributes little to understanding this important aspect of mathematics.

In either the tenth or the eleventh year the student also studies plane geometry, more correctly termed "Euclidean synthetic plane geometry." What does he learn here? He gets an introduction into the physics of a plane through the use of definitions, undefined terms, and a set of assumptions. A year-long chain of theorems follows, which in most cases results in large quantities of mere memorization. At the end of the year the student may be a bit more clever at discovering deductions to so-called originals, but is he really a better mathematician with a real understanding of the axiomatic structure of mathematics? The answer must be "No!"

Twelfth-grade mathematics in the American high school is the grandest fiasco of all mathematical programs. A half-year of solid geometry contributes nothing new to an understanding of mathematical structure. The geometry of the sphere, which could become a fine self-contained unit of study, is buried under a heap of useless applications.

To cap the climax, we have a semester of trigonometry, which is usually concluded with two months of solution of oblique triangles by the use of logarithms. The trigonometry of the general angle and topics such as reduction formulas, identities, and equations, as these are usually taught, contribute little to an understanding of trigonometry that is of value for further work in mathematics.

Society's Need for Mathematics

Now let us look at the role that mathematics is coming to play in our culture. I shall omit all reference to general education and the mathematical needs of all citizens as part of their general education. It suffices to say that all citizens need a working knowledge of arithmetic, elementary algebra, and geometric relations and measures. All secondary-school students should study mathematics until they have mastered these necessary facts, concepts, and skills. Here I would speak of the newer and more advanced mathematical needs of society.

The degree to which mathematics is applied to the other sciences and to so-called non-scientific social activities has increased tremendously during the past few decades and is continuing to increase. Mathematics has always contributed to the fields of physics, engineering, and technology. More recently mathematical methods have been applied to industrial planning, medicine, biochemistry, biophysics, and sociology. Even problems in philosophy and linguistics are being attacked through the use of mathematical logic. In all of this increased activity it is curious that, although the first investigations were begun by mathematicians, on the whole it is not mathematical propaganda or advertising that has made the situation what it is. The situation resulted from a genuine demand on the part of workers in these fields, who came to feel more and more helpless when they could not handle mathematical methods.

The number and the variety of mathematical disciplines have greatly increased in the last sixty years. New branches of knowledge based on mathematical methods have been created. Among these may be mentioned design of experiments, mathematical population theory, theory of risks, symbolic logic, biomathematics, factor analysis, quality control, mathematical theory of communication, information theory, theory of strategy and games, linear programing, periodogramanalysis and time series, statistical decision theory, and so on. While not all of these new theories have produced practical results commensurate with their mathematical structure, yet the judgment of workers in the field is that, on the whole, the mathematical approach has been beneficial to their particular domains.

Mathematicians themselves are creating new branches of pure

mathematics, much of it knowledge that did not exist sixty years ago. We may mention axiomatics; abstract algebra, including the theory of groups, rings, fields, and vector spaces; combinatorial topology and algebraic topology; lattice theories; general theory of sets; theory of linear spaces; tensor calculus; and even meta-mathematics, which is a study about, not of, mathematics.

I hasten to add that I know little of these fields of applied and pure mathematics except that they exist; that they have burst the existing compartments that house arithmetic, algebra, and geometry; and that their very nature makes obsolete much of the classical treatment of high-school mathematics. Note that I said the "treatment" of mathematics, and not the mathematics itself, becomes obsolete.

New Points of View

In the past one hundred years the nature of mathematics as a subject has been substantially altered by the results of mathematical research and by applications of the research. Some of this research can have significant impact on the high-school program. We can mention only a few of these newer areas of mathematical thought, without, however, developing their content.

In the field of algebra we mention first the concepts of group, ring, and field, all dealing with *structural*, rather than manipulative, aspects of algebra. None of these concepts is difficult to grasp. The concept of field enables us to study the structure of algebra rather than merely to manipulate algebraic expressions. This concept has given rise to studies of different algebras: linear associative, vector, multilinear, etc. This aspect of algebra has reshaped the thinking and the type of research that is now being done at the frontiers of mathematical knowledge.

In the 1920's and 1930's an advanced treatise in mathematical analysis always had a first chapter that treated the real number system, upon which, of course, the rest of the development rested. If you pick up treatises today, whether in advanced algebra, analysis, or geometry, the first chapter is always a treatment of the theory of sets, upon which the rest of the development rests. Set theory is the newest unifying concept to enter the field of mathematics. The ideas of sets in modified form can be applied to every portion of the present high-school program.

In the field of geometry, new points of view are also emerging. A hundred years ago non-Euclidean geometries became firmly established as worthy structures of mathematical study, thus freeing the subject from the absolute authority of Euclid. With the advent of these new geometries there arose a critical examination of the axiomatic foundations of Euclidean geometry. This study revealed in the subject subtle ideas that proved it to be too difficult a subject for rigorous treatment at the high-school level. The researchers also established other geometries, called "projective," "affine," "elliptic," and "hyperbolic," and shattered forever the idea that there is only one kind of geometry. Finally, a new approach to the study of space, called "topology," has opened fields of investigation in which the very first findings are of importance to the present high-school geometry program.

The Curriculum of the Future

Considering society's demands for mathematics and the modern developments in mathematics mentioned above, we can draw some inferences concerning the curriculum of high-school mathematics of the future. We consider here both the junior and the senior high school.

Seventh and Eighth Grades

The first two years of the junior high school will offer an intuitive and informal study of arithmetic, geometry, and some elements of algebra. More precisely, at the end of this informal study, a student should have a mastery of the four fundamental operations with whole numbers, common fractions, and decimal fractions. This includes skill in the operations at adult level (that is, adequate for ordinary life-situations) and an understanding of the rationale of the computational processes. A place-value system of numeration, with special reference to our decimal system, should be understood. Systems of numeration with bases other than ten, particularly the binary system, should be investigated. Students must be able to handle very large numbers (greater than 1,000,000) and very small numbers (less than one ten-thousandth, 0.0001). A knowledge of square root and the ability to find approximate values of square roots of whole numbers by dividing and averaging the divisor and the quotient (Newton's method) are recommended.

An understanding of the language of per cent (rate), percentage, and base is essential and, in particular, the ability to find any one of these three designated numbers when given the other two. The ability to treat with confidence per cents less than 1 and greater than 100 must be acquired. Applications of per cent to business practices, interest, discount, and budgets should be given moderate treatment.

The study of arithmetic must include the understanding of ratio as used in comparing sizes of quantities of like kind, in proportions, and in making scale drawings. Students must develop the ability to operate with, and to transform, the several systems of measure, including the metric system of length, area, volume, and weight. The nature and use of an arithmetic mean should be stressed. The work should be directed toward an informal study of algebra.

The informal geometry must include the study of length of a line segment, perimeter of a polygon, and circumference of a circle, areas of regions inclosed by polygons and circles, area of solids, volumes inclosed by solids, interior of angles (by degrees). In this work the use of a ruler (both English and metric) and protractor is learned. The pupil should know the difference between the *process* of measuring and the *measure* of an entity and should develop the ability to apply measurement to practical situations. He uses measurement in drawing to scale and in finding lengths indirectly.

Further concepts of geometry that should be developed are those of parallel, perpendicular, intersecting, and oblique lines (in a plane and in space); acute, right, obtuse, complementary, supplementary, and vertical angles; scalene, isosceles, and equilateral triangles; right triangles and the Pythagorean relation; sum of the interior angles of a triangle; sides and interior angles of a regular polygon with six or fewer sides. The student develops skill in the use of instruments in constructing figures; he learns ideas of symmetry about a point and a line.

Further ideas to be included in these two years of study are the use of a line segment and area to represent numbers; the reading and construction of bar graphs, line graphs, pictograms, circle graphs, and continuous-line graphs; the meaning of scale; formulas for perimeters, areas, volumes, and per cents (introduced as these concepts are studied) as mathematical models; the use of symbols in formulas as place-holders for numbers arising in measurement; and simple expressions and sentences involving variables.

Algebra

The study of algebra will consist largely of the same subject matter as hitherto. The difference will be in point of view, and this will be concerned principally with concepts, terminology, symbolism, and the introduction of a rather large segment of work on inequalities. The idea of one-dimensional graphs (for example, indicating the set of points for which $x<3$) will be introduced. There will be a shift from emphasis on mechanical manipulation to emphasis on understanding the fundamental ideas and basic laws. The study of the nature of number systems, of the nature and use of variables, and of the basic laws for addition and multiplication, namely, the commutative, associative, and distributive laws, are focal points. The application of these laws in various algebraic systems, with emphasis on their generality, will be studied. The meanings of conditional equations and inequalities, of their solution sets, and of equivalent equations and inequalities will receive as much attention as the mechanics for finding the solution sets.

If this approach to algebra were merely something interesting but useless, something at an abstract level that could be learned by high-school students, merely an extension of the algebra of the eighteenth century, or a game for scholars interested in pure mathematics only, we could ignore it. But it is none of these. It is being used in all the sciences, pure and applied. The ideas are elementary and can give the "meaning" we have been looking for in the teaching of our algebra. It is new. It can be introduced at almost any time in the high-school program. It gives to algebra a structural and unifying approach. Hence we cannot afford to ignore this approach as we reconstruct our high-school program.

Mathematical concepts do not remain static. When Leibnitz in 1675 used the word "function," he used it as concomitant change. Euler in 1770 said it was the relation between y and x expressed by a freely drawn curve in the plane. Dirichlet said y is called a function of x if y possesses one or more definite values for each of certain values of x in an interval x_0 to x_1. But today a "function" is a subset of a Cartesian product in which the first element of an ordered pair occurs only once; that is, a "function" is a restricted set of ordered pairs of numbers; it is single valued. Added to this changing concept we have the introduction of the new word "relation," which is far more inclusive than "function." The nature of a function—in particular, the linear, quadratic, exponential, and logarithmic functions— will be treated as much as are operations with them. Function will be distinct from a relation, and both will be related to sets of ordered pairs of numbers, and a rule or set builder.

The distributive law may be cited as an example of meaningful algebra. This law is the basic idea behind both mental and written arithmetic, the use of parentheses, factoring, multiplication of polynomials, and the manipulations of fractions. If the law is understood, most *special* methods of treating these topics can be eliminated.

Algebra will be further enhanced by introducing deductive reasoning—a procedure that should be taught in all courses of school mathematics and not in geometry courses alone. Thus geometry can be relieved of the burden of total responsibility for deductive methods. For example, students will make certain assumptions and definitions, except certain undefined terms, and then prove, for example, that the square of an odd number is an odd number and that it is always one more than a multiple of eight. Through such deductive procedures, diverse bits of information become related and "hang together," thereby promoting understanding and assisting the memory. Further, such understanding contributes to the ability to use algebra to solve problems.

Throughout the presentation the concepts and language of set theory will be used. The set concept is elementary and closely related to experience. It permits a variety and richness of problems that call for creative and original thinking. It is one of the great unifying and generalizing concepts of all mathematics. Meaning becomes of utmost importance.

Geometry

The program in geometry will be vastly different from the present program. The usual one and one-half years devoted to plane and solid synthetic geometry will be reduced to considerably less than one year of study. Solid geometry as a half-year course of deductive methods will disappear entirely. Those aspects of solid geometry of importance will be developed, along with the corresponding concepts of plane geometry. The treatment of the sphere can be coordinated with the circle; locus will be treated simultaneously in two space and three space. The mensuration and construction problems of solid geometry will be developed on an intuitive rather than a pseudo-deductive basis.

Since deduction is to be stressed throughout the study of mathematics, it is not necessary to spend a year on deducing theorems and originals of synthetic geometry. In fact, the study of plane synthetic geometry will begin with an informal and intuitive introduction to geometric ideas, followed by a discussion of the nature of deductive reasoning. The formal study will then start with the postulation of the congruence theorems and proceed as rapidly as possible through a chain of six or eight fundamental theorems to the proof of the Pythagorean theorem. One-third of a year of study is sufficient for this.

With the Pythagorean theorem established, it is possible to proceed to analytic geometry, where the fundamental ideas of distance, division of a line segment, slope, equation of a line, and equation of a circle are developed. Thus a new, powerful geometry exists for the students to use. To prove or deduce theorems and originals, both analytic and synthetic methods are now at his disposal.

Trigonometry

Vectors is another topic of great importance both in physics and in further mathematical study. A unit on vectors, with its assumptions and undefined terms, and the ideas of displacement, multiplication by a scalar, addition, and subtraction, will give the student an added tool for proving theorems in geometry and solving problems in forces, acceleration, and rectilinear motion. The study of plane vectors also gives an approach to trigonometry that permits the easy development of periodicity properties of the trigonometric functions.

Today trigonometry has become an integral part of analysis and has hardly any support as a separate subject, isolated for a half-year of study. The trigonometry of real numbers has been developed as a wrapping function of the real axis, and the sine function, for example, then repeats its values with a period of 2π—in symbols $f(2\pi + x) = f(x)$. Further, the sine is an odd function—that is, sin $(-x)$ $= -\sin(x)$—while the cosine is an even function—that is, cos $(-x)$ $= \cos(x)$. This behavior permits the application of trigonometry to all sorts of periodic phenomena, such as light and sound waves, alternating current, business cycles, heat flow, and harmonic analysis. The concepts of amplitude, period, frequency, and phase, in relation to the sine and cosine as functions of real numbers, have had significant effects in all branches of pure and applied mathematics.

The study of trigonometry will, from the very start, be related to co-ordinates, both rectangular and polar. It is to be noted that co-ordinates are to be continually used throughout the entire study of mathematics in the curriculum of the future. This is a new emphasis. The solution of triangles will play a minor role, the solution of oblique triangles being limited to the use of the law of sines and the law of cosines, without the use of logarithms. The logarithmic solution of triangles, a speedy method fifty or more years ago, has been outmoded by the advent of electric calculators.

The analytic aspects of trigonometry will be emphasized. In the past, in applications to surveying and navigation, the solution of plane and spherical triangles was the central theme. In the newer uses of trigonometry it is the circular functions of real numbers that occupy the central theme. The study of these functions is greatly facilitated by the concept of a function as a set of ordered pairs of numbers. The usual formulas will be developed with the use of co-ordinate geometry and in the spirit that trigonometry is a study of periodic functions of real numbers.

Twefth Year

The elimination of parts of traditional algebra and much of Euclidean geometry gives us time to complete the high-school program with a study of those topics of advanced algebra that can properly be classified as modern analysis. There will be a study of the elementary functions—polynomial, rational, exponential, logarithmic. This leads to study of absolute value and limits, followed by a unit on polynomial calculus developed from a meaningful and conceptual viewpoint and not one that is formalistic and mechanical.

I would add to the high-school curriculum of the future one more item of study, namely, the topic of probability and statistics. Just where and how this topic is to come in to the curriculum must be worked out. Many of the newer applications of mathematics are those underlying chance, that is, probability and statistical inference. These applications involve problems in safety, genetics, longevity, industrial planning, cost of living, occupational choice, testing, measuring, public opinion polls, theory of games, and so on. Statistical thinking is playing a greater and greater role in the life of educated men and women. An introduction to statistical inference with probabilistic conclusions is as important as the study of deductive systems with universal conclusions.

The two important aspects of statistics are: (1) in a distribution of attributes arising from chance causes, there is a coexistence of stability (a central tendency) accompanied by a variation; (2) by proper sampling techniques based on mathematical probability theory, both the stability and the variation of the entire population can be predicted to a high degree of confidence. The study of the first aspect is accomplished in descriptive statistics, that is, the collection, organization, and analysis of numerical data through the use of frequency tables, graphs of distribution, arithmetic mean, mode, and median, range, and standard deviation. The second aspect is acquired through the study of combinatorial analysis and partitioning of sets. Both these aspects will be in the mathematics curriculum of the future.

Summary

The aim of this entire curriculum is to enable those who are capable and who desire to study science, mathematics, technology, or engineering to enter college prepared to begin a rigorous Freshman course in differential and integral calculus. Realizing this aim will be a necessity for the development of our country's scientific progress in the immediate years ahead of us. All highly capable students must pursue the study of mathematics. For the other college-bound students, the more advanced part of the proposed curriculum may be delayed and studied as a first-year college program such as that proposed by the College Undergraduate Program Committee of the Mathematical Association of America.

Any seventeenth-century mathematician reappearing upon earth today could enter most classrooms in our high schools and, without any preparation, teach the present traditional curriculum, so far is it behind the times. But in order to handle the curriculum proposed here, the seventeenth-century mathematician would have to bring himself up to date with respect to fundamental concepts in every field included in the curriculum—algebra, geometry, trigonometry, calculus, statistics, logic. Most important of all, he would have to catch the spirit of modern mathematics, which began in the twentieth century—a spirit wherein we seek *patterns* of thought, mathematical forms, rather than specific tricks. It is in this sense that the proposed curriculum is modern and for the future.

I should like to add only one word concerning those in high school who are not capable of going, or are not planning to go, to college. Many of the present courses and textbooks for these students are a rehash and stew of everything under the sun. There is no organization, structure, or systematic development of mathematics in many of the books or proposed curriculums. It is my hypothesis that the mathematics for these students will be, and must be, the same as the elementary portions of the curriculum I have outlined. The mathematics used in general education for enabling us to undertsand our universe and solve our daily quantitative problems is the same mathematics that the scientist uses in his research. The difference is one of complexity and depth. Nothing but longer time and more concrete illustrations are needed for the slow learner, and not a different type of curriculum.

Science Education in the High School of the Future

Education in science has moved from the wings to the center of the educational stage. One can no longer discuss educational problems in the United States on the assumption that science may appropriately be left principally to the higher institutions. The relevance and the appropriateness of education in science at all educational levels have become central educational concerns.

We might find it possible to develop close agreement on aims for today's science education. However, I must admit a bit of cynicism about agreement on aims, for it seems to me that such agreement is largely a result of keeping terms so general that no one can quarrel with them. For example, we probably would not generate serious differences over statements such as these:

Science education should develop skill in modes of scientific thought.

Science education should help youngsters develop control of the basic principles and the basic facts of scientific knowledge.

Science education should develop a level of public interest in science, of public control of skills in scientific thought, of control of principles of scientific knowledge, which will insure effective public policy in the realm of science.

Science-education programs should deliver enough highly trained, able people to insure the maintenance of the scientific and technological innovation on which we depend for economic growth, social well-being, and military strength.

Virtually every responsible educator and scientist wants these things; the trouble is that translating these attractive aims into specific educational targets is extremely difficult. How much skill should be developed in modes of scientific thought? How effective shall be the control of basic scientific principles? What is an appropriate level of public interest and understanding? How many persons, with what training, are necessary to insure adequate innovation?

These questions, recently the concern of only the school man and the university scientist, today are foci of anxiety and fear, scapegoat-hunting, and rabble-rousing attacks on education, as well as of serious, responsible, and informed search for appropriate action. When detailed discussion of questions such as these takes place in today's anxiety-charged atmosophere, the productive lode turns out to be hidden by a thick overburden which effectively screens off the serious questions to be posed and answered.

My effort, therefore, will be developed along four lines. First, I shall seek to remove parts of the overburden in order to get at the vein of productive questions. Then I shall try to formulate several of the problems which seem to me to be visible parts of the vein which must be mined. Third, I shall attempt to predict answers for some of the productive questions. After that, I shall hazard some guesses about science education in the high school of the future.

Disposing of the Overburden

First, let us consider the overburden. One of its chief components is an overgeneralization of the term "high school." That term includes the Bronx High School of Science in New York, New Trier Township High School, and the Evanston Township High School. It also includes a little, ten-teacher high school sitting alone on the prairies of the Dakotas and a five-teacher school in an underprivileged section of the South. It includes schools with several faculty members who hold the Ph.D. degree, and it includes schools in which the fraction of faculty members holding the Bachelor's degree may be less than half. It includes school plants worth many millions of dollars, and it includes school plants which probably could be effectively replaced by good tents.

When one talks about "the high schools of the United States," one should be very careful, for any informed school person can contradict most of the popular assertions about American high schools simply by selecting an appropriate sample of schools. If one person asserts that schools in the United States neglect gifted youth, another can readily find several schools in which much attention is given to gifted youth and in which faculties include highly trained, intelligent persons quite dedicated to the location and development of gifted youth. If a person asserts that the preparation and the training of able youth are effectively done in the United States, he must be prepared for his opponent to take him to a half-dozen nearby schools which make little provision for individual differences and in which youngsters are herded through classes like so many sheep through dipping troughs. If we are to move ahead swiftly, we must resist as strongly as we can, the tendency to overgeneralize about schools in the United States. We must learn to talk about particular programs in specific settings.

A second obscuring feature is a corollary of the first. This is the frequent overgeneralization of "scientist" and its allied term "engineer." Each of these terms is proving to be extremely difficult to define even for census purposes. Who is a scientist? Is a university science teacher a scientist? In the census he is more likely to be counted as a teacher. Suppose a man has matured in an industrial laboratory and has become expert in an area of investigation of concern to his company. He may not have a Bachelor's degree, or he may have only a Bachelor's degree and in some field other than the one in which he is earning his living. Is this man a scientist? Or is he an engineer? The term "engineer," of course, includes persons who manage heating plants in buildings, men who operate railroad trains, and men like Dr. Vannevar Bush.

Generalization about scientists and engineers is extremely precarious. None of us would hold that only those students who intend to be scientists should be involved in secondary-school science classes, if by "scientist" we mean the research physicist, the research chemist, or the research biologist. Yet, unless a person is very careful, this assumption will govern his thought. This overgeneralization—that "scientist" means only "research scientist"—is a source of serious trouble in secondary-school science. Somehow the English teacher thinks that science classes are only for very able people; and the science teacher himself, if he is not very careful, may in due course come to think that science classes are for very able students only.

The fact is that a person can work constructively in electronics, for example, at levels from high-school graduation through to the Ph.D. in solid state physics. It is a matter of training, interest, and occupational opportunities. We might consider training below that of the high-school graduate and try to decide whether women who wire radio sets are working in electronics. They certainly are making electronic equipment, though most of them were not specially trained for the work in secondary or higher schools.

Another conspicuous section of the overburden is the notion that mathematics and science are "harder" than other subjects. No university faculty would tolerate serious discussion of the relative difficulties of physics and English literature. In any first-rate university faculty the very best minds available are working on problems in every field. The question of relative difficulty of subjects cannot be raised in seriousness at graduate levels. The question at hand, whether high-school science is more difficult than other high-school subjects, cannot be answered through demonstration of intrinsic differences between fields.

A secondary-school course is the result of selection from an enormous array of materials. Anyone of reasonable teaching competence in a given field can construct a course in that field which would frustrate all, or any desired fraction, of the high-school students who enrol in it. If, after careful investigation, science and mathematics should turn out to be more difficult at the secondary-school level than, say, English or physical education or social science, the appropriate question would be: Why are high-school science and mathematics more difficult than other high-school subjects? Any secondary-school teacher can make his material as difficult as he chooses for the students who come to him. Why should science teachers make their courses more difficult than social-science teachers make their courses?

Still another of the overburden items is the frequent assertion that science teachers are less well trained and less effective than other teachers and that coaches and administrators are more often science teachers. There may now be empirical support for the last statement, as a result of the exodus of science teachers from the schools. The administrator is most likely to be the person directly facing the need to do something about meeting science requirements for high-school graduation, and, when no one else can teach a course, the administrator is likely to teach it. However, studies of the qualifications of science teachers typically show only that many science teachers do not have majors in science and that they frequently have school assignments other than science-teaching.

Certainly it is desirable that everyone who teaches a high-school course in science should have at least an undergraduate major in the field in which he teaches. On the other hand, this level of teacher training is not universal in any other secondary-school teaching field. The appropriate questions are: Are science teachers less well trained than other secondary-school teachers? Are their teaching assignments more dispersed among other subjects than are the assignments of teachers of other subjects?

In the absence of accurate recent information, experience and contact with smaller high schools would lead us to expect some variation among teaching fields, owing to patterns of graduation requirements. However, one of the major and persistent problems in training teachers in the United States is the necessity of training teachers so that each can teach effectively in two or three fields. Outside the largest schools, it is virtually impossible for a teacher to stay full-time in a particular teaching field. The assertion that science teachers are less well trained than others, that current difficulties are to be ascribed principally to relative inadequacy of teacher training in the field of science, also is a part of the overburden, which must be dug out and laid aside.

Even the argument about supply of technically trained persons is part of the overburden covering the really basic problems of the science education of the future. Certainly the United States, right at this time and at current wages, can effectively use more scientists and engineers than it seems to be able to turn out. Actually, of course, this is a problem which has a strong economic aspect. Most of us have seen times of high demand and of low demand for technical people. The basis of the assertion that the present high demand will continue for an extended period is weak, and in any case the demand would disappear in the event that the desired people appeared in any substantial numbers. Whether the demand situation affects science education on a long-term basis is a question which every person will have to answer for himself. In my opinion, it does not affect long-term planning of science education, for I predict that we shall have "enough" scientists and engineers, and relatively soon, even in terms of current patterns of utilization of such skills.

This view, incidentally, does not minimize current difficulties.

I am communicating very poorly if I seem to be suggesting that our current difficulties with respect to the location of talented persons and so on are difficulties which will soon pass or are of no serious consequence. I merely hold the view that our "crisis" demand for scientists and engineers is likely to be temporary and that it does not bear significantly on long-range problems in science education.

Moreover, in the current demand for scientists and engineers there are at least two components which ordinarily are not distinguished. When we talk about scientists to design a rocket to put an American satellite into its orbit and about the general supply of scientists and engineers, we are talking about different things. In the first case we are talking about the amount of ingenuity, the amount of creativity, which can be brought to bear on a particular problem. This is the place at which Conant's comment of a few years ago bears most heavily—that there is no combination of second-rate minds which can equal one first-rate brain. The person who maintains that not enough really bright people are working at science, that we do not have enough people with bright ideas working in science and engineering, is illuminating one component of the discussion.

But this is very different from satisfying demands for scientists and engineers with the ordinary four-year college training. The latter group goes into the production of things of science. They are the persons who manage the production of guided missiles, of automobiles, of radios, and who manage the technical branches of the military. These are general executives, technical executives, and day-by-day workers in the technical side of a vast military and industrial plant. For purposes of educational planning, these two components must be separated.

Much of what I have said so far probably sounds very much like the erection and destruction of straw men. However, the questions and assertions I have sought to analyze are typical of those raised in the thousands of articles and speeches which have appeared during the past few years. This analysis could go much farther, but I think I have gone far enough to make my point: that whatever there is of future consequence in the current spate of argument is likely to be found below the screaming and the clatter.

Exploring the Productive Lode

One of these more basic facts is reported in the commonplace observation that the field of science is growing at an explosive rate— in techniques, in instrumentation, in content. This explosive growth is one of the conspicuous facts of what I have called the productive lode. During the last seventy-five years we have invented and developed a social gadget called an industrial laboratory. The laboratory provides an excellent site for the care and feeding of science and scientists. It also provides an agency through which our society undertakes the care and feeding of new ideas. The exploitation of this device—the laboratory—has succeeded in feeding research the equivalent of two boxes of wheaties every morning. Through the laboratory, the research-development social-change sequence has become the social Jack Armstrong of today's world. Not only are we getting more information faster, but we generate more demands for information than we can satisfy even with our present immense research structures. Research has become malignant; it breeds more research. It creates fresh demands for information. The more effective our research, the more information we get, the more unanswered questions we set ourselves, the more ignorant we feel, the more anxious we are for more information.

How does a society live with this situation? This fact sets a brand-new social problem. No society faced it before our Western society did; no society faces it now as acutely as does the United States, because of our explicit governmental commitment to a highly informed population.

Social science has also become an explosively growing field of knowledge. You have read of one of its recent developments: the advertising device which flashes a message on your television screen so briefly that you are unaware of it but which causes you to buy, anyway. Indeed the growth of knowledge in social science may have more serious impacts than that in natural science, unless we swiftly learn to get the new knowledge into our population in ways in which it can guide the decisions of individuals.

Another important element of the productive lode is the fact that science in our schools does not mirror science outside our schools. Suppose an anthropologist were making the reverse trip from Samoa, to assess the queer folkways of the Americans. If he made the public schools his last point of study, he would be forced to predict that public schools taught principally science and engineering. He would make this prediction from two facts: first, that the effects of science, the practice of science and engineering, the economic dependence on science and engineering in our culture, are very broad and deep and, second, that the public school is one of our basic social units. An anthropologist operating from outside our culture would be compelled to assume that the public schools are much concerned with training scientists at various levels, because applied science is used by almost everybody in the United States. Whether a person is a farmer or a manufacturer of automobiles, he is a consumer and an applier of science. Also, nearly everyone receives an important fraction of his social indoctrination in the public schools.

In fact, however, most elementary-school programs in science are scheduled for twenty to thirty minutes a day for two or three days a week. The time required in actual instruction in formal science in secondary schools is seldom above one-eighth of the total four-year period in high school and is more frequently one-sixteenth of the total program.

Our total school agency involves more than a million teachers, tens of thousands of school districts, tens of millions of students. All these people and governmental units interact intimately with our enormously science-oriented, science-integrated culture. American high schools and elementary schools are extraordinarily responsive to social pressures. Bands, typewriters, shops, drama, driving lessons —almost anything can be put into a school program by public pressure. How does it happen that group pressure to put science into high-school programs or into elementary-school programs is so low? Why has not the social order made high-level education in science an imperative in its schools, when it so deeply depends on science-based activities outside its schools?

A third fact lying in the productive lode is the flight of thousands of teachers from science-teaching. School systems like that in Chicago, which pay very good salaries even in comparison with industrial jobs, lose science teachers at a terrific rate, just as does every other school system in the United States. Simple salary differentials cannot explain the departure of science teachers from the schools, for the Chicago experience, as well as others, demonstrates that, even when salaries are good, science teachers continue to leave teaching.

A fourth important fact is the recent and rather sudden emergence of the national manpower concept as an important idea in the planning of educational policy. The manpower concept seems to be intrinsically attractive to Americans, but, if one ponders it for a moment, one asks: Manpower for what? For what do we need "manpower"? When is it appropriate to aggregate the individuals of a democracy into manpower measurements? Is the function of education that of providing manpower for various needs? If so, whose needs? Whose purposes? We use the manpower idea very readily and quite appropriately when we raise armies, navies, and airforces. Have we unwittingly carried a wartime concept into peace-time educational planning? Or, if this be a time of war, as many insist, are we failing to exercise the power of the government in an area of great national importance.

In education we have long held the conviction that the function of the public schools is to help each young person realize his own potentials. This is a man-by-man approach, however, not a manpower approach. The manpower-planning concept directly opposes the historic mandates given to American schools.

Attempts to use the national manpower concept in educational planning produces a serious problem: that of redesigning the relationships between local school-district policy and national policy in fields of high demand for people. Is it appropriate for public schools, for example, to recruit physicians or nurses? Do we carry on manpower studies in Washington; determine that current national policy requires so many teachers, so many nurses, so many doctors; relay the information to the public schools; and adjust local district policy to satisfy these demands? Of course such action might be held to be quite appropriate. On the other hand, this is a very different line of action from that which education historically has taken in the United States. We are a nation, and we do have needs which are best appraised at national levels. But the articulation of national manpower policies and local educational policies presents problems of governmental theory which are rarely formulated. Even the necessary questions are distressing to most of us.

A conspicuous aspect of manpower thinking is the appropriate division of educational labor between secondary schools and colleges. These two institutions must interlock and overlap to some degree, but for reasonable educational efficiency a college should have purposes that are different from those of secondary schools. Secondary schools now are being urged to accept a task which until recently has been assigned to the colleges: locating, and providing special training for, the persons who are to work at high intellectual levels. The argument is that we need more scientists; therefore secondary schools should deliver more prospective scientists to the colleges. Again, I submit, such a policy is not necessarily inappropriate. On the other hand, the argument is not usually presented in such a way that the policy question emerges; usually the argument appears as an attack upon the quality or standards of secondary education.

In the economic view the supply of scientists is not a policy problem; it is a problem of supply and demand. In the view of the typical economist, if the American people need scientists and engineers, raises in stipends and improvement of working conditions will make them available. The policy question, on the other hand, is: Should the secondary schools adjust their individual policies in peace time on the basis of Washington pronouncements? Or do we leave adjustment of labor supply to the market machinery? Should we deliberately alter educational policy school by school to fit situations as detailed as the current need for scientists and engineers?

Analyzing the Productive Questions

These are typical questions of the pay lode. How are they to be answered? Reliable information is at present inadequate, but some kinds of information could be gathered if they were seriously sought. Research in modern social-science frameworks can help, for example, in locating the causes of the departure of science teachers from the schools. Such research can map the controlling stereotypes of the scientist and engineer. Such research can tell us why, when a scientist turns up in a television program, in a comic strip, or in science fiction, he usually is presented as a gentleman of somewhat atypical appearance, with an intelligence which is unsafe because of its great flexibility and analytical power. We can describe the stereotypes, and we can identify the agents (perhaps TV, science fiction, and other media) which maintain the stereotypes to which our population is reacting.

We can learn whether science and education are sex-polarized activities in our society. Not many women choose science as a career. This fact is attested by the small fractions of the membership of scientific societies who are women. Is it true that science is men's work in our society? If true, this fact sharply reduces the number of persons who can be depended upon to have fresh technological ideas for our society.

If careful research should determine that science is men's work in our culture, we face a really serious educational problem, for it seems abundantly clear that, for us, care of the young is women's work. Elementary schools, for example, are staffed principally by women. If science is men's business and teaching the young is women's business, how do we get effective science courses into the elementary schools? Either women must accept parts of the men's roles or men must learn to share in women's roles. Those sophisticated in modern analysis of social groups will know that changing practices which are associated with sex differences is a really tremendous task for any society. With modern mass-communications media, such tasks can be undertaken, however, with hope of success—if we can develop accurate information on which to plan. It's a curious fact that in the present arguments, in which scientists and empirical social scientists are frequently conspicuous critics of public education, very little money is going into research which could provide guidance for improvement of public policy in education.

However, when modern social science has had its say, we shall still be far short of the information we need to answer the great questions underlying the current argument. How are decisions made when the necessary facts are unavailable, when such facts cannot be found, but a decision is nevertheless necessary? Each of us makes a tremendous number of such decisions; each of us learns to live with the process of decision-making when he not only does not have the information but can in no way get it.

Most of the real problems in science education are like those problems. For them, there is no escape from the painful work of democratic policy-making—just the plain public discussion and decision-making. Shall school boards use the national manpower idea to formulate educational policy? Is the location and development of talented youth a matter for national educational policy? What is an appropriate division of labor between secondary schools and colleges? Most public colleges now must accept everyone who satisfactorily completes a secondary school, or shall public colleges be permitted to select their students? Shall elementary- and high-school curriculums be adjusted to provide greater emphasis on science and mathematics? Shall we set out to adjust the present social roles of men and women with respect to science and the care of young children?

Under present limitations of knowledge, these questions will be answered in public debate and through the actions of our numerous district boards of education. As a result the role of the specially interested and specially trained person in science education must be that of the analyst rather than that of the decision-maker. The great debate must be cleared of its overburden. The policy questions must be properly posed, for no one can answer these great questions with precision. These are matters for the people of the United States to decide through their regularly constituted agencies, not matters for an oligarchy, no matter how constituted.

Americans are now engaged in one of the greatest and most far-reaching decision-making tasks ever faced by their nation: the determination of educational treatment of modern science, the most powerful intellectual activity created by man during the past five hundred years. We truly are deciding the fate of our nation through a debate on school policy.

Predicting the Decisions

Now, if you will permit me one assumption, I will undertake some predictions about the decisions our nation will reach in the field of science education. My assumption is that growth in science education in the elementary schools will continue, that science will become less of a man's job and more of a woman's job.

My first prediction, then, is that improvement in the teaching of elementary-school science will ease and expedite a steady pushing-down of scientific and mathematical information and skill from the college levels into the high school. As one of my waggish associates puts it, 'Today's problem isn't how you get more youngsters into high-school physics; it's how you get integral calculus into the tenth grade." The necessity to deliver people at the forefront of knowledge at something like twenty-five years of age results in defining a college Freshman as a youth who is seven years back from the frontiers of human knowledge in some particular field. He also can be defined as a youth twelve years up from age six in the public schools. There is no logical requirement that these two definitions provide individuals at comparable development levels or at the right time and in the right places. I expect that the college problem finally will control the decision-making, and that more dependence for technical control in mathematics and science will be pushed into the secondary schools. Too, as part of this movement, I expect that many colleges will provide double-track curriculums for general education and special education in science and mathematics. Some of the stronger universities may seek explicitly to abandon the general-education problems in science and mathematics to the secondary schools.

I also predict that the solution for the talent-discovery problem will be found principally through administrative innovation in secondary schools, because of a growing public awareness of our need for able people in all fields. A talent-discovery program in only science and mathematics cannot meet the national demands. The problem is that of viewing individual differences among students as a problem at the principal's level, as a school-wide problem instead of merely as a class-wide problem.

I expect much more articulation among science, mathematics, and social sciences in the secondary schools. The need to interpret the social impact of science has lain heavily on the minds of thoughtful people since Vannevar Bush's 1945 report, *Science the Endless Frontier*.[1] Also, secondary-school science of the future will almost certainly give much more attention to structure and process in scientific thinking. Both these tendencies will be encouraged by developments in two relatively new fields of study: the history of science

[1] Vannevar Bush, *Science the Endless Frontier: A Report to the President* (Washington: Government Printing Office, 1945).

and the philosophy of science. Though these fields have not yet had the full attention of many scientists or science educators, information from them is now trickling into the design of science-education programs in secondary schools.

More specific curricular trends are becoming clear. Abandonment of the ninth-grade course in general science may take place fairly quickly, particularly in the larger and stronger secondary schools. If elementary-school science programs continue to be strengthened and public interest remains high, fifteen-year-old students certainly will be ready for more sophisticated facts and more sophisticated modes of thought than those typical of present-day general science. The beginnings of this action are already apparent in some of the large schools. In place of the general-science course, I expect to see a co-ordinated program in mathematics and physical science at the ninth-grade level. The biology course will probably remain in the tenth and eleventh grades, and perhaps a new earth-science course, a combination of geology and geography, will be the phoenix which rises from the ashes of the old course in physical geography. My prediction of this emergent curricular division is based on the notably different types of scientific thought which govern these three fields of scientific work; each has its own distinctive characteristics of thought. As awareness of the history and of the philosophy of science spreads, these distinctive thought processes may be expected to emerge as bases for curricular division.

I have left until last the guesses that I would like to make about the short-range problems which have popped up so frequently in recent discussions. Since our nation is struggling anxiously with satellites and guided missiles, I expect Congress to decide that it cannot wait for the strengthening of science education district by district and school by school across the United States, though that strengthening can be rather clearly seen. Since the problem of maintaining effective science people in schools is considered so widely to be chiefly a problem of status and income for the teacher (though, as you now know, I do not wholly share this belief), I expect the Congress to allay its anxieties by trying to establish high-income, high-status school positions associated with science and the improvement of science education. I expect the first move will be to establish a state-wide position in each state, then as swiftly as possible to set up a specialized worker in each school district and perhaps in each school. The programs in agricultural education can readily be made to serve as a precedent for this type of activity; our government has already entered the field of education in everything from the great grants of land which produced the land-grant colleges to school lunch programs and agricultural extension.

This is enough forecasting. I am now far enough away from my support that I am sure to be embarrassed by any turn of events.

GERALD B. LEIGHBODY

Vocational Education Re-examined
for the New Era

If we are to examine the future of any aspect of education, such as education for vocational life, we can do so only by projecting and interpreting facts which already exist. Peter F. Drucker, in his thought-provoking book, *America's Next Twenty Years*, declares:

> The major events that determine the future have already happened—*irrevocably*. . . . Our forecasting is severely limited to those future happenings that are already under way. There is no need for crystal-gazing. We can find plenty to occupy us in what we *know* about America's next twenty years from events that have already occurred.[1]

In terms, then, of this future which, in a sense, has already happened, I presume to look at the place and the nature of vocational education in the schools of America in the years just ahead. In considering such a topic, it seems logical to look for evidence that will throw light upon questions such as the following: (1) In the future, will the majority of American youth continue their education beyond the high school and thus be able, in most cases, to defer preparation for work to this later period? (2) What will the occupations of the future be like? (3) Will they require much preparation? (4) Will the nature and extent of the preparation required to pursue the occupations permit such preparation to be postponed beyond the high school?

If answers to such questions lead us to conclude that vocational education has a place in planning for the high school of the future, then we must ask: (1) How great will be the need for vocational education? (2) What characteristics will such education have? (3) How can it best be organized and conducted?

We are all aware that the holding power of the American high

[1] Peter F. Drucker, *America's Next Twenty Years* (New York: Harper & Bros., 1955, 1956, 1957), pp. 2–3.

school has been increasing, that more young people are staying in school longer. Most of us are also aware that a greater and greater portion of our young people are going on into higher education. We are told to expect an explosive growth in college enrolments in the years ahead.

Not a few educational planners have accepted as a fact the conclusion that in the future all vocational education can be, and will be, deferred beyond the high school because all, or nearly all, young people requiring such education will be found in some program of higher education. This conclusion assumes, of course, that the decision can be made in terms of when the student is available to be prepared and that no other factors will affect the decision.

What Are the Facts concerning Need for Vocational Education in High School?

In spite of the improvement in the holding power of our high schools, a report issued recently by the American Economic Foundation shows that 35 per cent of all seventeen-year-olds, 48 per cent of all eighteen-year-olds, and 77 per cent of all nineteen-year-olds in our population are not enrolled in any school program.[2] We know that nearly all the young men not in school, and a large per cent of the young women, were in the labor market; except for the armed services, there was no place else for most of them to be. These per cents will surely decrease in the years ahead. Yet there is no solid evidence to indicate that the *majority* of our youth will, in the foreseeable future, continue their education for a substantial period beyond the high school.

President Truman's Commission on Higher Education issued a report based upon an extensive study of records available from the armed services, indicating the extent to which American youth have the ability to pursue higher education successfully. This report stated that, "even with the present inflexibility of college curriculums, a minimum of 49 per cent of the college-age population of this country has the ability to complete at least the first two years of college work and at least 32 per cent has the ability to complete ad-

[2] American Economic Foundation, "Here's Why Economics Must Be Taught at the High School Level" (New York: The Foundation [295 Madison Avenue], n.d.).

ditional years of higher education."[3] Even if every young person were to pursue education to the full extent of his intellectual capacity and if the facilities were available for him to do so—both unlikely prospects—half or more of the youth of college age will surely terminate their education with the completion of high school. Furthermore, recent estimates show that by 1965 we shall be short by at least 1,500,000 places of the facilities required to provide education beyond the high school for qualified students who will be seeking it. Even allowing for increases in the rate of growth of post-high-school education far beyond that of any known index, the majority of American youth will not, for many years to come, receive any education for work if it is deferred beyond the high school.

At least two other factors will play a part in limiting the formal education of the majority of young people to that secured in the high school. One is the serious and unrelieved labor shortage which will be a most important economic and social feature of the next two decades. This shortage is readily predictable from the age distribution of our present population. As a result great pressure will be exerted on every individual capable of contributing to the output of goods and services to induce him to make such a contribution. Despite all that can be done through counseling and advice, large numbers of young people will find, at the completion of their high-school education, that the opportunities for earning are too attractive to be resisted. We may hope that they will be motivated, and will have the opportunity, to continue their education on a part-time basis.

Another factor bearing upon the proper placement of vocational education is the rapid increase in the amount of basic and technical preparation required for success in the jobs of the future. This requirement can very well increase the necessity for basic occupational preparation at the high-school level. Assuming that we can persuade fairly large numbers of young people to continue their education for at least two years beyond the high school, it becomes increasingly doubtful that this span of time will be sufficient to complete the preparation needed for the jobs of the future. On the

---

[3] President's Commission on Higher Education, *Equalizing and Expanding Individual Opportunity* ("Higher Education for American Democracy," Vol. II [Washington: Government Printing Office, 1947]), p. 7.

contrary, it seems more and more likely that, to provide anything like the preparation needed, the basic elements of the preparation will have to begin not later than the eleventh year of school.

I have recently reviewed, in advance of publication, the data secured from a study of the need for technical manpower for radio-isotope work among more than ninety firms in New York State that employ radio isotopes in research and other operations. Their estimates of the additional trained personnel who will be needed during the next three years alone are as follows: (1) an increase of 161 per cent in the number of college graduates, (2) an increase of 164 per cent in the number of graduates of technical institutes or the equivalent, (3) an increase of 315 per cent in the number of graduates of vocational or technical high schools, and (4) an increase of 20 per cent in the number of high-school graduates with strictly academic preparation. Note the emphasis given to technical preparation at the high-school level.

Wherever serious studies have been made by economists, industrialists, sociologists, government agencies, or educators, the facts all point to this conclusion: while there will be a continuing expansion of vocational education at the post-high-school level, to suppose that the need for vocational-education offerings in the high school will diminish is to make a serious mistake. Rather than eliminating our concern for the vocational preparation of youth at this level, the American high school will be forced to concern itself, more and more, with meeting this need, at least in the upper years. In an address given in August, 1957, before the American Vocational Association, the chief of the Labor and Employment Statistics Branch of the United States Department of Labor estimated that by 1970 the need and demand for vocational education will be at twice its present level.

What Will World of Work Be Like?

If the high school of the future must play a part in the direct preparation of youth for careers, it is essential that those who plan educational programs understand, much more clearly than many of them now do, what the world of work is like today, what has already happened to change it, and what it will be like in the foreseeable future. The word "automation" has become widely used. It is associated in the public mind with new and almost magical methods for producing goods. It is that and much more. Few people, even those engaged in programs of automation, fully understand the implications of this phenomenon, which have been revealed by some of our most brilliant economists and sociologists. No educator of the future can afford to be ignorant of the full meaning of the effects which are already flowing from the truly revolutionary set of concepts described by the term "automation."

So far as preparation for careers is concerned, what it means is a massive upgrading of the skills required by the entire labor force of this country. The unskilled worker of yesterday has already disappeared from the industrial scene, never to return. Already the processes have begun which will upgrade the semiskilled and the skilled machine-operators of today into the highly skilled and knowledgeable technicans of tomorrow. And the term "skill" must be redefined, because the skills of one era are dead and the skills of the new era are just emerging. A visitor to the industrial plants that have begun to adopt these new processes is struck by the small number of workers actually on the production floor, and these workers will become fewer and fewer. In plants such as power-generating stations or oil refineries, practically no workers are in sight, but large numbers of persons are working behind the scenes in new, highly skilled jobs, as machine-builders, machine-installers, instrument technicians, trouble shooters, testers, data-processors, designers, draftsmen, programers, and mathematicians. These are the industrial jobs, and the prototypes of other jobs, of the future.

Agriculture has long been a declining field of employment. Today one worker in agriculture can produce food for himself and fourteen others, whereas in 1900 such a worker could produce food for only seven others. Of all young men born on farms today, one of every two must find a career in non-farm employment. Soon two of every three will find it necessary to leave the farm to earn a living. The application of scientific principles to crop production and livestock breeding, plus mechanization of farm processes, has brought about a complete revolution in agriculture. These changes in agriculture result in constantly shrinking opportunities for careers, and the careers are steadily becoming more technical and managerial in nature. The entire program of vocational agriculture in our schools will have to be re-examined in light of these facts.

The concepts associated with automation will probably have a greater impact upon office and business occupations than upon production processes. This fact appears to be little understood by leaders in commercial and business education. The only job below the managerial which will ultimately survive in the business office may be that of the private secretary. This fact must be reckoned with in any consideration of vocational preparation for girls in the future.

We are familiar with many of the recent innovations in merchandising and marketing, but these are only forerunners of others to come. For example, it is possible that the supermarkets of the future will be much larger than those we have today and that they will be electronic. You will select what you want, perhaps without even leaving your car, have the goods delivered automatically to your car, and pay as you drive out. Shopping by television is also a distinct possibility. It is too early to know exactly what all this will mean in terms of careers, but, as in the business office, it may reduce considerably the number of career opportunities of certain kinds. There will surely be many shifts in the job patterns in the distributive area of our economy, and, as in all other areas, we may expect these shifts to be in a direction which will require more and better preparation for those who hope to engage in them.

Many types of jobs which have required few workers in the past will use significantly larger numbers in the future. Some of these are outgrowths of our high standard of living, the widespread distribution of leisure, and our changing patterns of life. An illustration is the amazing increase in small-boat ownership, which has created thousands of new jobs in the construction, selling, maintenance, and servicing of boats and motors. This illustration could be multiplied many times.

There will, of course, be opportunities for great numbers of people in types of jobs which do not exist at all today. David Sarnoff has said: "There is no element of material progress we know today . . . that will not seem, from the vantage point of 1980, like a fumbling prelude."[4] He also maintained: "Whatever the mind of man

---

[4] David Sarnoff, "The Fabulous Future," *Fortune*, LI (January, 1955), 114.

visualizes, the genius of modern science can turn into functioning fact."[5] The important point for educators is that, as these new types of jobs come into existence, they will demand a level of preparation which is considerably more thorough and more technical than has ever been required in the past. The experts who prepared the study, *America's Needs and Resources: A New Survey,* for the Twentieth Century Fund wrote: "Technology . . . can be thought of as the primary resource; without it all other resources would be economically non-existent."[6]

These few brief glimpses into the future of the world of work will suffice to indicate that the working world will be far different from that in which many of us have labored. Many of the details are, of course, unknown at this time, but the main trends are unmistakable. Upon these clear trends, plans for vocational education for the future can be based.

What Do These Trends Mean for Vocational Education?

These trends show that careers of the future, at all levels, will require people with more, better, and different education. They will require trained brain power to an extent never imagined during the earlier period of our industrial and social development, and surely not fully appreciated today. The preparation for these careers cannot consist in developing skills in "gadgeteering." As Drucker puts it: "Even in routine jobs, Automation will require ability to think, a trained imagination, and good judgment, plus some skill in logical methods, some mathematical understanding, and some ability well above the elementary level to read and write."[7]

Viewed superficially, these facts may lead to the belief that a so-called good general education will be the only preparation needed for such a future. Penetrating analysis shows, however, that this is not the case. The quality of our general education, as well as that of other aspects of the educational program, will, of course, need to be

---

[5] *Ibid.,* p. 82.

[6] J. Frederic Dewhurst and Associates, *America's Needs and Resources: A New Survey* (New York: Twentieth Century Fund, 1955), p. 834.

[7] Peter F. Drucker, *op. cit.,* p. 30.

considerably enhanced. In addition, the high school of the future will have to provide, for the majority of its students, direct and applied education for the new vocations. The Educational Policies Commission, in its recent report, points out this fact with great clarity. The report says, among other things: "Among most young Americans, especially those of superior capacity, the career objective becomes an effective central strand in educational motivation. The education of these young people does not proceed best in isolated disregard of lifetime occupational activities.[8]

In terms of the future, then, we may conclude that vocational education in the American high school will become almost wholly technical education. I use "technical education" in the sense that it is used to describe programs now in existence in the few truly technical high schools and still fewer real technical departments in comprehensive high schools in America. The education provided there should not be confused with that in many schools and programs which are presently called technical but which are merely nonacademic. Too often these have been "escape programs"—combinations of industrial arts, miscellaneous trade courses, and various nondescript "shop" courses. Such schools and courses have been poorly adapted for meeting the career needs of youth in the past, and they will have no place in the program of the high school of the future.

The typical worker of the future, excluding those who can be unquestionably classified as professional, will be the technician, male or female (and the connotations of the word "technician" will be broadened). Technicians in the past have been thought of as akin to engineers. In the future they will be found in many areas of occupational life in addition to engineering and industry. The technician is a person who works at a job which requires technical knowledge and technical skill but little manual skill. The technician's work assignments are usually made by professionals, under whose supervision the technician works. Supervision, however, is loose rather than close, and an important characteristic of the successful technician is the ability to work independently under broad assignments.

[8] Educational Policies Commission, *Manpower and Education* (Washington: Educational Policies Commission of the National Education Association and the American Association of School Administrators, 1956), p. 68.

The technical education which is being described here will need to be offered in terms of broad areas of preparation, which provide directly for occupational life but go much beyond the requirements of the first job. It will not be enough to prepare solely for the first job, because the first job, and most succeeding jobs which the worker of tomorrow will hold, will change radically and often. Illustrations of such areas of technical preparation might be the areas of chemistry, of mechanical technology, of electrical technology, of health services, of business controls and analysis, of food preparation and service, of highway-maintenance technology, and many others.

Over the years, vocational education has met its responsibilities successfully in the schools of America wherever it has been permitted to develop properly. Where it has not been used as a dumping ground for those who did not fit well in other programs, it has generally served well the youth it has enrolled. At a few times and in a few places it has, in its attempts to be practical, become too narrow and shortsighted. Vocational education has always been more concerned with the total development and welfare of the pupil than its detractors have been aware of or willing to admit. Nevertheless, formulas of the past will not suffice for tomorrow. Those with the interests of vocational education at heart must be willing to review its place in the total program of education. There must be a willingness to reconsider, and if necessary to modify, the legislation upon which it has so long depended for direction as well as for strength; to seek appropriate changes in its pattern of administration and organization, in the nature of its offerings, in the qualifications of teachers and administrators. It must be sufficiently flexible to adapt itself quickly and frequently to the needs of the economy, of the society, and of the individuals who compose the society. It should play a strong supporting role in the great drama of American education, not demanding a separate stage of its own. Those who lead vocational education at all levels of the school program must be sensitive to the changes described. They cannot afford to stick doggedly to a program of training for skills which are disappearing or for occupations which are dying or dead.

How Shall Vocational Education of the Future Be Provided?

Only two studies of any depth have been made of the merits of the separate versus the comprehensive high school in offering programs of vocational education. Both studies indicate that, if a community is large enough to support more than one high school, the program in the separate school is more successful. Yet enough successful programs of vocational education are found in comprehensive schools to make it doubtful that this feature of the organization is critical. Other features are more vital. I suggest that, among the important features of programs of vocational education in the future, will be the following:

1. Youth enrolled in vocational curriculums will participate simultaneously in the same full program of general education available to all youth. This participation is quite possible and is being accomplished in several of the outstanding schools in this country.

2. Vocational curriculums will be planned so that they can, at one and the same time, offer terminal education for those who desire to give their entire school day to this program and offer college-preparatory education for those desirous of, and capable of, going further.

3. Courses and curriculums will emerge from the direct requirements of occupational life. Consequently the curriculum planners must be in continuous and understanding contact with the world of work and with research agencies which study occupations.

4. Curriculums will be broad and forward-looking yet thoroughly realistic.

5. Teachers will be recruited from among experienced practitioners of the technical activities which they will teach.

6. Facilities will be appropriate and will be kept up to date. Equipment will require frequent replacement, more because of obsolescence than because of wear. The practice of leasing, rather than purchasing, equipment, with regular replacement as obsolescence requires, may become widespread.

7. Vocational programs and schools can be, and will be, coeducational.

8. The best administrators of vocational programs will be persons whose professional qualifications have been augmented with personal experience in non-teaching careers related to the occupations being taught. An individual who lacks such experience can still administer a successful program if he is willing to become an active and intensive student of the vocations and careers represented in his school or program and if he will associate himself enthusiastically with leaders and workers in these areas. He will fail, and the program will fail, if he or his superiors or his professional associates have any doubts as to the educational respectability of vocational education or its necessary place in the school program.

Turning again to the report of the Educational Policies Commission, we are told:

> Concern with career need not be illiberal or narrow. Concern with career is in accord with the American educational tradition and with the highest cultivation of student abilities. Neither its devotees nor its detractors should suppose that there is anything in the nature of vocational education which requires it to be narrow or more limited than is needful in the best interests of the students.[9]

The issue of vocational versus liberal, or vocation versus culture, has always been a false one, and future events will make discussions of it seem more sterile and unprofitable with each passing year.

A recent report on the economic status and future of America released by the Twentieth Century Fund, quotes Adolf A. Berle, Jr., as saying: "The United States has not merely climbed to a new plateau, but is ascending heights whose upper limit is not yet measurable, and at an accelerated rate of speed."[10] The key to this rise is technology. For the individual, the key to success in the technological future is his readiness and preparation to take part in it. Vocational education must provide for the people of America the career preparation for this kind of future. The American high school will have a major role to play in this task.

[9] Educational Policies Commission, *op. cit.*, p. 69.

[10] Thomas R. Carskadon and George Soule, *U.S.A. in New Dimensions* (New York: Twentieth Century Fund, 1957), p. 2.

Commentary on the Conference

Commentary on the Conference

The National Citizens Council was happy to be offered the opportunity to collaborate with the University of Chicago in sponsoring the Conference on the American High School. We hoped that it would stimulate dispassionate discussion of means for attaining education of a high quality and serve as a springboard for broad cooperative action toward this goal.

Before the sessions began, I enlisted the help of other eyes and ears to let me know what went on in many group discussions. The reports I received came not only from the formal sessions—either general sessions or group sessions—but also from luncheon-table talk and dinner-table conversation, spontaneous hotel-lobby and hotel-room evaluations, and the even more animated and relaxed discussions that took place at many other more diverse tables around the city. After all, that is where opinions are expressed with the least inhibition.

With the multiple vision and understanding that my many eyes and ears provided me, in addition to my own extensive observations, I tried to identify the themes that ran through the entire conference. I shall mention six that appeared time and again, no matter what the subject under discussion.

First, it seems to me that the most conspicuous facet of the conference was the severe criticisms leveled at secondary education in the United States. But, and I immediately interpose a qualification, these criticisms came, without any shadow of doubt, from people deeply concerned about the welfare of the schools rather than from the type of headline-seeker so well known a few years ago. They represented not a "meat-ax" approach to high-school education, designed to destroy it, but rather the surgeon's approach: the scalpel was the instrument, and the objective was to cure current ills and promote the welfare of the patient.

447

Second, it seems to me that the criticisms came from people who recognize the great job the high schools have done, and are doing, in promoting the healthy development of democracy in our nation. Secondary education received, in the conference, the recognition it deserves as the bridge in our educational system which connects the activities of other educational levels.

A third theme that ran through all the discussions and speeches was the assumption that the objective of secondary education in the United States is to provide equal education for all our children. And there was the recognition of the fact that this is a more complex problem at the secondary level than we have been able to solve to date. There was also general acknowledgment of the fact that, in order to solve this problem satisfactorily, priorities must be established for the many demands made upon the schools, keeping in mind the responsibilities of the home, church, and other agencies which must also share some of the burden.

These first three observations add up to an overwhelming concern for quality in high-school education. The criticisms of our schools, the recognition of the tremendous job they have done and are doing, and the assumption that they must give every American youth equal educational opportunity—all add up to the fourth theme: a realization that we must have first-rate high schools if they are to meet the demands our generation is making on them and, even more important, if they are to come close to meeting the demands of the future.

The fifth theme that ran through all the discussions was the implicit or explicit realization that many of the questions that were asked cannot be answered until we have decided just what we expect our high schools to accomplish. The questions of what objectives we were setting for our secondary schools was seldom asked, but it was implicit in many of the other issues raised directly and indirectly in many of the discussions. In other words, the questions that seemed to be in the back of the minds of many persons were: What do we expect of a high-school graduate that we do not expect of a person who has not attended one of our high schools? What changes in the individual do we expect the school to bring about?

The sixth theme that I sensed was a new attitude on the part of all of us. The educators seemed to take a thoughtful look at new points of view and new ideas that were presented. As one of my reporters phrased it, the educators at this conference were more open-minded and less defensive than I have ever seen them at any conference before in my experience. And I was very much aware of the almost complete absence of irresponsible statements by uninformed laymen. Too frequently a few uninformed persons make it difficult for the other laymen to gain the full respect of the professionals in the field.

This, I believe, is a most hopeful sign, but we should not feel too complacent about it. One or two of the factors that contributed to this point of view may be mentioned. First, there is no doubt in my mind that the quality of the persons attending the conference materially influenced the reactions to it. Most of the participants were accustomed to thinking about education in a larger context than the narrow view of vested interest or personal security.

Second, the statesmanlike quality of the keynote speeches in the general sessions set a tone for the discussion groups that was almost unique in my experience at conferences. None of us could remain untouched by the vision of greatness that was presented to us time and again by the truly creative and imaginative leaders who gave of their knowledge and wisdom in the general sessions and in the group presentations.

But we should not be misled into thinking that all differences in the field of education have been resolved by the simple expedient of holding a conference. The nature of the conferenc itself was one of the determining factors. Here the discussions concentrated on the *big questions*. At the highly generalized or theoretical level it is easier to find agreement; the violent disagreements appear at the level of specifics. But there is no doubt in my mind that the broad perspective which the conference gave the participants will make it more possible for them to work effectively at the specifics of translating theory into actuality.

The American High School

Challenge of the New Era

A CONFERENCE

Sponsored by

THE UNIVERSITY OF CHICAGO

in collaboration with the

NATIONAL CITIZENS COUNCIL

for

BETTER SCHOOLS

THE UNIVERSITY OF CHICAGO

October 28–30, 1957

GENERAL SESSIONS

Monday, October 28

MORNING GENERAL SESSION, 9:00–11:30 A.M.

Presiding: RALPH K. GOTTSHALL, Chairman, Board of Trustees, National Citizens Council for Better Schools, New York City, and President, Atlas Powder Company, Wilmington, Delaware

Invocation: JERALD C. BRAUER, Dean, Federated Theological Faculty, University of Chicago

Address: "A Historian Looks at the American High School"

Speaker: HENRY STEELE COMMAGER, Professor of History, Columbia University

Address: "The Emerging American Scene"

Speaker: DEVEREUX C. JOSEPHS, Chairman of the Board, New York Life Insurance Company, New York City, and Chairman, The President's Committee on Education beyond the High School

Monday, October 28

DINNER MEETING, 6:30 P.M.

Presiding: JAMES E. DAY, Chairman, Citizens Board of the University of Chicago, and President, Midwest Stock Exchange

Invocation: JOHN B. THOMPSON, Dean of the Chapel, University of Chicago

Address: "The American High School in Prospect"

Speaker: FRANCIS S. CHASE, Chairman, Department of Education, University of Chicago

Address: "The University and the High School"

Speaker: LAWRENCE A. KIMPTON, Chancellor, University of Chicago

(Conference registrants are invited to the Dinner as guests of the Citizens Board of the University of Chicago)

Tuesday, October 29

MORNING GENERAL SESSION, 9:30–11:30 A.M.

Presiding: BENJAMIN C. WILLIS, General Superintendent of Schools, Chicago

Address: "Maintaining Balance between Science and the Humanities in the High-School Program"

Speaker: REUBEN G. GUSTAVSON, President and Executive Director, Resources for the Future, Inc., Washington, D.C.

Address: "Laymen Help Plan the High School of the Future"

Speaker: ROY E. LARSEN, President, Time, Inc., New York City, and Chairman, Board of Directors, The Fund for the Advancement of Education

Tuesday, October 29

RECEPTION AND TEA, 4:15–5:30 P.M.

Tuesday, October 29

EVENING GENERAL SESSION, 8:00 P.M.

Presiding: LAWRENCE A. KIMPTON, Chancellor, University of Chicago

Address: "An American Looks at European Secondary Schools"

Speaker: JAMES B. CONANT, Former United States Ambassador to the Federal Republic of Germany

Wednesday, October 30

NOON LUNCHEON MEETING

Presiding: HENRY TOY, JR., President, National Citizens Council for Better Schools, New York City

Invocation: WALTER HARRELSON, Dean, Divinity School, University of Chicago

Address: "The United States Commissioner of Education Looks at the American High School"

Speaker: LAWRENCE G. DERTHICK, United States Commissioner of Education, Washington, D.C.

GROUP SESSIONS

Monday–Tuesday, October 28 and 29, 2:00–4:00 P.M.

Ten concurrent Group Sessions will be held on Monday afternoon and Tuesday afternoon. The same general topic will be discussed on two consecutive days. An aspect of the topic is assigned to each day, and each day's session will be opened with a forty-minute address followed by a full hour of discussion.

GROUP 1: *"Science Education in the New Era"*

Presiding: HAROLD H. METCALF, Superintendent, Bloom Township High School, Chicago Heights, Illinois

Monday Address: "Science in American Life"

Speaker: ALAN T. WATERMAN, Director, National Science Foundation, Washington, D.C.

Tuesday Address: "Science Education in the High School of the Future"

Speaker: JAMES G. HARLOW, Executive Vice-President, Frontiers of Science of Oklahoma, Inc., Oklahoma City, and Dean (January 1, 1958), College of Education, University of Oklahoma

GROUP 2: *"Secondary Education for a Diversified High-School Population"*

Presiding: THADDEUS J. LUBERA, Associate Superintendent of Instruction, North Section, Chicago Public Schools, and Vice-President, Illinois Association of Secondary School Principals

Monday Address: "Educating Low-Ability Pupils"

Speaker: JOHN W. MELCHER, Assistant State Superintendent of Public Instruction and Director, Bureau for Handicapped Children, Madison, Wisconsin

Tuesday Address: "Educating the Gifted"

Speaker: MRS. DOROTHY E. NORRIS, Directing Supervisor, Major Work Classes, Cleveland Public Schools, Cleveland

GROUP 3: *"Resolving Conflicting Pressures on the High School"*

Presiding: GEORGE L. CLELAND, Secondary School Consultant, State Department of Education, Topeka, Kansas

Monday Address: "Clarifying the Role of the High School in the Face of Conflicting Demands"

Speaker: FRANCIS KEPPEL, Dean, Graduate School of Education, Harvard University

Tuesday Address: "Meeting Conflicting Demands on the High School"

Speaker: WALTER L. COOPER, Principal, J. Sterling Morton High School, Cicero, Illinois

GROUP 4: *"Mathematics Education for the New Era"*

Presiding: JOHN R. MAYOR, Director of Education, American Association for the Advancement of Science, Washington, D.C.

Monday Address: "School Mathematics for Tomorrow"

Speaker: MARSHALL H. STONE, Professor of Mathematics, University of Chicago

Tuesday Address: "The Mathematics Curriculum for the High School of the Future"

Speaker: HOWARD F. FEHR, Head, Department of the Teaching of Mathematics, Teachers College, Columbia University, and President, National Council of Teachers of Mathematics

GROUP 5: *"A New Look at the High-School Curriculum"*

Presiding: MAURICE F. SEAY, Director, Division of Education, W. K. Kellogg Foundation, Battle Creek, Michigan

Monday Address: "New Criteria for Curriculum Content and Method"

Speaker: RALPH W. TYLER, Director, Center for Advanced Study in the Behavioral Sciences, Stanford, California

Tuesday Address: "Innovations in the High-School Curriculum"

Speaker: ROBERT S. GILCHRIST, Superintendent of Schools, University City, Missouri

GROUP 6: *"Teachers for the High School of the Future"*

Presiding: ROBERT SARGENT SHRÍVER, JR., President, Board of Education, City of Chicago, and Assistant General Manager, Merchandise Mart, Chicago

Monday Address: "Teachers for the New Era"

Speaker: CLARENCE H. FAUST, President, The Fund for the Advancement of Education, and Vice-President, The Ford Foundation

455

Tuesday Address: "Preparing Teachers for the High School of the Future"
Speaker: HENRY H. HILL, President, George Peabody College for Teachers

GROUP 7: *"Better Utilization of Teachers"*

Presiding: ARTHUR F. COREY, Executive Secretary, California Teachers Association, San Francisco

Monday Address: "The Increasing Concern for Effective Teacher Utilization"
Speaker: JOHN I. GOODLAD, Director, Center for Teacher Education, University of Chicago

Tuesday Address: "Some Approaches to the Better Use of the Teaching Staff"
Speaker: J. LLOYD TRUMP, Professor of Education, University of Illinois, and Director, National Association of Secondary-School Principals' Commission on the Experimental Study of the Utilization of the Staff in the Secondary School

GROUP 8: *"The Layman's Role in the High School of the Future"*

Presiding: MRS. JAMES A. MASON, Immediate Past-President, Citizens Schools Committee, Chicago

Monday Address: "Responsibilities of Educators and Laymen in Developing the High School for the New Era"
Speaker: WILLIAM HENRY SHAW, Superintendent of Education, Muscogee County Schools, Columbus, Georgia

Tuesday Address: "Organizational Methods for Effective Co-operation"
Speaker: ERNEST A. GRAY, Vice-President, Fletcher D. Richards Advertising, New York City, and Member, Board of Directors, New York State Citizens Committee for the Public Schools

GROUP 9: *"Organizing and Administering the High School of the Future"*

Presiding: ROALD F. CAMPBELL, Director, Midwest Administration Center, University of Chicago

Monday Address: "Innovations in the Organization of the High School"
Speaker: LLOYD S. MICHAEL, Superintendent, Evanston Township High School, Evanston, Illinois

Tuesday Address: "Administering the High School of the Future"
Speaker: GEORGE W. CONNELLY, Principal, Roosevelt High School, Chicago.

GROUP 10: *"The High-School and College Relationship"*

Presiding: JOHN M. STALNAKER, President, National Merit Scholarship Corporation, Evanston, Illinois

Monday Address: "The Problem as Viewed by the High School"
Speaker: HOWARD A. LATTA, Principal, Webster Groves High School, Webster Groves, Missouri

Tuesday Address: "The Problem as Viewed by the College"
Speaker: CLYDE VROMAN, Director of Admissions, University of Michigan

Wednesday, October 30, 9:30–11:30 A.M.

GROUP 11: *"Achievement Standards in the High School"*

Presiding: FRED M. HECHINGER, Associate Publisher, *Bridgeport Herald*, Bridgeport, Connecticut, and Immediate Past-President, Education Writers Association

Speaker: I. JAMES QUILLEN, Dean, School of Education, Stanford University

GROUP 12: *"Pupil Personnel Services in the High School"*

Presiding: VERY REV. MSGR. WILLIAM E. MCMANUS, Superintendent of Schools, Archdiocese of Chicago

Speaker: KENNETH W. LUND, Superintendent of Schools, Oak Park–River Forest High School District, Illinois

GROUP 13: *"The Communications Revolution and the High School"*

Presiding: JOHN W. TAYLOR, Executive Director, Chicago Educational Television Association

Speaker: ALEXANDER J. STODDARD, Consultant, The Fund for the Advancement of Education, New York City

GROUP 14: *"Housing the High School of the Future"*

Presiding: EVERETT N. LUCE, President, National School Boards Association, Midland, Michigan

Speaker: ARCHIBALD B. SHAW, Superintendent of Schools, Scarsdale, New York

GROUP 15: *"The Acquisition of Values"*

Presiding: ELDRIDGE T. MCSWAIN, Dean, School of Education, Northwestern University

Speaker: JACOB W. GETZELS, Department of Education, University of Chicago

GROUP 16: *"Vocational Education Re-examined for the New Era"*

Presiding: CLIFFORD J. CAMPBELL, Deputy Commissioner, Department of City Planning, Chicago

Speaker: GERALD B. LEIGHBODY, Associate Superintendent for Instructional Services, Buffalo, New York

GROUP 17: *"The Emerging Economic Scene and the High School of the Future"*

Presiding: B. L. DODDS, Dean, College of Education, University of Illinois

Speaker: THEODORE W. SCHULTZ, Chairman, Department of Economics, University of Chicago

GROUP 18: *"The American High School and the Changing Dimensions of a World Community"*

Presiding: MAURICE B. MITCHELL, President, Encyclopaedia Britannica Films, Inc., Wilmette, Illinois

Speaker: GILBERT FOWLER WHITE, Chairman, Department of Geography, University of Chicago

GROUP 19: *"Freedom and Discipline in the High School"*

Presiding: FINIS E. ENGLEMAN, Executive Secretary, American Association of School Administrators, Washington, D.C.

Speaker: WILLIAM H. CORNOG, Superintendent, New Trier Township High School, Winnetka, Illinois

CONFERENCE COMMITTEE

HAROLD A. ANDERSON, *Conference Director*
Department of Education
University of Chicago

FRANCIS S. CHASE
Chairman, Department of Education
University of Chicago

WORTH McCLURE
Secretary-Emeritus
American Association of School Administrators
Washington, D.C.

HERBERT W. SCHOOLING
Superintendent of Schools
Webster Groves, Missouri

HENRY TOY, JR.
President, National Citizens Council for Better Schools
New York City

GEORGE H. WATKINS
Vice-President, Container Corporation of America
Chicago, Illinois

BENJAMIN C. WILLIS
General Superintendent of Schools
Chicago, Illinois

Index

461